California Odyssey

An Overland Journey on the Southern Trails, 1849

By William R. Goulding
Edited by Patricia A. Etter
Foreword by Howard R. Lamar

THE ARTHUR H. CLARK COMPANY
An imprint of the University of Oklahoma Press
Norman, Oklahoma
2009

Also by Patricia A. Etter

An American Odyssey: The Autobiography of a 19th-Century Scotsman, Robert Brownlee, at the Request of His Children: Napa County, California, October, 1892 (Fayetteville, Ark., 1986)

To California on the Southern Route, 1849: A History and Annotated Bibliography (Spokane, Wash., 1998)

Library of Congress Cataloging-in-Publication Data

Goulding, William R. (William Robinson), 1806–1865.

California odyssey : an overland journey on the southern trails, 1849 / by William R. Goulding ; edited by Patricia A. Etter ; foreword by Howard R. Lamar.

p. cm. — (American trails series ; 21)

Includes bibliographical references and index.

ISBN 978-0-87062-373-8 (hardcover : alk. paper) 1. Overland journeys to the Pacific. 2. Southwest, New—Description and travel. 3. Goulding, William R. (William Robinson), 1806–1865—Travel. 4. Trails—Southwest, New—History—19th century. 5. Frontier and pioneer life—Southwest, New. 6. Pioneers—Southwest, New—History—19th century. 7. Knickerbocker Exploring Company (New York, N.Y.) 8. California—Gold discoveries. I. Etter, Patricia A., 1932– II. Title. III. Series.

F786.G685 2009

917.904'2—dc22

2008050938

The paper in this book meets the guidelines for permanence and durability of the Committee on Production Guidelines for Book Longevity of the Council on Library Resources, Inc. ∞

Manufactured in the U.S.A.

---

1 2 3 4 5 6 7 8 9 10

Dedicated to
William Robinson Goulding
and his descendants in America, Australia,
and wherever else they may be

Contents

Illustrations

Figures

Maps

Foreword

As a teacher and scholar who has focused his career on the history of the Trans-Mississippi West, I have always been fascinated by the saga of the discovery of gold in California in 1848 and the dramatic rush of many thousands of migrants from the United States, Mexico and South America, Europe, and Asia to the new Eldorado between 1849 and 1859. Indeed, European observers said the gold rush was the most significant event in American history since the American Revolution.

Over the years, I have read at least five hundred overland journals and diaries, and given my special interest in the rich history of the American Southwest, I have read many diaries and journals of argonauts (as the forty-niners were called) on the southern trails. Three or four have been truly outstanding, among them the journal of the Knickerbocker Company published here: it is highly informative, articulate, and insightful. I learned much from this superb treasure, housed in Yale University's Beinecke Rare Book and Manuscript Library. But I remained mystified as to its author, for he never gave the reader any clue to his identity, his family, or his career. Only in the addenda to the journal is he identified as being forty-three years of age and a maker of surgical instruments.

Imagine my delight when my longtime acquaintance, Ms. Patricia A. Etter, the retired Curator of the Labriola Center, the American Indian Research Library at Arizona State University, informed me that she had edited and annotated this fine journal; discovered the identity of its author; and then spent several years searching for information about Goulding's origins, his professional career in New York City, his family, and his subsequent career as a United States Army medical steward at Lincoln Hospital in Washington, D.C., and later as a hospital steward at the Army Medical Museum. Before he could fully assume his duties, however, Goulding had become ill and died at Douglas Hospital in Washington on May 11, 1865.

Through assiduous research using resources found in New York, Washington, Great Britain, and Australia, Ms. Etter assembled enough facts to write the succinct biography of Goulding that opens this book. She then asked if I would be willing to write a foreword to her volume. I not only felt honored by her invitation, I realized it offered me an opportunity to thank her for her own earlier contributions to Southwestern history: first as editor of *An American Odyssey: The Autobiography of Robert Brownlee* in 1986, and later her valuable *To California on the Southern Trails in 1849: A History and Annotated Bibliography,* published by the Arthur H. Clark Company in 1998.

Her remarkable introductory chapter tells us that William R. Goulding was born in Canterbury, England, in 1806, the son of a sergeant in the British Army who had been in the famous Battle of Waterloo where the Duke of Wellington defeated Napoleon. At some point young Goulding received a good education and was trained to make fine surgical tools before he migrated to the United States. By the 1840s the products of his New York firm were in great demand by hospitals and prominent doctors and surgeons.

Excited by the news of the gold rush, he and his business partner, William Fraser Ford, joined the New York Knickerbocker Exploring Company of sixty-four men in 1849 to travel by way of Fort Smith, Arkansas, to Santa Fe and then across southern New Mexico and future Arizona to California. Because of Ms. Etter's exhaustive research, certain mysteries about the journal accounts immediately became clear. As a prominent maker of surgical instruments with some medical training, Goulding was inevitably welcomed by military officers and physicians at the various towns, forts, and camps throughout his trek west. On occasion he treated sick or injured members of his group. Military officers found him good accommodations, invited him to dine with them, and introduced him to well-known frontiersmen such as Kit Carson, Cherokee trader Jesse Chisholm, and prominent Indian chiefs. Frontier traders, farmers, and later ranchers treated him cordially throughout the overland trek.

Goulding had gathered information about the routes from Major William Hemsley Emory's classic guide to the Gila trails, *Notes of a Military Reconnoissance* (1848), written when Emory traveled with General Stephen Watts Kearny to California in 1846–47. He was also attracted by the route described in Josiah Gregg's *Commerce of the Prairies* and actually intersected with Captain Randolph Marcy's U.S. Army expedition that was exploring possible better routes from Fort Smith to Santa Fe. Goulding's own party chose to travel Gregg's route north of the Canadian River rather than Marcy's route south of the Canadian.

Many of the "feisty New York Knickerbockers," as Ms. Etter calls them, were young, educated, urban easterners who were impatient and impulsive, and in time they abandoned their heavy, overloaded wagons for pack mules and horses. Constant dissent led some members to join other groups, while Midwestern, Southern, and Texas emigrants often teamed up with the Knickerbockers. Throughout the journey Goulding remained a wise, realistic counselor to the others, and he met every challenge in a calm, cool-headed way.

The Goulding journal provides much information about the Indian tribes he encountered. On the route from Fort Smith to Santa Fe, he and his companions constantly bought food and game, traded horses and mules, and bought fodder for their own animals from the Cherokees and Choctaws, who greatly impressed them with their savvy trading abilities and intelligence. But in southern Arizona Goulding was appalled at the devastating Apache raids that had forced Mexican ranchers and townspeople to flee. He admired the Pueblos, Pimas, and Papagoes but reverted to the word "savage" to describe the Yumas when his party was crossing the Colorado River.

Goulding's group had a rough time crossing the Arizona and California deserts, but their dream of reaching "civilization" was finally realized when they arrived at Isaac Williams's Rancho Santa Ana del Chino where, in Ms. Etter's words, "thousands of fatigued and impoverished gold rushers arrived on his doorstep. . . . Fortunately, Williams liked to have people around, and as we learn from William Goulding, he was a gracious host to all who stopped at the ranch."

Williams kept a register book of those arriving at his ranch, in which Goulding provided a valuable detailed entry of his and the Knickerbocker Company's experiences. Fortunately, Ms. Etter has copied Goulding's entry, which constitutes appendix B of this volume.

Ms. Etter also tells us that Goulding provided one of the best descriptions we have of Williams's ranch, and that Williams was so impressed with Goulding that he asked him to deliver a letter to General Bennett C. Riley, the military governor of California in Monterey, asking for protection against Mexicans returning from the gold fields as well as others. Spurred on by this request, Goulding and his small party journeyed up the famous Mission Trail to Monterey, where he met with the governor, who was busy promoting a constitutional convention for California that hammered out a state constitution after only six weeks. Once again Goulding had the good fortune to meet important people such as John Augustus Sutter; Caleb Lyons, secretary of the convention; Edward Gilbert, editor of the *Alta California,* and other dignitaries. Curiously, Goulding returned to New York in 1850 without ever having visited the mines.

Clearly one of Ms. Etter's greatest "sleuthing" successes has been her unearthing of Goulding's subsequent return to his career as a maker of fine surgical instruments and, as earlier mentioned, the story of his participation in the Civil War as a medical steward in army hospitals in Washington, D.C. Learning of his 1859 trip to visit his son in Australia, she was able to track down Goulding's descendants in Australia and the United States. In addition, she was able to learn more about Goulding's devoted wife, Ann, and their children. Patricia Etter's impressive scholarship and exhaustive research have led to the creation of four maps that carefully retrace Goulding's route to California—a route she has explored over the past twenty years. Moreover, she has provided information about the location of Goulding's surgical instruments in medical museums and has illustrated several of her chapters with modern photographs of scenes along the route.

What is most important is that the Goulding journal is one man's account of people engaged in the largest voluntary migration in modern history, relying on their own strength and will and depending on their draft animals who bore them to the promised land of golden California. As John D. Unruh (1993) has written in *The Plains Across,* the overlanders were so convinced of "the uniqueness and the historical significance of their travels . . . that in the entire American experience perhaps only the Civil War has called forth a commensurate cornucopia of letters, journals, diaries, memoirs and reminiscent accounts, a veritable folk literature of one of the nation's greatest achievements."

Patricia Etter should be congratulated in providing yet another major scholarly contribution to this vast body of gold rush literature. She deserves high praise from gold rush historians and the general public; both will find her compelling, dramatic narrative a joy to read.

Howard R. Lamar

Preface

WILLIAM ROBINSON GOULDING's gold rush journal details his adventures on a seven-month overland trek with the Knickerbocker Exploring Company of New York. The handwritten journal, part of the collection of the Beinecke Rare Book and Manuscript Library at Yale University, contains daily entries between February 18 and September 18, 1849.

My study of the journal began in 1992, when I was preparing an annotated bibliography of travelers in 1849 on the southern trails. The Goulding journal, 325 pages in all, is divided into twenty-one chapters. Chapters 1–17 are written on loose sheets, while chapters 18–21 are contained in a notebook. Following chapter 21 are sixty-one numbered pages of addenda in Goulding's hand, dated from July 1864 to April 1865. These contain random notes such as copies of letters sent, accounts, his state of health, and his daily activities. Also included is a broadside of the Knickerbocker Company constitution and a list of its members, along with a printed diagram of Lincoln General Hospital in Washington, D.C. Interleafed in the notebook are three pencil sketches of Comanche Indians by Goulding. Regrettably, none of Goulding's other drawings that originally accompanied his journal have survived.

Chapters 1 through 6 are written in a different ink, paper, and script from the other chapters. Their style is easier to read than the balance of the document in Goulding's own hand. It appears that his son, William, copied those chapters for some unknown reason. The handwriting was compared with that written in 1910 on the reverse of a photograph of his father. It was also checked against 1910 entries from the younger Goulding's diary.

Goulding's handwriting is flamboyant, and he did not concern himself with commas, periods, or paragraphs. I have added indents and inserted or omitted punctuation where needed. Following the style of his day, he capitalized many common words, and I have lowercased these to concord with modern usage. He frequently used the orthography *fs*, as in "afsistance," which I have replaced with *ss*. As the reader will find, his spelling is often inconsistent. Such things as AM, PM, and o'clock have been standardized here.

Other changes I made as I transcribed the journal include adding chapter titles. Goulding prefaced each chapter with a list of topics. I have omitted these but added a brief introduction to set the stage for each phase of the journey. In Goulding's original chapter 19, he wrote down the dictation of fellow traveler John Hoyt, who later parted with the company. I have moved this chapter to appendix C.

Overlanders on the southern routes routinely tucked a copy of William Hemsley Emory's *Notes of a Military Reconnoissance* (1848) into their pockets. Like many other diarists, Goulding copied useful passages from Emory, uncredited, into his own journal. As these segments are not important to Goulding's story, I have removed them and noted their location in the text.

Over a period of twenty years, I have visited most of the sites covered in Goulding's journal by auto and off-road vehicle, on foot, and on horseback. However, numerous sites along the route are on private property; have disappeared under the plow, concrete, and water; or are not accessible from modern roads. Goulding's trip is shown on four accompanying maps by cartographer Tom Jonas. Footnotes further describe specific sites as far as can be determined. Fortunately, the daily journals of Goulding's traveling companions have been useful in identifying sites.

One does not write a book alone, and a number of individuals and institutions share in the production of this work. First is William Goulding's great-great-grandson Warwick Goulding of Sydney, Australia, who helped fill in many blanks in his biography. I am also grateful to Warwick Goulding's cousin Prue Goulding Crabb, who graciously supplied the Goulding photographs that appear here. George Baur, a Goulding relative by marriage also from Australia, compiled information on both William Goulding and his son. Ed Ford of North Carolina, a distant relative, also kindly supplied important family information and put me in touch with William Goulding's Australian descendants.

I am particularly grateful to David Miller of Cameron State University, Lawton, Oklahoma, for sharing the results of his own trail research in Oklahoma. In October 2007, he drove many miles to introduce me to areas both north and south of the Canadian River as we searched for a route that the Knickerbockers might have taken. My daughter, Janet Bull of Arlington, Virginia, also drove many miles to locate sites in Washington, D.C., and provided board and sustenance during my numerous trips to the National Archives. Jane Rosenthal, an adventurous friend and colleague, has risked a horseback ride over New Mexico's Guadalupe Pass; a mountainous drive to Janos, Chihuahua; and a search for a geological feature reminiscent of an overturned teacup in the Texas Panhandle. Over the years, Bill Cavaliere, past sheriff and historian of Hidalgo County, New Mexico, has opened doors in New Mexico's "boot heel" for me and members of Oregon-California Trails Southwest as we searched out trail segments in his county.

My appreciation also goes to archivists who provided information on Goulding's medical and surgical background: Terry Reimers, director of research at the National Museum of Civil War Medicine; Michael Rhode at the National Museum of Health and Medicine; and Michael Angelo, archivist at Thomas Jefferson University, Philadelphia. Michael Echols has preserved examples of Goulding's medical instruments and generously provided the photograph of the set that appears here. James Edmonson of the Dittrick Museum of Medical History at Case Western Reserve University graciously shared materials from his own research.

Colleagues have contributed expertise in other ways. I am grateful to Susan Gray and Steven Semken, Arizona State University; Gary Kurutz, California State Library; C. Arthur Louderback, Historical Society of Western Pennsylvania; Reba Grandrud and Stephen Williams of Phoenix; and Alex R. Waugh of Toronto. Dennis Copeland, Monterey Public Library, supplied a heretofore unknown diary by Goulding's fellow traveler George Churchill. Archivist Betty Bustos, Panhandle Plains Museum, Canyon, Texas, retrieved treasures to assist my research, and Andrew Masich of the Senator John Heinz Pittsburgh Regional History Center can always be counted on for military-related questions. I am especially grateful to my colleague Peter Blodgett, Curator of Western Historical Manuscripts, Huntington Library, for his help in identifying rare resources that enrich this work. In addition, unnamed librarians and archivists at libraries and historical societies, including the National Archives and the Library of Congress, followed up on numerous requests. Especially noteworthy is the Inter Library Loan staff at my own university, Arizona State University, who filled numerous esoteric requests with nary a complaint.

I am grateful to my colleague George Miles, Curator of Yale Collections of Western Americana, who has for many years supported this project and especially helped with details of the Goulding journal. ASU student Ann Leonard patiently checked citations and bibliographic entries and applied her skills to my promotional photograph. Cartographer Tom Jonas enthusiastically researched and created the fine maps that show Goulding's route cross-country as it might have been in 1849. Tom's daughter, Holly, performed her magic on a 150-year-old glass plate, giving it light so we can clearly see Goulding showing off his Eastern Woodlands suit. I also want to express my thanks to the Emeritus College, Arizona State University, for its generous grant to support my work. I am both honored and grateful to Howard R. Lamar, Sterling Professor Emeritus of History, Yale University, for supplying the foreword to this book. No less important are my editors, Julie Shilling and Katrin Flechsig, University of Oklahoma Press, who not only kept me focused but provided valuable suggestions for improvement. Robert Clark of the Arthur H. Clark Company, a University of Oklahoma Imprint, has been most supportive of my effort to produce the story of the trials and travails that one group of men experienced on a two-thousand-mile adventure, and I thank him for his confidence in me and my project.

California Odyssey

Introducing William Robinson Goulding

WILLIAM ROBINSON GOULDING's gold rush journal narrates his daily experiences on a cross-country trip to California with the Knickerbocker Exploring Company in 1849.[1] His journey led him on the less-traveled southern trails from Fort Smith, Arkansas, to San Francisco, California. Goulding records his frequently extraordinary adventures on his long-distance trip in detail. By contrast, he refers to himself only obliquely in his writing, rarely mentioning his own background or his family in New York. As a result, Goulding's biographical sketch still contains some mysteries.

Nevertheless, we can infer from his penmanship and style that the writer was educated and sophisticated. The journal reveals an already well-traveled and deeply religious man who appeared to take the frequently extreme difficulties of travel in unknown territory in stride. Goulding was evidently well liked and trusted by others as both a leader and a doctor, to judge by his recollections of encounters with a variety of individuals. Though he could be blunt in his observations, he showed real interest in the people he met on the way: frontiersmen; the military; Hispanics of New Mexico, Arizona, and California; and members of numerous Native cultures.

Goulding began his overland adventure at Fort Smith, where the town's paper listed him as one of sixty-four members of the Knickerbocker Exploring Company of New York.[2] This group of gold

[1] Goulding's middle name was kindly supplied by George Baur, "Journey of William Robinson Goulding, Sr.," n.d.

[2] Constitution of the Knickerbocker Exploring Company, *Fort Smith (Arkansas) Herald,* March 21, 1849.

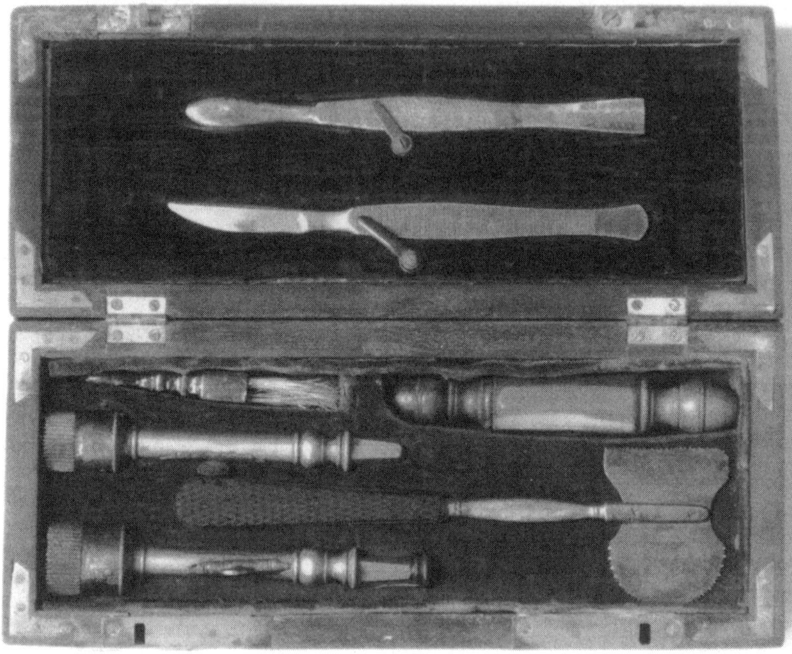

FIGURE 1. Military trepanning set in mahogany case, supplied to the U.S. Army Medical Department in 1846 during the Mexican War. 9½ × 4 × 2 inches. The name "Goulding" is imprinted on the bone rasp at top of photo. The boar's-hair brush and all the instruments have seen extensive use. *Courtesy of Michael Echols.*

seekers planned to travel the Fort Smith–Santa Fe Trail on the first leg of their California journey. We learn from the newspaper that he was forty-two years old, married, and a surgical instrument maker.

In fact, he was one of the top designers of surgical instruments in the country. He had worked with some of the major surgeons of the day: Alfred C. Post, a surgeon at the New York Hospital; Valentine Mott, founder of the University Medical College of New York; and obstetrician Gunning S. Bedford, Professor of Midwifery and the

Diseases of Women at the University of New York.[3] Many of the high-quality instruments Goulding designed for surgeons have since become collector's items (see figure 1).[4] The United States Army provided boxed sets of these tools to its surgeons, and civilian doctors often owned their own sets. Goulding's medical background served him well as he traveled cross-country, as it gave him entrée to the surgeons in charge of the military posts he passed on his way to California. If they did not own one of his surgical sets, they no doubt knew of him by reputation.

Thanks in large part to the work of Goulding relatives Warwick Goulding and George Baur, it is possible to fill in some of the gaps in his biography. William Robinson Goulding was born on September 28, 1806, in Canterbury, Kent, England, son of an Anglo-Irish father, Robert R. Goulding (b. 1782), and a French mother, Henriette Audebert.[5] Robert Goulding was a sergeant in the British Army and was present at the Battle of Waterloo in Brussels, Belgium, on June 18, 1815.[6] Henriette traveled with her husband to his various duty stations and brought her son along, which was not unusual at the time. Thus our diarist, William Goulding, recalled being present at the Battle of Waterloo when he was a child of nine (see chapter 11). Robert Goulding was discharged from the British Army in 1821, when we lose track of him.[7]

Sometime between 1821 and 1826, William R. Goulding emigrated to the United States, either alone or with his parents, for he married Ann (Nancy) Loring (1809–80) in Portland, Maine, on January 3,

---

[3] James Edmonson, *American Surgical Instruments*, 1997, 75. Edmonson's fine book provides a detailed history of surgical instrument manufacture.

[4] Some examples are a circa 1845 amputation set with ivory handles and a circa 1848 military surgical set in a mahogany case lined with red velvet, furnished to the United States Army Hospital Department at the time of the Mexican War. Goulding's name was often stamped on the instruments. See illustrations in Edmonson 1997, 74–79.

[5] Baur, "Journey of William Robinson Goulding, Sr.," 1.

[6] Robert R. Goulding served in the 12th Prince of Wales Light Dragoons in Capt. Edwin Sandy's Troop 4th Army Brigade, part of Lt. Col. Hon. Frederick Ponsonby's Regiment. Baur, "Journey of William Robinson Goulding, Sr.," 1; *Waterloo Medal Roll* 1992, 46.

[7] Goulding's Australian descendants treasure the Waterloo Medal, the first general medal issued by the British government to all soldiers present at Waterloo. Warwick Goulding, personal communication; *Waterloo Medal Roll* 1992, 46.

1826. He was twenty, she seventeen.[8] It is not known if the young couple began married life in Maine, but by 1837 they were living at 166 Rivington Street, New York City, a few blocks from East River Park. By 1839, Goulding had set up his business at 35½ Chatham Street, and by 1844 he was using steam-powered machinery to produce surgical and dental instruments. The machinery consisted chiefly of grindstones and light machine tools such as lathes and drill presses. Where Goulding received his training is unknown, but he may have started out as a cutlery maker, a trade that employed many of the same techniques as surgical instrument making.[9]

During the years 1826–43, Ann and William raised six children: Henriette (1831–1902), who married John Wesley Hoes; William R., Jr. (1834–1913), who worked in the Goulding business until he moved to Australia; Ann Elizabeth (1835–1905), who married William Fraser Ford in 1854; Joseph Henry (b. 1838); Alice (1841–52); and Carolyn "Carrie" (b. 1843). Two other children, Robert and Charlotte, died in 1829 and 1834, respectively.[10] Goulding joined the Independence Guard, 264th Regiment of the New York State Infantry, at the rank of private on October 17, 1844. It is not known if he continued service in the regiment over the years.[11]

Between 1841 and 1848, Goulding's creativity as a surgical instrument designer blossomed. He was "ambitious as well as innovative and succeeded in cultivating a clientele among the leading surgeons of New York."[12] Goulding capitalized on his collaborative relationships by featuring surgeons' endorsements in advertisements and securing their support for appointments as instrument maker to several city institutions. Dr. Valentine Mott wrote one testimonial:

---

[8] Ancestor.com lists her as Nancy. I have been unable to trace the Goulding family in immigration records.

[9] Edmonson 1997, 74, 218.

[10] Warwick Goulding, personal communication; U.S. Census Bureau, 7th Census of the United States, 1850.

[11] William R. Goulding, Certificate of Membership in the Independence Guard, 1844. Neither the New York State Military Heritage and Research Center nor the New York State Archives could supply information on the Independence Guard. Goulding is probably wearing the uniform of the guard in the frontispiece photograph.

[12] Edmonson 1997, 75.

> Mr. Goulding: — Dear Sir, — It is with great Pleasure I inform you that I have just received from one of my particular friends, a most flattering account of the beneficial effects of your "new Patent Truss."
>
> He has been afflicted with an Inguinal Hernia on each side, for many years, and latterly with one at the navel also. He has tried a variety of the most improved trusses of the day, without finding any one effectual until he made use of yours. . . . The successful adaptation of your Truss to my friend's case, encourages me to believe that it is well calculated to relieve the worst forms of Rupture.
>
> This improvement, with others you have made in the manufacture of Surgical Instruments, which I have had an opportunity of knowing, warrant me in recommending you to the Public and Medical profession.
>
> Very respectfully yours,
> Valentine Mott[13]

James M. Edmonson, in his 1997 history of American surgical instruments, comments that William Goulding and his overland traveling companion and future son-in-law, William Fraser Ford, were "the last Englishmen to attain prominence in the instrument trade of New York City." Goulding's work, he adds, displayed the "level of elegance and finish commonly associated with the work of John Weiss, the premier London instrument maker of the 1830s and 1840s."[14] We also learn that William Goulding was not the best of businessmen; he would face financial reverses, lose his share in the company, and ultimately stop designing and manufacturing surgical instruments.

Goulding was known as "Doctor" to his traveling companions and other acquaintances. His work with noted medical doctors in order to design the best surgical instruments had probably given him better training than that of many nineteenth-century doctors. He regularly dispensed potions from his medical chest to care for the sick and injured he encountered during his travels.

---

[13] Mott 1846, 135–37.

[14] Edmonson 1997, 74–75. Goulding's surgical instruments are found in the collections of the Menczer Museum of Medicine and Dentistry, Hartford, Connecticut; the Dittrick Museum of Medical History, Case Western Reserve University, Cleveland, Ohio; and New York Academy of Medicine Library, New York. Edmonson 1997, 77–79.

An economic depression in the late 1840s and the discovery of gold in California were the impetus for thousands of people to consider a journey to California. Now middle-aged and married for some twenty years, his business on a downturn, Goulding was no doubt eager for a change. First, he needed to consult his family and make arrangements for their support while he was away. Some men left wives and children under the protection of a relative; some borrowed money for their family's upkeep or left their wives in charge of the family farm or business. Some were gone for two years or more; others never returned; and still others arrived home poorer than when they started. Goulding turned his business over to Montagnie Ward, presumably to help finance the California trip and provide for his family during his absence. Almost immediately, Ward published a catalog noting that "W. R. Goulding has retired from the Agency of the Surgical Instrument business . . . and the business will be conducted in the future by the Subscribers at 45 Ann Street, where the Instruments are manufactured by the same workmen as heretofore."[15]

The California gold rush was a traumatic period for wives, whose lives were turned upside down while their husbands sought adventure and escape from the humdrum of Victorian urban life. One Arkansas wife, Catherine Rector, a pregnant mother of three, was left in charge of the plantation when her gold-seeking husband departed for California. "I feel low spirited and depressed in feelings," she wrote. "Have I not enough to make me feel sad?"[16] Ann Goulding may have had a similar reaction. Known as a pious woman, she may have sought comfort in her Bible.[17]

William Goulding's investment in the trip was probably between two hundred and five hundred dollars—a hefty sum in those days. In contrast to many gold seekers, he seemed always to have money to spend. He was one of the senior members of the Knickerbocker Company, according to twenty-one-year-old George Churchill,

---

[15] Edmonson 1997, 75.

[16] McArthur 1986, 180.

[17] Baur, "Journey of William Robinson Goulding, Jr.," 1.

who wrote, "Old Mr. Goulding is the largest man in our company. He weighed 230 pounds."[18]

There is no evidence that Goulding actually visited the mines, because he was back in New York in time to be counted by the 1850 census. About this time, the family moved 125 miles north of New York City to the town of Stockport, New York. This manufacturing and mill town, the smallest in Columbia County at the time, was established in 1833 and named for Stockport, England. Snugly laid out on the banks of the Claverack and Kinderhook streams, it is five miles from the Hudson River and has a railroad connection to New York. Stockport registered only 794 males and 842 females in 1875. The major employer in town was Reynolds Empire Loom, established in 1852. The town also supported the Cotton Print Works (established in 1828), two churches, and a number of stores.[19] Four mineral springs, known as the Hudson Medicinal Waters, were located in Stockport and advertised cures for those who "suffered from cutaneous, rheumatic, or other physical ills."[20] High in the nearby Catskills was the exclusive Mountain House hotel, which the Gouldings visited (see chapter 8).

Stockport was a fine community for Goulding's wife and children, and for a while Goulding commuted to New York by train, returning home on weekends. Ann Goulding regularly taught her children the scriptures and they went to the Sabbath school in Stockport. On Sundays, they attended St. John's Evangelical Episcopal Church, built in 1844.[21] The Goulding children undoubtedly attended the Christmas Eve children's service organized and supported for some fifty years by a Miss Jane Scott, who provided presents for all the young people.[22] As time went on, members of the Goulding family would be laid to rest in the adjoining cemetery.[23]

[18] Churchill, May 17, 1849.

[19] F. Ellis 1878, 350, 383.

[20] Columbia County, New York, Historical Society subject file.

[21] Baur, "Journey of William Robinson Goulding, Jr.," 1.

[22] The church was affectionately known as "the little brown church." *Chatham* (*New York*) *Courier*, 1970.

[23] St. John's Evangelical Episcopal Church Cemetery records in the editor's files.

Goulding's son William, Jr., also started a diary, beginning in 1856 and adding to it for the next fifty years. That diary is now in possession of his Australian descendants. From it we learn that he was sixteen when the family moved to Stockport and he began his own career in the surgical instrument business in New York. He gives us a brief insight into life in the small town, recording three consecutive days of shooting blackbirds: "Got 15, lost 4 in the bushes." He went riding, and in winter, sleighing. A masquerade ball was held in the family home on Boxing Day, "the merriest day of the whole year."[24] During one wintry day in Stockport, he wrote, "Clear and cold. Took a sleigh ride with Cousin Harriet W—— ran over 2 pigs and upset in Hudson injuring Harriet's nose. Got home safe."[25]

There is no doubt that Goulding senior arrived home from his overland journey to California a changed man. He had overcome enormous physical and emotional challenges in the deserts and mountains. He had participated in one of the greatest mass migrations in history and had met all manner of fascinating people. Was he able to drop back into his old life, revitalize his business, and return to creating surgical and dental instruments? Evidence suggests that he found readjustment to his former Victorian lifestyle difficult.

However, he had a family to support, and between 1852 and 1853, he attempted to reorganize his business in two locations: 85 Fulton Street and 33 Gold Street. But things did not go well. First, the family suffered the death of eleven-year-old Alice on December 3, 1852. Goulding sold the business on December 29, 1853, to Thaddeus H. Walsh, who assumed the company debt and operated as "T. H. Walsh & Co. (Successors to Goulding & Co.) & Proprietors of the United States Surgical Instrument Manufacturing Company." Goulding's son William was expected to remain with the company and take over the firm when he obtained majority. At that time, the younger Goulding was described as a "practical surgical instrument

[24] The first weekday following Christmas; a legal holiday in many Commonwealth nations, when service workers are given Christmas boxes.

[25] Baur, "Journey of William Robinson, Jr.," 2.

maker [who] at present superintends the mechanical side of the business."[26]

His father briefly retained ties with T. H. Walsh and Co., then moved his end of the business to Stockport. According to the *New York Times*, the senior Goulding

> had exclusive charge of the manufacturing department of the firm, at Stockport, did all the business of that department, economized to that end, proposed the employment of boys as being cheaper than that of men, who often grew saucy and overbearing. In fact, Goulding was the "great gun" of the Stockport establishment for the manufacture of surgical instruments, and the New York City branch were small muskets or little pistols in comparison—though this latter branch were great in finance. (January 18, 1855)

This statement was made by the defense in a trial in which Goulding was accused of fraudulently endorsing a three-hundred-dollar check made out to Thaddeus H. Walsh and Co. on June 12, 1854. The jury found Goulding not guilty of the deed.[27]

The following April, William Goulding, Jr., went into partnership with William Fraser Ford, now his brother-in-law, but by May 1855, they were forced to hold a sale of surgical instruments to pay off a mortgage debt.[28] They soon dissolved that partnership, and young Goulding, now twenty-two and needing to fly on his own wings, sailed for Australia on April 21, 1856, where he remained for the rest of his life.[29]

The Panic of 1857 led to another economic downturn, and perhaps as a result, the Goulding name ceased to be connected with the business, which would be carried on by George Wade.[30] Finally, on March 19, 1861, the business became Wade and Ford. Ford had been working for the firm all along but his name did not appear until he obtained full discharge of the creditors of Goulding and Ford. By

[26] Edmonson 1997, 75–76.
[27] *New York Times*, 1854 and 1855.
[28] Boyd, May 12, 1855.
[29] Baur, "Journey of William Robinson Goulding, Jr., 2.
[30] *Dun & Co.*, New York City, 374:111; Edmonson 1997, 79–85.

this time, the company employed twenty-five workers in steam-powered shops and manufactured both surgical and dental instruments. In 1860, the business was worth thirty-nine thousand dollars, and Ford would remain successfully in the surgical instrument business until the end of the century.[31] The senior Goulding may have continued to create and supply surgical instruments to Wade and Ford from Stockport for a few years, but in 1859, he decided to sail to Australia to visit his son.

He was back in Stockport by 1860, when census records listed his occupation as "Gentleman."[32] Five youngsters are listed at the address along with Goulding's wife, Ann, and daughter Carrie. They were the children of D. W. Eames of New Orleans, and Ann was caring for them although Eames was no longer paying her. An 1864 letter from Goulding to his son implies that Eames was the owner of the house, and that he had rented it to another family and given Ann a life lease on a different house, presumably as payment for her child care.[33] These complex living arrangements suggest the severe financial problems the family was experiencing.

Goulding wrote that he was deeply in debt and hounded by lawyers. He had eighty dollars in his pocket, and with his wife's consent, he considered going back to San Francisco or leaving the country altogether. He began to sell tobacco and cigars, but that business was not profitable. He tried to join the navy as a surgeon's steward, to no avail, as Goulding confided in an 1864 letter to Henry S. Van de Carr, a Stockport businessman.

> So I went to my old friend Dr. V.[alentine] Mott, and who received me very kindly. I had often assisted him in my younger days in his surgical operation in the New York Hospital where I had been an officer for nine years. He gave me a letter to Surgeon General McDugal and the result was an appointment in the McClellan Hospital [illegible], 4 miles from Philadelphia. I did not like that position and seeing an advertisement for

[31] *Dun & Co.*, New York City, 377:119; Edmonson 1997, 79–80.

[32] U.S. Census Bureau, 8th Census of the United States, Stockport, 1860. Listed were David, aged eight; Jane and George (possibly twins), aged five and born in Louisiana; and Clarence and Henry, no age given, born in New York.

[33] Goulding to William R. Goulding, Jr., October 10, 1864.

surgeons at Washington I came here and succeeded to get a contact with J. C. McKee, the Surgeon in Chief.[34]

"Here" was Lincoln U.S. General Hospital in Washington, D.C., where Goulding obtained the position of medical steward on September 28, 1864. In a letter to Brigadier General Joseph K. Barnes, the U.S. Army surgeon general, he wrote: "I have the honor to request an appointment as Hospital Steward, U.S.A., for duty in the Army Medical Museum." The surgeon general responded the same day, recommending that he enlist, be appointed hospital steward, and report to the surgeon general.[35] (Barnes was Abraham Lincoln's personal surgeon and treated him after he was shot by John Wilkes Booth on April 14, 1865.) On October 13, 1864, Goulding filled out his papers for a three-year enlistment in the U.S. Army at Washington, D.C. He wrote that he was fifty-six, married, and from Canterbury, England, and he claimed to be an "artist." He described himself as having blue eyes, brown hair, a fresh complexion, and a five-feet-eight-and-one-half-inch frame.[36]

Lincoln Hospital had opened on December 23, 1862, at East Capitol and Fifteenth streets. It was founded specifically to treat soldiers injured in the Civil War. A map of the hospital complex found with Goulding's journal shows twenty pavilions arranged in two lines forming a V, and twenty-five tent wards with 2,575 beds. The thirty-acre complex included many outbuildings. By August 22, 1865, the hospital had treated 20,228 white troops, 18 colored troops, and 1,113 prisoners of war. The hospital was dismantled shortly after the Civil War.[37]

Goulding's first assignment to Lincoln Hospital was as a medical steward—a noncommissioned officer ranking above the first sergeant of a company. Goulding was responsible for procuring medical supplies and surgical instruments, and he arranged a contract for the army

[34] Goulding to Henry S. Van de Carr, January 31, 1865. The four-hundred-bed hospital was named for the leader of the Union Army, Gen. George McClellan, and was located at Germantown and Cayuga streets some four miles from Philadelphia (F. Taylor 1913, 226–27).

[35] Goulding to J. Barnes, September 28, 1864; J. Barnes to Goulding, September 28, 1864.

[36] Goulding, enlistment papers.

[37] Plan of Lincoln U.S. General Hospital; [Otis] 1865, 155–58.

surgeon in charge, Brevet Lieutenant Colonel J. C. McKee, to buy them from his old business, now Wade and Ford. During his tenure at the hospital, he continued doing business with Wade and Ford to supply medical instruments to the various doctors serving there.[38]

According to an 1862 manual, a hospital steward was expected to perform minor surgery and should be "industrious, temperate, patient, good-tempered and actuated by a desire to minister to the sick and wounded under his charge."[39] Stewards received a clothing allowance, one room as quarters in the barracks, and one cord of wood each month from October to April. Some particularly able stewards could be promoted to assistant surgeon. In an October 10, 1864, letter to his son, Goulding wrote, "My department is on morbid anatomy. My pay is $100 per month . . . I am allowed one orderly man who attends to my quarters and does all my dirty work, etc. He is a U.S.A. soldier or corporal." He added that there were "about an average of 5 deaths occurring every day and from 3 to 6 capital operations performed every day. . . . The scenes are awful."[40]

Goulding now began to outfit himself for duty. On October 15, he noted in his journal that he purchased a military cap with insignia, $4.00. On October 25, he added a dress coat, first quality, $58.00; dress pants, $20.00; 2 vests, cloth and 8 white, $20.00; trimmings, $5.00; 2 pair gloves, $3.00; 1 pair suspenders, $1.25; fatigue military vest, $4.00; and scarlet stripes for pants, $1.50. On November 1, he recorded an expense for a military sabre, belt, and sash amounting to $33.00, and shoes to order, $33.00.[41] He must have presented quite a grand figure in his single-breasted frock coat of dark blue cloth, collar and cuffs edged with a cord of crimson, and a red worsted sash with bullion-fringed ends, wound twice around the waist and tied behind the left hip.[42]

---

[38] Lists of these purchases and subsequent payments to Wade & Ford fill many pages of the addenda to Goulding's journal.

[39] Woodward 1862, 13–25.

[40] Goulding to William R. Goulding, Jr., October 10, 1864.

[41] Goulding addenda, 21–22.

[42] Woodward 1862, 27.

During this time, he admitted in a letter to a friend that he had visited the "old shop" and that it was "just as of old. Better for me I pitched that in final trade and gone in the service 20 years ago—that's just my fort—I was born and bred a soldier—and the life and sound of the drum is my delight—I love it . . . we have a band and drum corps, a parade every afternoon, and inspection on Sunday."[43]

Goulding obtained leave on November 5, 1864, to travel to New York to visit his daughter Annie, now married to William Fraser Ford. Goulding's wife, Ann, came from Stockport to be at the gathering. This may have been the last time he saw his wife. His daughter Annie presented him with a copy of *The Book of Common Prayer* that Goulding had given his son William in 1847. The younger Goulding had left the book with his sister before going to Australia. Goulding wrote that "it was again presented to me by my beloved daughter on November 13, 1864 in Brooklyn."[44]

Not long after that visit, Goulding wrote that he had been very ill and confined to his quarters for a week or so and "could not stand up, violent pain in the left knee, the shoulders and neck also the hands and wrists."[45] He must have been feeling better by January 27, 1865, for he began working at the Army Medical Museum, the position he had originally applied for when he joined the army in the previous October. He soon moved out of his quarters at Lincoln General Hospital and rented a room from Mrs. Elza Klemm at 424 Fourteenth Street for ten dollars a month.[46] President Lincoln had signed a bill in April 1862 reorganizing the medical department of the army and had appointed William Alexander Hammond as head. Hammond announced his intention to open a museum and instructed medical officers to "collect specimens of morbid anatomy" from battle sites to assist future research and treatment.[47] Goulding reported to curator

---

[43] Goulding to John Wolfel, December 20, 1864, in Goulding addenda, 16–17.

[44] Goulding addenda, 5.

[45] Goulding addenda, 60.

[46] It was reasonably close to the Medical Museum (formerly the Corcoran Building) at 1325 H Street, between Thirteenth and Fourteenth, across from the New York Avenue Presbyterian Church.

[47] Henry 1964, 9, 11, 25.

George Alexander Otis, who assumed charge of the museum on October 3, 1864, the same day that Goulding joined the army.[48] There is an item in the National Museum of Health and Medicine that arrived following the Battle of Gettysburg in July 1863. It is the severed leg bones of Major General Daniel E. Sickles, who was aware of the importance of collecting for the museum. Those bones continue to be displayed in the twenty-first century; an accompanying label notes that the general visited his leg from time to time. We will be left to wonder if William Robinson Goulding made casts of those bones.

By 1865, Goulding was evidently quite ill, and he ordered a carriage to take him with his baggage to Douglas General Hospital on March 12. Based on his earlier complaint of pain and the "Rheumatic Medicine" he was taking, he was probably suffering from rheumatic fever.[49]

During his last days, Goulding wrote and received many letters at the hospital, the dates of which he noted in the final pages of the addenda to his journal. On the day of Lincoln's death, he wrote that he had sent newspapers recording the event to his wife and to his son in Australia. He also remembered to send valentines to his "dear wife" and his daughter Carrie. He made his last entry on April 29, 1865.[50]

In his 1865 annual report, Goulding's supervisor, Dr. Otis, wrote that the "Quartermaster's Department had fitted up a workshop for a moulder in plaster in the building in rear of the museum, and also floored the lower hall of the main building with a large glass case. Hospital Steward Goulding, U.S.A., was assigned to the duty of making plaster casts of pathological specimens and died before he had perfected any of his work."[51]

---

[48] Lamb n.d., 33, 36.

[49] Goulding addenda, 42, 47. Douglas Hospital was one of three brick houses that had been converted to hospitals during the Civil War. They were owned by Stephen Douglas, Henry M. Rice, and John C. Breckenridge. Often referred to as "Douglas Row" or "Minnesota Row," they were located where New Jersey Avenue, I Street, and Second Avenue meet. The hospital opened in January 1862 and was closed in November 1865. "Military hospitals," finding guide, National Archives.

[50] Goulding addenda, 54–60.

[51] Lamb n.d., 36.

Goulding died on May 11, 1865, and was buried in Stockport's Episcopal Churchyard Cemetery beside his daughter Alice.[52] Ann Goulding wrote to her son in Australia informing him that his "Father died a Christian, this is indeed a blessed thought." She went on to write that "his last letter showed a deep spiritual change—and even before his last sickness he had set his house in order and was bound for the land of bright spirits above."[53] Ann Goulding and her daughter Carrie remained in Stockport. Ann would be laid to rest next to her husband following her death fifteen years later on August 25, 1880.[54]

William Goulding appears never to have fully adjusted to the daily routine after his return from California. Here was a creative, artistic individual who had already achieved the ultimate as a designer of surgical instruments. Coming home from the adventure of a lifetime, he undoubtedly realized the California gold rush was a momentous event. His brush with history was heightened by the number of illustrious figures he had met and talked to. He had literally walked through history in the making as he crossed the United States on the brink of change: Indian Country in flux, the newly organized Territory of New Mexico governed by the United States; and the beginning of the decline of the great Spanish and Mexican land grants in California.

Though he went back to manufacturing surgical instruments for a while, economic downturns in 1854 and again in 1857 had weakened his former business considerably. Things had begun to look up when he had the opportunity to join the United States Army during the Civil War; he was able to do good works for the medical community once more and make a small contribution to the beginnings of the Medical Museum, which later became the National Museum of Health and Medicine. It is to be hoped that in his last days, Goulding reflected on his family, his travels across the continent,

[52] St. John's Evangelical Episcopal Church Cemetery records. The *Register of Enlistments in the United States Army, 1798–1914*, confirms the date of Goulding's death at Douglas Hospital.

[53] Baur, "Journey of William R. Goulding, Jr."

[54] U.S. Census Bureau, 9th Census of the United States, 1870; St. John's Evangelical Episcopal Cemetery records.

the people he met, and his accomplishments in the medical field and was satisfied that he had led a very good life.

Following Goulding's death, his journal was sent to his son William in Australia. It was eventually sold to the Beinecke Library at Yale University by a grandson, Philip Arthur Goulding, also of Australia, sometime before 1950.

The journal is unique in a number of ways. Whereas most emigrants starting out at Fort Smith followed the south bank of the Canadian River to the New Mexico border, Goulding was among the minority of travelers who followed trader Josiah Gregg's 1839–40 route along the north bank of the river in Oklahoma as far as the Texas Panhandle, then headed south of the river to New Mexico. Once in New Mexico, Goulding was again among the minority who left the Rio Grande near Truth or Consequences to follow in the wake of John Charles Frémont's return trip to California after his disastrous fourth expedition in 1848. Unlike other travelers, Goulding had letters of introduction to men in the various military posts. The interesting individuals he met along the way included Native peoples from some fifteen tribes. In California, Goulding followed the Mission Trail to Monterey, meeting and conversing with numerous rancheros. He reached Monterey at a time when delegates were gathering for the constitutional convention, where he met with the military governor, Bennett C. Riley; John Sutter, and many other figures important in early California history.

I

The Adventure Begins

William Robinson Goulding was starting out on the trip of a lifetime. He was about to leave New York for Wheeling, West Virginia, where he would join sixty-three other men who had signed up to travel to California with the Knickerbocker Exploring Company of New York. Since 1848, newspapers all over the country had been filled with news of the discovery of gold. The gold rush began in earnest after President James A. Polk's State of the Union message in December 1848, when he confirmed that there was enough gold in California for all who wanted to risk the journey.

As a result, a group of interested individuals gathered in New York on January 19, 1849, to write a constitution for the Knickerbocker Exploring Company, elect officers, and decide on a route (see appendix A). They agreed to start out on the Fort Smith–Santa Fe Trail by way of the Canadian River, probably as a result of reading Fort Smith's "Ho! for California!" circulars, published in eastern newspapers, which encouraged prospectors to take that route as the best and shortest.

Additional encouragement came in the form of a hundred-man military escort that was to protect the forty-niners and also survey a national road between Fort Smith and Santa Fe. An army appropriation bill was approved on March 3, 1849, to cover the expense. Captain Randolph B. Marcy of the Fifth U.S. Infantry was selected to escort the emigrants, and Lieutenant J. H. Simpson, a topographical engineer, was appointed to survey and construct the wagon road. The Knickerbockers eventually decided to forgo military protection and begin their westward journey through Indian Territory on trader Josiah Gregg's old trail along the north bank of the Canadian River (both Gregg's route north of the Canadian and Marcy's route south of the Canadian would ultimately be referred to as the Fort Smith–Santa Fe Trail).

In the first chapter of his journal, Goulding details his trip to from New York to Fort Smith, which took almost twenty days by rail, stagecoach, and steamship. At Wheeling, West Virginia, Goulding and friends boarded the steamship Hudson, which one of the Knickerbockers, Phineas Blunt, had chartered to take them along the Ohio, Mississippi, and Arkansas rivers to Fort Smith.

Leaving New York on Sunday, February 18, 1849, in company with two friends, and travelling by way of Philadelphia, Baltimore, and the Great Western Rail Road, I arrived at Cumberland [Maryland] on the evening of the 20th.[1] The scenery by the way was, for the most part, interesting and attractive. I was particularly struck with the abundance of wild duck, brant & teal at Harpers Ferry & hovering along the shores of the Potomac.

From Cumberland, the night route over the mountains in coaches was no less amusing to some than fatiguing to others of the company. It was my privilege to secure a seat in the coach which conveyed the only female passenger, and somewhat addicted to gallantry, I duly appreciated the honor. In both slumber, with interludes of talking, laughing & grumbling, the night passed away, and morning found us still rumbling over mountain & valley, with eager appetite for the long delayed breakfast.

[1] It is questionable whether Goulding traveled to Baltimore via the Atlantic and Great Western Railroad, since it was not chartered until 1859. Once in Baltimore, Goulding more than likely boarded the B&O Railroad, which had been in service to Cumberland, Maryland, since 1842. Another 78 miles by stage would bring him to Brownsville, Pennsylvania (Dunbar 1937, 3:1113). His two companions were probably William Fraser Ford and John A. Hunter, also listed as surgical instrument makers (see appendix A).

A little after noon, we arrived at Brownsville [Pennsylvania], where we found abundance of good cheer, admirably flavored with the never-failing humor of our worthy & facetious host, Dan Brown. But all Dan's fun & wit cannot make his place look clean & home-like to a northerner. Black & dingy with the smoke of coal, not only the houses, but the fences, the trees, and the very ground seems to need washing.[2] It is impossible to keep anything clean. It is so in all the coal region west of the mountains. The men & the boys & even the ladies show marks of it on all occasions.

Smutty hands & smutty faces,
Smutty linens, smutty laces,
Smutty houses, shops & stables,
Smutty beds & smutty tables,
Sooty water, sooty air,
Smouched & smutty everywhere.

There are coal pits all along the road. Many families have them just in the rear of their houses, like wood-yards, to which they go as the coal is wanted for daily use.

Brownsville was all alive with excitement, [illegible] expecting the arrival of General [Zachary] Taylor on his way to Washington and determined to give him a worthy reception.[3] We did not stop to enjoy the fun, but met the brave old soldier with his retinue about five miles out of town. With many hearty cheers, we sent him on his way and pursued our own, through mud & mire, to Washington, Pensy [Pennsylvania], where we arrived at 9 PM.

The next day at noon we reached Pittsburgh, where I expected to overtake my company. To my great disappointment, they had left but an hour before. Taking the steamer Michigan to Beaver [Pennsyl-

[2] When Col. James Burd uncovered a vein of soft coal near Brownsville in 1759 and "burned a bushel of it in his fire," western Pennsylvania was soon found to sit on an almost unbroken bituminous coalfield. By 1831, the area had become chiefly dependent on the production of coal (Writers' Program 1940, 598–99). One gold seeker, George Pattison, wrote of Pittsburgh: "It appears in fact, to be one huge blacksmith shop, and clouds of smoke rain all day upon it" (April 3, 1849).

[3] A hero of the Mexican War following his victory at the Battle of Buena Vista, Zachary Taylor (1784–1850) was traveling from his home in Baton Rouge to Washington, D.C., where he would be inaugurated as twelfth president of the United States on March 5, 1849.

vania] & thence by country waggons over horrible roads, travelling day & night without rest, twice capsized & once losing our way in the darkness, I reached Wheeling [West Virginia] on the evening of Friday, February 23, worn & almost exhausted with the fatigues of the journey.[4] Here we overtook our company and were duly installed as members of "the New York Knickerbocker Association."

Passing down the Ohio in the good steamer Hudson,[5] we reached Cincinnati on Monday, February 26, with no incident of much importance except that during the night of the 24th, we were so much impeded by ice that it became necessary for all hands to lend a hand in clearing a way. It was hard work & bitter cold. But the interest & excitement of the scene were so great that it went off as a first rate frolic. Some of the party went on shore and kindled large fires on the bank to give light to those engaged in the work. After about three hours duration, the boat went on her way and met with no further obstruction.

On Sunday, February 25, we had divine service on board the boat, conducted by the Rev. Ira M. Allen, one of our company.[6] At Cincinnati, we were cordially welcomed by many good friends and when we left that hospitable city, the Queen of the West, our departure was cheered by hearty & long continued demonstrations of kind & affectionate good will from young men & maidens, old men & children, that would have satisfied the ambition & compensated the sacrifices of soldiers returning from the wars.

On Thursday, March 1, we stopped a few hours at Louisville, the most thriving place in Kentucky. The next day, passed the Cave

---

[4] The *Michigan* was a 103-ton stern-wheel packet steamer manufactured in Shousetown, Pennsylvania in 1847, with Captain Wolf at the wheel (Way 1994, 321).

[5] According to the *Fort Smith (Arkansas) Herald* (March 14, 1849), the Knickerbockers chartered the steamer *Hudson*. The 94-ton stern-wheel packet was built at Smiths Ferry, Pennsylvania, in 1846 and sold to James McMillan, Master, in December 1848 (Way 1994, 218). George Churchill (1849) remarked on February 14 that each man paid $39 for the trip to Fort Smith, which included provisions, and that the captain ultimately pocketed a total of $2,700 for the trip.

[6] The topic of the service, according to Phineas Blunt, was the question: "Would have all men to be saved and come to the knowledge of the truth?" (February 25, 1849). There would not be many more Sunday services, although the men had planned a day of rest on Sundays, for as time went on, the difficulties of travel and survival took precedence.

Rock, which from its resemblance to the Palisades on the North River, attracted the attention of every eye in our company. This rock is about one mile in length, perfectly perpendicular, to the height of 60 feet, and forms one of the banks of the river. It seems to the eye more like masonry than the work of nature. Near one end of it, there is an opening leading to an extensive cave, from which the name of the rock is derived. It was formerly occupied by a desperate gang of banditti commanded by the celebrated Captain [Henry] Neal, who was the terror of all the early settlers.[7]

On Saturday, March 3, we found ourselves at Cairo [Illinois], a small but very important place at the junction of the Ohio with the Mississippi. This place is rendered important by its [illegible] position at the confluence of the two great rivers. A vast deal of money has already been expended here to lay the foundations of a city sufficiently high to brave the terrors of an annual inundation. Whether money can accomplish this grand object is yet a question. If it can, there is no point in the great West which would concentrate more & greater advantages for the site of a mammoth, great city.

The wharf boats at this place & at Memphis attracted my attention as a peculiar feature of the rivers. It is one of the largest class of river boats, no longer fit for service on the river, and now firmly moored to the levee, where it serves the purpose of a wharf for the other boats to make fast to. It is stripped of all its machinery & gear of every description, in order that every portion of the hull may [be] brought into use. The lower hold, well lighted & ventilated, is divided into various apartments, which are well fitted up & furnished, one as a butcher's shop, another as a drug store, a third as a grocery, a fourth for dry goods, a fifth for hardware, a sixth for a post

---

[7] No doubt the cliffs reminded Goulding of the palisades on the southernmost part of the Hudson River between New York and New Jersey, a familiar sight near his Stockport home. Cave-In-Rock looks down on the Ohio River from a limestone cliff in Shawnee National Forest in southeast Illinois. Its reputation dates to the Revolutionary War, when deserters from the Continental Army sought refuge in the cave. It also proved to be an ideal hiding place for pirates and desperadoes who attacked and plundered passing flatboats from the site. Henry Neal, whose job it was to track down criminals, was indicted for murder after firing some seventeen bullets into James Ford in 1833 (Snively and Furbee 1968, 158, 171, 175–76).

office, a seventh for a telegraph office &c., while the upper or cabin decks are metamorphosed into a first rate hotel, furnished with every comfort & luxury which the most fastidious wayfarer could desire. Memphis has a fine appearance from the river. It is situated on high ground and is well built. Leaving at 7 in the morning, we were again favored with religious services on board by Rev. Mr. Allen.

Early on the morning of Monday, March 5, we reached the mouth of the Arkansas River, 360 miles from Cairo. The landing is called Napoleon, a small, mean, dirty place with a mighty name.[8] The squalid appearance of town was, however, somewhat compensated by an excellent breakfast of venison & eggs at the hotel, as it was called, served up by a very handsome landlady.

At 11 o'clock, we got under way to ascend the Arkansas, [illegible] having a distance of 570 miles to accomplish before reaching Fort Smith. The day was fine. Peaches & other small fruit trees were in blossom. We promised ourselves a pleasant trip. But the appearance of the country was monotonous & dull—one "boundless continuity of shade"[9]—one dense, unbroken forest of cottonwood & butternut. Here and there a log cabin, erected perhaps by some independent squatter, will show itself on the bank with a few acres of clearing, from which, without fear of landlord or claimant and with no reverence for parchment deeds or recorded titles, the hardy settler draws a comfortable living for his family, and it may be lays the foundation of a planters' fortune.

Moving slowly up against the current, we found the scenery gradually improving. The dwellings of the primitive settlers became more numerous and the aspect of their little farms more thrifty. Some of them had abundance of cattle & some from 20 to 50 slaves & plenty of cord wood piled upon the bank to supply the boats passing up &

[8] Until 1874, when the town at the confluence of the Mississippi and Arkansas rivers was submerged, Napoleon, Arkansas, was a wide-open, lawless river town with few comforts. Lorenzo Aldrich (1851, 7) bedded down in an abandoned wharf boat on May 3, 1849, and counted ten buildings, none of which was a school, a church, or a jail, observing that "the state of society is bad."

[9] Goulding was quoting from popular English poet William Cowper (1731–1800), "The Timepiece": "Oh for a lodge in some vast wilderness / Some boundless contiguity of shade" (Cowper 1889, 198).

down the river. We lived luxuriously. Game was very abundant—blue crane—wild duck and many other favorites of the gourmand were continually tempting us to waste our powder in securing more than was wanted for each day's consumption.

On Tuesday, March 6, we reached Pine Bluff [Arkansas], about 170 miles from the mouth of the [Arkansas] River. This was at that time a place of about 400 inhabitants, situated on a bold point of about 30 feet high & remarkable for containing the only pine trees that are to be found in the lower courses of this river. As we proceeded, we saw immense numbers of wild geese, ducks, cranes, pelicans, swans, plover &c. The whole county teems with them. They find their houses around the borders of the numerous lakes & ponds with which this part of the country, on both sides of the river, is liberally dotted. Amid this profusion of game, there was a plentiful scarcity, sometimes, of ordinary provisions, which gave rise to some portentous grumblings around our table.

On Wednesday, March 7, we reached Little Rock, the capital of the state of Arkansas. It takes its name from a small rock which projects into the river in front of the town.[10] A rock is of so rare occurrence in these alluvial bottoms that this was the first we had seen for several days. It is therefore a sufficiently prominent feature of the place to claim the right of naming it.

Little Rock contained, at that time, about 3,000 inhabitants and

---

[10] Little Rock is on the south side of the Arkansas River. In 1822, French explorer Bernard de la Harpe bestowed the name La Petite Roche (Little Rock) after a stone outcrop on the bank of the river where the city now stands (Herndon 1922, 5).

The *Arkansas State Democrat* (*Little Rock*) on March 9, 1849, took note of the group's arrival: "HO FOR CALIFORNIA! The Knickerbocker Mining and Exploring Company, numbering seventy members under the command of Capt. Ebbetts, arrived at our city, on Wednesday last, on the steamer *Hudson*. . . . This Company have along with them, their wagons, and every other necessary for their outfit, except mules and horses. . . . The members of this company were all in good health and fine spirits."

The small city had a few impressive buildings. Lorenzo Aldrich (1851, 7) arrived in town on May 6 and described an imposing State House on the banks of the Arkansas River, which he learned had been built of brick, coated with plaster, then scored to look like marble. Now a museum, this historic building has undergone several face-lifts over the years and has long been a favorite of former president William Jefferson Clinton.

appears to be a place of considerable business. Our dinner at the Anthony Hotel we shall not soon forget.[11] In the [illegible] phrase of the epicure, it was "capital," and made us all forget our table grumblings till the bell rang for supper.

Above Little Rock, the face of the country assumes a very different appearance: the dead flat [page torn] place to beautiful undulations of land. Hills [page torn] to rise on either bank of the river, some of the sufficient height to be dignified with the name of mountains. The pine and other evergreens, till now not seen anywhere except at Pine Bluff, make their appearance along the dark sides of the hills and on the banks of the river. This variety is agreeable & inspiring, the more so because it resembles the features of our own beloved land—the land of the north. We were often reminded of the highlands of New York and the scenery of the Catskill Mountains.

On the night of Wednesday, March 7, an alarm was raised that brought all hands on deck in their night clothes like so many frightened spectres. The boat struck on a sand bar, when, partly through ignorance of the nature of our danger & partly from mischief, the fearful cry "a snag! a snag!" was raised by one of the deck hands. This was followed by shouts of "Fire!" "Water!" "Snag!" "Wreck!" with a violent ringing of the bell, till all was bustle, terror & confusion on board. It did not continue long, however. The true nature of the accident was soon ascertained—the shouting ceased—order was restored, the affrighted passengers skulked back to their berths, the boat backed off from the bar, and choosing a deeper channel, proceeded on her way without further hindrance.

In this part of our trip, we had no occasion to complain of our fare. Game of every kind was in great abundance and to be purchased at so

---

[11] The three-story, red-brick Anthony House was a few steps from the steamboat landing on the south side of Markham between Scott and Second streets. The 28-room establishment had been rebuilt after an 1840 fire and was managed by 29-year-old James Brown, who maintained "his wide reputation as an excellent land-lord. All those who stop at his house will find themselves so well gratified by his attention and table, that they will not need an invitation to 'call again'" (*Van Buren Arkansas Intelligencer*, May 3, 1845). Goulding and friends feasted in the 60-foot dining room and very likely sampled the offerings in the hotel's well-stocked bar. Perhaps they also enjoyed after-dinner cigars in one of the hotel's two parlors (M. Smith, n.d.).

cheap a rate that we had no temptation to trouble ourselves with shooting it. At any of the stopping places, chickens could be had at 10 cents each, turkeys at 3 to 4 shillings, eggs at 8 cts. per dozen, butter at 10 cents per pound, and other things in proportion. Of these, we laid in a plentiful supply, expecting soon to reach our camping ground and our line of march across the country. We made an [page torn] upon the milk of that region, which was very abundant & cheap. But we were unable to drink it. It made us sick in every instance, and we were informed that it always has the same effect upon northerners when first used. As with the water, it gives us some considerable time to become accustomed [to] it. Whether this is owing to anything peculiar in [the] feed of the cows, or to the water they drink, I am not informed. A chemical analysis of the milk [would] probably decide the question. The fact is referred to the philosophers.

A heavy fog ushered in Friday, March 9, which we supposed would be the last day of our steaming up the Arkansas. About 9, the fog cleared away and the weather became intensely hot. The time was fully occupied in organizing our company & making arrangements for our future movements. The company was divided into twelve messes of six men each, with a council man to each mess.[12] These were nominated by the mess and elected by the votes of the whole company. There was also a captain & two lieutenants and it was decided that all our affairs should be conducted under a sort of military discipline. I was placed at the head of Mess no. 3. In the distribution of our stock, each mess was allowed 406 pounds of pork & bacon, 400 of pilot bread, a half barrel of flour, 150 pounds of pinola (sweet corn, dried & mixed with sugar), 150 pounds of moist sugar, 65 pounds coffee, 1 bag of salt, 5 pounds of tea, 1 box of soap, 2 pounds of mustard, 2 pounds of pepper, 50 pounds of Indian meal, two gallons each of molasses & vinegar, 400 pickles, two bushels beans, one bushel of peas, a set of cooking utensils, six shovels, two axes, a handsaw, two crowbars, two hatchets, with screws, nails, gimlets & hammers, and two pans, two plates, knife, fork & spoon

[12] Goulding's six messmates would share a wagon and the chores of driving, cooking, hunting, and tending the animals.

for each man, also a waggon & four lots of mule harness for each mess. These last were purchased by a committee of three [page torn] from the council men.[13]

On the morning of Saturday, March 10, we arrived at Fort Smith on the borders of the [page torn] bade a final adieu to our steam boat. And here a scene of confusion ensued, our military organization altogether forgotten in the excitement of getting [page torn] on terra firma. Every man was captain, and with [page torn] independence, was determined to have his own way. And that way, in most cases, was by no means a gentle or a gentlemanly one. Helter-skelter, like a company of mad men rushing hither & thither, shouting, carousing, swearing & swaggering, flinging things about, breaking & smashing anything that [was] capable of being broken, the quiet people of Fort Smith must have thought bedlam let loose upon them. Early in the day, the course things were likely to [page torn] quietly withdrew from the scene & went with my baggage to the hotel, awaiting the return of our captain, who had gone out into the country to select a suitable place for our first encampment.[14]

---

[13] Phineas Blunt (March 6, 1849) was one member of the committee of three that bought the wagon and mule harnesses.

[14] Goulding found lodging at Capt. John Rogers's brick hotel at the corner of present-day Second and A streets. Rogers had been sutler at Fort Smith, 1822–24, and was one of the town founders (Tomer and Broadhead 1992, 181n28). Years later, Balduin Möllhausen, a Prussian artist traveling with the 1853–54 Whipple expedition, wrote that he stayed at Rogers's hotel for two dollars a night, where he enjoyed a "pleasant and festive time" (1858, 13).

2

The Feisty New York Knickerbockers

GOULDING'S FIRST ACTION on arrival at a military post was to visit the quartermaster's office or that of the surgeon on duty. At Fort Smith, Arkansas, he met Dr. Joseph Howard Bailey, a U.S. Army surgeon, who may have owned a set of Goulding's surgical instruments. Goulding's surgical background gave him the opportunity to meet a number of interesting men during his travels: Jeremy Francis Gilmore, a future Confederate chief of engineers; Matthew Arbuckle, Jr., a future brigadier general; Delos Bennet Sacket, a future inspector general of the army; John Marshall Washington, military governor of New Mexico; Bennett C. Riley, military governor of California; Kit Carson; and John Charles Frémont, the "Pathfinder." Whether Goulding later followed the fortunes of any of the illustrious people he met on his trip is unknown.

During his stay in Fort Smith, Goulding explored his surroundings, made his first foray into Indian Territory, and briefly visited General Matthew Arbuckle, Jr., commander of Fort Smith. Goulding and John A. N. Ebbetts, captain of the Knickerbockers, consulted the commander about the merits of two possible routes. Captain Randolph B. Marcy of the U.S. Army, who was already at Fort Smith, planned to open a road south of the Canadian River and did not leave with his troops until April 4, 1849. The Knickerbockers, on the other hand, who already felt well prepared, left on March 26 and remained in advance of Marcy's troops all the way to Santa Fe. They followed the trail north of the Canadian River that Santa Fe trader

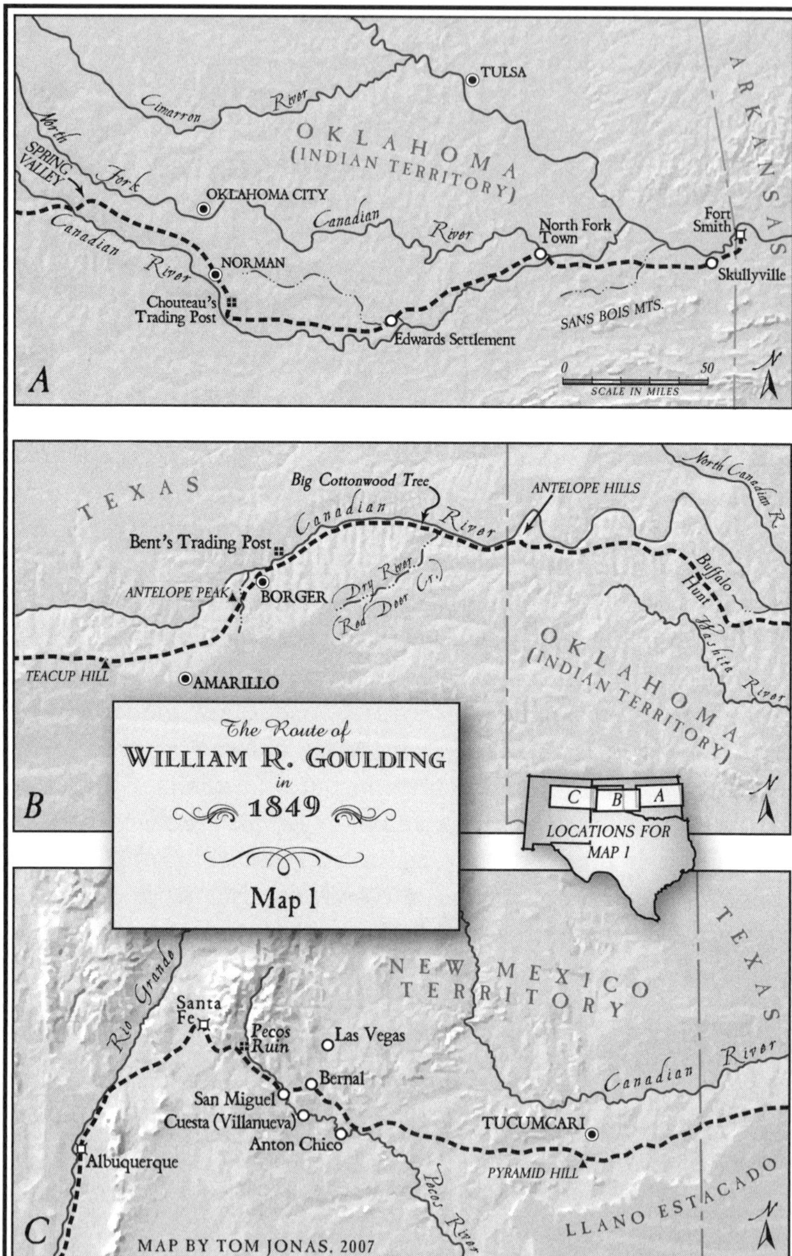

Map 1. Fort Smith to Albuquerque

Josiah Gregg had opened during 1839–40. Perhaps someone brought along Gregg's book, Commerce of the Prairies, which introduced the people and customs of New Mexico to travelers and described the merits of the route. Along with the Heath Pack Mule Company, which had left Fort Smith on March 12, the Knickerbockers were among the first to travel along the north bank of the Canadian River as far as a place called Spring Valley, where they crossed and continued on the south bank of the river.

Saturday, March 10, late in the afternoon, the Captain of our company, John Ebbetts,[1] came galloping along the bluff, drenched to the skin with the rain which had been falling all day, and informed us he had selected a site for the encampment about two miles from Fort Smith, called "Sulphur Springs." Immediately all was bustle and activity for the removal. Waggons were loaded with great dispatch, & mules, such as they were, & in some cases oxen were lured to draw them to the camp. It was a scene of unusual interest and variety. The road was almost impassably bad. Mud, soft and almost knee deep, made it difficult to move at all, and in some places impossible, without all hands turning out and giving a lift. It was new business to many of the gentleman Knickerbockers, and they certainly did not appear to the best advantage. Pulling at the wheels, poking at the oxen, or whipping the mules with noisy vociferations, abundance of oaths, drenched with ceaseless rain, and woefully bespattered from head to foot with mud, they would scarcely have

[1] The *Fort Smith (Arkansas) Herald* reported on March 14, 1849, that the 33-year-old "Captain" from New York was "a gentleman who has experience in Prairie life and appears to be an enterprising, persevering man." John A. N. Ebbetts had a number of years' experience with the Union Fur Company in the northwest (*Niles' National Register* 1844, 224). But he was not a good leader of men, and as time went on, dissension rose in the ranks of the Knickerbockers, who ultimately split into small groups and followed their own destinies. Ebbetts would continue his explorations in California, and on December 19 and 20, 1853, the *San Francisco Daily Herald* published his Pacific Railroad Survey on the discovery of Ebbetts Pass in the Sierra Nevada (Ebbetts 1853). Sadly, those who opened the *Daily Alta California* on April 16, 1854, were horrified to learn that the steamer *Secretary* had blown into atoms a few hours after departing from Sacramento for Petaluma. Some thirty lives were lost—among them, that of John A. N. Ebbetts.

been recognised by any of their old companions in Broadway. Some four or five of the messes succeeded, with prodigious effort, in reaching the camp that night. Others were hopelessly stuck in the mud and compelled to remain there all night, the tenfold darkness of which was occasionally relieved by tremendous flashes of lightning. I succeeded in getting my waggons to the camp ground and returned late at night to my lodgings at Fort Smith.

I had fortunately made the acquaintance of Dr. [Joseph Howard] Bailey,[2] surgeon in the U.S. Army at Barracks, who introduced me to the officers of the station and made me welcome to their mess. About 200 men were then at the station under the command of Gen. [Matthew] Arbuckle.[3]

The next day was Sunday, March 11. I was too entirely exhausted with the labors of the previous day to be very early at my post. I kept my room till noon & then rode out to the camp. All the stragglers who were left the night before in the mud, were in, and the camp assumed quite an orderly appearance. Cooking of various kinds were going on among the different messes, and all seemed to be enjoying themselves highly. It was like anything but a Sunday scene at home. After assisting my mess in some of their culinary operations and enjoying for awhile the general good cheer, I returned in the dusk of the evening to my quarters in the town.

While on my way, going at full gallop, I was suddenly arrested and thrown into such a fright as I never before experienced. I nearly lost my wits. My horse was no less frightened than myself. He trembled like an aspen leaf and could scarcely stand. The cause of all this alarm was an immense flock of parroquets that flew like a cloud over

---

[2] The *Fort Smith* (*Arkansas*) *Herald* published a letter from Dr. Joseph Howard Bailey on February 14, 1849, in which he enthusiastically promoted travel on the Fort Smith route to California as "not only a nearer, but a better way than the northern one." He said he obtained his information from personal experience, conversations with military men, and the Indians and traders. Bailey, a New Yorker, had come to Fort Smith from Fort Towson, where he served as post surgeon (G. Foreman 1968, 66). During his tenure at Fort Smith Barracks, Bailey became Fourth Grandmaster of the Belle Point no. 20 Masonic Lodge ("Grand Old Belle Point," 2006). Following retirement in 1862 (Heitman 1903, 1:181), Bailey stayed on in Fort Smith and over the years acquired considerable property in the area (Faulk and Jones 1983, 30).

[3] Brevet Brig. Gen. Matthew Arbuckle, Jr., was on his second tour of duty in Fort Smith, having previously served there in 1822–23 (Thrapp 1995).

FIGURE 2. Fort Smith, Arkansas, as it looked in 1855. Painting by Francis M. Treseder, 1911. *Picture Collection, Special Collections, University of Arkansas Libraries.*

the trees and lighted down on the road just before me with such a confused, unearthly chattering, mingled with loud, shrill screams & shrieks, as almost made my hair stand on end. If a troop of wild Indians had encountered me or if the earth had opened at my feet and a thousand ghosts had emerged from the regions below, I should scarcely have been more startled, though the alarm might have [been] more lasting & serious and the company less agreeable. They almost took my cap from my head with the flapping of their wings as they swept by. I was not prepared for so sudden & noisy an apparition, which, by the contrast of their red feet & bills with the deep leaf green of their plumage, had an effect as surprising as it was singular. They are very abundant in this part of the country. They move in flocks like pigeons. They are very quick on the wing, but their motion is irregular and fitful like that of the swallow, darting up with a sudden jerk, and then swooping down to the very ground, chattering & screaming with every variety of tone, as if they had just been let out of Babel. There are many other birds of fine plumage in this part of the country. The taste & science of an Audubon alone could do them justice.[4]

This fright over, my horse & myself fully recovered from our agitation, and my own equanimity & self respect restored by a hearty laugh, I made the best of my way to the village. My adventure was the subject of tea table talk; and my friends of the mess amused themselves vastly at my expense, declaring that if every parrot that flapped across my path was to bring me & my horse to the ground, quaking with terror, I should never reach the gold diggings alive.

In the evening, I went to hear a sermon from Rev. John N. Moffitt,[5] who had just arrived at the place. As usual, he attracted great attention. His fame had preceded him, and so had all the stories of his strange conduct and of the severe treatment he had received from those who had once been his friends. I was pleased with his eloquence, and with the ease & polish of his address, but never having had much confidence in his sincerity, I was not prepared to derive benefit from his preaching.

There were now several days of busy preparation for our contemplated march across the country. Horses & mules were to be purchased and many other things that were essential to the comfort of our journey. The animals were for the most part furnished by the Cherokees, a considerable company of whom resided in the neighborhood. I bought for my own use a fine looking, able bodied black

---

[4] According to John James Audubon, the now-extinct Carolina parrot (*Psitacus carolinensis*) was a handsome bird whose brilliant mantle of green feathers was topped with a bright yellow hood. These birds emitted a nasty, ear-splitting screech. They swarmed in flocks that stripped fruit trees and corn plants and gobbled up seeds of any kind, including those of the mulberry and the dogwood. As a result, farmers felt no guilt in aiming their shotguns at what they considered a destructive pest. Plume hunters and sportsmen also got in on the act, driving the birds to extinction (Audubon 1940, 217–23). George Churchill, traveling with the Knickerbockers, reported on April 2 that a traveling companion shot fifteen of the birds near the San Bois River in one hour. The last sighting of the birds in Indian Territory was in 1886 (Tomer 1992, 29).

[5] The *Fort Smith (Arkansas) Herald* (March 14, 1849) reported that the Reverend John Newland Maffitt, a well-known and controversial evangelist, was leading revival meetings for a large crowd every evening, and that many overlanders had heeded the call. Another traveler to California, William Chamberlin, attended on Sunday, March 25, and wrote that he "knew [Maffitt] by reputation, but had never seen or heard him before. He is certainly an eloquent speaker, but I came to the conclusion that he is more renowned for eccentricity than either piety or the future of his listeners. . . . Although upwards of 50 years of age, he does not appear to be more than thirty and I am inclined to think he spends more of the time at [his] toilet than at his bible" (1945, 25). Charges were brought against Maffitt's moral character following his second marriage in 1847.

horse & gave him the name of "Billy Black Hawk." For the horse & saddle I paid $55. To test his qualities, I rode out to the camp & then made a circuit of some 12 miles in the country, calling by the way at a Cherokee encampment of several hundred Indians. Some of them speak a little broken English, enough for the purpose of an ordinary bargain, but the greater part of them have no language but their own. I also bought a young pony for 25 dollars & a mule & pack saddle for 42.50. The pony I called Nancy, & mule, Tad.[6]

Many things which we had procured at Cincinnati & other places along our route, we found, could have been had at Fort Smith at much more reasonable rates, and many others could easily be dispensed with. We had a great deal of unnecessary baggage, which had been transported thus far at considerable expense & trouble. We paid six dollars for buffalo robes at Cincinnati when a better quality could have been purchased here for four. Our blankets, saddles &c. cost us too much in the same proportion.[7] It is a common mistake with explorers, as well as with travellers, to overburden themselves with unnecessary baggage. For the edification of any who may wish to follow our track, I will say that if I were going again on the same expedition, I would carry only a single suit of clothes, two good red flannel shirts, two check shirts, a good rifle or double shot gun, a pair of horse pistols or one of Colts six barrel revolvers, a good jackknife & a pair of riding boots with spurs. More than this would be not only useless, but cumbersome.

Our camp was frequently visited by the Cherokees, who supplied us abundantly with a great variety of game. Prairie hens, quails, rabbits,

---

[6] Goulding rode to the Choctaw Agency at Skullyville, a major trading, political, and social center catering to nearby tribes. It had been established in 1832 after Choctaw removal to Oklahoma Territory. No doubt he encountered the Cherokees en route as they came to Skullyville to trade. The pony was named for his wife, Ann, known as Nancy.

[7] Among the multitude buying, selling, and exchanging goods was forty-niner William Chamberlin, whose own journal details his trip with the Lewisburg Company of Pennsylvania that trod the Fort Smith–Santa Fe and Gila trails to the Yuma crossing on the Colorado River. He got rid of his provision chest, exchanged his tent for a larger one, and purchased saddles and other items (Chamberlin 1945, 25). The sudden influx of travelers proved a boon to Indian economy, as both the Choctaws and Chickasaws began selling surplus produce and livestock to the California emigrants. Grant Foreman (1934, 165) tells of an enterprising Shawnee chief who, along with members of his tribe, obtained mules and buffalo robes from western tribes, then sold them to needy emigrants.

squirrels &c. &c. were our daily luxuries, on which we fared sumptuously, doing our own cooking in the most approved style. General Arbuckle, with some of his officers, also honored us with a visit & shared our good cheer. For the most part, our encampment was a kind of holiday, preparatory to the toils & hardships of our long journey. Amusements of various kinds were plentifully interspersed with the more arduous business of preparation. And some parts even of our necessary business were converted into frolics of the richest kind.

Among these, the scenes of the 15th March will not soon be forgotten. On that day, the Cherokees came to the village with large numbers of horses, ponies, mules & jacks to furnish our company for their expedition. Every animal was tried, and every man must take part in the trial. Some of them had never straddled a horse before, and of those who had, few had seen the inside of a riding school or had training experience even in the ordinary horsemanship of a town or country life. Several of them were thrown, though none were seriously hurt. Their awkwardness, their fears, the plunging & kicking of the animals, who instinctively spurn the acquaintance of a clumsy rider, the sharp criticism, the stinging jest, the sparkling repartee of the members, the surprise & amusement of the Indians, and the general interest & excitement pervading the little community, together with the spirited jockeying & bargaining, betting, swapping & drinking, made that a high day in the village, a scene of continual bustle, merriment, noise, and good cheer.

The Fort Smith Herald issued on the 14th contained a copy of the Constitution of our company with the names, ages, professions & residences of the members, which, for the purposes of preservation and as a specimen of the combined wisdom of our association, I here subjoin [our] Constitution [see appendix A]. On Friday, March 16, there was quite an accession to our numbers in the arrival of a new company, bound, like ourselves, across the country to the newly formed ophir.[8]

Saturday, March 17, was distinguished by a revolution in the camp. The same untamed democracy which can make a constitution

[8] Goulding is referring to the biblical land of Ophir, reputedly rich in gold. Stanislaus Lasselle of Logansport, Indiana, arrived in Sulphur Springs, Arkansas, on March 25, 1849, leading a company of men who caught up with and joined the Knickerbockers on April 25 near Chouteau's fort and trading post (Lasselle 1991, 4, 9).

can also unmake it. The small communities, as well as in nations, the inalienable right abides—of reforming the works of their own hands. I do not mean by this to admit that all revolutions are of necessity reforms, or are conducted with a just regard to the rights & welfare of the whole. In this case, a small minority of agitators, of whom it would be no abuse to call them rowdies, who are resolved to have everything their own way, succeeded in breaking up our entire organization. On my return to camp that morning, I found every thing in confusion. A regular quarrel was in progress and the parties were in a high state of excitement.[9] Capt. Ebbets was too quiet a man to manage such discordant elements. A stern & rigid disciplinarian was needed to prevent the first rising of discontent from turning into an outbreak. Two meetings were held during the day, and after much discussion and many sensible endeavors to heal the breach, it was resolved that the constitution should be annulled, the association dissolved, and all the property, mules, waggons, stores &c. sold at auction on the following Monday.

Monday, March 19, at this sale, I purchased four mules for my mess, paying eighty five dollars for one pair and a hundred for the other. The entire property being thus redistributed by the sale, and the rioters being satisfied with the mischief they had done, a new plan of travelling was entered into. A roll of guard duty was arranged by Capt. Ebbets, the different messes binding themselves to march in company, to perform guard duty in regular course, and to support each other in case of accident or danger. In this, the mal-contents were not solicited to join. Some of them soon after abandoned the enterprise altogether and returned, while others, unwilling to submit to the rules we had established, proceeded to California by other routes.

My acquaintance at the Barracks was a source of great comfort & advantage to me during the continuance of our encampment at Fort Smith. I passed nearly all my evenings there & some parts of the days, and thus escaped many of the vexations which those experienced, who

---

[9] On March 17, 1849, fellow Knickerbocker George Churchill wrote of the fracas: "I never in my life saw such a set of babies calling themselves men and I trust I never will again. I kept quiet to see what the next move would be knowing well our funds were all invested in this expedition and it was hard work to get them out. We either had to abandon them or go on."

were compelled all the time to endure the noise & confusion of an ill-managed camp and the presence of discontented rowdies.

One day, I took a pleasant stroll on the opposite side of the river, where I had a fine view of the new & thriving town of Fort Smith & the adjacent country.[10] I was most agreeably surprised at the discovery I then made of the advantages of its position. The site is a very promising one. The river banks are high and the landing convenient for boats. The surrounding country is rich & will ultimately yield a large amount of produce for this market. The Barracks, on the right of the town, are of brick & will accommodate 600 soldiers. The river was crossed in canoes, which are numerous & always to be had on both sides of the river, the Indians being prompt & accommodating ferrymen & very moderate in their charges.

On Wednesday, March 21, it became necessary for me to enter upon regular camp duty. I therefore packed up all my baggage, took leave of my quarters, and removed to my own tent. On my way out I called at the Catholic College about a mile & a half from the town and purchased from one of the priests, 300 lbs of hay. The old gentleman was quite conversable & amusing, giving me much information respecting the college & the history of the neighboring settlements. The buildings occupied by the college were erected for Barracks & originally occupied as such. They are situated on a kind of mound in the center of a tract of about 300 acres, which is well covered with trees. There are two regular rows of one story wooden houses facing each other, with kitchens & other outbuildings in the rear of each and a large common well in the center between the

[10] Maj. William Bradford established Belle Point (later Fort Smith) in 1817 on a bluff on the south side of the Arkansas River, where it served as a supply base for shipping and a commercial center at the head of navigation. As the first military installation in the Southwest, it also served to promote tribal relations and keep order after relocation of the Five Civilized Tribes: Cherokee, Creek, Seminole, Choctaw, and Chickasaw. The post was strategically located at the junction of the Arkansas and Poteau rivers. A two-story enlisted men's barracks housed four companies, and officers' quarters were contained in two elegantly furnished brick buildings, two stories high, covered with slate, and a gallery on each side. A parade ground and other outbuildings were enclosed by a rectangular brick wall (Mapes 1965, 13–14; Bearss and Gibson 1969, 4, 194). When Fort Smith was shut down in 1871, one of the buildings became a federal court. It was here that the well-known "hanging judge," Isaac C. Parker, handed down his often unwelcome decisions.

rows. When new, they must have made a very fine appearance; but they are now falling into decay. These buildings, with the land, were sold to the Catholics for the purpose of promoting the education of the children of the Indians.[11]

Having performed my first camp duty, I went with Capt. Ebbets to Fort Smith & called upon General Arbuckle at his quarters.[12] From him we received a great deal of valuable information relative to our contemplated tour. He entertained us very hospitably, showing us his maps, from which we transferred to our own such lines & directions as were deemed most useful. The next day, the General returned our call, accompanied by some of his officers. We entertained them to the best of our ability and enjoyed highly the rational amusement of a free social interchange with intelligent & refined gentlemen.

On Saturday, March 24, the quiet village of Fort Smith was thrown into a fever of excitement by a rumor that a steamer was coming up the river, filled with passengers for California, with the cholera raging among them. It ended in a perfect farce. A public meeting was called in the street, and a committee appointed to wait on General Arbuckle with a request that he would go down the river with his force and prevent the further progress of the boat. This requisition was promptly responded to. With drum & fife & bristling bayonet, the detachment marched out to meet the invading pestilence, and summoning the boat to an instant anchorage, threatened to fire on her if she attempted to proceed an inch further. The Captain, though a brave man, deemed prudence the better part of valor, and seeing such a formidable array of soldiery backed by a still more

---

[11] Goulding is describing Cantonment Belknap, which was built on school land in 1838 to serve as temporary army headquarters while the new Fort Smith was being built. A one-story log house was constructed for the commanding officer at the head of Garrison Avenue at 22 North 13th Street, behind the modern Church of the Immaculate Conception on the grounds of St. Anne's Academy. The soldiers' quarters were built south of the log house. Gen. Zachary Taylor lived in this log house between 1841 and 1845 (Faulk and Jones 1983, 27, 29; Mapes 1965, 13).

[12] Following many years of service on the frontier with the 7th Infantry, the ageing Gen. Matthew Arbuckle, Jr., had many contacts with the various tribes and was able to gain their confidence and work with them fairly and effectively. This son of a woodsman and Indian fighter was born in Virginia in the year of Independence. His long life of service ended in Fort Smith on June 11, 1851 (Thrapp 1995).

numerous band of excited but unarmed people, backed to, and sent a boat on shore to inquire the meaning of such strange proceedings. Whether he took the precaution to send a flag of truce in the boat I did not learn. It was permitted to land, however, with[out] a single act of violence, and was then sent back with a message that the steamer must haul up on the other side of the river, and not a man be allowed to leave her till she had undergone an inspection by a medical committee. This was done. The committee went, when they learned that, while on the Mississippi, one or two passengers had died of cholera, that no case of sickness had occurred since that time, and that the boat was in a perfectly clean & healthy condition. On this report being made, the soldiers marched back to their quarters & the people to their tents. The steamer was permitted to come up to her landing, and so the farce ended.

Twice during our stay here, I visited the Masonic Lodge and was much pleased with the character & condition [of the] craft. On one occasion, I heard a very good lecture from a young brother whose name I did not learn.[13] I also attended church regularly while there.

Monday, March 26, being fixed upon as the day for breaking up our camp, the previous day was not much like Sunday at home. All kinds of business were going on. In the town, blacksmiths, saddlers & other artisans, as well as all the shopkeepers, were in a full tide of active business. Horses & mules were to be shod, waggons to be mended, purchases to be made, farewells to be said, and all the thousand & one things which are always left till the last moment to be done. In the camp it was bustle, noise, merriment, grumbling & confusion worse confounded. Loading waggons, arranging harnesses, buying, selling, swapping, drinking, shouting, carousing, stampedings, these were but a part of the desecrations of that day. Late in the afternoon, all were ready for the march, and two of the waggons started a short distance on the advance.

[13] The first Masonic Lodge there was organized in 1847, soon after Fort Smith was completed (Faulk and Jones 1983, 34). Dispensation to found the new branch was granted by W. Claude Jones, of the rank of Worshipful Master, on December 10, 1847, and the charter to Belle Point no. 20 was granted on November 15, 1848. Goulding, a Mason himself, had no difficulty attending the meetings since they were held in the officers' quarters in the early days ("Grand Old Belle Point," 2006).

3

Travel in Indian Territory

Back on the road, Goulding faced his first challenge as he tried to ford the Poteau River near its junction with the Arkansas River at Fort Smith. Finally making it across, the men drove their teams to Skullyville, the Choctaw capital, where they watched a ball game, the national sport of the Choctaws that came to be called lacrosse. The Knickerbockers traveled slowly at first, especially as seasonal rainfall hampered their efforts to negotiate the increasingly miry roads. Among several Indian farms in the area was one belonging to Choctaw doctor Adam Nail, who provided the travelers with campsites and sustenance. About forty-seven miles out of Fort Smith, the Knickerbockers crossed the San Bois River and continued west toward the Creek Agency at North Fork Town on the Canadian River.

Subsequent to the forty-niners' continental crossing, the U.S. government sponsored a number of surveys across Indian Territory. Amiel Weeks Whipple surveyed a railroad route from Fort Smith to the Pacific Ocean in 1853, and Edward F. Beale followed with a survey for a wagon road to the Colorado River in 1859. These reports have helped the editor considerably in defining the Knickerbockers' journey.

The next morning, Thursday, March 27, all hands were early on the move. Tents were struck & packed, and as fast as each wagon was ready, it wheeled into line and moved on, the members of the mess to which it belonged accompanying it on horses or ponies. At half past nine, my mess fell into the line all in good order and in fine health & spirits. Our great work was now begun. We were about to pass the bounds of civilization and to plunge into the great uncultivated and almost uninhabited wilderness, with many hundreds of miles of travel before us over hill & valley, over mountain and gorge, through forest & prairie, over rapid rivers and swollen streams, over trembling morasses and arid sands, without highway, or road, or reliable landmarks to guide our way. Few of us were sensible of the toils & hardships & self-denials of that wilderness journey. But if we had known them all, our self-reliance and our hopes were then fully equal to the encounter.

When about two miles out from the camp, my progress was arrested by a man, apparently lifeless, lying across the path. Dismounting, I found it was John Murphy,[1] one of our company, who had been thrown by a fractious pony that he had purchased of an Indian the day before. Poor fellow! He thought it was all over with him and believed in his heart that pony riding, though it might do for an Indian, was totally unfit for a civilized Christian. I took him into my wagon, dressed his wounds, which proved not very serious, and sent off a detachment in search of his fugitive steed.

About one o'clock, being in advance of my wagon, I halted at an Indian farm-house and ordered a good dinner for my mess. In a little while, the party sent out in quest of Murphy's pony came up, having had the good fortune to capture the unruly deserter at some distance in the woods. We then sat down to an excellent dinner, to which we did ample justice, not only by actions, but by words. Their bacon was excellent, the very best we had seen since leaving home. This farm, consisting of some 300 acres, was the property of two Indian boys, the one, eleven & the other, twelve years old. Their parents were dead, and they were now under the sole care and protection of their slaves, eight in number, who lived with them in

[1] John Murphy arrived at the Rancho Santa Ana del Chino in California with John Ebbetts on September 2, 1849 (Bynum 1934, 12; see appendix B).

common, cultivating the land and looking after the interest of their young masters with a fidelity & attachment that was equally creditable to themselves and to the family in which they had been trained.[2] They all appeared contented with their lot & happy in the opportunity to set before us the best of their fare.

A short distance from this place, we came to the river Oporta [Poteau], which it was necessary to ford.[3] The banks were very steep and the descent difficult. It proved too much for the tongue of my wagon, which snapped in going down and caused us considerable delay. We had an extra one, however, and rigged it with all possible dispatch and proceeded on our journey without further accident or hindrance. Our travelling was necessarily slow, but not disagreeable. It was enlivened with conversation and sometimes with story & song, which made the old words ring again.

About dark, we reached the ground which Captain Ebbets had selected for camp no. 2, having travelled twenty three miles during the day. Our tent was soon pitched and supper ready, during the preparation of which I was engaged in dressing the wounds of the unfortunate Murphy. He was considerably bruised by his fall & was very stiff & sore. We made the best arrangements in our power for his comfort & soon had the satisfaction of seeing him fall into a sound sleep from which he did not arouse until morning. As this was the first day of our march, the wagons were considerably scattered and rather irregular in coming into camp. They all, however, came up in safety. Guard was set and the night passed in quiet repose.

The next day, Wednesday, March 28, after travelling through some fine wooded country and passing several very good farms owned by the Indians, we arrived about noon at the Choctaw

---

[2] Following removal to Indian Territory in the 1830s, many Choctaws, along with their slaves, settled on farms close to rivers such as the Poteau. These young men were fortunate that their servants were keeping the small family together.

[3] Goulding must have crossed downstream from other travelers, for there was a ferry of sorts on the Poteau River on March 26 when fellow traveler Phineas Blunt crossed. Stanislaus Lasselle (1991, 7) also mentions his ferry crossing on March 31. The Choctaws had established the ferry, which was created from a wagon bed made watertight and held together with rawhide and canvas (Writers' Program 1941, 150).

Agency. This place is called Schuleyville, or Money Town, the Choctaw word for money being Schuly. Mr. [Samuel M.] Rutherford was the agent.[4] Having dined & ordered a new tongue for my wagon, I was much amused by a stroll about the place. Some of the Indians were playing ball on the common.[5] They are very expert in this game, which calls into exercise their wonderful agility & quickness of sight, as well as their ready cunning in gaining an advantage by stratagem. They enter into it with intense spirit, and it often seems as if some of them must be injured in their violent & fearless struggles for the prize. Yet it is seldom that any accident occurs. They scarcely ever disagree about the principles of the game or get angry with each other for any occasional hurt. In this they teach an admirable lesson of moderation & forbearance to their more civilized, but not more civil, neighbors.

The costumes of the Choctaws at this place were various & fanciful. The men wore loose frocks of printed muslin, some of them

[4] The U.S. government's first Indian agency in the Southwest was a sturdy log structure built in 1832, fourteen miles from Fort Smith, to serve the Choctaw people, who had been removed to Indian Territory that same year. The LeFlore County site called Skullyville was a thriving center of Choctaw cultural and political life and the capital of the Choctaw Nation. Most of its thirty buildings were stores that sold merchandise to western travelers. The name derived from the Choctaw *iskuli*, a piece of money, and was the place where Native citizens showed up to receive annuity payments and government rations. Following the Civil War, Skullyville declined, and activity moved to nearby Spiro, Oklahoma. The Skullyville Choctaw National Cemetery, the first burial ground for the Choctaw people west of the Mississippi, marks the site of the once active town (Morrison 1938, 234–40; Domenech 1860, 1:155). George Pattison wrote that the Choctaws were well dressed and friendly and brought dairy products to sell to the emigrants (May 2, 1849). Samuel Morton Rutherford was Acting Superintendent of Indian Affairs at the time, and had first come to Little Rock from St. Louis with some $90,000 to disburse among the tribes on the frontier (*Fort Smith [Arkansas] Herald*, March 15, 1848).

[5] This location is Charby Prairie, southwest of Skullyville, where George Catlin had observed "ball play" in 1834, commenting that some three thousand Indians were present. Forbidden to touch a leather ball with their hands, players used curved sticks with webbed ends to move the ball between goalposts. There was no limit to the number of men on a team, and perhaps one hundred would participate from dawn to dusk or until one team achieved one hundred goals. Hitting an opponent was not allowed, but tripping, bumping, or stomping could and did cause many injuries to participants. Betting was vigorous. Opposing villages might have settled disputes with a ball game; it was also a way to release aggression. A number of other tribes played the game, which was also a national sport among the Cherokees. Women had their own version of the game (Morrison 1938, 234–40; Keoke and Porterfield 2002, 152–54).

neatly ornamented with red & blue flannel, & some with handsome worsted fringes of the same colors. Some of them had sashes highly ornamented with beads. They all wear loose pants, gaiters & moccasins. Some of the latter are very beautiful and are worn with pride as love tokens from some favorite Indian maiden. The hair of the men is generally drawn into a tuft on the top of the head, tied tightly, and cut square off a few inches above the knot so that it looks much like a thick shaving brush. This, with their faces painted in red & blue streaks, gives them a very uncouth and savage appearance. They generally carry bows & arrows for shooting game and are extremely skillful in the use of them. They are great lovers of whiskey, which has been the one great bane of all their race, having done more to exterminate them from their fatherland than war & pestilence united. It is the Delilah by means of which the pale faced Philistines have stolen their reason & shorn them of their strength.

The women are, in general, less attentive to their dress than the men. They are extremely careless about their hair, leaving it hanging loosely about their shoulders, or flying in all directions at the mercy of the wind. While engaged about their servile work in their huts, they wear loose muslin frocks, like the men. When they go out, they wear blankets, partly for covering & partly to assist them in carrying various kinds of burdens upon their backs. Some of them wear shoes, but the greater part of them go barefooted. They are, for the most part, ugly & disagreeable, presenting in the strongest possible light, and at a point where it is most observable & always felt, the immeasurable chasm between the savage & the civilized state.[6]

Having dined and rested, we took up our line of march again, passing in the course of the afternoon several beautiful streams, the water of which was as clear & limpid as morning dew. It was quite refreshing, both to man & beast, to pass through them. Prairie hens were

---

[6] Many travelers saw the American Indians through Victorian eyes, regarded them as a curiosity, and had a tendency to compare them unfavorably with their white cousins. They failed to understand that, although the Indians were slowly adopting or copying white ways, there naturally continued to be a strong link to cultural traditions. According to Stanislaus Lasselle (1991, 8), most had adopted Western clothing but still wore the traditional headdress, a turban.

abundant. We saw, also, some very fine cattle & large numbers of hogs belonging to the Indians. They run wild in the forests & prairies & find abundance of food without any care on the part of their owners. This day, we made twenty five miles and came to our third encampment a little after sunset.

During the night, there was a very heavy rain, which perfectly flooded some of the tents and made their occupants feel very much as if they were "out." The tent occupied by my mess was sound. It is called, in the army, a cavalry tent. It sheds the rain better than any other. I was also well provided with gum elastic cloaks & blankets, as well for my horses as for my men, so that we suffered very little inconvenience from this source.[7] The rain continued during the following day.

Thursday, March 29, gum elastic of all kinds were in great demand. After a hurried & rather disorderly, not to say uncomfortable, breakfast, we struck our tents & moved forward. The march was heavy & slow. Several wagons got stuck in the mud, so that all hands were obliged to turn out & put their shoulders to the wheels, which even then were extricated with great difficulty. In the course of the forenoon, we passed a creek, the banks of which were very steep. The ascent was very difficult, so that [we] were obliged in all cases to double our mule teams, and in some, to bring up the oxen, for which we had two yoke in the company. The purchase of these was objected to by many, but they were now found eminently serviceable. We were two hours in crossing this creek, having thirteen wagons to get over. The rain continued to pour all the afternoon. The members of each mess kept close to their wagons to render assistance in case of need. Our march was slow & straggling. We saw no Indians nor any signs of human habitations. About night the foremost of our train reached a small Choctaw farm called "Neils"

---

[7] Charles Goodyear had accidentally discovered the process of vulcanization in 1839 by treating South American gum elastic or India rubber with sulphur. By 1849, therefore, Goulding and the emigrants had access to rubber ponchos, canteens, and blankets that could be used as ground cloths or tarps (Goodyear 1853; Marcy 1859, 132).

[Nail's].[8] It was on somewhat high ground and offered a good encampment. With all our delay & hard travelling, we had made twenty miles, with which we were quite satisfied. One after another, all the wagons except two came up. These were hopelessly stuck in the mud, where it was impossible to help them until the return of daylight.

The proprietor of this farm was a half-breed—a very smart, intelligent man, and exceedingly accommodating to his numerous & unexpected guests. He was thriving, industrious & independent, and had an abundance of all the comforts of life around him. To us, in our wet & weary condition, they were more than comforts, they were luxuries indeed. The rain continued far into the night, but the morning rose clear and pleasant. Two of our wagons being in the rear, and one of the company sick from the fatigue & exposures of the previous day, we concluded to remain with our worthy host till the next morning. A volunteer detachment of one from each mess was sent out to assist in bringing in the missing wagons, which soon made their appearance, all hands being in as good health & spirits as if they had enjoyed the shelter & shared the luxuries of the half-breed's hotel.

---

[8] Adam Nail welcomed a steady stream of visitors beginning on March 29. On that date, Phineas Blunt paid Nail twenty-five cents for a meal of cornbread, bacon, and coffee. George Churchill lightened his load on the same day and left much of it with Nail. In May, George Pattison stopped by and enjoyed fresh pork, warm bread and butter, and coffee. Pattison (May 3, 1849) wrote that Nail "had relapsed into his Indian habits," although he said Nail was intelligent and well educated in the States. Goulding and Pattison might have been surprised to learn that they had been speaking with Dr. Adam Nail, a graduate of Choctaw Academy in Scott County, Kentucky, who had become the academy's resident physician in 1839. In his 1837 report, Dr. H. T. N. Benedict noted that "the Choctaw youth, Dr. Adam Nail . . . has engaged as student and assistant to this department. His attention and acquirements, his assiduity and morality have been of the most praiseworthy kind, and have gained the full confidence of his superiors, and bid fair to make him an ornament to the profession (C. Foreman 1932, 79–80, 89–90, 100). Nail, now thirty-three, had returned to his farm. Writing in 1860, Henry C. Benson noted that the "Choctaw Academy did a vast amount of good; the best men in the nation had there received their education." He added that many thought the academy a failure since graduates returned home as strangers, neither Indians nor white men (Benson 1860, 37). According to George Churchill, the Nail farm was about four miles west of Skullyville, which would be near modern Spiro, LeFlore County, Oklahoma.

The experiences of the past had satisfied us all that our wagons were too heavily loaded and that we could not hope to accomplish the long & arduous journey before us without considerably increasing our retinue or lightening our overloaded vehicles. The former expedient was impossible without sending back to Fort Smith, which would delay us a week or more. The only alternative was to dispose of such things at this place as could be most conveniently spared, leaving it to the discretion of each mess to decide what they should part with. This, after a full discussion, was resolved upon in a meeting of the company.

Then ensued a scene of reckless & foolish wastefulness such as I never before witnessed. I could not have supposed that full grown men would behave so like children, or rather, like mad-men. Everything like discretion seemed to have abandoned them. They had no regard either to the value of articles or to their probable necessity for the journey that was before us. Flour, bacon, pork, biscuit were thrown away as if it had been laid in for ballast only. Of these, the Indians in the neighborhood had fine pickings. Trunks of clothing were lightened in the same reckless manner and articles of great value thrown out upon the ground. Some of the natives obtained what they had never had before—a white shirt; and the ground was strewed with trunks, valises, boxes, kegs &c. as if a caravan had [been] wrecked or robbed. Such is the folly & weakness of men when they [are] away from the natural influence of home. If there had been one prudent wife among them, they would not have had occasion, as they often did afterward, to regret the wild mismanagement of this day.

On Friday, March 30, all being well and in good order, we took up our line of march at half past six in the morning. The day was fine and the country through which we travelled beautiful. The fields were covered with a rich carpet of green and there were scattered here & there, in the valley or on the hill slopes, the most beautiful groves or copses of wood I ever saw. Many of them were as regular as if planted by the hand of man and seemed like fairy islands in the prairie seas. Flowers of various kinds beautified the landscape

& filled the air with perfume. Several flocks of upland or horned plover passed over us. Prairie hens also, & meadow larks, were every where in abundance.

Being somewhat in advance of the main train, I halted for a little while in the midst of a beautiful plain, attracted by a large drove of wild horses that were feeding on the rich, green grass. I galloped towards them. They remained perfectly quiet, though with heads up & ears erect, till I approached very near them. They were in beautiful order, as clean & sleek as if they had just been groomed. There were about 40 of them. If I had been acquainted with the use of the lasso, I could easily have taken one of them. After viewing them a few minutes, I cracked my whip at them, when off they flew with the speed of lightning. It was a beautiful sight. Tossing their heads, their flowing manes & tails flying in the wind, they seemed to spurn the ground, scarcely touching it, as like an animated cloud they skimmed over the surface, till suddenly halting on the other side of the plain, they turned as if looking defiance at their pursuers. But pursuers they had none. We were not prepared for such a chase. We enjoyed it more highly than if it had been the best race course in the world, and having lost nothing by betting our favorites, we again pursued our plodding way toward the west.

In the afternoon we traversed a beautiful valley running between two mountains. The scenery on either side was in the highest degree romantic & picturesque, the road now winding round the projecting spurs of the mountains & then stretching along a plain & level course, sometimes overshadowed with a tall & luxuriant growth of forest trees, and sometimes opening beautiful vistas into deep ravines & spreading valleys on this side & on that. The picturesque effect of the whole was greatly heightened by the long train of well appointed vehicles, each attended by its little guard of outriders in various costumes, and all moving on in quiet & stately procession, or, under the pleasing excitement of the scene, passing & returning from front to rear & from rear to front with gay shoutings and joyous song to enjoy again from favorite points of view, the fairest portions of landscape. On the farther side of this pass, we found a few Indian cabins and one very comfortable farm house, where we replenished our larder with fowls & eggs and laid in a small stock of corn for our animals.

It was near sunset when we reached the river Sans Bois (no woods),[9] no very appropriate name if this part of its course may be taken as a sample of the whole, the banks being plentifully lined with trees, which are every where [interwoven] with a luxuriant growth of grape vines. The passage of this river was somewhat difficult. But we all reached the other side in safety before dusk and pitched our camp in good style on the bank of the river. A fine supper of game, which we had taken by the way, closed the operation of this day. The night was still & beautiful. As captain of the watch, I enjoyed it highly, though I cannot deny that after the fatigues of such a day, a few hours of sleep would have been gladly taken in exchange for all the romance of star gazing.

The following day, Saturday, March 31, we made twenty five miles through a country even more beautiful than any we had passed. We were early on the march and soon encountered a burning prairie, which obliged [us] to change our course in order to come pass it. These fires are kindled by the Indians to burn off the high old grass. But when once underway, they are not so easily extinguished. They burn sometimes for days, carrying every thing before them, consuming the dwellings of the natives & often destroying their cattle & crops. The principal feature in our journey this day was the prodigious abundance of strawberry blossoms, which for miles covered

[9] Balduin Möllhausen of the Whipple expedition wrote that the "San Bois Mountain road winds between a chain of rocky hills, and an occasional Indian farm" (1858, 42). He added that it was a fairly easy ride up the north side with an abrupt and precipitous rocky drop on the south side. He noted that the character of the country changed as they left the mountain and moved toward San Bois Creek, usually about two feet deep, and easily fordable, but spring rains were swelling the rivers and streams, adding considerably to the difficulty of travel. At Edward Beale's recommendation in 1859, an iron bridge was built at the crossing; it appears on modern maps as "Iron Bridge," southwest of Keota on State 26, Haskell County, Oklahoma, about forty-seven miles from Fort Smith. The bridge was burned and destroyed during the Civil War (Beale 1934, 77n9). The Robert S. Kerr Dam and Reservoir on San Bois Creek have since inundated many miles of land in the county, including the crossing place.

the ground to the exclusion of almost every other kind of flowers. Several deer crossed our track in the course of the day, but we did not think it worth while to trouble them. Flocks of wild geese & turkeys were also hovering about. No man need go hungry in this part of the country. He has only to take what nature has liberally provided.

In the evening, we encamped in the regular "corral" by the side of a small brook of pure, sweet running water. It was a fine place, altogether suitable for a Saturday night's rest. Every thing was arranged in unusual good order. The whole company had travelled in close column all day, and all arrived in camp at the same time. Refreshed with a good & well cooked supper, and truly grateful that we had accomplished so much of our way in health & safety, we retired early to rest and were soon lost in sound & refreshing sleep.

4

Edwards Trading Post at Little River

Working one's way across Oklahoma by wagon in the 1840s was a challenge even to the most intrepid traveler. There were some military roads and Indian trails between farms and trading posts, but travelers steered primarily by the stars, physical features of the landscape, and word of mouth. It had been ten years since Santa Fe trader Josiah Gregg had taken this route, and any tracks he left had long disappeared.

After crossing the Canadian River, Goulding and friends arrived at James Edwards's trading post near modern Holdenville, where Edwards made him comfortable at his home. Heavy showers kept the rest of the company on the other side of the river until the weather improved. In the meantime, Goulding became a tourist, strolled through the village, and purchased seven deerskins for an "Indian costume" he was determined to own.

Sunday, April 1, the morning rose clear and cold. A meeting of the company was called at an early hour to consider how we should spend the day. It was resolved to rest in our present camp. But it was not, to many of us, a Sabbath rest. The day was passed in various occupations according [to] the taste & convenience of the company. Some employed themselves in repairing their trappings, rearranging their baggage, and putting everything in order for another week's journey. I took my gun and strolled along the bank of the brook a few miles in quest of game. A pair of snipe was all the result I could boast of. But I found what was more refreshing in a beautiful, clear, sparkling basin, in which I enjoyed a most luxurious bath.

Returning to camp, I took upon myself the responsibilities of cook. My stock for the occasion consisted of two prairie hens, six meadow larks, two English snipe, three squirrels, and a suitable allowance of pork. This I prepared in the most approved style and made up into a grand pot pie such as would have done honor to an experienced housekeeper. The pastry was excellent, though I say it, and very fair to look at. This was followed by a first rate plum pudding, served up with brandy sauce. The whole was eaten with a high relish. The cookery was abundantly praised and the cook quite satisfied with his show of the spoils.

On Monday, April 2, we took up our line of march at 6 o'clock, passing still through a rich, well watered country, capable of the finest cultivation and offering every inducement to the hand of industry & skill. There are no bounds to the fruitfulness of this region, and when the time comes, as it inevitably must, that it shall pass from the lazy, unthrifty race who now occupy it, to a race of industrious & intelligent cultivators, it will furnish ample support to many millions.

A little before noon, we approached a very high hill which in some parts of the country would be deemed worthy to be called a mountain. In company with Rev. Ira M. Allen, I ascended it to reconnoitre the way before us. The view from the top was extensive & beautiful. Within an horizon of from twenty to thirty miles, lay a country of rare beauty & fertility, abundantly watered with lakes & streams and elegantly diversified with hill & valley and far stretching plain. Below, our diminished train wound slowly along its serpentine way, seeming in the distance like a procession of pigmies moving in pantomime.

Having taken a wide survey, we returned to the company in season for dinner. This was furnished in comfortable style at an Indian farm house where also we obtained a good supply of corn &c. for our animals. At 5 in the afternoon, we pitched our tents at the foot of a mountain, where we had plenty of good water and grass. Our distance this day was only eighteen miles.

The next morning, Tuesday, April 3, it was ascertained that we must climb this mountain or make a three days circuit to get round it, so resolved to try the shorter course of going over.[1] Napoleon had crossed the Alps with an army. Why should Yankees flinch at the sight of an ordinary hillock? It was a matter of no small labor, though we continued to make it a matter of some sport also. We doubled our mule teams and then attached ropes to the tongues of the wagons so that we could all take hold & pull together. Here we halted and refreshed ourselves and our animals. It was the tallest table we had yet sat down to, overlooking a wide reach of country and fanned by the best breezes that swept along the sky.

This mountain seems to be composed, in great part, of an excellent quality of grindstone, equal in grit to that of Boylston. Huge masses lay on the surface for many miles in extent. Millstones of the largest size could easily be procured here. The descent from the mountain was comparatively easy. The road lay through a beautiful wood, entirely free from underbrush, the trees standing from ten to thirty feet apart, so that we could gallop through them in all directions.

The Canadian River washes the western base of this mountain. We reached it about two o'clock and found a respectable barge, under the management of natives, ready to ferry us over. We paid a dollar for each team and were occupied two hours in getting over. The Indians were much surprised when they found we had climbed the mountain with our heavy wagons [and] would not have thought it possible to accomplish such a feat.

A short ride from the river brought us to the Creek Agency [North

---

[1] Three of Goulding's contemporaries also commented on the mountain in their diaries. William Chamberlin (1849, 20:30) noted that the hill was difficult of both ascent and descent; Stanislaus Lasselle (1991, 9:8) wrote that they "past over a small mountain" that day; and Phineas Blunt said they had to use ropes to help them to the summit. It was probably the same mountain that 1859 surveyor Edward Beale (1934) called Winchester Mountain, which he described as steep and rocky. He wrote that the road was probably an old Indian trail that went straight up the mountain, but with some engineering would "make a capital road over the mountains" (Beale 1934, 12:79). Now known as Broken Mountain, it is west of Enterprise, near Oklahoma State Highway 9, Haskell County, but the area is much changed due to the creation of Eufaula Lake in 1964.

Fork Town],[2] where we encamped for the night. This [is] a very considerable settlement, much the largest than any we had hitherto met with. There is one large central store, which serves for the whole community. There is also an apothecary's shop and a smithy.

The Creeks are not as good looking as the Cherokees & Choctaws. They are very much addicted to whiskey and are ready to traffic in it on all occasions. They had some execrable stuff at the ferry at the time we crossed it. Some of our men tried it, at a "bit" a glass, and having repeated the dose after our arrival at the village, gave us much trouble in the evening. The riot ran so high that it became necessary to call a meeting of the company early the next morning to consider what should be done. The result was the expulsion of one of the members, who appeared to be incorrigible.

Wednesday, April 4, at 8 o'clock we resumed our march. The country was hilly & broken, and the land inferior to that through which we had passed. Log cabins & Indian huts were scattered thickly by the way, but there was nothing inviting about them, and the natives, who were very numerous, were poorly clad & miserable. About 3 o'clock we opened upon a splendid prairie as smooth & level as a floor and covered with a luxurious growth of grass. After traversing it a distance of five miles, we came to a beautiful brook bordered with trees, where we planted our camp for the night. It was a splendid place. The views in all directions over the plain were admirable. We enjoyed them highly and found it was much more refreshing to encamp amid beautiful scenery than on a bleak & barren heath. Our camp was visited by a considerable number of Indians, who supplied us liberally with chicken, turkeys, eggs, corn &c. Many of them remained all night, sleeping on the ground by the side of our watch fires. We did not admit them within the guard. The delinquent member who had been expelled from the company for disorderly conduct at our last encampment followed us to this place, expressing his regret for what had

[2] The men arrived at North Fork Town, McIntosh County, Creek territory, on April 3. The town thrived during the gold rush, when traffic increased so much that a post office (called Micco, after the Creek chief) was established in 1853. The town was relocated in 1863 to the new town of Eufaula, some two miles to the west (G. Foreman 1939, 165). Ultimately the old town disappeared under the water of Eufaula Lake that inundated huge areas in Haskell, Pittsburgh, and McIntosh counties. As a result, the best we can do is identify a probable route.

passed, and asking to be restored to his position. He was accordingly received into full fellowship again.

Thursday, April 5, at six o'clock in the morning, we were all ready and on our march. Taking leave of the shady brook, we soon began to ascend a steep hill, from the top of which a magnificent view was obtained. I amused myself with taking a sketch.[3] Behind us was the beautiful prairie we traversed the day before, stretching away like a sea of verdure shut in among the hills. Before us was a fine reach of valleys & country which it was a feast to the eyes to behold. It seemed as if another "sea of verdure" similar to that behind us had been tossed by some night wind, or by some subterranean convulsion, into a wide reach, billowy agitation, and then suddenly hardened into solid & durable form, with all its pleasing variety of meadow & grove, of lake and brook & winding stream.[4] Rarely have I seen so enchanting a picture. And the interest was greatly heightened by our long train slowly winding up the hill like a caravan of emigrants coming to take possession of the promised land. It is indeed a region of excellent promise, especially if the report of the Indians be correct, that there is abundance of coal in the hills.[5]

Here we met, for the first time, the native <u>cactus</u> (Agave americana), the beauty of which is rarely equalled by any other product of nature.[6] The varieties of game we had often seen before continued also to be abundant, and we took care to secure enough for the day's demands. In the afternoon, a brisk shower of rain made the travelling heavy. We succeeded, however, in making our twenty five miles before five o'clock, at which time we pitched our camp in the edge of a wood in the midst of a heavy thunder storm. It was not a very agreeable night that followed, and none the more so to me for the necessity of standing guard. A sentinels duty is never to be envied; but it is subject, like

---

[3] Sketch missing.

[4] It appears that Goulding was familiar with the writings of Sir Walter Scott, who used "sea of verdure" to describe the view from Richmond Hill in his novel *The Heart of Midlothian* (Bain 1890, 302).

[5] Amiel Weeks Whipple (1941, 46) wrote that the whole area outside Fort Smith was believed to be rich in bituminous coal. He especially noted that coal strata were found near his camp no. 14 at Coal Creek north and west of McAlester, Pittsburg County.

[6] Soapweed yucca, *Yucca glauca* Nutt., native to the Great Plains.

adjectives, to degrees of comparison, of which the superlative is a cold drenching; a drizzly night's clearer star-gazing is quite another affair.

Friday, April 6, taking an early start in a fine, windy morning, we soon reached a small Indian settlement where we halted & procured a supply of feed for our animals. From this place, a detachment consisting of Samuel Kelly,[7] John P. Hoyt, John Murphy, and myself was dispatched in advance to Little River, about twenty five miles distance, to make preparations for our journey across the Great Desert, or to speak more properly, the Great Central Prairie. This was to be an important port in our route, being the last at which we could procure supplies for the more difficult part of our enterprise.

Our ride was by no means an agreeable one. We had thick wood, wide prairies, dry river beds with high, rough banks, and tumbling brooks to pass. In the midst of an open prairie, we were met about one o'clock by a heavy, pelting thunder gust right in our teeth, brilliantly illustrated with thick-coming flashes of lightning and enlivened with a copious outpouring of hail stones. It called into requisition all our courage & patience as well as our India rubbers, and made us think much, not only of home, but of Goodyear, to whose ingenuity & skill we were indebted for our only shelter from this pitiless storm. On we pushed, the storm thickening upon us at every step. At length, as we emerged from a wood which had been scathed by lightning the year before, we saw, to our great joy, a log cabin not far ahead. Hastening up to it, we dismounted and made earnest application for instant admission. But our urgent knocking brought no host to the door. On examining the premises, we found the house deserted. There was the appearance of a newly made grave in the center. The furniture was standing in orderly arrangement and the household utensils all in their places, as if they had just been left for the night. It was a lonely, dismal place, and it seemed as if a long and dismal night must pass before that lone sleeper would awake to reclaim his solitary cabin.

Preferring the shelterless road and the pitiless storm to the hospitality of such an abode, we took again to our saddles and dashed on

[7] See appendix A.

over hill & dale and through dense, dark forests, resolved that a shelter and a place of rest must be found before nightfall. A few milcs brought us to another cabin on the top of a hill. Here we found a very civil half-breed, whose name was Reed. His wife, a very polite, obliging woman, immediately set about preparing us a dinner of such as she had. It was soon ready—bacon, eggs, coffee & Indian bread—and was eaten with unusual relish by all of us. While dining, Reed explained to us the mystery of the deserted cabin, or house of death, in the forest. It is a custom among the Creeks that when the head of a family dies, to bury him in his own house or close to the door of it and then to abandon the place, with all its furniture, to his sole possession. Such a tenement is never occupied again, but is suffered to decay with the bones of its proprietor. And such is the reverence for the departed among this people, that no article left in such an abode is ever liable to be disturbed.[8]

We would gladly have remained here all night, if there had been provender & shelter for our horses. For want of these, we found it necessary to push on to Little River, which was two miles from Reed's. The rain continued to pour, with heavy & almost incessant thunder. At 7 o'clock we reached the river, and fording it, arrived at the long wished for village on the opposite side. We immediately made ourselves acquainted with Mr. Edwards, the proprietor of the village, with whom we soon found ourselves at home.[9] Every possible attention was paid to our comfort & that of our horses; our host, his wife, daughters & servants vying with each other in their kind & considerate regards. Mr. Edwards is a native of Missouri but has

---

[8] Though the custom was modified over time, Goulding and friends were right to leave the house alone. One Creek tradition involved wrapping the body of the deceased in a blanket, lowering it into a circular pit in a sitting position, and covering it. The house contents were supposed to remain undisturbed. Eventually, graves were placed outside the family home (Malinowski et al. 1998, 416–23).

[9] Edwards's settlement was about 5 miles south of present-day Holdenville, Hughes County, Oklahoma, on the west bank of Little River, 1½ miles above the mouth, and about 3 miles from the Canadian River. Edwards had a flourishing trade with local tribes and in addition owned a large farm worked by Creek Indians, who produced corn, sweet potatoes, and other vegetables. Lt. James W. Abert of the U.S. Army visited the settlement in 1845 and remarked that "Edwards was the patriarch of the settlement" consisting of log huts (1970, 62–63). Edwards had married a Creek woman, and a daughter, Eliza, married Jesse Chisholm, the famed Cherokee guide and trader, who opened a post not far from Little River (G. Foreman 1939, 157, 159).

been with the Creek Nation forty five years. His wife is a full blooded Indian but speaks perfectly good English. When the tribe removed from their old settlements to this new territory, Edwards & his family accompanied them. They are much pleased with the change, and so, they informed us, is the entire nation.

Little River village consists of some 30 or 40 small houses built with logs and dashed with mud. Mr. Edwards and his son-in-law, Joe, own them all. They have a store, well supplied with provisions, drygoods & hardware, which they are obliged to transport in wagons from Fort Smith over the same route by which we had just passed. His teams were out at that time, having taken a load of peltries [hides] to Fort Smith. Edwards has also a blacksmith & a carpenter shop on his premises. He had then nearly completed a fine two story frame house, which looked quite like a palace in the midst of the dingy cabins that surrounded it. After a long evening chat by a comfortable fire, we retired to rest, having, for the first time since leaving Fort Smith, the luxury of a bed "wherein to lay our weary bones and sleep."

Saturday, in the morning, we found the river so swollen that fording at this place was no longer practicable. Having nothing else to do, I looked about the village & made some purchases at the store. Among other things, I resolved on having a full Indian costume. For this I bought seven deer skins, handsomely dressed, of a delicate smoke color, and engaged one of Mr. Edwards' daughters to make me a hunting coat, breeches & leggings, after the most approved native style.[10]

In the afternoon, Mr. James Broadmeadow[11] and some others of our company came up to the opposite bank of the river and reported the company all well in camp about twelve miles distant & unable to advance, in consequence of the swollen state of the streams. Our own Little River was also impassable, so that having made their report and received such messages as we had to send, they were compelled to return to their own camp.

---

[10] Goulding describes his new outfit in the next chapter. His fellow diarist George Churchill also purchased "Indian dressed deerskin" with which to make "riding pantaloons." Churchill made his own after finding some Texans who could help with instructions (March 12, 1849).

[11] See appendix A.

5

The Creek Indians

DURING HIS SOJOURN at Edwards's Trading Post at Little River, Indian Territory, Goulding had the opportunity to meet a number of unforgettable people. The well-known Delaware guide Black Beaver even presented Goulding with his gloves as a sign of esteem. This was a rare honor, for when Captain Randolph B. Marcy arrived toward the end of April, he hired Black Beaver to guide the troops and companies following in his wake to Santa Fe.[1] *The famed Cherokee Jesse Chisholm was also at the post, and he and Black Beaver may have been responsible for encouraging the Knickerbockers to continue along Gregg's route north of the Canadian River. Goulding was also lucky that one of the major Creek ceremonies, the Green Corn Dance, took place at this time of year, and that Creek chief Echo Harjo invited the group to observe. Despite Goulding's ethnocentric remarks—typical of gold rush diarists, who often found themselves in the midst of ceremonies they did not understand—his description of the dance and of his own participation in it are unique among diarists.*

Sunday, April 8, the storm continued with great violence. Finding we were likely to be detained several days longer, Mr. Edwards had some of the rooms in his new house fitted out for our convenience. Here, with a good fire and nothing to disturb me, I employed myself a considerable part of the day in writing to my friends.

[1] G. Foreman 1939, 158.

In the afternoon, I walked, or rather, waded, through the woods about a mile and a half to another small settlement, owned by a Mr. Hurd.[2] Here I purchased a mule for forty dollars, an excellent match for my mule Tad, and called her Dot. I also purchased a bridle for two dollars, and mounting my mule, returned to the village in style much more to my taste than that by which I went out.

The next day, Monday, April 9, the streams being still impassable and all communication with our company being thereby cut off, I continued my surveys of the village and its appendages. About a quarter of a mile from Edwards' house, I made an interesting discovery. This was no other than the village dancing hall, or square. It was quite a curiosity to me as I had heard much of Indian dances, but had never seen one. Hoping, before leaving the place, to witness one of these high festivals, I continued my stroll along the bank of the river and made other discoveries which interested me much more than this, and in quite a different way. There were several very neat log cabins, surrounded with gardens in a pretty state of cultivation, with several acres of cultivated clearing in the rear. They were owned & occupied by Creek Indians. This looked like progress and improvement, and presented an interesting & promising contrast to the general condition of that part of the nation which I had thus far seen.

On Tuesday, April 10, the weather being fine, we all went down the river a few miles, where the water being deep & comparatively slow, we obtained a good crossing in a canoe. Struggling through the woods for some time with no little difficulty, we struck upon the road by which we had travelled a few days before, and soon fell in with the advance of our company. They had come to a halt and were spreading out their clothes to dry and examining their provisions, which had been sadly drenched in the late flood. Having obtained a few changes of clothing & rendered all the assistance in my power to my comrades, I returned to my quarters at Little River.

The next day, Wednesday, April 11, the rain began to fall afresh. Some of the company became discouraged, & symptoms of open disorder appeared. Captain Ebbetts, with some others, came to the vil-

---

[2] Edwards ran his farm while Thomas Aird conducted the trading post nearby (G. Foreman 1925, 106). Mr. Hurd either worked for Aird or lived in the area.

lage by the crossing which I had made the day before, and after waiting & consulting there awhile, went out to reconnoitre the roads in advance. They had been represented as almost impassable with wagons, and some of the party had on this account resolved to dispose of them altogether and pack every thing on our mules. In the evening they returned with quite a favorable report of the state of the road, though the late heavy rain had made it much worse than usual. The weather continued severe during the whole week. It was very cold, with a constant succession of heavy showers with hail & snow.

On Sunday, April 15, snow fell to the depth of three or four inches, the like of which the oldest inhabitant had never seen before.[3] Tired & sick with their long & miserable blockade, and resolved not to endure it any longer, two of the messes, nos. 7 & 9, cut their way nearly a mile through the woods to the river. Then, taking off their wagon wheels, they sent them over with their baggage in the canoe and floated the [wagon] bodies over with ropes. The next day, all the others followed suit, so that, with great exertion, our whole caravan was comfortably lodged in the village on the ninth day after my arrival there.

During my stay there in the village, I became acquainted with several remarkable Indian characters. One of them was the celebrated Black Beaver, who made us a visit on the 12th.[4] He was once a terror to all the white settlers on the border. He had been several times

---

[3] The unwelcome weather did little to improve the travelers' attitudes. Fellow diarist David Jordan summed it up: "worse roads I never saw—6 miles from the camp five of the [mules] mired at once the horse I rode fell, got my leg under him & in plunging to extricate himself threw me over his head on the mud" (April 16, 1849). Jordan stayed with the Knickerbockers as far as California and went to the "diggings" on the San Joaquin River, where he made a fortune, later stolen by Mexicans. Not one to give up, he made a second fortune, which he invested in land in Santa Cruz. He returned to his family in Dayton, Ohio, but died in 1857 before he could return to his property (Hackenberger 1938, 11:250–53).

[4] Black Beaver (1806–80), scout of the Delaware-Lenape tribe, was forty-three when Goulding met him at Little River. Black Beaver's Indian name was Se-ket-tu-ma-qua (*Biographical Dictionary,* 1991: 1:60). He told Balduin Möllhausen (1858, 93) that he had been to the Pacific Coast seven times and spoke English, Spanish, and eight Indian languages. He had previously escorted both John James Audubon and Stephen Watts Kearny. He would continue service to the United States in the Civil War and as a delegate to the International Indian Council held at Okmulgee, Indian Territory (Oklahoma), in 1870. He later became a Baptist minister and made a point of setting a good example for others. He died at age seventy-four in 1880 in Anadarko, Indian Territory (C. Foreman 1946, 291).

among the Comanches, trading for horses & mules. He told us the Comanches were not to be feared. He gave us a great deal of information about the wild Indians and also about the Creeks. He also entertained us with the story of his own exploits, which, if they could all be believed, were marvellous enough. His adventures with Col. [John James] Audubon were very amusing, and he evidently felt a great pride, not only [in] the splendid musket given him by the Colonel, but in the aid he had been enabled to render that gentleman in making his grand collection. The Black Beaver remained with us all night and made a very long & interesting evening with his conversation about the customs, habits & laws of the various Indian tribes. He speaks remarkable good English and has a fine address. He traffics in mules, peltry &c. and usually has some six or eight attendants. When he left us he presented me with his gloves, a courtesy which I reciprocated by requesting him to accept mine. This was his mode of holding on the hand of friendship.

I also became acquainted with Chism [Jesse Chisholm], a man of some note among the Creeks, and one of the chiefs of their nation.[5] He also had been among the Comanches and gave us much valuable information respecting them. He represented them as friendly to the Americans but irreconcilably hostile to the Mexicans.

On Friday, before any of our wagons came up, my Indian dress was completed.[6] I was quite proud of my appearance. With my fancy belt, sash, and fox-skin cap, it was acknowledged on all hands that I

[5] Jesse Chisholm (1805–68) was born in Tennessee, son of a Scottish father and a Cherokee mother, the daughter of chief John Rogers. The family moved to Arkansas early on, where Chisholm became a guide and interpreter for many expeditions. He was said to have the command of some fourteen Indian languages and to have excellent rapport with both Indians and whites (Dockstader 1977, 50–51). He was, no doubt, operating out of his nearby post at Camp Holmes, the westernmost supply outpost until the Civil War (G. Foreman 1939, 197). The meeting with Goulding's party took place on April 14, and according to Stanislaus Lasselle (1991, 9), Chisholm "was a very intelligent man" and stayed overnight to share both supper and breakfast with the men.

[6] The costume is in classic Eastern Woodlands style. He would have purchased the beaded sash, also classic to the culture, already made, since those creations take many months to produce. The turban was common among the Five Civilized Tribes and was usually made from cotton material. The gloves Goulding wears may well have been Black Beaver's gift.

In 1853, Möllhausen found the Creek Indians to be "tastefully dressed with handsome shawls gracefully twisted around their heads. They wore leggings and moccasins of buckskin, handsome calico shirts, and a beautiful pouch with broad belt ornamented with massive beadwork" (1858, 62).

FIGURE 3. William R. Goulding poses in
Woodlands-style Indian costume during a trip to Australia, 1859.
Batchelder Brothers collodiotype.
Courtesy of Warwick Goulding and Prue Goulding Crabb.

was a very respectable looking Indian. The girls looked shy at me. If I had been willing to remain with them, they might have made me a chief or a medicine man and offered me the choice of their daughters for a wife. But on the following day, I saw enough of their daughters to rob the latter temptation of all its charms. The women of the place, from the oldest to the youngest, as if by previous arrangement, had a regular Indian spree. It was a scene of riot & confusion of the most loathsome and disgusting character. They were all in a state of beastly intoxication, in the shameless indecency of which they far surpassed the lowest rowdies I had ever met with. It made me heartily sick of the place and of everything in it.

On Monday, April 16, the day before our wagons came up, Mr. John Hunter, one of our men, narrowly escaped being drowned in the river.[7] He attempted to ford at the usual place, but the water was still very deep. Hunter lost his confidence in himself and was carried, with his horse, a considerable distance down the stream. He would have been lost, inevitably, if some of the Indians, who are excellent swimmers, had not gone to his rescue.

Our whole company was now together in the village. But the recent storm had done as much to disturb our harmony as to abridge our comforts. A very important question had arisen as to our future movements. The experience of the last week had fully satisfied some of the company that to cross the desert with wagons was utterly impracticable. Others entertained a different opinion. The dispute ran very high. Some of the men were determined to have their own way, without any reference to the will of the majority or to the comfort & safety of our future journey. We had thus far, in addition to our mess wagons, had a general commissary wagon, drawn by four oxen & carrying the heavy stores of the company. As we could no longer agree to act harmoniously in common, this wagon with its team was sold at auction. I purchased the wagon, with four sets of mule harness, for eighty dollars. Black Beaver and Chism bought

---

[7] Yet to be investigated is whether John Hunter, a New York surgical instrument maker (see appendix A), was a descendant of John Hunter (1728–1793), the English surgical instrument designer, known as the "father of scientific surgery."

the oxen. Several of the messes were broken up & reformed, and thus, in the course of the day, a kind of order was restored, though not without a deep undercurrent of grumbling in some quarters. In the new arrangement, Mr. John Hoyt joined my mess, bringing two mules, which, with my two, made a full team for my new wagon.[8] I had thus ample means for transporting my baggage, which I was resolved should be sufficient in any emergency for me and my mess.

On the evening before our departure, the great Corn Dance of the nation took place. Many of our company attended as invited guests. It was a ceremony I had often desired to witness, having from my boyhood felt a great interest in things relating to the manners & customs of the Indian tribes of our country. The whole scene was new & original as it was amusing. I entered into it, with one or two others, with great zest, dancing three times in the same circle with their chief, Echohoys [Echo Harjo].[9]

This dance is a national religious festival.[10] It is held on the evening before the annual corn planting and is intended to propitiate the favor of the Great Spirit and thus to secure a good harvest. The dancing hall or enclosure consists of four long sheds on each side of an open parallelogram, which is about two hundred feet

---

[8] John Hoyt and George Churchill traveled with Goulding as far as Santa Fe, where they joined a contingent of dissenting members of the Knickerbockers traveling by pack mule. They packed the full length of the Gila Trail to the Colorado crossing at Yuma, Arizona. Goulding would meet up with both men in the Yuma area.

[9] Tuckabatchee Micco was chief during the gold migration through Creek territory in 1849. Second Chief Echo Harjo succeeded Micco as chief of the Upper Creeks in 1859 and served until 1861. Grant Foreman (1934, 203, 216) wrote that Harjo lamented the rapid decrease of the buffalo, the main source of subsistence, and worried that his people would be compelled to abandon their wandering habits and find other ways to earn their living.

[10] The dance has also been described by John Howard Payne, who was in the town of Tuckabatchee, Georgia, in 1835—before removal to the west—as Creek residents prepared to celebrate the annual Green Corn Dance. It was an eight-day festival divided into two parts of four days each: gathering of people, women's dance, lighting the fire, hunting interval, woman's second dance, fast day, address by chief, and dispersal. Corn was the centerpiece of the festival, and the ripening of the corn signaled the beginning of the Creek New Year (Payne 1932, 170–95).

Goulding's fellow Knickerbocker George Churchill also "went down to the Indian Dancing Ground." He was not sure if he understood the ceremony but observed that the grounds were "beautifully arranged for sight seeing—elevated seats on either side covered with a thatched roof to keep off sun and rain" (April 16, 1849).

square. These sheds are constructed of logs, & all are open inwards. The roofs are thatched with branches and then covered with sod and cane brake. All round on the inside are seats, composed of logs, for the accommodation of the company. In the center of the space thus enclosed is a small shed, with an opening in the roof under which a fire is made. This fire is the great object of interest in the festival, and, as such, the center of the dance.

The ceremony is commenced by the men. One of the inferior chiefs, taking the lead, begins, with a measured jumping pace, to move round the fire, singing, or rather grunting, as he goes, in a very monotonous strain, "He, ho, ho, ho, hah, eh, ho, hah." Soon, other[s] follow in the same manner and with similar monosyllabic ejaculation, keeping pretty good time, but with no regard to harmony or melody. Presently, the whole dance becomes a kind of short dog trot. At certain intervals, the dancers all stop short with a sudden shriek or yell, "Ha, hoy!"

Occasionally, the step is changed to a short jump, in which the advance is very slow, the dancers all making signs with their hands towards the fire, invoking the aid of the Good Spirit, deprecating the power of the evil. When they stretch out both hands open to the fire, they are understood as saying, "Hell fire to bad corn!" Stretching up the right hand over the fire is a sort of promise, or vow, that they will be good, as if they took an oath of allegiance to the Good Spirit. Clapping their hands together signifies that, as they intend to be good, they will have plenty of corn, and is a kind of recognition of the covenant between the Great Spirit & their nation. Laying their hands upon their mouths is a confession of their sins and a prayer for forgiveness.

These various ceremonies are often repeated in the course of the dance. When all the men who desire to enter the circle have taken their places, the women begin to fall in, forming circles outside of them. After them, children of all ages enter the ring till the space is filled. The women do not make signs with their hands nor join in the singing or shouting with the men. They have a kind of moccasin or buskin prepared for the occasion, into which are loosely wrought various kinds of shell, bits of coral or slate, brass buttons &c., which as they dance make a regular, tinkling music and add much to the effect of the ceremony. They carry themselves perfectly erect, making no motions with head or hand. Their movements are so equable and uniform, regulated by the tinklings of their ankle ornaments, that they seem as if swayed up & down by the gentle undulations of the sea rather than moved by any exertions of their own. Their quiet, regular, wavy movements form a peaceful & beautiful contrast to the short, vigorous trot and noisy ejaculations of the male dancers. Though the Indians treat their females with less deference & kindness than we do, it seems that even in savage life, the gentle, the graceful & the beautiful are reserved for women.

The Chief Echohoys, who led off this dance, was a fair looking fellow, fully six feet high. He could not speak a word of English, but readily communicated with us through an interpreter. About midnight, in one of the pauses of the dance, I requested him to allow us to see the women dance alone as we understood they sometimes did. He immediately assented, and turning to the people, addressed them in a very grave and respectful manner. When he had finished, the men very quietly took their seats under the shed, all but one, who sat near the fire & commenced tapping a sort of drum. The women then came forward one by one, very slowly, jumping slightly in time with the tapping of the drum, but not advancing till the circle was complete. When that was full, they began to move—there was life and music enough. The regular jingling of such a multitude of ankles keeping time to the monotonous drum had a singular effect. It was unlike anything I had ever heard, and forcibly reminded me of the censure which the Prophet Isaiah passed upon the wanton ladies of Jerusalem, who walked mincingly & made a tinkling with their feet. Ever and anon, the dancers would all stop short as if by magic, for I saw no signal & heard no sound by which they could be guided. Then they would go on as before, all moving at the same instant & continuing to move in perfect harmony till the dance was finished. Not a man moved from his seat during this ceremony. Not a child interrupted by word or motion the order of the dance. In all my acquaintance with balls, assemblies & parties of all kinds, I never knew a festive gathering conducted with such admirable order and regularity. No single incident occurred to disturb the peace or mar the festivity of the scenes, though from six to seven hundred persons were present.

About two o'clock, I presented the chief with a gold ring, and taking a few whiffs from his tomahawk pipe by way of friendly salutation, took my leave of the assembly, much pleased with the evening's entertainment and more favorably impressed with the character of the natives, & especially of their women, than I had heretofore been. On passing out of the enclosure, I noticed several parties on the outside, gathered around their fires and busily but very quietly engaged in preparing a feast for the company. As we were to re-commence our march early in the morning, I did not care to remain to this part of the ceremony, though the lateness of the hours, and the somewhat fatiguing exercises I had gone through, enhanced not a little the savory odors that were wafted to my olfactories.

6

The Great American Desert

In their conversations with Black Beaver and Jesse Chisholm at Edwards's trading post, the Knickerbockers were probably advised to stay north of the Canadian River on an old Kickapoo trail for the next seventy-odd miles toward Spring Valley. On the way, they passed through Hughes, Seminole, Potawattomie, and Cleveland counties before stumbling across the ruins of Colonel A. P. Chouteau's trading post near modern Purcell, Oklahoma. They finally arrived at the lovely spring-fed valley that Josiah Gregg had named years before. It was here that they planned to cross the river.

The morning of Tuesday, April 17, was clear & fine. All was bustle in the village preparatory to our departure. But such had been the disorder & confusion in our camp, that but few of the messes were ready for a start. My two wagons, with [Mess] no. 7, being in perfect trim, I bade adieu to hospitable friends and took the lead in the march. The travelling was very heavy. Our road lay through [page torn] of bog, made beautifully soft by the recent abundant rain.[1] [Page torn] quick sand and across ugly ravines, more broken than usual by the rush of the swollen torrents. After pulling at this rate about six miles and finding we were not likely to have the company

[1] Those traveling across Oklahoma during March and April can expect the same kind of weather. It was here at Little River that Stanislaus Lasselle (1991, 9) and a number of others stretched a cable across the river in an attempt to get the wagons across, became frustrated, and began to dispose of wagons and other unnecessary items.

of all our comrades, we concluded to pitch our tents by the side of a small creek and await the coming up of the main train. Nine only of the wagons arrived at this place that [day].

The travelling for the remainder of this week was very difficult & fatiguing. Several serious accidents happened. The train was seldom all together and there was but little of the courtesy & good humor necessary to the comfort & success of such an expedition. On Wednesday, April 18, one of the no. 9 wagons, in attempting to cross a wet ravine, was capsized and plunged, bottom up, into the water. All the baggage was thoroughly drenched, much of the provisions was spoiled, and many articles of value were lost beyond recovery. My mess rendered them such assistance as they could in getting out of this scrape, and exchanged dry biscuit for their wet ones to supply their immediate wants. The next day, my own wagon was broken, so that we were obliged to take every thing out in order to repair it. These accidents brought us considerably in the rear of our company, and there was no disposition to wait till we could come up.

On Thursday, April 19, a little after noon, we came to a steep, rocky mountain, which we ascended by a circuitous path, winding almost entirely round it. There we struck the Kickapoo trail leading to Shoto's [Chouteau's trading post] and opened upon a fine, rolling country. We were still much in the rear, though there were other wagons yet behind us. At one encampment that evening, Rev. Ira M. Allen overtook us and requested us to halt till their party, which was seventeen miles in the rear, could come up. He then pushed forward to the advance & made the same request, but without success; the captain was not in the humor then to wait for any one.[2]

The next morning, Friday, April 20, several of our animals were missing, among them my mule Tad and my horse, Bill. They were

[2] Unable to keep up with the Knickerbockers, Allen and a companion, Joel G. Candee, traveled cross-country together. They were befriended by a company of Cherokees and Mississippians and safely reached Santa Fe under their guidance (Candee 1850). The journey ultimately took its toll. Allen died and was buried on the banks of the Gila River some 120 miles east of the Colorado River crossing, a fact noted in numerous diaries and recorded in the Rancho Santa Ana del Chino Register Book on August 30, 1849 (Bynum 1934, 25).

stolen by the Kickapoos, several of whom had dogged our track all the previous day. We sent out six men, mounted, in search of them. They were all recovered except my mule, which by offering a reward of five dollars to some Creek Indians who came to our camp, I hoped yet to secure.

On Sunday, April 22, about three o'clock, we overtook the advance of our company encamped just within the borders of the long expected "Grand Prairie," having passed a little way back the ruins of Shoto's trading houses.[3] Immediately waited upon Captain Ebbets and suggested the propriety of waiting here till Rev. Mr. Allen & his party came up. But my request was refused. He was resolved to go on early in the morning, leaving those in the rear to come up when they could.

Accordingly, at 7 o'clock on the morning of Monday, April 23, we commenced our march over the Great Desert.[4] The air was cold & bracing, and for a time, we made good head-way. About noon we reached a ravine, which it was necessary to bridge over before the wagons could pass. During this delay, I went out in search of game, when about half a mile from the place, I was surprised by the sudden appearance of a wild Indian. I made signs to him to come to me, instead of which he turned & ran away. We made twenty five miles this day. We had now fairly entered upon the Great Desert. The travelling was easy. Game was abundant, buffalo & deer were often seen, as well as a great variety of birds. We had also other company

[3] A West Point graduate and friend of the Indians, A. P. Chouteau entered the fur trade, erected a frontier military post on the north side of the Canadian River in 1835, and traded successfully with the Comanches and other nearby tribes. The military post was west of the Cross Timbers on Chouteau Creek, east of Lexington, and about five miles from Purcell on Route 77 to Norman, Cleveland County, Oklahoma. The post burned down a few years after Chouteau's death in 1838; the site has long since disappeared (H. Van Zandt 1935, 316–37). William Chamberlin described the remnants of several buildings built within a court about 150 feet square, enclosed on three sides and opening to the east (1945, 40). When Josiah Gregg approached the post on his way to Santa Fe in 1839, the Indians began to gather, expecting Chouteau's return, and "great was their grief when they were informed that their favorite trader had died at Fort Gibson the previous winter" (1990, 231).

[4] "Great American Desert" was a nineteenth-century term used to describe the High Plains or Great Plains east of the Rocky Mountains. As travelers anticipated, it was buffalo country.

not quite so agreeable. Rattlesnakes crawled in our path & wolves hovered about our track.

About noon on Tuesday, April 24, we were overtaken by Mr. David C. Buchanan from one of the companies in the rear,[5] who were making forced marches to join us, as it was not safe to cross the desert in small detachments. To my great surprise & pleasure, he was mounted on my lost mule, Tad. He had purchased her of an Indian for five dollars and cheerfully restored her to me for the same sum. At 5 o'clock we encamped, having made thirty miles in ten hours, giving the rear a very hard task to overtake us, and exciting no very kindly feeling on their part, by the want of courtesy we had shown them. We were much annoyed by mosquitoes during the night and by the wolves yelling round our camp, which on account of our watch fires, they did not dare approach. But though they kept at a respectful distance, their music was by no means agreeable.[6]

By forced marches and with great difficulty, the rear had now come up. Our whole company was all together, in full force, and was sufficiently formidable for any danger we might be expected to encounter. We numbered one hundred & fifteen men, with thirteen wagons and three hundred horses & mules. Having a wide, level plain to travel over, we moved in comfort and regular order, with something of the sway of an army on its line of march. The wagons were arranged two abreast, with the packed mules in the center and the mounted men on the flanks and rear. In lieu of [illegible] & miners, we had in the advance a detachment of one man from each mess, a sort of pilot's rear guard, who travelled some distance ahead, each man bearing a small United States flag and ranging due west by the compass. This was necessary in order to make a straight course, for we had no landmarks. We were on an ocean plain, without a tree, rock, or hill, without a

[5] During the Mexican War, David C. Buchanan had been an enlisted private in Capt. Stanislaus Lasselle's company from Cass County, Indiana (Helm 1886, 1:331). While following Stephen Watts Kearny's trail along the Gila River in Arizona, he was seriously injured by a shot from his own gun. Lasselle (1991, 22) wrote that his colleagues carried Buchanan to the Pima villages on a litter.

[6] Chamberlin (1945, 37) mentioned the nightly music of the prairie wolves. He learned that the Indians say they sleep well when the animals "sing," but if they stop it is a sure indication that wolves are around.

track, save that of the buffalo, without a bound, save that of the ever changing horizon.

Rattlesnakes were now very numerous. Some of them were daily killed by the whips of our riders. Wolves were our constant attendants, prowling around our path by day & our camp by night, with a remorseless talent at thieving and an insatiable appetite for blood. We often met with the trophies of their forays in the fresh picked bones of the deer or buffalo which had served for their night's repast. We camped at night without the shelter of a single tree, like a ship becalmed in the boundless water of waters. We had not fuel to cook with but buffalo's dung. This, when once kindled, makes a very hot fire. It burns like peat and keeps all night like coals in the ashes.

Sunrise on the prairie, like sunrise at sea, is a magnificent sight, and when witnessed for the first time, makes a deep impression on the mind.[7] My Indian friend Black Beaver had spoken of it with more enthusiasm than I thought an Indian capable of. Perhaps he acquired it from Audubon, who in all things was his [illegible] Apollo.

On Thursday, April 26, I rose at the dawn of day and walked out some distance from the camp to get an uninterrupted view of this great sight. It was ever more grand & majestic than my imagination had painted. First the deep, glowing blush overspreading the front of day, on the approach of its lord; then the long, sudden blaze in the very edge of the horizon, as if heaven & earth were beginning to fuse; then the broad, full disc, rising slowly & majestically like a god from his couch, with no intervening object to break the view, or to cast a single shadow over the wide plain that rejoiced and brightened in his coming. It was a boundless expanse of green below, melting into a boundless expanse of blue above, with no cloud to break the surface of the one, and nothing but our little camp, which seemed an insignificant speck on the broad bosom of the other.

[7] Amiel Whipple, caught by the magic of a prairie sunrise in 1853, wrote that "while the sun was still 20 minutes below the horizon an extraordinary refraction placed a crown of light in the east, of sufficient brightness to cast a shadow" (1941, 89). Möllhausen, the artist with the Whipple expedition, described "broad shafts of light" shooting upward to the zenith "dividing the whole firmament into regular spaces" (1858, 240).

As I turned this survey to the ordinary duties of the morning, I was much amused with the grotesque appearance of our company. The whole army, which in our marches we had thought so formidable and imposing, appeared now, in the midst of that useless field, like a single bird in the sky or a [page torn] of tiny nautili on the boundless ocean. The men [reduced] to pigmies, and the animals to insects, and as they [moved] busily about, cooking over their low fires their singular breakfast, grooming their horses, leading up their mules, arranging their lading or harnessing up their teams, presented a picture such as Gulliver might have described, had he met a caravan of Lilliputians just breaking up their camp in the midst of a Brobdingnagian meadow, in whose gigantic measures he was himself an atom too diminutive for notice.

At seven o'clock, Friday, April 27, we were all moving on again toward the west, our line being composed as on the previous day. Our front was changed every morning, the wagon that took the lead yesterday, falling in the rear today, and the vanguard of one day, relieved from the ranks on the next. Thus every man had his share of every service, and all were satisfied.

In the course of this day, we were surrounded with immense numbers of birds & blackbirds, yellow-birds, sparrows, crows, plovers, curlews, and many others. A drove of wild horses also came up from the south but did not approach very near. On the north, at a great distance, the horizon was slightly broken by a few clay hills, while here & there a tree was seen in the opposite direction.

About noon, we met with a prairie dog town, which is one of the most curious things in the history of animal instinct.[8] The prairie dog is a small wild animal, not larger than a good sized squirrel. It has a head like a cat, with the tail of a dog. They live together in large communities, burrowing underground for shelter like rabbits. Their holes are dug in regular order and at equal distances and often cover a very large area, the earth drawn out from each hole, so

[8] The black-tailed prairie dog (*Cynomys ludovicianus*) was popular with travelers on the Great Plains. The vociferous rodents exist on grass and weeds that grow around their extensive colonies.

remaining like a large mole-hill at its mouth and giving to the town the appearance of a city of mounds or gigantic ant-hills. Their subterranean dwellings often communicate with each other, forming hidden passages some [miles] in extent, by which they keep up a social [page torn] intercourse among themselves and retreat from the pursuit and annoyance of their enemies, the chief of which are owls & rattlesnakes. Some of the latter I shot in their holes as we passed along. We have often seen the little dogs sitting by the hundreds at the doors of their houses, squatting on their haunches like squirrels, watching our approach and then, as we came near, suddenly disappearing in their holes and popping up again at some distance in advance. They seem to have an aversion to water, their habitations being chosen in the driest parts of the prairie. Their food appears to be prairie grass, especially grasshoppers, which exist in [such] prodigious quantities that the air is often darkened by them as they fly. We cut them down by hundreds with our swords as they fluttered by us in swarms, like a live cloud sweeping over the prairie.

Not long after leaving dog-town, we found a small valley in which was a fine spring of water. Here we halted for dinner. At five o'clock, we reached a place called "Spring Valley,"[9] where there was plenty of water, excellent grass, and beautiful clumps of trees, abounding with

[9] Spring Valley does not appear on modern maps. It was first mentioned by Josiah Gregg, who passed there in 1839 on his outward trip to Santa Fe and again when he returned in 1840. He described "one of the most charming prairie vales that I have ever beheld . . . on account of the numerous spring-fed rills and gurgling rivulets that greeted the sight in every direction; in whose limpid pools swarms of trout and perch were carelessly playing" (1990, 235). His 1844 map locates Spring Valley somewhere between the Canadian River and the North Fork of the Canadian, northwest of Chouteau's old trading house (Gregg 1926).

Both Maurice Garland Fulton, editor of Gregg's diary (1941–44, 1:64), and Grant Foreman (1925, 105) speculated that Gregg crossed to the south side of the Canadian River at some point west of Spring Valley in the southern part of Blaine County, while Max Moorehead, editor of Gregg's *Commerce of the Prairies* (1990, 235n17), thought Spring Valley was in the northern part of Blaine County.

Going on-site in 2008, I found that a wide area in southern Blaine County and in northern Caddo County could easily fit Gregg's description. Using the mileages and descriptions left by the emigrants and traveling the area using Terrain Navigator software, my cartographer, Tom Jonas, and I came to the conclusion that the location of Spring Valley and the crossing of the Canadian were most likely south of Interstate 40 and ten miles east of Hinton at Powder Face Creek in Caddo County.

game, from which we were soon provided with a luxurious supper, which, whatever the ladies may say, was well cooked, and eaten with a relish seldom known in the comfortable precincts of home.

In the evening, when everything was cleared away and our camp parlor put in the best order for company, we had a regular ball, at which we celebrated the Indian Corn Dance in right good style. For this purpose, a large fire was made in the center of the camp, around which we danced to the Creek song, "Ta ho, hah, oh, ha, ye, hoy, ho, hah," &c. There were some variations to the dance, as well as to the song, each dancer occasionally changing step, modifying his ejaculations, and interspersing extempore antics, grimaces, and gesticulations to suit his own whim. It was grand sport & was kept up till a fashionable hour. The festivities were greatly enlivened by a good song, composed for our special use by Mr. McColly [James H. Cooley] of Mess no. 7.[10] In the chorus, "over the mountains capped with snow," all the company joined with heart & voice, making the old words ring again and startling the owls from their "melancholy musings" in the caves & hollow trunks around.

At seven o'clock the next morning, Saturday, April 28, we took up our line of march again, all in fine order & spirits, across the beautiful valley on the edge of which we had pitched our camp. An hour's travel brought us to a narrow stream of running water with high steep bank and a channel too deep to admit of fording. We

[10] The song was published in the *Fort Smith (Arkansas) Herald* on March 21, 1849. The first stanza and chorus are presented here.

Song Composed by James H. Cooley
for the Knickerbocker Exploring Company
Tune—Dance Boatman, Dance

The New York Boys and Yankees too,
With some of the real old Jersey Blues
Have thought it would be a very good plan,
To make a draw on Uncle Sam.
So draw while you can, the Gold is free and plenty,
'Tis very fine, oh! how it shines—hurrah for California!

Chorus:
Hy ho! away we go, o'er the Rocky Mountains, O!
Hy ho! away we go, o'er the Mountains cap'd with snow.

accordingly came to a halt and commenced preparations for building a bridge. The timber was felled and dragged to the spot by our oxen and in one hour a bridge constructed, sufficient to convey over our whole company with ease and safety.[11]

In the course of the morning, we met with several other streams, which we crossed without difficulty. At twelve o'clock, we struck the Canadian River in one of its majestic windings through the Great Prairie. We knew that this river would cross our track again, but we had reached it too soon, showing that we had made too much southing in our march hitherto. Halting on the bank, a party was sent to reconnoitre for a suitable place to cross, while the rest were busy in preparations for dinner.

A respectable ford having been found at no great distance, we commenced our crossing about two o'clock. The bank on the north side, by which we descended to the river, was rather steep & difficult, so that we were compelled to lock our wagon wheels and hold them back by drag ropes attached to the axles. The river was low, having only three feet of water in the channel. On the south side, there was scarcely any bank at all, but a shelving up into the level plain, which was richly covered with a luxurious growth of grass. It seems as if the river, instead of flowing in a channel of its own through the prairie, wound along the edges of a bottom which it once entirely overflowed, the northern bank being the abraded shore of a mighty lake, now dwindled to a comparatively narrow river. I was the first one to cross the stream. Staking my horse in the tall grass on the other side, I amused myself with taking [a] sketch of the company in their difficult & somewhat comical position while fording.[12]

At four o'clock we were all over, and again on the march. Bending our course up the stream about two miles, we came upon an Indian encampment but recently abandoned. A feeling of alarm, or rather of excited attention & inquiry, pervaded the corps. It [was] impossible to conjecture who our neighbors might be [and] what their disposi-

[11] George Churchill (April 27, 1849) wrote that the men constructed two corduroy bridges over the slough; that same day, Phineas Blunt also mentioned building the bridges.

[12] Sketch missing.

tion towards us should we chance [to] meet. By a common impulse, every man began to examine his gun, to overhaul his pistols, and take a peek into the state of his ammunition. A little beyond this deserted camping ground, we chose our own position for the night and pitched our tents in the best possible order for defence in case of an attack. The guard was set and maintained with unusual care and every precaution taken to avoid a surprise. I was captain of the midnight watch; and the night being pleasant, and the prospect of an approaching danger furnishing excitement enough to overcome drowsiness and fatigue, the service was by no means disagreeable.

There was abundance & variety of game at this place, as well as excellent fish in the river and the best of feed for our animals on its bank. We therefore determined to rest a day in order to recruit and prepare for the difficult passages which were yet before us. It was a day of bustle, business & sport. Various were the employments about which the company were to set themselves. Rearranging the packings both of the wagons & the mules, cleaning guns & pistols, washing & mending clothes, repairing harness & wagons, cooking, hunting, fishing, bathing—these were all going on together and by turns, and made our camp as busy from morning till night as a small town on market day and as gay as the court of the prince of harlequins. Our bill of fare that day would make a gourmand smack his lips & feel ashamed of his favorite hotel. Turtle soup, trout, cat-fish, craw-fish, fried bull frogs, roast turkey, venison, squirrels, rabbits, hare, with sundries in the way of wild fowl, and other sundries for dessert. It is seldom that such a table is spread in the desert.

In the afternoon, I took a survey of the last Indian camping ground. From its extent, and from other indications, I judged that there were not less than a thousand persons in the company which so recently occupied it. Their wigwams, still remaining as they left them, were composed of branches of trees stuck into the ground, bent over so as to meet at the top. A large quantity of buffalo bones was strewed over the ground, and the stakes were standing in which they had dried the meat for future use. It was evident they had been there a number of days and were bound on a long expedition. They might be crossing the desert on the same track with ourselves, in which case we should no doubt encounter them. Among their relics was the shell of a very large turtle,[13] which they had doubtless taken in the Canadian River. It must have weighed, when taken, thirty five to forty pounds. The Indians have a high esteem for this luxury and know how to make savory dishes of it, as well as their more refined neighbors.

Towards evening, we had a general bathing in the river, every man being disposed to have a thorough washing preparatory to the approaching Sabbath. The dance that followed was no improvement upon this preparation, though it was quite in keeping with the manner in which the day was spent. When it arrived, the evening was enlivened with songs, of which the following may serve as a specimen, "Going to California, with a wash-bowl on our knee," &c.

[13] Some nineteen species and subspecies of freshwater turtles are currently found in Oklahoma. Native people roasted them over a campfire or cut pieces up for a delicious soup. They also relished turtle eggs. Warriors ate turtle meat before battle, believing that it protected them and made them difficult to kill (Kimball and Anderson 1968, 94).

FIGURE 4. Modern view of Caddo County mounds, Oklahoma, 2007. *Photo by Patricia A. Etter.*

7

The Buffalo Hunt and More

Crossing the Canadian River, the Knickerbockers entered a new environment. The landscape featured vertical-walled canyons and red sandstone formations known as Permian red beds. They sighted their first buffalo, and responding to the excitement of the hunt and anticipating steaks for dinner, rode into the herds. After a few mishaps, they trudged westward over miles of gypsum beds until Antelope Hills in Roger Mills County came into view. Moving on for some seven miles, they crossed the boundary into the Texas Panhandle, where the Knickerbockers' trail and Marcy's subsequent trail crossed. The Knickerbockers continued on Gregg's trail close to the south bank of the Canadian River, a few miles north of the trail Marcy followed. Both Marcy and the Knickerbockers met a large group of peaceful Kiowa Indians who were in the area waiting to trade.

The morning of Sunday, April 29, we took up our line of march at 7 AM, all in good order, and prepared to meet with any foes that might aproach us. Great display of arms was now made and great feeling manifested by all the company as to the present occupants of our last encampment, and the greatest caution was observed by all hands, and the waggons were kept in a proper double rank, with the packed mules in the center, in perfect battle order of march. The advance guard being sent out had four hours ahead of the company, and at ½ mile distances, the centinals were left to their post, all in good and strict order; in fact, this last camp of the Camanches inspired our Yankee boys with a true spirit of strict attention to their new position. Our rout was now over a fine, clear, sandy soil. As far as the eyes can see, not a tree or scrub of any kind was to be seen. The wind was very high and caused the dust to be of great [line illegible] now put them to the test and were found of great use.

At 10 AM we came in sight of a great number of mounds. I took a sketch of the first, approaching them at a distance of nearly two miles; when near to them, they were about 50 to 100 feet high and of a red gravelly kind of soil, the tops covered with grass. We marched through the center of two of them, and after passing them some two miles, innumerable quantities of all sized mounds appeared to us in all directions, some of them looming up like the Pirimids of Egipt.[1]

During the afternoon, the signal of alarm was announced to the main body from the advance guard, of some large body of Indians being in sight. So then their became such a time of talking and loading and capping and preparing arms just as if we were going into the battle field, as would make any old Napoliatur soldier laugh right out to split himself. So, after many conjectures of what tribe they might be or of what force, or how we should do and what we should do if we went to take them prisoners &c. &c., at last we overtook our advance guard, who had come to a stand after assertaining that our great "Camanche" tribe was the great heards of buffaloes on their spring

---

[1] (Sketch missing.) The emigrants found themselves among the "red beds," geologic formations predominant in Caddo County, Oklahoma, carved by tributaries of the South Canadian and Washita rivers. This area also contained some of the most diverse forest of the Great Plains (Little 1939, 1–10; Suneson 1996, 88–105). George Churchill described, in his notation for that day, "several mounds on the prairie from 60 to 100 feet high and deep ravines 100 feet deep with large trees growing in them" (April 29, 1849). George Sniffen (1849, 33) with the Havilah Mining Company described one broad ravine as being a mile long and two hundred feet deep. He added that the prairies abounded with these ravines, many filled with timber. William Chamberlin also crossed deep ravines, then passed over rolling prairie before camping near a "running stream of very red water." Here they gathered a "mess of mushrooms for their dinner" (1945, 42). The red formations they saw are known as the Caddo County mounds: Dead Woman Mound, Lone Mound, and Twin Mounds are some of the dominant features they might have seen in the distance.

travels to the north plains.[2] The sporting part of [the] company now became enraptured and fired with the sport of hunting buffalo; some 30 to 40 of the best mounted imediately left for the chase and captured 5 fine bulls, which were skinned and divided amongst the company during the evening, when we enjoyed ourselves to the fullest appetite. The buffalo were now in all directions about us.

The next morning, Monday, April 30, we continued our march amidst heards of miriads of buffalo in all directions as far as the eyes could reach. The wind was still blowing very high and caused clouds of dust to blow over these immense heards of buffalo, and which made a most splendid sight. After travelling some 8 miles we approached some very extensive rocks of red looking sand banks to the south and at sight of which we became alarmed, for it was very evident we had made too much south and were fast approaching the sandy deserts of Texas. After a consultation in regard to our march, a counter march was taken to the north, when we again struck on

[2] The emigrants first sighted the American buffalo (*Bison bison*) in Custer County, Oklahoma. Without exception, the diarists confess their eagerness to join the hunt. As soon as the word was given, "Buffalos Ahead," David Jordan was amused to see men scampering about and riding off with their guns. They killed two buffalo in half an hour, then "feasted on the meat, rather tough" (April 5, 1849). Stanislaus Lasselle (1991, 10) admitted to hunting for sport and left a wounded buffalo to the wolves or to rot on the prairies. He also remarked that the horses suffered because the buffalo ate much of the grass. John Boyer of the Van Buren Company, one of many companies formed in Arkansas that followed Marcy and his troops, had looked forward "to the delicacy of a prairie supper." When the feast was finally laid before him, he lamented, "O cracky! In vain our grinders brought to bear upon it; its toughness was a quality that absorbed all others; it was abandoned" (September 7, 1849). Jacob Alfred Kanouse, a 34-year-old lawyer from New Jersey, was in hot pursuit of a buffalo when, as he described it: "I let [my] gun fall back to rest on my shoulder to pass under the bushes when it went off and the flash communicated fire to my cotton coat . . . I ran down the ravine again to the water and put out the fire on my clothes and when I returned for the mare, I could see nothing of her" (1849). George Pattison perhaps summed up the excitement travelers felt around buffalo: "Their advance is somewhat frightful; their thundering rumble over the dry plain; their lion-like fronts and long beards; their open mouths and hanging tongues as they come puffing like an engine at every bound" (June 9, 1849). Pattison was among the minority who wrote of the importance of the buffalo to the Native residents, who depended on the animal for food, housing, clothing, bedding, ropes, meat bags, sinews for bow strings, sewing thread for moccasins, leggings, etc. Travelers found buffalo chips to be a great substitute for wood in their cooking fires. Writing in his log on May 15, Chamberlin remarked that he had not yet "used buffalo chips for fuel, but I find that one answers the purpose of a writing desk at present" (1945, 43). George Churchill summed up on May 1: "Our company has eaten so much buffalo meat that we all got sick."

the grass covered prairies. Buffalo were still all around us, and numbers of our company were tempted to hunt them, and several of the men were thrown from their horses, and some lost their pistols, all of them amongst the heards in stampeding them of their calves, and a Mr. [Jacob Alfred] Kanouse lost his horse altogether. When he was thrown, his horse was carried off in the immense heard of the buffalo and such quantities of dust [word illegible], it was not possible for him to find out in which direction his animal had gone. The hunters got enough of sport this time, for with the loss of the horse and the narrow escapes of several broken necks and the loss of pistols and the breaking down of their horses—many of which got gored by the buffalo bulls—it gave them enough of it. So we camped early in a deep and extensive revein with thousands of buffalo all around us. The sportsmen took a goodly quantity of calves this afternoon and we all enjoyed a hearty supper of veal cuttlets. 8 men volunteered to go with Mr. Kanouse in search of his lost horse.

Next morning, Tuesday, May 1, we left this camp at 7 AM, wind abated, the buffalo in all directions, but our hunters were rather shy, got enough of the sport. Our travel today was very rough. Several deep reveins and dykes and some small timber [illegible]. Met with some few flocks of turkies, also a river, supposed to be the headwaters of the Washitaw. Here we encamped to await the party in search of the lost horse and had plenty of turkies and other small game as well as buffalo.

Wednesday, May 2, after enjoying a good breakfast of stewed turkey, we commenced our march again. We met with some rolling stray hills this day, covered with sea shells such as oyster, conk, mussels &c., also a soft kind of white stone which you could cut with a knife like pipe clay.[3] No doubt that at some remote period of time this

---

[3] The Knickerbockers' route took them past modern Weatherford, Oklahoma, and westward through Custer County. There they came upon immense beds of gypsum. Marcy later found gypsum and limestone ledges in which he and his men "discovered the petrefactions of oysters and mussels," the first fossils he had seen on the road (G. Foreman 1939, 218). Möllhausen (1858, 163) wrote that it took five days for the Whipple group to cross the gypsum fields, and Phineas Blunt (May 2–3, 1849) remarked that the fields were some six to twelve inches thick over a field of red earth.

Great Desert was covered by the sea, for the present appearances shows distinctly that such was the case. Our travels were very ruff and [over] much ridge land. We met with an extensive revein during the afternoon with some good spring water, and we camped early to wait the return of our scouting party, who returned during the evening without success after an unsuccessful search amongst several heards of the buffalo. They finally abandoned the horse with his bridle & saddle & 1 Colt's revolver all compleat. This was a good lesson for them.

Thursday, May 3, we commenced our march this morning at 7 AM and traveled over much range land, when about 10 AM we met with a revein with a river, which we crossed, and travelled by this river for 3 miles, when we stoped to noon and rest. Here we found the first horned frog, which is some[what] like our northern frog except it has a bony kind of prominence over the eyes like small horns, also on the tail part is covered with prickly prominences and so up the back.[4] We then proceeded on our march and left this river, and during the afternoon we were deluged with a heavy rain and a severe thunder storm through which we traveled till 6 PM, when we camped in an extensive revein with good grass and plenty of wood, but no water but what was collected by placing our tin pans and camp kettles by the edges of our tents and waggons. It rained all night.

Friday, May 4, this morning was very cold, and 2 oxen & 1 mule were missing and after some 2 hours search were found. We traveled over some extensive plate lands, and during the morning we struck with a trail, supposed to be Gregg's trail.[5] One of the men found a piece of a broken Haines [axe] and an Indian stone sledge hammer.  During the afternoon we again met with a river and which was thought by some to be the Canadian River again or the Dry

[4] The Texas horned lizard (*Phrynosoma cornutum*), also referred to as the horny toad, has been added to the protected species list in Texas and Oklahoma in the twenty-first century. This tract was probably located in or near the Black Kettle National Grasslands, Roger Mills County, Oklahoma.

[5] According to Goulding's traveling companion Phineas Blunt, on this date the men passed Antelope Hills or Boundary Mounds, which he described as "pyramid hills with flat tops." These are a dominant feature in a deep bend of the Canadian River north of modern Durham, Roger Mills County, a few miles east of the Texas boundary. There are six of these hills rising from 120 to 150 feet almost perpendicular to the prairie. Lt. James W. Abert (1970, 51–52) described and sketched them during his 1845 reconnaissance of the area.

River.[6] We seen but few buffalo during this day's march, denoting we were getting well through their regions. We met with great quantities of agat[e] and jasper and beautiful stones, all strewed over the surface, many splendid specimens of which were picked up by our men.[7] The howlings of the wolves were the music of the night.

Saturday, May 5, we travelled over some rolling hills by the river bed. At noon we stoped to feed up in a most beautiful or natural garden in the river bottoms, of dwarf grapes and wild gooseberrys and excellent grass and a few very old oak trees of immense size, on some of which we put our names and date of the month and where we came from, &c. &c.[8] We continued over this vast desert of country. During the afternoon we flushed a fine flock of wild turkies and a few dear and one buffalo. We left the river and came in sight of some very high and prominent hills and mounds. The travel was continually raising until we approached near to this mound, which we observed to be the remains of an extensive volcano. All the broken fragments of stone and rocks had the appearance of being at some time burnt, and many portions of lava which we handled was very light and resembled pumistone, but darker coloured. Here we could not find any water so continued our march till dark night, and we became so tired out, was obliged to camp in a small revein with very little water.[9] Some few Indians were seen during our march this day, but they did not approach us. The night was cold.

Sunday, May 6, early this morning a party went out to reconnoitre

---

[6] The Knickerbockers crossed the border into the Texas Panhandle in the vicinity of State Route 33, just south of the Canadian River in Hemphill County. The travelers negotiated sand beds that some described as quicksand. There the animals strained to pull the wagons over a "Dry River" (Red Deer Creek) that emptied into the Canadian River near the town of Canadian in the Texas Panhandle. Marcy described the quicksand phenomenon: the sand absorbed much of the flowing water, which further evaporated in the daytime. At night, when evaporation was less, the water flowed over the sand (G. Foreman 1939, 221–22).

[7] John P. Sherburne (1988, 82), traveling with the Whipple expedition in 1853–54, also found agate and jasper along the route, east of Dry River, Hemphill County.

[8] Phineas Blunt (May 7, 1849) and others feasted in the garden of grapes. The trees Goulding calls "oaks" were actually cottonwoods.

[9] Blunt also described traveling along the bluffs of the Canadian "over hills and deep vales and shallow ravines" and fighting the insatiable sand flies (May 7, 1849). Whipple made his camp no. 38 about eighteen miles west of Dry River and noted that they "passed hills similar in character and form to the Antelope Hills" that "appear[ed] to be the last remnants of a llano or prairie that once covered the whole region" (1941, 79).

and find water & grass so as we could stop and camp, it being Sunday, when they were met with by one Indian chief whom they fetched into camp mounted on a small mule. He was a fine, yellow looking fellow and appeared to be well pleased with his visit. He staid with us nearly 2 hours and by signs and grunts, we learned that he was from the south, and their was more of them in that direction. His hair was plaited and fashioned on a long strip of buffalo hide with silver plates of oval form laced on, and extended nearly to the ground. He had a striped red & white [buffalo hide], also a black one, which he used on the saddle when mounted. He had also a piece of buffalo hide wrapped around a portion of his body. He had a large black & white necklace of bone beads about his neck, which were braided together very thick, and a belt with silver plates laced on around his waist, and on his wrists and arms above his elbows were several large brass wire rings. His skin seamed to be either died or painted a pale yellow color. He had a gun with a raw cowhide over on it with 9 strands of white hair fastened to the top of the barrel and which looked in the distance like a flag. He had a pouch and powder horn ornamented with small round beads, and of which several of his straps and dress were ornamented. His stirrips were wood and covered over with raw hide like the gun. I took a sketch of him on the mule, also when he was dismounted, and altogether he was quite a novel sight to us, particularly in our present wild and desolate condition.[10]

He appeared to be of a most jovial and excellent disposition and he talked by signs—but so as we could easily take the hint that Capt. Ebbets, who first seen him, ran away as he approached him, and he

---

[10] Sketches missing. Stanislaus Lasselle confirmed the sighting of the old Indian:

> His face was painted all over with yellow clay while red paint surrounded his eyes. He had on a buffalo robe with pins from the back of his head reaching to the ground. His wrists were covered with brass wire rather large. He had a rifle covered over with white cow hide and at the mussle of the gun was ten or twelve strings of white cow hide. He also had a small bag where he kept his looking glass, and he seemed to take as much care of it as a lady would of her toilet. (1991, 11)

With the introduction of the horse, the Kiowa, Comanche, and Apache tribes had gradually moved southward from Montana and Wyoming, choosing a nomadic lifestyle adapted to the buffalo culture of the plains. Since 1790, the Comanches had allied with the Kiowas, who settled mainly in the Southern Plains area of Oklahoma and Texas. The Comanches became one of the most feared tribes on the plains for their depredations, as white settlement threatened their traditional way of life and subsistence. Ultimately, following many years of battles and U.S. military conquest, they were forced onto reservations.

would laugh with us at the "courageous captanio." We understood by him he was of the tribe called "Kiowayes," and his party were after buffalo. He was about 80 years old, by his appearance and by the information we obtained from him. We proceeded on our march and met with the river some 4 miles further on, when we found plenty of grass and a good camp. When we stoped for the day, the Indian again visited us. He appeared to like our fair, and eat hearty with several of the messes and remained with us all night.

Next morning, Monday, May 7, we proceeded on our journey and the Kioway Indian parted with us. The appearance of the country now was more hilly and ruff than in our recent travels and evidently seemed we were approaching New Mexico by the change of soil. The travelling was very difficult, up one hill and down another, great hardship on mules and horses. One waggon got broken down and caused some delay, but we still kept near and in sight of the river and camped in excellent grass and water with the croaking of frogs for the music of the night.

Tuesday, May 8, several bears was killed by the men and we all had bear steaks for breakfast. We travelled over many extensive white sand beds by the river during the day and [it] was heavy work for the mules at times. About 2 PM we met with a very large old cottonwood tree in a flat meadow-like bottom by the river. This tree consisted of 5 main trunks which spread its extensive branches over upward of one hundred feet of land; in fact, our whole company could camp under its branches. See drawing.[11] We only stayed here an hour when we proceeded on our march, which was very heavy and difficult, and camped with good grass but very poor water.

Wednesday, May 9, the weather was now very fine and warm. Some more black bears were shot this morning and bountifully supplied our messes with bears grease to fry our flap jacks. Sand bluffs and ridge

---

[11] Sketch missing. The cottonwood was still there when Balduin Möllhausen and the Whipple expedition passed four years later. Möllhausen marveled at "a tree that rose solitary on the plain, and was remarkable for its gigantic growth and for its strangely twisted and entangled boughs and branches. It was a cotton-wood tree, centuries old, and had a diameter of twelve feet; at the height of about six feet from the ground, it divided itself into two mighty arms, which stretched themselves far out, and with their numerous boughs shaded the arid ground" (1858, 195). Lasselle (1991, 12) noted that the Knickerbockers dined under that tree, the limbs of which spread in every direction. The tree stood south of the Canadian River between Whipple camps 38 and 39 at East Dry Creek and Indian Creek (J. Morris 1997, 282), both in Roberts County (Whipple map 1, 1853–54).

FIGURE 5. Balduin Möllhausen, Alamo, 1853.
Big cottonwood tree on the Canadian River, Hemphill County, Texas. Graphite on paper. Whipple Collection. *Courtesy of the Research Division of the Oklahoma Historical Society.*

hills seems to be in our continued progress this day, which made it heavy drawing for the animals. Sand beds 2 to 3 feet deep of clear white sand and up steep, gravelly hills and down reveins were our Macadamised road this day. About 5 PM we met with a tolerable good camp place so we camped. We passed an old Indian encampment during our march this afternoon and we had a smart thunder storm.[12]

[12] The men were camped on White Deer Creek south of the Canadian River. Across the river was Bent's Old Trading Post, also known as Fort Adobe. A modern traveler can reach the area by driving east from Stinnett, Hutchinson County, over some thirty-four miles of winding country road, partially graded and partially paved. William Bent and Ceran St. Vrain, partners in a trading enterprise called Bent's Fort near La Junta, Colorado, opened the satellite trading post of Fort Adobe on the Canadian in the early 1840s. They constructed an adobe fort some eighty feet square, surrounded it with nine-foot walls, and cut one entrance for trade with the Comanches. However, resistance from the Jicarilla Apaches and other Native tribes made trading difficult, and frustrated with the continued hostility, Bent simply blew up the fort's interior in the early spring of 1849 and abandoned the place. On May 15, David Jordan was among the first who wrote about the devastation of Fort Adobe, describing the stone wall from his campsite on the south bank of the Canadian. On April 18, 1849, Asa Scarborough of the Heath Pack Mule Company hiked over to the other side of the river to take a look, and described the ruins as being thirty-five yards square with three stone bastions on which had been mounted six guns. "Most of the fort has been burned," he said (1969, 25).

Thursday, May 10, it was now very evident that we had come into a new species of climate and country, for the trees, grass, birds, and everything seemed to be all in their bloom and evidently in the hight of spring or summer; a great variety of plants and flowers was indeed most cheery and beautiful. Wild currant and grapes, &c. &c. were in great abundance. The river now was walled in on both sides with high sand or gravel bluffs and leaving a wide river valley or river bed, in some places 6 or 7 miles wide, and scenery evidently intended by Madame Nature to become a great resting place for the generation to come. Hereafter we passed another old Indian camp of lodges during this day's march,[13] and in one of the reveins we met with a great encampment of Mexicans, as it appeared, by an old Mexican waggon which had broken down. The wheels were of solid wood as cut out of a large cottonwood tree. Here, there was alone 2 cattle pens and the bones and remains of a slain ox. In a short time, we discovered the tracks of waggons and evident signs of a regular trail towards Mexico.[14]

Our men were attacked during this day by the sand fly, and many of them suffered much by having their eyes bandaged up and face very much swollen.[15] In fact, we were so much annoyed, we had to

[13] The emigrants wrote about a number of deserted encampments as they trudged along the Canadian River. These belonged to the Comanches, who left each spring to hunt buffalo and returned before winter set in. Whipple made his camp no. 43 in this spot, known as Shady Creek, in September 1853, and counted not less than three hundred dome-shaped lodges covering several acres on both sides of the stream (Sherburne 1988, 82; Whipple 1941, 87–88).

[14] In addition to following Indian trails, travelers would find a trace the Comancheros (native New Mexican traders) followed to Santa Fe and the western settlements in the area. While encamped at Dixon Creek near Borger in Hutchinson County, Lieutenant Abert wrote in 1845 that the traders would often stop to repair their clumsy, two-wheeled *carretas* at this spot. Coming along the trail, he correctly surmised that the carts' axles broke as they rolled downhill (1970, 27). In 1846–47, Frederick A. Wislizenus, with Doniphan's expedition, "heard in the distance of several miles a singular, awful noise, like a combination of falling rocks, breaking bones, screams of anguish and cries of children, but the deep impression which the mysterious concert had made upon my ears was but surpassed by the surprising effect, when with my own eyes I descried the wonderful machine whose action produced that unearthly music—a Mexican carréta" (Wislizenus 1848, 6–7).

[15] Gregg called this insect "a species of prairie tenant . . . generally known to prairie travelers as the buffalo-gnat . . . its bite is so poisonous as to give face, neck, and hands, or any other part of the person upon which its affectionate caress has been bestowed, the appearance of a pustulated varioloid" (1990, 238–39). Lasselle noted that one of the Knickerbockers was severely kicked by a mule that day because he could not see, as his face was wrapped with a green veil to keep out the gnats. He added that "several of the K's today have their faces tied up with eyes so swollen that . . . they can't see ten feet" (1991, 12).

leave the river bed and take the ridge land. We camped on upland, and a terrible thunder storm came up & hail stones as large as walnuts fell in great quantities. Several tents were blown down, and quite a time [illegible] amongst the companys animals, several of which stampeded and caused much trouble to be found again.

Friday, May 11, the day was fine and warm, and we struck into the regular waggon trail this day, and now we were satisfied we were in the regular rout to Santifee. A Mr. Hide, [Steven Hyde; see appendix A] got a severe kick this day by one of the pack mules in passing him by. The cactus in endless varieties, with other flowers, were continually feasting our eyes today as we progressed on our march, also the great varieties of birds singing, and the living and domestic cooko; of that innocent bird, the cooko is a species of doves which are in great quantities in these regions.

We crossed a beautiful river or stream of clear running water during the day, coming from the south and emptying in the muddy waters of the Canadian River. It was near to this river we struck into the regular waggon road or trail, which no doubt had led over the Canadian River at this point. By fording far beyond this, we seen no signs of waggon tracks excepting those of our men.[16] We met with a recently packed mule encampment; also, we were still troubled with the sand fly.

Saturday, May 12, through some bad management, the regular waggon road was lost this morning and a counter march of about two miles had to be taken to enable them to take the road. During this operation great numbers of hairs and antelopes were disturbed and were running in various directions to the view of many of us, who enjoyed the scene. Here we left the Canadian River (if that was the Canadian River) altogether and struck south on the open prairies, which were splendid and extensive, but we met with no water [illegible] after 9 o'clock at night, when we camped on the edge of a great

---

[16] The Knickerbockers left the Canadian River at Dixon Creek, Hutchinson County, and trod along Gregg's trail as far as modern Borger and Bunavista, on State Route 136. Archambeau (1954, 7) writes that Marcy found and followed this old wagon trace when he arrived in the area on June 9, 1849.

revein and went to bed supperless, completely fatigued out, and some of the messes did not get up till midnight.[17]

Sunday, May 13, by descending a very rugetty & dangerous revein, we obtained sufficient water to make our breakfast. The scouting or reconnoitering party came to breakfast and had discovered some fine spring holes of water within 200 yards of us. So we remained here all day to rest ourselfs, and parties went out for abundant supply of water. Two fawns or antelope were taken this morning and added a sweet addition to our messes. The [illegible] and rest cured the most of the company eyes so we were the better able to progress our journey the next morning.[18]

Monday, May 14, we commenced our march this morning, all in good spirits, and felt quite refreshed after our rest and much improved in our sight. Travelling over prairie land covered with small chaperal and cactus and small shrubs, about noon, the signal from the advance guard came that Indians were in sight, so the alarm became as before. Every preparation was [made] for making the attack, and arms examined and caps put on, &c. &c. In a short time we halted in a regular coral when the Indians were allowed to enter, and as their was but 9 of them, we gave them some tobacco & biscuit and a few charges of powder, as they were in search of buffalo and were peacable Apaches. They had bows & arrows and their chief had a rifle. They proceeded on their way, as we did, once in a [illegible] direction.

Several flashes of lightning and rowling thunder in the distance denoted we were surrounded with a terrible storm, and during the afternoon, after its making a circle around us, struck us about 3 o'clock. I never seen anything like this before. It blew and lightning, a perfect sheet of fire, and in fact, we thought it was all over with us.

---

[17] This camping spot was about two miles southeast of Antelope Peak, near Deal, Carson County. It was visible for several miles around, lacked wood, and had soil unfit for cultivation, according to Marcy (G. Foreman 1939, 228).

[18] Gregg turned south toward modern Amarillo, then west, closely following the route of old U.S. 66, while the Knickerbockers and later Marcy would take a more northerly route crossing U.S. 87 near Glick, then passing Gentry, and crossing Tecovas Creek at State Route 1061 north of Bushland on Interstate 40.

The ground trembled and their we were all huddled up together, mules, horses, and men and waggons, and not a soul could speak a word. Even the poor brutes were struck dumb and trembled with fear. Many of the men got under the waggons, and the horses got as close to each other as possible.

The hail stones fell as large as hens eggs and large walnuts and fell some 6 inches deep. I filled a camp kettle full and placed in a waggon to have a cherry cobbler at camp in the evening. Several of the men were effected by the flashes of lightning. It was the most awful storm I ever witnessed, and lasted about 25 minutes. The covers of several of the waggons were torn by the violence of the hail, and my shoulder was collered several weeks after from the pelting I got by the merciless storm, as well as many others of the company.

About 2-1/2 PM we met with a valley with a pond of water in which their was fish, so we camped, having abundance of grass and wild gooseberrys &c., we living very comfortable, and experienced our hail stones (which were now melted down to the size of marbles) in some delicious cherry cobblers. Through some mismanagement, a pack mule was lost during the day's march, supposed to have lagged behind, and was stolen by some Indians, as their was some seen in our trail during the afternoon. Mr. [Phineas] Blunt went in search of the mules and was chased into camp at 9 o'clock PM by two Indians armed with spears. The guards were doubled this night and every precaution attended to as to watching well on animals, but we were not troubled or molested by any Indians during the night. The mule lost was a pack mule belonging to no. 11 and was lightly packed with tobacco, some ammunition, and 2 doz. jack knives—just the very articles the Indians wanted.[19]

Next morning, Tuesday, May 15, we proceeded on our march sloly as 4 mounted men, well armed, were sent in search of the lost mule,

[19] Blunt wrote that his pack was worth fifty dollars and held his long boots, six or seven pounds of lead, and locks. When he arrived at the spot where he thought he could find his mule, he saw two Indians coming toward him on horseback with two long spears in hand, so he ran as fast as he could back to camp (May 14, 1849).

and at 1 o'clock we met with a good grass spot and stoped to rest and bath in a small pond of some spring water, when the scouting party overtook us but without success, for they did not discover any signs of either the mule or Indians. No doubt the Indians made tracks during the night far from us, as they made about as good and profitable a haul in that pack as they could select out of the whole company and therefore were satisfied. We traveled till about 5-1/2 PM and camped in good grass & water.

8

New Mexico and the Comanches of the Plains

As the men made their way through the Canadian River valley in the Texas Panhandle, Goulding sketched a teacup-shaped feature he saw in the area of Vega, Oldham County. Marcy mentioned the same feature a month later; thus we are able to locate a small area of trail winding its way through the bluffs of the Canadian River.[1] *Goulding continued across Texas into New Mexico in the area of modern Glenrio, Quay County, near the route of Interstate 40. Continuing west, he passed between Little and Big Tucumcari mounds on his way to the Pecos Valley. The company stopped to visit and trade with a large Comanche encampment, where Goulding made a one-of-a-kind sketch of the chief.*

Wednesday, May 16, we commenced our march at 7 AM in good order and kept the old waggon track till 1 PM, when we met with water and stoped to rest to 2 o'clock. Our travelling was now very level and we passed several dog towns. Several of the dogs were shot by the company, as they are considered good food. A long ridge of highlands made to our view, supposed to be the Pecos Ridge. About 5 o'clock we

[1] This would not have been possible without Ernest R. Archambeau's (1954) detailed reconnaissance, in which he compared Marcy's route with that of Gregg. In addition, by 1954, surveys had been made and streams named. Using these guides and others, it has been possible to recreate Goulding's route in this area with some accuracy.

FIGURE 6. Modern view of bluffs, Canadian River valley, Oldham County, Texas, 2007. The geologic features are similar to ones Goulding describes. *Photo by Patricia A. Etter.*

 passed through the ridge, where their is a wide pass, when imediately comes to view a splendid large knoll or mound with a cap on the top looking like a large stone laying in the top.[2] After passing this mound, we camped by a good spring. The bottoms here are lined with small brush—chaperal—and alive with hair and antelope. Took a sketch of the mounds and highlands, also the camp with the sun setting. We are now very well satisfied that we are in the true rout to New Mexico, for the road seams to have been travelled by many thousands.[3] The night was very warm & fine.

[2] On June 13, Marcy passed the same feature, describing it as being "in a gap or notch formed by the bluffs of the 'Llano Estacado' . . . there is one near our camp, detached from the main bluff, this can be seen for many miles; and as it is round, very symmetrical, and crowned with a stone cap in the form of a reversed plate, it is a good landmark" (G. Foreman 1939, 230). This feature is about eight miles northeast of Vega, Oldham County, Texas, on Interstate 40. Many similar features making up the bluffs of the Canadian River can be seen for miles around. Goulding's sketch shows the form, and figure 6 illustrates the various shapes and features that cover a wide area south of the Canadian. Continuous erosion by streams flowing from the Canadian River has no doubt created and reshaped these mounds over time.

[3] On the same date, Lasselle wrote that the men were following wagon tracks over a wide expanse of prairie dog villages and cactus (1991, 14). These were probably the tracks of Comancheros or Indian trails since very few, if any, companies had preceded the Knickerbockers.

Thursday, May 17, we started early on our march this morning, and about 8 o'clock, I was ahead of the company waggons, and meeting with a nice patch of grass in a small hollow, I stoped and made my lariet fast to my large Bowie knife, which I used as a stake in the ground to let my horse grase a bit. In the meantime, wrote up my notes, when some of the pack mules, coming suddenly up with their packs covered with buffalo robes over the brow of the hills, and my horse, supposing them a heard of buffalo, made a sudden jerk. And before I could grasp my knife hilt, he was off, knife and lariet, up the hill in the opposite side. Some of the company nearby, mounted, went in pursuit, and coming up with him, finding him all of a sudden come to a halt, and on examining him found the Bowie knife had choped off his rear hind leg close by the fetlock, leaving but a small portion of the skin holding in the hoof. Here my fine black horse, Bill, which was the pride of the whole camp, stood on 3 legs trembling in the most pitiful manner. I soon came to the conclusion what was best to be done in this case. No case or remedy now, and leave him to be eaten alive by the infernal wolves continualy bawling after us I could not think of. So I requested one of the company to put the poor animal out of pain by shooting him at once and proceeded on our march. With the thought of the loss of this valuable and beautiful horse, my mind was much disturbed during the day.[4]

About 3 PM we were amused by the appearance of a caviat [herd] of wild horses. They came up within 3 hundred yards of us and stared at us with as much curiosity as we had of them. Their was 27 of them, and after treating their eyes sufficiently and satisfied that we were the folks who hold horses as slaves, they came to the right about face and made quick tracks for the south, and it was a splen-

[4] Stanislaus Lasselle wrote that Goulding lost a very fine horse "foolishly" by sticking his Bowie knife in the ground and tying his horse to it (1991, 14). Phineas Blunt confirmed that they had to "kill him on the spot." George Churchill wrote that it was a "beautiful creature, jet black . . . and had carried him [Goulding] every step of the way so far." He further added that George H. Blake (see appendix A) shot the horse in the head to put him out of his misery.

did sight to look on; as far as the eyes could reach, we gazed after them, till they became as small pigmies.[5]

Some highlands being in our sight, we were desirous of making them. Consequently, our days march was very long and we did not camp till 9 o'clock at night and but little water. The company was very much scattered and fatigued and many of the camp came in late.

Friday, May 18, in the morning, it was discovered that 2 mules were missed this morning and a party was sent out in search of them but could not find any traces of them. We continued our march through a fine open valley towards the south with ragged looking hills & reveins, and far to the north appeared some high mountains and blue looking highlands. About 4 o'clock, appearance of a storm, and meeting with a good spot, we camped for the night; and one of the oxen being lame, he was slaughtered and served out to the different messes—and we had beef stakes of the real sort this time and a good supply of suet to fry our flap jacks. It stormed during the night but was not cold.[6]

---

[5] Lasselle recalled that

> the great anxiety I had to see wild horses was to day gratified. A[b]out three o'clock in the afternoon we saw a drove of about twenty about a mile off scattered in small squads. The leader of them all was a grayish roane. They had long tails dragging on the ground and heavy manes which seemed to be divided on either side of the neck. They would advance within a quarter of a mile of us and stop several minutes when again they would wheel around and take a quick trot from us. . . . Most of the horses were jet and shining black trotters. . . . They were much larger than [I] expected wild horses to be. (1991, 14)

These were Comanche horses. Acquisition of the horse in the late seventeenth century gave the Comanches mobility, and they gradually spread into and dominated the Southern Plains, where the buffalo was abundant. The horse soon became a measure of Comanche wealth, and therefore a valuable trade commodity. At the same time, having perfected horse stealing to a high art, they easily increased the size of their herds.

[6] On this day, several of Goulding's traveling companions mentioned striking a wagon trail that they rightly believed would lead them to the Mexican settlements (Blunt, May 18, 1849; Churchill, May 18, 1849). It was the old Comanchero Trail that swung around the southeast side of Tucumcari Mountain and west to the Pecos Valley (Gregg 1990, 260n9). The Knickerbockers did not descend to Rocky Dell Creek, where Möllhausen (1858, 259) found numerous pictographs. Instead, they moved on a few miles to Trujillo Creek and crossed into New Mexico in the area of abandoned Glenrio on Interstate 40, where the cart road might have been (Archambeau 1954, 4).

Goulding's sketch of Tucumcari Mountain and other mounds, New Mexico

Saturday, May 19, we proceeded on our march, travelling over a beautiful, level country with some mounds in our front, which varied in shapes as we approached on to them. Sometimes looking thus ——. Then after a few more miles they appeared thus ——. Then again thus ——. Then again, in a few hours, their shapes would change thus ——. These mounds or hills kept changing their views during our march all day and was very interesting.[7]

Our ox teams were very backward now and lagged very much in the rear and caused us to much delay. The advance guard met with a Comanche Indian who informed them of the scarcity of water and pointed out a hole or pool of water as being the only water for miles in this direction and that a large encampment of Comanches were ahead of us about 16 miles. It being now 7 o'clock, we encamped. The night was cold and windy and we were in an open plain and but one pool of water about 8 feet by 4 feet wide, and that well impregnated

[7] The shapes Goulding described were bluffs bordering the Llano Estacado near the Tucumcari Hills, Quay County, New Mexico. On May 23, David Jordan passed "high bluffs & a number very high mounds or pyramids several hundred feet high and standing entirely alone," while Chamberlin, with the Lewisburg Company, saw "a large peak having the appearance of a perfect dome; and others having peculiar shapes," adding that their road "continued through a valley containing pyramid shaped hills and mounds covered with a scrubby growth of cedar" (1945, 47).

Goulding's sketches give us a good idea of what the various features looked like. Tucumcari Mountain is easily recognized, and the feature with two "turrets" could be the 500-foot Pyramid Mount about ten miles southwest of Tucumcari, so called by Möllhausen when he sketched it in 1853 as a member of the Whipple expedition. Emmanuel Domenech also noticed that "in the same valley can be seen rocks of gritstone resembling towers or fortresses . . . Gothic castles, cathedrals in ruins, minarets, broken columns or even enormous vases that look as if they had been fabricated by giants" (1880, 1:163).

with "awa de mula." Strict guards were put on tonight in consequence of the alarm of Indians ahead of us, and the strictest caution observed.

Sunday, May 20, in consequence of the scarsity of water and neglect of those whose duty it was to attend to the oxen, they had strayed, and a party was sent off to the rear in search of them. This caused considerable delay. In looking with my spy-glass I seen the dust and appearance of a company in our rear, and when they came up, proved to be a packed mule company that had followed us all the way from Fort Smith and had just now overtaken us. They left the latter place on April 18th. We had a hearty time altho their was not one of the party of 11 packed mule men we had ever seen before. Still, we were as sociable as though we had been natural brothers—well how did you leave the States, have you any letters for me, and you got the late papers—did you not stop at the post office—and all such questions. They informed us that their was 20 waggons about 4 days march in our rear and that they had followed our blazing march and camp places all the way. They informed us of our 13 oxen about 5 miles in our rear, but the scouting party had gone after them. Great preparation was made now to treat our new cousins, for we had plenty of beef.

Just as this excitement was over, another party came in sight but from the other direction, consisting of a black covered waggon drawn by 4 oxen loaded with maze, farina, and biscut and 12 mules packed with the like etceteras for trafic with the Indians. These were conducted by 6 Mexicans of small size and one female.[8] The boss of the party gave us all the information we wanted, as he could speak tolerable good English. He told us all about the Camanches being friendly, and we were on the regular Santa Fe road and only 5 days march from the first Mexican settlements. I bought a lariet from him

[8] The latter group were Comancheros, native New Mexican traders from Santa Fe, Las Vegas, and other towns. They were well acquainted with the country and traded especially with the Comanches, preferably for stolen horses and cattle. Their wooden carts left tracks across the Llano Estacado of west Texas, which covers some fifty thousand square miles of flat and almost featureless landscape. It was an area that all forty-niners would have been wise to avoid.

for 75 cents & 4 cakes of hard brown bread for 20 cents & 2 pans full of wheat flour for a few charges of powder, and our men were supplied with many luxuries from this carivan. Our scouting party having now returned with the lost oxen, we hitched up and proceeded on our journey.

About 3-1/2 PM, the advance guard came to a halt and waited till the whole body came up so as to consult and make the best and most grand and formidable appearance we could, and the consequence was that they also turned out their warriors and received us in a most hospitable manner and led us to a very fine camping ground. The sight was indeed a grand one. This encampment was situated in the Pecos Valley, and to any one who has been at the Catskill Mountain House and remembers the extensive and magnificent view then seen, just such a plain was before us, excepting the river was not so large, the Pecos being only a small stream.[9] When we formed our ranks and commenced our march from the rising ground descending towards the Indian encampment, their camp and tents looked splendid, they being all white and regularly pitched, and their cattle in large caviats or heards extended far up the valley as far as your eyes could reach, with guards in all directions mounted, minding them, and as a matter of course on our formidable looking force approaching them, of which they had not the least knowledge of until they all at once seen us descending sloley the mountain opposite them.

This we seen at once caused their heard keepers some alarm, for we notised their guards or horsemen galloping in several directions and many chasing up their different heards in compact bodys, showing us that they are prepared in the ways of protecting their animals in case of attack. The advance guard of our corps now thought it adviseable to approach the chiefs as quick as posible so as to prevent any continuation of alarm. So since 10 of us, all mounted, continued

[9] The Catskill Mountain House, known as American's premier resort and a favorite retreat of New Yorkers, opened its doors in 1824. Built high atop South Mountain and reached by stagecoach, it commanded sweeping views of the Hudson River Valley. It was not until the 1880s that other hotels were built to match its grandeur. The 150-year-old hotel was demolished in 1963 (R. Van Zandt 1966).

some ahead and were met by their principle chief, who was intirely naked and without any kind of ornament about him, not even the brass rings on the arms, but simply a blue britch cloth & a thing around his body. The chief and his interpreter, who could speak Spanish (not English), even dressed enough to make up for him. After we all dismounted, we laid down our arms and approached these Lords of the Plains and were all most cordially hugged and shaken. As brave connoisseur of the party, we were escorted and shown a camping ground by [the] side of the river, and about 80 mounted warriors were mounted as guard to keep off their own people, such as their women & children and old men, who, like our own people in cities, run to see and rush to every show.

After our waggons came into camp and our coral properly formed and tents pitched, they started and grunted in a most formidable manner in token no doubt of surprise & joyfulness at our appearance, and near night, at sunset, they all returned to their lodges—except some few who were curious to look at us cooking, and they were astonished at our method of making fire by the locofoco match.[10] This seems to surprise them more than anything else. The guards being mounted and all our animals properly staked out, we retired to rest.[11]

Next morning, Monday, May 21, we were visited by several hundred of these people, old and young, and some whole families, and we were indeed surprised at seeing such a vast number of wild creatures. It was thought advisable to stop here some time and trade with them and exchange some of our animals, now pretty well jaded or broken down. I bot a fine black horse for my dress sword.[12] The chief who traded with me wanted the blade to make a spear of it, as he broke the hilt of the mount. The trade was made, and [he] threw it in the ground as they do everything that they consider of no use to them.

---

[10] A friction match, also known as a lucifer match.

[11] Marcy arrived at the Comanche campsite, west of Tucumcari and at the western edge of the Comanches' territory, on June 18 (G. Foreman 1939, 237). New Mexican authorities were making an effort at peace-keeping with this group of Native people.

[12] Blunt noted the exchange on May 20: "Goulding got a good horse for an old rusty sword."

Many of the company bought and exchanged animals with them for pieces of cloth, beads, paint, and blankets. They think much of red paint and of red & blue blankets and cloth and no. 8 brass wire, which they use for rings on their arms. The kind of beads they like most are bone, ivory & ebony, anything substantial. Several of their aristocracy came out to see us, their young princes mounted on horses a la Dutches Dubery [Madame du Barry] without saddle or bridle, poppouses lashed on a kind of frame carried by their breading [breeding] women, all curious in seeing us, as much so as we were to see them. Our company made a collection from the different messes and made a present to these chiefs, which they cordially accepted.[13]

During the height of our pleasure trading with these wild Lords of the Plains, we were abruptly intruded upon by our officer with a party of United States Dragoons who came to this encampment from the town of Begas [Las Vegas, New Mexico] for the purpose of escorting the chiefs of this tribe to Santa Fe for to make a treaty with the garrison their of New Mexico. This officer, the alcalda of San Miguel, which he afterward proved to be, requested us not to trade

---

[13] Phineas Blunt recorded that "we have at last fallen in with the much dreaded Comanches. They are as good looking as any Indians I ever saw, the men are about middle size with broad shoulders and chests, short muscular arms, complexion copper colored. Their dress is a pair of moccasins with leather drawers attached and come up to the lower part of their bellies, all naked above, only when covered by a buffalo skin. They wear nothing on their head" (May 20, 1849).

Goulding's illustration of a Comanche (figure 7) is one of few extant images of their hairstyle, which shows a long braid almost to the ground, decorated with silver buckles. Fellow traveler George Churchill described the form in which Comanche men arranged their hair:

> The Comanche pounded silver coin in a thin bowl shape perfectly smooth and in the center they made two slits. They then arrange their hair so they string one larger piece of silver next to their neck and then another smaller one and each subsequent one still smaller until all the hair is taken up. They braid in horse hair until the tail of the queue is about five feet long. The silver ornaments are polished up and being bowl shape, glisten in the sun. The Indian having the most silver ornaments on his hair and on the bridle of his horse is considered the richest and the bravest. (May 20, 1849)

Until then, the only comprehensive drawings of Texas Indians before removal in 1850 were executed by Lt. José María Sánchez in 1828 (Berlandier 1969, 156). According to Marcy, who met the chief on June 10, some twenty days following Goulding's visit, the chief's name was Is-sa-ki-ep or Wolf Shoulder. Correspondent "C" traveling with the Black River Company also met the chief, whom he called Issakeep. This company left Fort Smith on April 17 and met the chief a few days before Goulding caught up with the large tribe (G. Foreman 1939, 237, 239, 262).

any more with them, as the sherriff of the County of Santa Fe would not allow it.[14] But we had just finished all the trading we wanted, so their was no umbrage manifested on our part, or disappointment.

I visited these lodges, which consisted of upwards of 200, all in 3 rows, regularly apart about 40 feet, and were washed or rubbed over with a kind of white clay like whitewash. These tents hold some 4 to 6 or 8 people and look very well in the distance but rather filthy when close in connection with them. Their women are mostly bad and homely looking and carless in their person, as so are the smaller children. Those of 14 to 18 years old are more cleanly, and some of the best of the females carry a sort of fan made from fine cane & leaves to keep the flies off them. Some have white or striped blankets carelesly wrapped around them and some have pieces of buffalo & other furs around their person. They all leave their hair carless and flying about in a moppy manner, that is, the women and old men.

The body and the faces of many of them are painted in stricks, and some of the young women look tolerably handsome. I noticed many of the tents closed up intirely with the occupants peeping out at us. I was informed afterwards that in them they have captives whom they take from the other tribes of Indians or from the Mexicans in their [illegible] against them. In addition, that this tribe is one of the leading tribes of the plains, Camanches, and have upwards of 2,000 warriors, who are now away on a hunting scout in the great buffalo region and these few only left here to protect their families and their oldest chiefs. They had upward of 2,500 animals consisting of some very excellent mustang horses and many poneys and mules and a large number of oxen and cows. This tribe consisted now of about 5 or 6 hundred, as far as I could see, and take them altogether as a very good specimen of the Camanches. I gave several of them presents of rings and beads & figs and pieces of ribbon and returned to our camp well pleased with my visit.

We then hitched up our teams to commence our march. So at 1 PM we left the place and to our amasement and great surprise these

---

[14] The alcalde may have been Miguel Sena y Romero (May 12, 1849). George Churchill (May 21, 1849) said that the army told the Indians they could not follow the emigrants.

FIGURE 7. Comanche Indian by William R. Goulding, 1849. Inscribed: "Drawn from life by W. R. Goulding in the Camanche Encampment. Pecos Vally." *Courtesy of Yale Collection of Western Americana, Beinecke Rare Book and Manuscript Library.*

people struck their tents, and such a scene of confusion and running and gallopping in all directions as I never before looked on. It was grand in the extreme to see this great camp all in the act of packing their horses and mules and loading on their tents and raw hides painted white, of which the tents are formed of, and their dried meat and traps, and getting out of the camp as fast as each one was ready and continued on after us. On some horses you would see an old man and 2 or 3 young children mounted and a lot of hides on another and a female on behind with her 2 poppouses fastened in the frame, and during the whole afternoon we were amused by the passing and repassing of these people on our line of march. About 6 PM we were overtaken by the party of U.S. Dragoons with the alcaldas and with 8 of the chiefs, escorting them to Santa Fe, and as they advanced on us, I noticed all these Indian followers of us were stoped by these chiefs and returned back to the great valley of the Pecos Ridge, so about dark we seen no more of them except the party of chiefs and a few warriors with the dragoons who were encamped near us during the night.

Tuesday, May 22, we travelled during the forenoon in company with these dragoons and at 12 PM we stoped to rest on the battleground of the Kendles [George Wilkins Kendall] Expedition, so we were informed by these dragoons, who now left us and went on their way, as we found their travelling to fast for our waggons.[15] Our travels now was through a very mountainous country, and at 6-1/2 PM we met a party of Mexican pack mule traders camped on some salt springs where was excellent grass, so we camped for the night. Our

[15] Goulding was approaching Anton Chico, New Mexico, and was referring to the capture and imprisonment of one contingent of the 400-man Texan–Santa Fe Expedition in 1841. George Wilkins Kendall, founder and editor of the *New Orleans Picayune,* traveling with the expedition, recorded the saga of his own capture near La Cuesta (Villanueva), San Miguel County, and imprisonment a few miles away at San Miguel del Vado by then governor Manuel Armijo. He went on to record the subsequent forced march of some 1,300 miles over the Jornada del Muerto to Mexico City (Kendall 1935). History suggests that the New Mexicans believed the Texans were intent on military conquest, not a trading expedition as advertised (Beck 1982, 124–26; Fugate and Fugate 1989, 123–24, 277–78). Anton Chico, Guadalupe County, is one of the oldest communities in New Mexico and was founded in 1822 by residents moving southeast from San Miguel (Julyan 1996, 18; Pearce 1965, 9).

company became seen to be very disorderly and many refused to do guard duty and manifested munitinus disposition to go ahead and break up our sistem of marching.

Wednesday, May 23, this morning their seamed to be no kind of order. Every mess [illegible] to be his own company, and as fast as they were ready, left camp in straggling order. About 8 o'clock the long wished for mountains capted with snow made their appearance. During the day, the company got men together and the grand scenery before us was all the talk during the march. We travelled over hill & dale and through small groves of the dwarf oak and pine & cedar trees and the high, rocky mountains continually looming up before us, when about 5 o'clock we discovered the party of U.S. Dragoons coming towards us with their Lords of the Plains all [illegible] and making on a dashing, warlike appearance as they passed by us. The dragoons wore the native umbra large hat so as to keep the sun off them, and the clashing of swords and trappings made quite a pleasing noise to us. They had been to a place called Begas and changed their escort since we seen them yesterday.[16] We overtook them in their camp this evening and camped along side of them and amused ourselves by getting considerable information respecting this country. Their was also another party of these Mexican traders in this camp with whom we traded and got a goodly supply of bread & dried mutton.

[16] Las Vegas was a port of entry to New Mexico for those traveling on the Santa Fe Trail. It was here on the village plaza that Stephen Watts Kearny announced the peaceful conquest of New Mexico in 1846. It became a temporary military outpost, "Post Las Vegas" (Gottschalk 1999, 62). The Third Artillery companies C and K were stationed in Las Vegas and in May 1849 were commanded by Capt. Henry P. Judd (Post Returns, Las Vegas, National Archives).

9

Santa Fe Beckons

Everything seemed new and different in New Mexico, where the diarists among the group were kept busy writing about the manners and customs of Mexican citizens and Native people. Many anticipated (and sometimes regretted) attending the inevitable fandangoes, which could go on for hours, and the people at San Miguel del Vado were happy to help the men relax and celebrate after their difficult trek. Goulding, as might be expected, discovered the quartermaster's office on arrival in Santa Fe and met with the Camp Marcy officers, the military governor of Santa Fe, and the famous Christopher "Kit" Carson.

Thursday, May 24, this morning the tumult still continued amongst our members in regard to breaking up the order of march. Some were for going on ahead and forfeiting their obligation as to the forming [of] guard duty and protecting each other as was heretofore practiced and understood by the different messes of our corps. When our captain, Mr. John A. Ebbets, came out in front of the whole company and said, "O, gentlemen, you are now near the Mexican settlements and so far you are out of danger, and as many of you are dissatisfied and appear to be inclined to go on your own hook, I therefore resign any further command, so you can now do as you please." This statement and resignation of Captain Ebbets took many by surprise, and a general conversation was entered into. Several wanted an imediate settlement and division of the surplus funds as received for the company commissary department and which was in the hands of the treasury. Mr. Peter Lodewick, being the treasurer of the company, said he would be responsible to all for the funds in his hands and would account to all the members therefore at Santa Fe. This settled the matter. So all hands packed up as fast as posible and the march continued in a straggling and undivided manner, to our disgrace, before these U.S. Dragoons, which were witness to our mutinous and undisciplined galiwags.[1]

I travelled in company, riding with a sergeant of these dragoons, of whom I got a great deal of valuable information respecting this country. At 11 AM this escort and the Indian chiefs took another rout, a bypath through the mountains but by which we could not travel with our waggons. So we parted [with] them, continuing the direct camino. We arrived at the Pecos River at 12 PM. Here we stoped to noon. This was the first clear runing stream we seen since we left the Arkansaw Territory. Consequently some of us enjoyed its refreshing waters, often resting our animals. We again proceeded on our march over a very fine, rolling, hilly country. During the afternoon we came up to an imence flock of sheep, goats & lambs headed by one man and several dogs. Our men purchased several of the lambs and sheep. We continued our march till 7 PM, when we met with good grass by some salt licks where we camped and enjoyed a hearty supper of lamb and mutton chops to our fill.[2] We also seen a large drove of cattle grazing on the side of a high hill during our march, which was indeed cheering to us as we had heretofore only being looking at the wild cattle of the Great Prairies.

Friday, May 25, I got up this morning at five o'clock and went out to examine our horses and I found my horse, Camanche Bob, quite

[1] It was not unusual for members of a company to break up, re-form and decide to take a different route. Phineas Blunt, John Hoyt, and Stanislaus Lasselle split off and packed along Kearny's Gila Trail to the Pima villages with John Ebbetts as guide. See the Lasselle diary (1991, 1–34).

[2] The gold rushers were in the area of Gallinas Creek and the Pecos River on May 24 when George Churchill observed that a herd of "four thousand sheep had been here grazing." On the same day, Phineas Blunt said he "bought a sheep for my mess, paid for it $1.50 . . . such a baa, baa, baahing I never before heard."

lame, caused by the small thorns in the prickly cactus which was in great quantities amongst the grass where he was startled during the night. This caused me some delay as I had to through him down and annoint his fetlocks with bears grease, and with a scalpel and a pair of artery forceps, in this way I extracted the greater part of the prickles out and wrapped up the limbs with rags. By this means he was enabled to walk sloley along. After 2 or 3 hours march, he however came up to the train and was much improvd. We met with some small woods of yellow pine and ceder during the day and several roads crossed our camino, and about 5 PM we met the first settlement. This was a few huts made of logs and daubed all over with mud and whitewashed. They had their little place all fenced in with brush wood from the tops of pines. They had a black-smith shop and quite a number of cattle and a large flock of sheep and were very polite and civil to us and gave us plenty of (latha) milk and (carney) meat, as we wanted. Between this farm and a small chapel we encamped for the night. During the evening I amused myself taking a drawing of this place with its chapel and farm house in full view of our camp.[3] The natives fetched us abundance of eggs, milk, polmera (sugar), and lamb. So we lived well.

Saturday, May 26, having been informed that San Miguel [del Vado] was but 4 or 5 miles from us, we were all anxious to see this first Mexican town. After a substantial breakfast of fresh lamb chops and eggs, we hitched up and vaumised, travelling over a very good road in a valley of about three miles long. At 9 o'clock the long talked of city of San Miguel came in sight, so after gazing some time to see something in the shape of a town with houses, but seeing nothing but what looked like a very extensive brick yard, we concluded to find the Pecos River, which again presented itself to our

[3] Sketch missing. According to Stanislaus Lasselle (1991, 16), the settlement was Bernal (Serafina), San Miguel County, a stop on the Santa Fe Trail. George Churchill was impressed with the houses "built of large mud bricks made of mud and straw and dried in the sun." The floors were packed adobe, and the "thatched roofs . . . made the little houses look comfortable." He added that they built their houses against trees to keep the rain, which always came in the same direction, from washing down the adobe (May 25, 1849). The land is on a grant given to an ancestor of the Bernal family, said to be a member of the 1598 Juan de Oñate expedition (Pearce 1965, 16).

front, directly crossing our road. After crossing, we passed two small rancherias by a small hill, then turning to the left, and then to the right, rounding a small mountain or mound, we soon came to a halt in the grand plaza of "San Miguel." This was a square of about 3 hundred yards wide each way with a number of poor, low, and misirable looking mud huts with flat roofs—3 of them occupied as small stores—two of which were kept by French men, who gave us considerable information.[4]

In front of this square or plaza, there is a small chapel with a kind of dome used as a belfry in which was 3 bells. The chapel is also made of logs and daubed all over with adobies or mud and white washed.[5] The priest I was introduced to by one of these French store keepers, and he amused me very much in stating to me of the War with Mexico and how the U.S. troops first took the place, and he showed me the barricks for the company of native dragoons occasionally quartered their, but were now at the town of Bagus [Las Vegas] after their pay and clothing. At these stores we purchased bread & cheese and the native wine at 30 cents a quart. After staying here some three hours and seeing enough of that place, which looked more like an extensive brick yard than a town, we started; or rather, but 6 of our waggons took up one line of march, leaving the other 6 waggons to enjoy the Mexican wine and fandangoes of the evening.

[4] San Miguel del Vado, also known as St. Michael of the Ford, San Miguel County, New Mexico, had been the port of entry to New Mexico for Missouri merchants since 1831. There they had to deal legally (or illegally) with Mexican officials, who assessed heavy duties for each wagon load (Etter 2000, 18–19). Asa Scarborough wrote that two Americans, two Frenchmen, and two Germans were living in the village in 1849 (1969, 34). One of the American storekeepers was Thomas Rowland, brother of the well-known pioneer John Albert Rowland. John had joined one of the early caravans for California in 1841 and became a major figure in Southern California history. Thomas began trading between Santa Fe and Missouri in 1835 and ultimately moved to San Miguel, where he recalled the arrival and imprisonment of the Texan–Santa Fe Expedition in 1841. He was murdered in his store in 1859 (Rowland 1999, 48).

[5] The community dates to the mid-1790s, with construction of the church, built with native stone and adobe, starting about 1805. Legend records that the townsfolk contributed earrings, rings, and other jewelry from which to cast the bell. The village ultimately faded into obscurity as nearby Las Vegas gained in popularity resulting from increased activity on the Santa Fe Trail (Stanley 1964, 19). In 1841, prisoners from the Texan–Santa Fe Expedition were forced to walk here from the village of Anton Chico and were imprisoned in the church before being marched off to Mexico City.

FIGURE 8. Abandoned adobe at San Miguel del Vado, San Miguel County, New Mexico, 1988. This example is typical of abandoned ruins in the village. *Photo by Patricia A. Etter.*

We proceeded through a broken and uneven kind of country, some mountains and some heavy timber such as pine and ceder. On our way we met 3 waggons with 4 mounted U.S. Dragoons on their way to Bagus. One of them had a wheel broken and had to lash a tree to the body and drag on the [illegible]. They directed us to a very good place to camp off the main road by the Pecos River by a ranch where we arrived by 5 o'clock and camped. Their was 4 different rancheros here, all of which supplied us with abundance of eatables and milk. We also caught several fine black trout in the beautiful river. During this evening an attempt was made to again to try to have order restored in the company and a resolution was offered and a committee appointed to wait on Captain Ebbets to have him again to command us as far as Santa Fe.

Accordingly, the next morning, Sunday, May 27, the committee consisting of Messrs. [Jacob Alfred] Kanouse and [Jessee] Brush were dispatched to the rear to inform Capt. Ebbets of our resolution.[6] So about 8-1/2 AM we hitched up our teams and proceeded sloley in our march, taking it easy so as to allow sufficient time for our committee to overtake us before the afternoon. About 11 o'clock we were overtaken by some of our party of the pack mule trail and who informed us of their good time last night and of the night of the neglect of the "boys" in not mounting guard, but all at the fandango, in consequence of which they had three of their animals stolen and considerable of their clothing and stock from their waggons. They gave us a discription of how the Knickerbockers enjoyed the native wine as well as the native brawny senoritas and how they gloriously huzzed for the red, white & blue, and how blue they were in the morning laying about the cazas "minus their ladies and dunkies."[7]

At 12 PM we met with good water, so stoped to noon. A 1/4 of mile to our right was an old ruined caza. A party of us went over to examine, where we found a Mexican boy minding some goats, who informed us this was the ancient town of Pecos.[8] [Emory extract

---

[6] See appendix A for Kanouse and Brush.

[7] William Chamberlin wrote that the fandango "was a curiosity to me; it was certainly a shade faster than anything of the kind I had seen before—a medley of Mexicans and Americans dancing upon a ground floor with the 'Marguerettas' of the country, the face of each of these ornamented with a cigarette . . . the gentlemen being obliged to treat their partners to a glass of wine at the end of each set. But the noise and confusion, heat, smoke, dust, fumes of liquor, and the strange 'lingua,' made it sorry enjoyment." (1945, 20:51)

[8] The Pecos ruins, several miles north of San Miguel, were established as Pecos Historical National Park on June 28, 1965. There Hernando Alvarado saw a thriving village of some 2,500 Tanoan farmers in 1540. Pecos had two parts: the church, which was built by Spanish padres in the 1700s, and the Indian village of about six hundred rooms. A smallpox epidemic ravaged the pueblo in 1788, but the survivors stayed on until 1838, when the last seventeen residents abandoned the crumbling ruins and moved to Jemez Pueblo (Kidder 1968, 61–139).

omitted].[9] The "estuffa," or square bed on which was once their everlasting fire, was of stone apparently cemented together with clay and was about twenty feet square & about three feet high. The walls of all these places were disfigured and mutilated by the many visitors or passers[by] whose many names were scribbled on the walls with pieces of charcoal or cinders. The whole town was about a quarter of a mile square but all in a compleate state of ruins. We stoped at this place till about 3 PM, when we again proceeded on our march.

When arriving on the main road, we were joined by some of the rear of our company, who gave us a better and more correct discription of the exploits of our boys at the fandango the last night. The discription of the bell[e]s was rich. Their was some black spotted senoras with their hair beautifully soaped up and a velvet skirt with nothing but a chimise without sleeves, and sandles on their feet and the everlasting reboso over their head with its fringed flaps dangling about their sides. Some of these short, dwarfish & common colour looking ladies sported fans and fancy silk handkerchiefs, occasionaly dashing them in the faces of their beloved new amie, "Americano Cavaloris" and "mouncha amerous capitanios," so while our duped

---

[9] Both Goulding (May 27, 1848) and David Brainard (July 16, 1849, traveling with the Walworth County Mining Company from Wisconsin) copied the description of Pecos from William Hemsley Emory, *Notes on a Military Reconnoissance* (1848), into their journals. The reader is referred to archaeologist Alfred Vincent Kidder (1968) for the Emory material and a complete description of the Pecos Pueblo.

Phineas Blunt carried out his own extensive search of the Pecos ruins and left a unique and detailed description of his findings on May 28, 1849. He located a number of rooms adjacent to the church, one with a fireplace remaining. In addition, there was a "large portico made of cedar wood, the floor is hard mud, the halls inside have several coats of whitewash . . . top ceilings and timbers are painted with images of various sorts, principally in black and white colors the whole is in a state of decay, the roof in one place has fallen in. Over the alter is these characters *F C A R O E U S* with letters recessed being more easily read by standing at the back of the alter." He also found a tower about 8 feet square and rising about 10 or 15 feet above the building. He found the courage to drop into a small hole to examine a lower room, which he "found to have been a cellar as the strings are still there on which the people hung their provisions. In the place is 3 large cisterns which once contained water."

John Robert Forsythe, another gold seeker from New York, had his own adventure in Pecos on August 8, 1849. He wrote that "at night a few of the men explored the ruins with torch & dug up a part of the floor which was found full of human bones. One of the mummys was in a perfect state of preservation. Money was the object of digging, but none was found."

ole hunkers were envelloped in the pleasures of "des los Angeles," the "laderon umbras" were busily engaged taking charge of their baggage and mules—Messrs. [Samuel] Kelly, [James E.] Baker, [John] Hempseed, [James] McNally, [Peter] Lodewick &c. were the lions at the fandango of San Miguel.[10]

Our journey now was through a cañon with hills on each side of us from one to two thousand feet high above the road, in some places as close as a musket shot. The scenery wild and grand.[11] About 6 PM we came to a small valley coverd with some grama [pasture grass] where we camped for the night. The committee during the evening reported unfavorably and were discharged.

Monday, May 28, we hitched up early and proceeded on our journey. The road [was] rather difficult, with an immense pine forest of full grown trees on both sides of us. During our march we were passed by a troop of U.S. Dragoons on their march to Santa Fe. All of them had on the native umbra "sombrero" to keep the sun off their faces. They had 3 Indian chiefs with them of some different tribe of them which we seen before. The travelling was ruff and pretty much the same as yesterday. We met with several dried up streams or water beds. In some of them were the dried up carcass of numerous oxen and cows which died last year in consequence of the great drought.[12] We lag[g]ed considerable this days march so as to give every available

---

[10] See appendix A.

[11] Leaving Pecos ruins, emigrants negotiated the south end of the Sangre de Cristo Mountains through what is known as the gateway to Santa Fe, Glorieta Pass, at an altitude of more than seven thousand feet. The trail was enclosed between high canyon walls, and James Josiah Webb described its condition in 1844 as a road that "winds and turns, crossing steep pitches and ravines over rocks, and around boulders, making short and difficult turns" (1931, 76, 79). Kearny and his Army of the West were at Glorieta Pass in 1846, expecting to meet resistance from Gen. Manuel Armijo and his Mexican army. Fortunately, Armijo had decided not to do battle and had retreated. William Hemsley Emory (1848) wrote in the report of the trip: "the road leads into a cañon, with hills on each side from 1,000 to 2,000 feet above the road, in all cases within cannon shot, and in many within point blank musket shot; and this continues to a point but 12 or 15 miles from Santa Fé. The scenery is wild" (1848, 31). Goulding's description of the pass evidently paraphrases Emory's.

[12] Robert Brownlee, with the Little Rock, Arkansas, Company, said the area was "lined with dead carcasses of horses and mules, lying just as they fell, the skins perfect, the eyes gone, but you could raise the skeleton on its feet and it could stand; and at a little distance looked lifelike" (1986, 60).

chance to the rear to come up for the purpose of our own credit sake, to make some kind of a respectable aperance in entering Santa Fe. Consequently, about 6 o'clock their was 8 of our waggons together in a small valey about six miles from Santa Fe, and their being no grass and our poor animals attached to our waggons now being mostly faged and worn out, we concluded to proceed on sloley. A party of us proceeded on ahead and arrived in Santa Fe at 9 PM.

The United States Hotel I and my party put up at, altho the hour being late, their was evident signs that it was early for them.[13] Some twenty to thirty of Americans and natives were at a long table playing cards and piles of dollars heaped up on the table for which they were busily employed to win and lose. After reporting to the landlord, who was an American, the number of my company & being informed he could accommodate us all, we ordered supper, and our waggons coming in at ten o'clock all in good order. We soon enjoyed our repast, and had a comfortable drink and retired to my room, which was the billiard room, but as this game is not the fashion just at this time, they applied the room to our comfort as a bedroom by placing matrises on the floor for such as had not room on the table.

Tuesday, May 29, early this morning, after looking about this city of Santa Fe (a big and noble name but) a poor and miserable place, and ever so much more so must it have been before the American troops came here, which very much added to its appearance by the half dozzen pieces of ordnance now in the center of the plazza, and them, with the noble standard of the "Stars and Stripes" then waving over them, was the first thing that I observed when turning out in the morning. I walked over to the quartermasters office, & Capt. Bob [Thomas Lee] Brent, then acting quartermaster, kindly received me,

[13] Somewhere along the way, William Chamberlin picked up a handbill that encouraged the emigrants to stop at the U.S. Hotel in Santa Fe "for comfort, convenience, good living, etc." He and his companions soon learned that was an overstatement. They entered the hotel through a courtyard filled with horses and mules left by other emigrants—typical of Mexican hotels of the day. Here was "a small uncleansed stable, infested with fleas, bedbugs, and other vermin, the stench being horrible" (Chamberlin 1945, 53). Andrew Smith (July 27, 1849) also negotiated the "dirty courtyard" and found the hotel full, though he did mention that it was managed by two Americans, Raymond and Murphy.

as well also Lieut. [F. D.] Thomas of the artillery.[14] And incidentally I was introduced to Dr. [Lewis A.] Edwards, Lieut. [Oliver Hazard Perry] Taylor & others, and during the morning to Colonel [John Marshall] Washington, then the Governor of New Mexico.[15] During the day I visited the hospital with Doctor Edwards, also the new fort,[16] which was built and planed imediately after the troops entered Santa Fe during the late war by Lieut. [Jeremy Francis] Gilmor of the engineers.[17] It is within 600 yards of the center of the town and is about 100 feet above it. This is the only part which commands the town. It is computed to garrison about 280 men. It was built princeply by the men composing the U.S. troops and some few of the native masons or brick makers.

The pueblo square is the next place of note. On the north side of it is the military store houses, governors rooms, and officers quarters. In front or the south is the city hall and a number of stores and hotels as also on the east and the west wings, all occupied by stores or shops for the selling of provisions, cloths, and articles of luxury, all of which comes from the United States in waggons. In the rear of the public square or plaza runs the Santa Fe River, a small runing stream of pure spring water, and from which the inhabitance get their supply of water, boards being placed across it for the purpose of passing and repassing.

---

[14] Because there was no water at Fort Marcy, troops stayed in rented quarters adjacent to the Palace of the Governors (Giese 1995, 7–8). Thomas Lee Brent, an 1830 Military Academy graduate, had become a captain and quartermaster in 1847 (Heitman 1903, 1:242). Although Goulding refers to him as "Bob," his identity as Thomas Lee Brent is confirmed by Captain Marcy (1939), who referred to the quartermaster as "Thomas L. Brendt." F. D. Thomas is listed in the Post Returns, Fort Marcy, National Archives.

[15] Dr. Lewis A. Edwards served his country for many years, becoming assistant surgeon in August 1846, promoted to major surgeon in 1861, and to brevet lieutenant colonel and colonel in 1865 for faithful and meritorious service during the war (Heitman 1901, 1:398). Lt. Oliver Hazard Perry Taylor was an 1842 Military Academy graduate, became second lieutenant, dragoons, in 1847 and served in the Mexican War (Heitman 1903, 1:948). John Marshall Washington, a Virginian and 1814 graduate of the Military Academy, served as civil and military governor of New Mexico between October 1848 and October 1849 (Post Returns, Fort Marcy, National Archives; *Virtual American Biographies*).

[16] Fort Marcy, begun in 1846, was named for then Secretary of War William L. Marcy (Prince 1912, 4; Fugate and Fugate 1989, 122).

[17] Jeremy Francis Gilmer became Confederate chief of engineers during the Civil War (Gilmer papers).

I visited several private rancherias owned by merchants of the town, and the interior of many of these was most splendidly fitted up and furnished. I dined at the officers mess and we had as fine a dinner as I ever sat down to. Captain Beufort [Abraham Buford][18] of the dragoons took the head of the table, and the cellebrated "Kit Carson"[19] and "Cown," the chief muleteer for the government envoy, with myself were the guests or the "Lions of the day," as Lieut. Thomas called us. Many were the jokes and stories that were told during the afternoon, and you may rest assured that good disciplin was displayed with the butter and glasses.

Several "charges" were made and the retreat did not take place till nearly 8 o'clock, when we all retired to Lieut. Thomas and Capt. Brents rancheria to participate in a native fandango got up by their ladies and the senoras of a number of merchants of the town. Two violins, one guitar, and an umbra singer were the orchestra. The party consisted of some 25 couples of the first class merchants of the place and oficers of the station, all of which had their senoras or senoritas their and who were dressed in as splendid and fashionable style as I ever seen in the States, and as for jewellry they far excelled our ladies, altho I was informed their was not one married couple present. I never, in any assembly when I have been before, seen more genteel and better behaved ladies. Their etiquet and modesty and sedate manners could not be beat. Nevertheless, they were all concubines. About 11 o'clock we had a cold cut and coffee and then danced till a late hour, when I retired to the quarters of Dr. Edwards with a much better opinion forming in my mind of the inhabitance of Santa Fe.

Wednesday morning, May 30, I did not get up till after eight this morning. After breakfast, I went over to the U.S. Hotel and found

---

[18] Capt. Abraham Buford, an 1837 Military Academy graduate, was in Santa Fe following exploration of a new route to that city by way of the Cimarron River, and would leave Santa Fe on June 6 to escort a U.S. mail contractor back to Fort Gibson, Oklahoma (G. Foreman 1939, 211).

[19] Kit Carson and his exploits have become an integral part of the "Myth of the West," but when Goulding met him, Carson was simply farming his property in Rayado, New Mexico. Charles Edward Pancoast (1930, 209), who met him a month later on July 29, 1849, wrote that Carson sat by their campfire and entertained them with stories of his adventures.

all of our company had now arrived and that their was a great time amongst the Knickerbockers now as to the division of the commissary stores and monies, and a general break up of the company took place. My mess consisting of eight men, and we soon settled our property. Sold the mess waggon & mules as well also my own waggon to Capt. Beuford, who was just about preparing himself to return to the States to see his family. Having purchasd four of the men of my messes interest in the waggon (the rest being my own) for ten dollars each, I now was determined to go the rest of the journey by packed mules, so I dispensed with everything weighty and unnessary, which consisted of the following articles,

2 waggons & harness for 8 mules for $60 each	120.00
1 mule partly broken down the others being stolen at San Miguel	25.00
1 trunk, 3.00, 1 small valice 1.00, 3 seives 2.25	6.25
1 basket 1.50, 1 munkey rinch 2.50, 1 rifle 15.00	18.00
Lot of garden seeds 2.00, 1 tin box 25/100, 2 shovels 1.50	3.75
2 picks 1.00, 20 lb shot 2.50, 3 bottles medicine 1.00	4.50
Lot of glass beads, chains & rings of brass	4.50
2 pair common shoes 1.50, 1 G.E. bed 10.00	11.50
1 gun case I gave to Dr. Edwards and a lot of medical powders and instruments	$193.50

My tent I reserved and I purchased

1 blanket for 5.00	1 frying pan 1.00	6.00
1 camp kettle 2.00	1 holster 1.00	3.00
1 water goard .50	1 gal native brandy 2.50	3.00
7 [illegible] 7.00	100 lb. biscut 10.00	17.00
3 pack saddles 9.00	50 lb. flour 3.00	12.00
5 larriets 7.50	54 lbs sweet [illegible]	14.65
Shoeing horses & mules and extra shoes & nails		7.00
Tea coffee and sugar rice &c. &c. &c.		9.00
		71.65

Paid Mess [James E.] Baker, [John] Hempseed, [James] MacNally & [James M.] Hutchings each 10.00	40.00
	111.65
Leaving a ballance from the above sale	81.85
	193.50

The New York Knickerbocker Association was now entirely disolved and their was now several captains and several companies forming, some to go the northern rout and some to go the Spanish Trail, and I took every opportunity I could to advise with "Kit Carson" and others whose judgement I could rely on to give all the information I could, so decided with my own party to take the southern rout by the south pass[20]—Kit Carson advised me by all means to go that way if I was not in any haste, as I was sure to have grass and water all through, but his rout, which is called the Indian trail, was very uncertain that time of year and particularly so with a large party of undisciplined nondiscripts. I now set all my men to work to fit up our packs and employed myself busily constructing paniards and bags out of a number of black bear skins I had previously bot or dried on our journey, having it always in my mind to dispence with the waggons the first opportunity that offered. I wrote some letters to my friends and family in the States and amused myself taking observations about the town the rest of the week till Saturday afternoon, June 2nd. [Emory extract omitted.]

The escort of U.S. Dragoons with several Indian chiefs arrived following my stay here and had a "counsel talk" with Colonel [John Marshall] Washington, which lasted for about two hours. After some presents of blankets, pieces of cloth &c. being given to them, they all went away. Well pleased with the reception and in high glee, they made a very grand appearance as they filed out of the plaza. Their was some fifteen to twenty of them all mounted on splendid mustangs, and they did look like Lords of the Plains. After they got

[20] By "south pass," Carson was referring to the Gila Trail, which he had taken many times—not Wyoming's South Pass.

outside of the town, they gave a shout, something like the war-whoop, when they all dashed off at full speed.

On Saturday afternoon, having settled my bill at the U.S. Hotel for the fodder of our animals &c., amounting to 24.50, I parted with all my friends, the officers of the post, with a cordial shake [of] hands and with right good hearty cheers we left Santa Fe at 3 PM, June 2. I received several letters from Capt. [Thomas L.] Brent & Beufort [Abraham Buford] and Lieut. Stinus & [Alfred] Pleasanton to Lieut. Taylor & [Delos Bennet] Sacket, and other brother officers in the various stations where we were likely to stop.[21] We travelled till about 8 o'clock PM by the valley of the Santa Fe River nearly west for about five miles, when we left the river and struck across a dry plain intersected by arroyes (dry bed streams), which caused us much fatigue, and seeing a rancho nearby, which we found a small hollow in which was some tolerable good grass, so we stoped and camped for the night and a beutiful moonlight night it was. Mr. [William F.] Ford visited the rancho and got a fine pailful of new milk which we enjoyed very much.[22] Our party consisted of but 6 men and 13 animals, all well packed.

---

[21] Lt. Alfred Pleasonton, class of 1844, Military Academy, was assistant adjutant general to Gen. Persifor F. Smith's staff. Pleasonton left Santa Fe for San Francisco on June 3 in command of a small detachment of Second Dragoons (G. Foreman 1939, 285). Following a long and successful military career, he became United States collector of revenue (Heitman 1903, 1:795; *Virtual American Biographies*). Delos Bennet Sacket, Military Academy graduate of 1845 (Heitman 1903, 1:856), was assigned to accompany Capt. Randolph B. Marcy on his return journey to Fort Smith (G. Foreman 1939, 341). Sacket was destined for an illustrious career and replaced retired general William L. Marcy as senior inspector-general of the army with the rank of brigadier-general in 1881 (*Appleton's Cyclopedia*, 1887–89).

[22] William Fraser Ford, a 29-year-old Englishman and surgical instrument maker and Goulding's future son-in-law, stayed with Goulding for the entire trip and appears as the third entry in Isaac Williams's Rancho del Chino Register Book on August 12, 1849.

10

Down the Rio Grande

The reduced company of Knickerbockers passed a number of Pueblo villages, including Santo Domingo, San Felipe, Angostura, and Bernalillo, before arriving at Albuquerque Post. Goulding made new friends among the military there. Leaving Albuquerque, the company traveled down the Rio Grande, passing numerous small villages: Peralta, Tome, Belen, and La Joya. They forded the river at Lemitar, the town to which General Manuel Armijo had retired following the recent war. Somewhere near Socorro, the Knickerbockers added to their numbers and teamed up with the Cherokee and Mississippi Company from Fort Gibson, Oklahoma. In the town of Polvadera, Goulding witnessed a funeral procession and described a unique method of burial among the Mexican people.

Sunday, June 3, all hands in good spirits this morning, we saddled up and proceeded on our march. Passed by an old lime kiln and some ranches. About 10 AM we came to a small chapel where we seen several of the native inhabitance assembling for their worship. Some were mounted on very good looking animals, and occasianly would arrive [on] the primitive animal of this neighbourhood, the donkey, with some wealthy senora or senorita sitting on the posterior prominence of this faithful "bouricker." Sometimes a young "machichu" belabouring him in the rear to the tune of the bell now ringing fast for the commencement of the ceremonies. We crossed an extensive open plain on which their was some large troops of

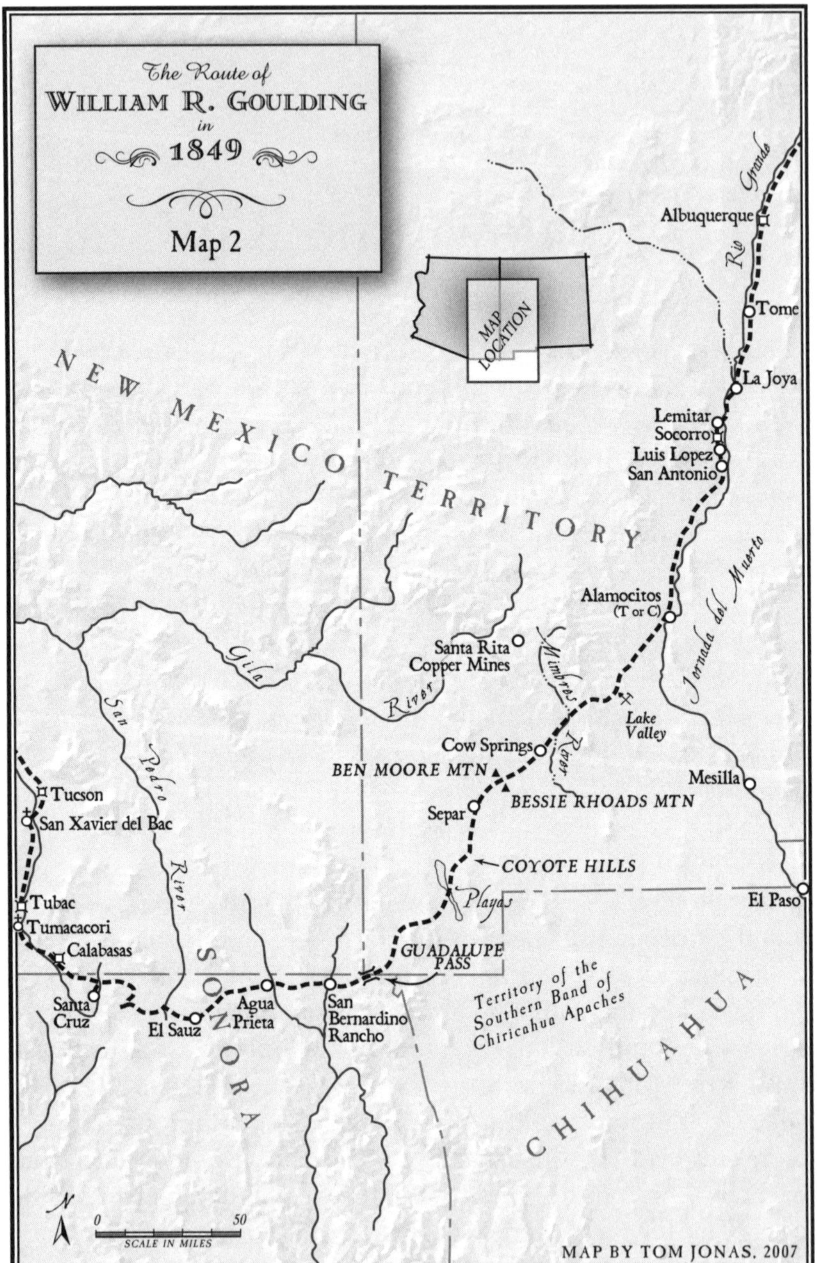

Map 2. Albuquerque to Tucson

horses and heards of cattle grazing. To our right was several (farms) ranchos, one of which we stoped at where was a small water mill. [Emory extract omitted.]

This town [Santo Domingo] has the appearance of some ancient monestary or castle from the hills as you approach to it. It is inhabited by the tribe of "Pueblo Indians" of which their is about from five to six hundred.[1] On near approach to the town, the houses are made with much better taste than any I seen at Santa Fe. The roofs of their casas are all flat and all walled in, the same as those we have before described. Some few of the men approached us but were naked, the same as wild Indians, but were very civil and polite and spoke the Spanish language very well. They have about five hundred acres of land under tillage, which they all work as one common community for their support. They have large troops of horses and very extensive heards of cattle. These Indians are said to be a very useful and warlike tribe and turn out the best warriors on the Rio Grande in time of need. They use the lance, shield & bows and arrows. The steep clifts which overhang the town gives it a romantic and Gothic appearance in the distance. [Emory extract omitted.]

Leaving Santo Domingo, we struck the high way, where we met a pack mule company consisting of nine men who were on their way also, as we were, to California. We soon became acquainted, and they proposed forming a company with me and party, agreeing to conform to the rules of guard duty and to protect each other. Our road was a very good one, and after travelling about six miles from Santo Domingo, the pretty village of San Felippe presented itself to our view.[2] Near to this place, after selecting a good spot, we encamped for the night. San Felippe is also a Pueblo Indian village and has a most beautiful appearance. It is overhung by a steep, craggy precipice,

---

[1] Santo Domingo Pueblo, Sandoval County, is a village of Keresan speakers some thirty-five miles south of Santa Fe on the east bank of the Rio Grande. In the twenty-first century, the conservative village is home to 3,106 citizens who are particularly well known for their production of fine jewelry. Farming comes in a close second in employment (Tiller 2005, 761).

[2] Residents of San Felipe Pueblo, Sandoval County, are also speakers of the Keresan language. The modern village counted a population of 3,185 in 2005; its economy is based on tourism, agriculture, mining, fine jewelry production, and the casino industry (Tiller 2005, 748–49). Goulding has paraphrased Emory (1848, 38) in his description of the village.

upon the summit of which are the ruins of a Roman Catholic church, presenting in the sketch I took this evening, the appearance of the pictures we see of the castles on the Rhine.[3]

The population of this village is about three hundred and are the same sort of Indians as the last discribed. [Illegible; Emory extract omitted] made us a visit and appeared to be very friendly. He informed us their were many Americanos on before us, that he had come up the Rio del Norte a few days back and had seen several encampments of men like us. The night was very fine but our camp was much annoyed by the moschetoes [mosquitos].

Next morning, Monday, June 4, we commenced our march this morning at 8 o'clock, having had much trouble with our pack mules, some of which were very fractious. When about three miles on our journey, to our surprise, we met one of our late companions, a Mr. [James P.] Burr, one of the fractious "Knickerbockers," who had again got dissatisfied with his company and was now on his way going back to Santa Fe. He turned back with us, when a few miles further on, we met two more of the same sort, a Mr. [Melvin S.] Gardner and [James E.] Baker, who also came on with us [see appendix A; Emory extract omitted]. We passed the Pueblo town of Angostura, also an Indian community.[4] This is some six or seven miles below San Felippe.

Early in the afternoon we came in sight of a kind of grove of dwarf oak and cottonwood with tolerable good grass. Here was five waggons and a number of pack mules. Part of these were of the late New York Knickerbocker operation company, now encamped, waiting for a party who had gone to prospect some noted gold mine in the neighborhood.[5] By our conversation with them, it appeared evident

[3] Sketch missing.

[4] Angostura, Sandoval County, was part of the Angostura Grant deeded to Andrés Montoya in 1745 (Julyan 1996, 17).

[5] Anxious to begin hunting for gold, many men diverted to the mining community of New Placers, Santa Fe County, some twenty miles southeast of Santo Domingo on New Mexico State Road 14 near Golden. Arriving there on June 3, Phineas Blunt and his companions found the town in ruins and the countryside barren from earlier mining. He also found Captain Ebbetts, who had been at the mines since the previous day, according to David Jordan of Ohio (June 3, 1849).

they intended to loiter here in these bottoms until September and recruit their animals, as their was abundance of fish and game and abundance of vegetables to be bought from the natives.

My party consisting now of 18 men, we camped here for the night but we could not induce any of these slow "boys" to come on with us, so on Tuesday, June 5, we saddled up our packs and "vaumised the camp," bidding good by to our late "cow team" party. The travelling was rather heavy, the road being very sandy. Indeed, this valley of Angostura has been ever since we left the latter town, and gradually getting wider in some places. The valley is nearly seven to nine miles wide. We passed several ranchos and hicendias [haciendas], also the neat small town of Bernallilo.[6] This is inhabited by Mexicans and is the neatest town I have seen.

Our party encreased today as we met with a few straggling Californians sloley travelling on their way. At 12 o'clock noon today, our party, when stoped to noon, numbered 25 men and 32 pack mules and horses. While at this camp, we were joined by a young man named Loring who was on his way to Albuquerque after a horse,[7] so I concluded to go on ahead of my party with him by a short byroad which he said he knew, theirby making the distance much shorter, and that we would reach Albuquerque before dark—this gave me a good opportunity of seeing the gardens and fields of vinyards and varieties of produce through the country as we cantered along through these fields, our narrow trail for miles sometimes passing straight through the very yards of the hicendias or farm lands.

At 4-1/2 PM we arrived at the splendid rancho of Madam Armijo.[8] After rapping with a stick at the gate some time and Mr. Loring sending in a letter from Dr. Jackson of Santa Fe, we were requested to enter the center court of this extencive place. [Emory extract omitted.] In a short time the seignor (a Mr. Armijo and brother to

---

[6] Bernalillo, the county seat of Sandoval County, is seventeen miles north of Albuquerque and was the site of a Tiwa pueblo in the days of Coronado.

[7] A. Loring is listed as First Lieutenant, Second Dragoons, Company K, Albuquerque (Post Returns 1849, Albuquerque, National Archives).

[8] The former governor had a number of siblings, many of whom had property in the general area. The Madame Armijo whom Goulding mentions was probably the wife of one of the Armijo brothers living on a nearby ranch.

the General of that name who so figured in the late war) came in, and after the accustomed salutations, politely gave me an invitation to come and see him with Lieut. [Oliver Hazard] Taylor, with whom he was on familiar terms, and after treating me to a glass of wine and cake, he directed me a nearer way close by the river to the quarters of Lieutenant Taylor. During the afternoon, I had gained considerable information from this young man respecting this country and whom I had now left and continued on alone, flushing here and their a few wild ducks on the banks of the Del Norte.

At last, after travelling upwards of thirty-five miles since 12 o'clock today, I arrived at this U.S. Post in the Mexican town of Albuquerque.[9] Coming up to the quarters of Lieut. Taylor, I met him just at the door, and heartily glad was he to see me. Instantly calling one of his dragoons, who took charge of my horse, I was soon comfortable seated in the room of my hospitable friend. After partaking of a sumptuous supper of red peppers stewed with mutton and tortillas & chocolate, and being much fatigued from my long ride, I went to bed on a "bed" and which I had not before done since I left Santa Fe, having a good nights rest and sleep.

I woke up in the morning about 5 o'clock, Wednesday, June 6, when the first thing I seen was a naked boy standing by my cot with a tray. We were shown into their best parlour and on it a bowl of chocolate and a plate of sweet bread. This is one of the habbits of this country amongst the most wealthy. At 7 o'clock we had breakfast, where I was introduced to the Lady, the senora of the rancheria, with whom Lieut. Taylor boarded. Since he has been at this post, the place was most beautifully furnished. The parlour was all tapestried with rich silk velvet curtains [Emory extract omitted].

---

[9] A garrison and supply depot was established west of Old Town Plaza, Albuquerque, on November 17, 1846, a few months after Emory's visit. It was abandoned on August 23, 1867 (Giese 1995, 7). Troops were quartered in an extensive barracks adjacent to Governor Armijo's former home, the same building where the general had once housed his military escort. The stables were to the west, between the plaza and the river (M. Simmons 1982, 149). When the post was first established, the army rented housing for the officers and men from local citizens. Second Lieutenant Oliver Hazard Taylor, First Dragoons, to whom Goulding had a letter of introduction, was listed on the camp roster along with Maj. M. S. Howe, Second Dragoons, Commander of the Albuquerque Post (Post Returns, National Archives).

After our morning smoke, Lieut. Taylor ordered two dragoon horses up from the barrack stables (leaving my horse to rest), and after his morning parade of his troop, which consisted of 44 men all mounted, he took two of them, dismissing the remainder to the ordinary duties of the day, and we took a ride outside the town to see and meet my party about two miles east of the town.

We seen a party encamped, and thinking them to be my men, proceeded on toward them but found them all strangers. They were a party who had just arrived the evening before across the mountains from Texas. They consisted of 17 men, mostly "Cherokee half breeds," apperantly very fine looking men, all of which were well mounted and armed. While here with this company, a Mr. [Gerard] Banker came up and informed me my company were some five miles east.[10] Lieut. Taylor sent his dragoons with a note from me to Mr. Ford, to forward to that place and camp. Accordingly I made arrangements with Mr. [J. N. A.] Carter, who was the leading man of the Texan party and to which he cheerfully agreed so to do.[11] Lieut. Taylor and myself then proceeded across the fields, passing some beautiful vinyards and peach orchards, to Seignor Armijo's hicienda. A message having been sent in by the umbra at the gate and the names of Lieut. Taylor and the Senior Doctor Cavalero being announced, we were instantly escorted in by some half dozzen little naked "michitas" who act as their slaves and who are always rejoyced when the American visitors are arrived. Our nags were taken from us by the rancherio, a tall, fine looking fellow and dressed in the true Mexican style, with his pants open on the sides and a red silk sash around his waist, with a (hat) sombrero at least

[10] Gerard Banker was one of the original Knickerbockers and remained with Goulding throughout the trip. See appendix A.

[11] On June 4, 1849, David Jordan met Capt. J. N. A. Carter and his Cherokee and Mississippi Company from Fort Gibson while sojourning at New Placer mines, and they decided to join forces and travel the rest of the journey together. Carter was elected captain of their newly reorganized company. Goulding and his men joined Carter's group a few days later while encamped near Socorro. The Texan party referred to was led by David S. Terry. At least one of Terry's men, John A. Fairchild, joined the Knickerbockers (Powers 1849, 1). Terry ultimately became a justice of the California Supreme Court. He was known to be hot-tempered; incensed by statements made by Senator David C. Broderick in his 1859 campaign speeches, Terry challenged the senator to a duel and fatally wounded him (Hoover, Rensch, and Rensch 2002, 407–408).

three feet wide in the brim on his head. The lady senora with her two daughters were now present and received us very kindly, although they were in trouble for the loss of one of their daughters, who died some few days ago, and also of news of one of their sons, who was now absent in the United States and of whom they had been informed was also very unwell [Emory extract omitted].

The senora and her two senoretias were very fond of talking about the United States and appeared to take a great interest in my travels, of which I recited many incidence of which I had seen. These ladies, as is with all the Mexican ladies of the higher classes, seem to be well informed and well educated and are very free in their conversation with American gentlemen. Our napkins being removed by their female serfs in waiting, we walked through their numerous rooms, the most of which opened to the court yard around which was a piassa some twelve feet wide covered in on top, the ground of which was cement, the same as the floor all through the palace, except here and their a part was covered by splendid matts and rich embroidered carpets and blankets. We arrived in their private chapel were we took a quiet siesta. Here again I was overwhelmed with numerous questions about the United States and of "Nueva York," which I could only stop by questioning them, in return, of this country. [Emory extract omitted.] In the end of this salon was an alter on which were several wooden candle sticks, all handsomly carved and gilt, in each one a long wax candle about 1-1/4 inches thick. A figure of Jesus Christ and the Holy Virgin kneeling at the foot of the cross was covered over with a large remnant of pink crape. On a small table close by was some priest's garments and a silver chalice, a small silver bell, and a pot for burning incence, apparently of copper plated with silver around the sides. A bass violin and two banjos with a tambourine were laying on a seat near to. Such was the appearance of this chapel and which looked more like a suitable stage for theatrical representations than for a place of worship of the true and ever living God. During my observations here, I notised two young Indian Pueblo's with red hair. On making inquiry, I was informed that several of these Pueblos are red headed. The senora very politely apologised to us for the absence of her seignoro, who had gone to "Tom's" on some business respecting the sale of cattle, in which he done much business. At five o'clock, our horses being [illegible] up for us, we bid adieu to our accomplished and very polite and hospitable friends with a right good invitation for us to visita "once oter foia."

We soon galloped back to town, where we arrived in time for the evening parade of the dragoons, all mounted. Going down to the "Del Norte" to water their horses during the evening, Mr. [William F.] Ford and [John A.] Hunter visited me and reported of their being in camp along with the Cherrokee or Texan Company, who had decided on leaving this place on the next morning.

After supper, Lieut. Taylor and his sergeant major, a very fine young man, an American, went to visit the fandango of the town, which was held in a much larger and more spacious hall than those I had seen at Santa Fe. Here was quite an assembly both of the native umbras as well as the soldiers of the U.S. troops, with some of the Californians of the parties now encamped in the neighborhood. The music was excellent. They had 3 violins, a tambourine, and a banjo and drum, and two singers, who did make a most grand and noisey sound [Emory extract omitted].

Next morning, Thursday, June 7, having taken a hearty farewell of Lieut. Taylor and his accomplished, talented bride, I mounted and proceeded to join my companions, who were busily employed in packing and preparing for the march. We had some trouble with our pack mules. One of the mules stampeded and compleatly broke and smashed all the contents of her load, to the perplexity and vexation of the man who had her in charge, and caused much delay. The company got considerably ahead of my imediate mess, consequently we had to push on pretty fast to overtake them.

The country suddenly contracts below the village of Perdilla between Isoletta [Isleta] and the pretty little Mexican town of Peralta. This place had a very neat little church or chapel. Our road led directly by it about two miles beyond this town. Passing a number of rancherias, we stoped in an open plain or field with a number of casas in sight of us and camped for the night. I visited one of these houses to obtain some milk and eggs and found the seignor and senora were related to the Armijo family, and when I told them of my visit at the rancheria of their kinsman, they felt much joy and kissed my very cloak and sent abundance of tortillas, milk, and eggs to my camp for the men. Even their dog felt proud in escorting me about the premises, and he proved his faithful attention to me more particularly before morning. I stood smoking and talking with these friendly people, whose name was "Quanbihiler," until after ten o'clock.

The night was most splendid, with the moon as bright as day, when I returned to camp. I kept guard till 12 o'clock, when I laid down to sleep, giving up my guard duty to one of my men, named Wm. Cunningham, who had been my mulateer all the way from Fort Smith. It apeared that him and John Hunter, also one of my party, had had a falling out respecting the [trouble] with the troublesome mules the day before and at various other times, and this night was picked upon for him to "vaumis" the camp. It seems that when I laid down he went right to work with all hands being asleep and packed his kit, taking one of my mules, saddle, and one pistol & some bacon and biscuit.

About two o'clock, as I looked at my watch at the time, I was awakened up by this little dog, with whom I became acquainted in the evening at the rancheria. He kept licking my hands, which I usually have over my head on my saddle when asleep, and by this means I was awakened up. And in not being answered by Mr. Cunningham when I called, and looking sharply to our animals, as they had all been staked nearby and it being very light, the moon being at its hight, I missed one of them. So I called Ford and Hunter and we soon discoverd that this chap had made tracks for the east. In examining our traps, we found nothing missing of consequence except the mule and saddle and pistol, and these I intended to give him when I got to our journies end, so under the circumstance of the dispute between him and Mr. Hunter and which was now all told to me for the first time, I therefore concluded not to go after him but felt thankful he had not robbed us of something of importance to us in our present condition. Mr. Ford kept guard the remainder of the night.

On the morning of Friday, June 8, our friends from the rancheria sent us a fine large pail of milk and a dish full of tortillas, fresh baked, so we had a first rate breakfast and proceeded on our march by eight o'clock. Mr. Ford and Mr. Hunter now had to act as M.D. (mule driver). Our travelling was very heavy—mostly barren, sandy, and hilly sort of country with a few scattering casas and ranchos in the distance, the small towns and villages being mostly on the opposite side of the river. During this day we flushed numerous flocks of wild foul such as black ducks, teal, brant, wiggeon, and sand crane, most of which appeared to be very tame [Emory extract omitted]. We passed by the village of Tomé, also the pleasant little village of Belen, also the village of Sabinal. After these, the settlements became far between. At La Joya we overtook the main body of our party and here we all camped at this place [where] the Del Norte makes a bend [Emory extract omitted].

Saturday, June 9, we were all in good order this morning and took up our line of march at seven o'clock. When crossing over some sand hills, one of our mules stampeded, and the packs became entangled under the belly of the animal and caused considerable merriment at the cost of my own mess, for all our camp kettles and cullenary utensils were all kicked and dinged into all sorts of shapes and some of them compleatly distroyed. The balkey Miss Taddy, however, soon became tired out of her frolic and again allowed her packs to be replaced, and proceeded on her journey. About 11 o'clock, we "arrived at the town of Pulvidera [Polvadera], which we found, as its name implies, covered with dust."[12] We stoped at this place to noon, and the major domo of one of the most wealthy rancherias and who was a Texan by birth and could speak very good Spanish, French, and German, as well as English. He amused us, while resting, with

[12] Emory 1848, 50.

a story of an attack been made on this town during the late war by the Apaches [Emory extract omitted]. Our United States Dragoons have now put a stop nearly to the revellings and scenes of plunder and violence of these reckless banditti.

In consequence of the disorder and breakage of our [stampeding?] frollick in the morning, and our present camp being a very good one, our company were tempted to remain during the afternoon and night in this place. It is said they make the best brandy in the territory. Some of the women are very beautiful and very tastey in the manner they fix up their hair, which is very long [Emory extract omitted].

A strange sight presented itself, in a sort of sedan borne by four men, on the top of which was apparently a lifeless body sewed up in a coarse canvas bag or blanket. Following imediately were eight men dressed up in their best of style, followed by three woman with the "reboso" over their head and partly covering their faces. Also, two small girls dressed with pure white skirts and carr[y]ing small baskets of flowers. A few steps before the sedan was two men, one playing the violin, the other a banjo, and one woman singing, or rather shouting, a kind of melancholy song. Occasionally all the troop would shout in a kind of corous. I followed on after this singular procession.

[In] about [a] quarter of a mile, the whole band came to a sudden halt without any word of command, and in confusion were jostling each other, when one of these men, who appeared to be the padre, commenced to chant, and the women then all joined in a squeling sort of noise. Another of the 'umbras' commenced digging a hole in the sand or gravelly soil about three feet square and some five deep, when the body was tumbled head first into this hole, and the others threw in stones and gravel with their hands, and one of the believed kinsmen, with a huge stick some six inches thick, commenced pounding in and on the body of the deceased so as to make him conform to the size of the hole.

All the time this was going on, the padre and the women kept on shouting or singing and crying, while the men kept pounding and grunting to the time of the banjo and fiddle. The little girls, leaving them their baskets of flowers all in the hole during the performance, came over to me, and in answer to my inquiry said it was their brother who had been drownded and this was the place of interment. On looking about, I notised several stakes denoting the grave of many others, no doubt deposited here in the same wretched and diabolical manner. After the grave was well jumped on and a large stone put or rolled on top, the party all continued back, a dancing and singing and keeping time in the most joyful manner till they came to the casa of the late diceased, at which place a fandango was held during the evening, the wife of the buried man taking the lead in the dance with just as much gaiety of manner as if she never had even been a wife or lost a husband.[13]

A party of Mexican muleteers were encamped near this town and they added much to the festivities of the evening, as they had a great quantity of dried fruits, figs, and preserved meats and sweet bread and cakes and wines and cordials in any quantity and smoked salmon, the first of this luxury I have seen since leaving the States, and which they sold us at ten rials per pound (one dollar). The evening was most beautifully bright and serene, the air was of the most delightful temperature, varied occasionally by a gentle breese from the south wafting along the perfume from the vineyards and fine cottonwood trees by the banks of the river. On arriving at our camp, we prepared ourselves a collation of some of the provisions we had purchased, and our guards being all posted for the night, we soon fell into a sound sleep.

Sunday, June 10, this morning all our party were up early and concluded to cross the Del Norte at Lamitas [Lemitar], a small village

[13] Josiah Gregg (1954, 185) reported that New Mexico's lower classes were rarely buried in coffins; the corpse was simply wrapped in a blanket. Gregg was repulsed at the operation of filling the grave, where the earth was pounded down with a large maul. He added that there was nothing to indicate the place of any previous graves, and often, decayed relics were dug up and thrown again into the earth with the recently deceased. During Colonial times in New Mexico, the act of burying the dead was not as important as ritual preparation for death, which included the last rites and was followed by annual *novenarios* in remembrance. It was known as preparing for a good death. The body could also be interred under the floor of the local church (Will de Chaparro 2007, xv, 123–25).

about two miles below our present camp.[14] Quite a number of the natives of this neighborhood, having been informed of our determination, came on with us to assist and partisipate in the sport, it being Sunday. The river winds here in a beautiful semicircle bending to the west. On either side is excellent grass and shaded by large cottonwoods [Emory extract omitted]. After passing over some unoccupied strips of ground and some sand hills, we arrived at the crossing place. Here is a small valley on each side of the river with the banks nearly [level] with the water. The river makes a sudden bend, consequently the current is running at about five miles an hour.

All hands now formed in close order close to the bank of the river and every man commenced unharnesing the mules and horses and strapping or tying all the saddles and packs, panyards and baggage as compact as possible, all of which was stowed in small canoes provided to us by the natives for a few rials each, ourselves sitting on the top of our luggage. All the property being safely carried across and placed under guard, as was necessary, as on the opposite side their were several hundreds of the Mexican natives and Pueblo Indians, all curious in looking at our movements and watching [for] an opportunity to plunder.

All our mules and horses were driven into the river in one large body by all the men and who were assisted by the natives, shouting and chasing them to the very edge of the river, in which they plunged, followed by ourselves in the canoes and hundreds of the Pueblo Indians enjoying the sport by swimming after them, some holding onto their tails and some hanging on to the necks of the horses, all of them shouting the most shrilling Indian yells you ever heard. By this hurried and abrupt manner of forcing them in the water and the noise made by all hands, with the rapid current just at this bend of the river, soon caused them all to be safely landed

[14] Many California emigrants crossed the Rio Grande at the farming community of Lemitar, where Manuel Armijo was in residence since his return from exile in Mexico. The fast-running stream was about 250 yards wide at this spot, and William Chamberlin (1945, 150) and his men hired Mexicans to ferry them across in a "dugout" for eight dollars plus three dollars for them to swim the animals across.

obliquely down on the opposite side of the river. One of my horses unfortunately got drowned in crossing. The poor thing was much jadded and almost had given out with us some days before.

It was late before we all got over, and being eight miles from Socoro, we concluded to camp by the very bank of the river. By that means we had but one side to guard. The excitement of the day was great and very fatigueing to many of us. We paid our umbras a few rials each who assisted us in crossing and they all vaumised the camp apperently well pleased.

During the evening we were visited by a Frenchman who resided in this country for many years and who seemed to be much feared and respected by the present spectators of the imediate neighborhood. He informed us of the road and said we would be well welcomed at Socoro, that the soldiers their were fine fellows and were under the command of their Sergeant Major ([A.] Williamson), a very clever man, a Cherokee half breed, and with whom some of our present company had known was in the army but not till now knew in what post he was stationed.[15] The informant said he was going to Socoro this night on business, as he was the Prefect of this district, and he would have quarters prepared for us next morning.

Monday, June 11, we continued on our march through rather rugged kind of country. The prospect is forbidding. From the Sierra Lescadon [Ladrón Mountains] opposite the amphitheatre, as far south as the eye can reach, on the west side of the river is a chain of precipitous, basaltic mountains traversed by dykes of trap.[16] At last, about ten o'clock, the Sierra Socoro [South Baldy], the mountain overhanging the town of that name, and which is about three miles distant from the river, came to our sight. On nearing the town, we heard a gun fired and the brave flag of the United States was hoisted

[15] Companies D and E of the Second Dragoons were stationed at Socorro between 1849 and 1851. Records confirm that Sergeant A. Williamson, Infantry, was in Socorro during that time but by January 1850 had moved to Albuquerque (Post Returns, National Archives).

[16] Goulding borrows from Emory (1848, 51) in this paragraph. The rugged terrain of the Ladron Mountains with their rocky cliffs, steep slopes, and deep canyons provided a hideout for Navajo and Apache raiding parties, and later, for Anglo rustlers and thieves (Greene 2006, 92). Dikes of trap can be described as fractures in a volcano into which magma intrudes.

at the same moment, and soon afterward, we were met by our visitor of last night, the Prefect, and eight of the dragoons, all mounted in fatigue, to escort us into the town of Socoro, where we arrived at eleven o'clock. Sergeant Williamson informed me that Lieut. Sacket, the commandant in command, had gone to Duyanon [Doña Ana] and he did not expect him for a month. The party of dragoons here were of the Second Dragoons and consisted of twenty-two men. They have here a branch of the commissary department under the charge of Sergeant Clark, who had his wife with him and who was the first American woman we met with since we left Fort Smith, and a very polite and lady-like woman she proved to us, for their was nothing spared on her part to make us all comfortable as well was it with all of these dragoons.

They had all of our horses and mules sent down to the beautiful grass meadow vales by the banks of the river, and placed lots of straw in some casas which were empty close by their own quarters, where we had sufficient rooms for our whole party without being crowded. During the evening they gave us a splendid fandango to which all of the most respectable ladies of the town figured in the native dances of the country in a most pleasing manner, and Mrs. Clark and her obliging husband provided coffee and chocolate with other refreshments during the evening. The festivities of the evening did not seace till twelve o'clock, when we all retired to our quarters, well pleased with our first days reception. Mr. Baxter, one of the company, had just come up, being all the day in the rear looking for his horse, which had got lost in the cottonwood vales near our last camp, but was not successful in finding it, but had seen the dead body of Mr. [William F.] Ford's poor nag which belonged to my imediate party and which had been drownded at the crossing.

11

Fandangoes and Festivals

On arrival in Socorro, New Mexico, Goulding assumed his role as "doctor" and attended to a wounded colleague as well as townspeople who lined up for medical advice. He later joined Sergeant A. Williamson in San Antonio, New Mexico, to watch the villagers celebrate the Feast of Saint Anthony and to participate in the fandango that typically followed such ceremonies. It was here that he was introduced to, and hired, a man who the previous February had guided John Charles Frémont to California. This event was the determining factor in the route they were to follow after leaving Socorro: through Alamocitos (later Truth or Consequences) on the Rio Grande, then west on the Gila Trail and south at the Mimbres River. In the meantime, they continued their trek along the Rio Grande.

Tuesday, June 12, this morning a very serious accident occured to one of the men, a Mr. [John A.] Fairchild, in making up his mess fire.[1] In some way his powder flask blew up and burned his face in a most shocking manner. He was a very clever young man, so we determined on stopping here a few days to await the result of his case. During the day, in consequence of the loss of the horse in my mess, it became necessary to dispence with some of our kit so as to get an animal for Mr. Ford to ride. We sold upwards of one hun-

[1] David Jordan confirmed the accident, adding that the burnt man's "eyes are swelled shut & looks very bad" (June 12, 1849).

dred dollars worth of clothing and article[s] for about twelve dollars [Emory extract omitted].

The town of Socoro had a population of about one hundred & fifty souls exclusive of the U.S. soldiers.[2] It has a small chapel with a square steeple [San Miguel] and is prettily situated in the valley of the river which is here almost circular and about five miles in diameter. The church meets the eye at a great distance. During the evening I enjoyed a cup of tea with a nice plate of toast with Mr. Clark (orderly sergeant of the troop of dragoons) & Mrs. Clark, and which reminded me of my own dear home. I retired to bed early after attending to my patient, Mr. Fairchild, who I had taken under my immediate charge.

The next morning, Wednesday, June 13, my quarters was very much thronged with visiters. The inhabitance having been apprised of a "Senor Doctoro" being with the "Americano Cavelerios" and no phisisian being in the town, several of them came begging for some medencino, crying pitifuly they were mucho malo &c. Amongst the group their was some of the handsomest females of the place, some with soar eyes, others with pains in the breast and some with georoneré and some with cut fingers and sore legs. After attending to my own men, two of which were sick, as well as Mr. Fairchild and two of the dragoons, I served the whole lot of the applicants with powders, pills, plaster, decoctions, and physick so that all were satisfied and went away praying for the "mucho bravo Seignor Doctoro Americano Cavelerios."

News came into the town this morning that their was a company of Americans in camp about twelve miles of this place, near San Antonio. So after dinner, myself with Sergeant Williamson and one dragoon took up our march to see them, all of us mounted on very

[2] The Post of Socorro was founded in fall 1848 to protect the surrounding settlements from Indian attacks and to establish a U.S. presence following the Mexican War. Companies D and E, Second United States Dragoons, were settled in rented quarters in town. The post was abandoned in 1851 (Giese 1995, 25). Arriving emigrants observed a town surrounded by cornfields, the Stars and Stripes flying high in the plaza, four stores from which to purchase supplies, and a force of twenty-two dragoons, who treated the new arrivals generously while they rested and attended fandangoes (Forsythe, August 23, [1849]; Blunt, June 19, 1849; Hunter 1992, 10; Harris 1960, 53).

fine, fresh dragoon horses. We left Socoro at three PM. During our ride over sand plains and a barren kind of land, [we saw] several extensive rancherias looking in the distance like some old forts or walls of some garrison.[3] During our ride we passed by several of the people from all parts of the country who were flocking in crowds to San Antonio to partisipate in the fete of the patron saint of the town [Emory extract omitted].

At six and a half o'clock we arrived in the plaza and stoped at the casa of the alcalda of the town, who was acquainted with Sergt. Williamson, and he gave us a cordial wellcome.[4] Our horses were instantly corraled in a fenced in kind of yard close by and we were kindly received by the senora, the wife of the alcalda, who appeared to be on very familiar terms with my friend Sergt. W[illiamson] of the dragoons. We were now informed that the "Campo" of the "Americanoes" had taken up their march this afternoon but could not have gone very far, so we let the alcalda have one of our horses and we dispatched him to overtake them with a note I wrote to them informing them of the number and strength of our company at Socoro and of our destination, and requesting of them to await us at some good camping ground they might meet with on the river. We now were ushered into the sala of our worthy hostess, who had roasted a kid for our supper and baked a large heap of tortillas and a stew of mutton and onions and chilé and the frijolé [Emory extract omitted]. We were furnished with spoons and bowls of excellent coffee, but not a knife or fork was their to be seen. We each of us had dragoon swords, but unfortunately none of us had knives except myself happened to have a loose scalpel and which now came of use in disecting the roasted kid and which we did ample justise to in

---

[3] One of these rancherias was Luis Lopez, Socorro County, a tiny estancia named for the man who settled there in 1667 (Julyan 1996, 214). William Hunter (1992, 104), with the Callaway County (Missouri) Pioneers, remarked that for some five miles south of Socorro, it was one nearly continuous plantation.

[4] San Antonio, Socorro County, is eleven miles south of Socorro. The town has a long history through both Spanish and Mexican regimes, but in the twenty-first century it is better known as the birthplace of hotelier Conrad Hilton, whose father once owned the saloon in the popular Owl Bar and Café, 77 U.S. Highway 380.

devouring the whole of it. In fact, I thought it the sweetest morsel I had ever eaten in all my life.

After eating a hearty meal, we promenaded to see the preparations for the grand theatrical representations now making in the public square [Emory extract omitted]. [On] each side were numerous boys carrying torches and numbers of men firing off carbines and pistols and [shouting?] the greatest noise imaginable when they came up to the capilla (the chapel). In the grand plaza they all formed a half circle and all at onced became perfectly silent when the grand spectacle—the host of priests and padres—came on in processional. First came two fidlers and two banjos and a drum & tamboreen, and four men chanting, and eight men all dressed up in the most curious fantastics imaginable. Then came some twenty young women all dressed in white skirts, and rebosos over their heads, and then six little girls dressed up like angles with small wings attached to their shoulders, with small trays of pasteboard fastend on their waists containing small bouquets of flowers. Then was three boys, with each a chalice in which was the burning incence, as they walked along swinging them in the faces of the host of priests and friars imediately behind them. In the center of this crowd of priests was four men, their legs only to be seen, their bodys being entirely covered with a black velvet cloth under which was the sedan in which was the patron saint to which they were now cellebrating this fete [Emory extract omitted].

When the grand sedan with its contents arrived at the chapel portal, their was a general silence, all the spectators falling down on their knees, and the boys and friars, who all carried long wax candles, surround the God of the time. When after an interval of a minute, their commenced a distant chant apparantly in the chapel and the sound gradually approached to us, when the priests then commenced chanting, accompanied by the ladies, then the men commenced, and gradually the whole congregation joined into a regular shout or yell. All at onced again they stoped when the head padre or bishop spoke some words in Latin [Emory extract omitted].

It was now nearly ten o'clock and our messenger, the alcalda, returned and gave me an answer to my note. It was signed by a Messrs. Stout and Callahan from Texas on their journey to the South Pass, and in reply to my request, they would wait for our party at the first good grass they would come to on the Rio del Norte, as their animals were much used up and wanted rest. Their party consisted of twenty men and thirty-five asses, ponies, and mules.

The procession being now broken up and the great assembly of people scattering in various directions, the alcalda led us along through the plasa to a species of public building or guardhouse where a number of Mexicans were collected, some of whom had just figured in the fantastical part of the show and were laughing and talking of the various exploits of their various visits as made during the evening at the rancherias in the neighborhood. One of these fellows was the umbra which Col. Fremont had as a guide when he crossed through or by this place on his way to California, and the alcalda informing him of my company being in want of a guide, now said he would go with my company and he promised to be at Socoro the next day and make the arrangements.

The alcalda's lady and her accomplished niece were the admired and gazed at bells of the place. The senora was dressed up in her very best equipments. She had on a royal purple silk velvet skirt and spencer open in front with a rich lace vest ornamented with scarlet edgeing and so neatly arranged as to develop her prominent bosoms—her size being rather of the corpulent order, her dress was arranged in a loose manner. Her niece was dressed in a striped silk dress with a very costly reboso, fringed with gold lace, over her head. Her arms and neck down to her breast all bear except as to what was covered by the folds of the reboso. Several senoras and senoretas of the town and neighborhood were also present and many of them dressed in the most richest and costly manner, exhibiting great quantities of jewelry, consisting of necklaces, breastlets, ear and finger rings, buckles, stars, and sandle springs, some with sockets in which were neat pearl handled dirks.

The senora alcalda very politely asked me to lead the dance with her in a cotillion. Accordingly, a set was formed by my party and the ladies of the family of our worthy alcalda, and you may rest assured that the two corpulent dancers in this set were much gazed at for the time during that dance. Several cotillions were danced, in all of which we indeavored to change our partners so as all our ladies would be pleased, after which the more joyous dances of the country were introduced, such as the Coona, and the Italiana, and the Bolera [Emory extract omitted].[5] Of those who may feel inclined, in one end of this hall was a barrel of wine, of which those who wished could quench their thirst when they pleased. The dancing was kept up to a late hour. About one o'clock we returned to the alcalda's where skins for mattresses and these with our dragoon cloaks and the saddles as pillows served us to sleep on till day light.

On the morning of Thursday, June 14, we saddled up early this morning and proceeded on our way back to Socoro, where we arrived in time for breakfast, which I took with the soldiers mess. At my quarters, again this morning was I much annoyed by numbers of the inhabitants soliciting medicines and complaining of various diseases. Giving them all gratuously doses of physick, they all went away satisfied. Mr. Fairchild was much improved and his sight was saved, so I reported to the company of the result of my visit to the Texan corps ahead of us. It was unanimously agreed upon to take up our line of march the next morning. Our guide being now present, it was agreed with him to proceed with us as far as Cow Spring Valley, a place noted in the rocky mountains for a resting place, for fifty dollars and his grubb. Each mess agreeing to feed the fellow in their turn day about, and he was to find his own way of conveyance with us. Accordingly, he left us, now promising to join us on our march down the river during the next day. After this I took a walk about the town to find some new points of observation [Emory extract omitted]. During the evening we visited the fandango, which was a repetition

[5] Forty-niner diarists who managed to get caught up in a local fandango frequently borrowed Emory's terms "the Coona, the Bolero, and the Italiana" (1848, 43).

of the former one, the dragoons seemingly to be as well trained in the Spanish waltzes as if they had been at it all their lifetime.

> "And every man, had his lass,
> but never, a lass was their for me.
> O what can the matter be, O what
> shall I do, no body coming to have me,
> no body coming to woo." "Ford" ditty

We all retired to our quarters early tonight and slept comfortable till the morning of Friday, June 15. A party was sent down to the river bottoms early this morning, who drove up all our horses and mules and which was in fine order after the rest, all being put into a corral. The Mexicans of the place lassood our animals and each man got his own. The scene resembled more of a horse fair or market than anything else as trade and exchange with the party. By ten o'clock we got all ready for a start. All our packs being now compleated and our column formed, Sergt. Williamson and four of his men escorted us for a few miles, so with three times three right good hearty cheers, we parted in opposite directions.

We kept up near the base of the highland during the most of our march. The air was quite elastic and fragrant with the perfumes of the wild sage from the adjacent hills. The sun burned out bright and red till after the meridian. About one and a half o'clock we came up to a patch of grama grass, where we found our guide in waiting for us with his large jackass staked out, mowing it down with his teeth at a great rate. After a rest of a short half hour we again pushed forward, our road leading down towards the river. Here we met with a large flock of sheep and goats and of the shepard we purchased a sheep for each mess for one dollar each.

By the aperance of the country now, it was evident we were leaving the settlements, for the roads began to disapear as well as the rancherias, and the mountains looked majestic and wild, looming up before us to the right and left from three to four thousand feet in hight. We notised on the opposite side of the river this afternoon a large train of wagons and packed mules escorted with a troop of dragoons on their way to Santa Fe. I viewed them with my spy-glass and it was indeed a pretty sight.

About five PM we came to a cannon of the river, which our guide informed us was the first cannon off the river and we must camp here, their being some cottonwood trees and some good grass. Our guide informed us we had thus passed the last settlements and henceforth a new road must be trodden, for very few marks of the old trail are left. The land we travelled over today, although not much settled, is incomparably the best I have seen in New Mexico. The valley is broader, the soil firmer, and the growth of timber along the river larger and more dense. The ruins of a deserted and modern town [Valverde] we passed this afternoon.[6]

The remains of ditching for irrigation were quite visible. The frequent incursions of the Indian is said to cause the desertion of this part of the valley. During the evening we had a company meeting and Mr. [J. N. A.] Carter was elected as Captain, Mr. Tyler as Lieutenant, and Mr. Lovely [Rogers] Sergeant of the guard duty for the remainder of our journey, whose duty it was to make out the suitable guard for each day, to act as advance guard, and mount guard during nights.[7]

Saturday, June 16, at seven o'clock this morning our troop were on the march, our guide leading the way mounted on his donkey, thumping his sides occasionally with his knees after the fashion of these people. At 9-1/2 o'clock we came up to the new Texan troop, who were on their march and who joyfully joined into our ranks. Altho there was not a man of that party that any of us ever knew before, still the marks of the Anglo Saxon race was so apparent that we soon became as brothers, and many were the exciting stories that were communicated during our march this day. These men had seen much harder times than we had, for they had at one time been intirely robbed of all their animals and left intirely destitute of the means of

[6] Valverde, Socorro County, twenty-nine miles south of Socorro, was at the northern terminus of the Jornada del Muerto and was considered a modern town until the populace abandoned the site due to Navajo raids (Julyan 1996, 370).

[7] Capt. J. N. A. Carter and Lovely Rogers, a mixed-blood Cherokee, were members of the Cherokee and Mississippi Pack Mule Company from Fort Gibson (Fletcher, Fletcher, and Whiteley 1999, 182). Goulding mentioned Carter's arrival in the Rancho del Chino Register Book (Bynum 1934, 5).

proceeding with their kits. But being determined and courageous fellows, they dogged the Indians for many miles, leaving all their baggage to the mercy of the winds, and by a cunning night attack they again came in possession of the most of their mules, who like themselves knew they had been stolen and that they were now in the hands of their right owners. They made extra forced marches both day and night, feeding their animals from their saddles as they travelled on their way. Part of the time and the greatest suffering they had was the want of water. They did not know where they were for several weeks and not till they came over the mountains of Zandia and they crossed the river at San Antoine at a place that never was crossed before.

Our rout led over hills and dales through a great variety of vegetation, all totally different from that of the United States. Their was the cactus in endless varieties and a large species of tall grama grass, very coarse and as good as oats for our animals, and several varieties of chaperal and mezquite. And as for the varieties of that department, the flora, it is beyond my comprehension and must leave that for some traveller more versed in the knoledge of that beautiful discription of the production of this southern Mexico.

Fra Cristobal Mountain presented itself to our view [Emory extract omitted]. We have heretofore revelled in the perfect stillness and quietude of the air and scenery of New Mexico, but today has been an exception, for the wind has been very high from the south and the dust overwhelming. At five o'clock we camped, their being some slight signs of rain, and is the first rain we have seen since our arrival in this New Mexico. Our guide tells us that by or near this Fra Cristobal Mountain their is slight rains all seasons of the year. We are now camped on the bank of the river with considerable growth of cottonwood, among which are found some signs of the otter or beaver, some patches of grama grass in spots, with small hills of white sand. We were much anoyed during the night by the gally nipper, but our mosquitto net helped us to some degree.[8] The road or camena to [Chihuahua] runs on the eastern side of the Fra Cristobal Mountain, where the agriculturing part of the country ceases and the muleteer

---

[8] The gallinipper is any of a variety of insects, including the mosquito.

traveler meet with a dreded "Jornada" where their is no water for upwards of ninety miles during most seasons of the year.[9]

Sunday, June 17, our squadron made a fine appearance this morning at seven o'clock, our guide taking the lead, following the river for about two miles, passing another deserted town all in ruins in heaps of adobes or walls of clay almost covered up with the luxurious growth of chamisa and the atriplx [saltbush] and varieties of the cacti or the prickley pear, all in full blossom. Also several trees of the mesquite tribe, also the "dalea fermasa" [*Dalea formosa*], a many branch shrub about three feet high with beautiful purple flowers, and many of the cacti were of a gigantic size, with a few white ceder trees.

Immediately on assending the hills above this last ruined town, our travelling became very broken and uneven with stones and large rocks looking like clinkards just as if they had resently been thrown up out of some great mountain volcano. About 11 o'clock, we came to the second cannion of the river, where our guide informed us we must now assend the ridge land, and we are now two hundred miles from Santa Fe and in the extreme end of the valley of Valverde, which makes a kind of half circle near the point where we left the ruined town and which terminates at this cannion.

The valley of the river narrows here into a canon which sweeps at the base of Fra Cristobal Mountain, making it necessary to rise to the table lands on the west side and which we found very ruff travelling, being covered with basalt and burnt rocks and meeting with deep arroyes. Distant ranges of mountains are continually in our view running north and west, and nearly parrallel to each other; the deep reveins between are very broad and show the beds of immence dry streams. Several clay buttes were seen in the distance and had the appearance of adobe houses surrounded by trees, but on a near approach showed them to be a kind of clay or lime hills washed away by the rains.

At four o'clock we again approached the river, where we met a party of the native Pueblo muleteers who had been a trading with the mountain Indians. These chaps informed us the Apaches were

[9] The Jornada del Muerto (Journey of the Dead), is a desolate, rock-strewn trail through the desert. It cuts off a bend in the Rio Grande between Fray Cristobal, Socorro County, and Rincon, Doña Ana County, on the Camino Real that connected New Mexico towns with Chihuahua.

friendly to the Americans and we would meet with them in about five days. This being a fine valley of about a hundred acres in extent, well grassed and wooded, we camped for the night close to the river. This valley apparently was untrodden by the foot of man. Here was considerable signs of game in the tracks of bears and deer. I took my gun and strolled off and flus[h]ed several covies of the blue quail. This bird differs in the plumage from those of the States but is similar to them in their habbits. The noise they make is a kind of scream like the English pheasant. The male bird has a top knot with two long, beautiful feathers projecting like horns and of a gold purple color. Several black tailed rabbit or hair were also seen, and a flock of wild geese and several ducks about the river. Several crows and a hawk were also seen and were the first of these latter birds we have seen in New Mexico.

Abundance of an intirley new kind of currant was growing here and perfectly ripe, of which the most of us eat with a good relish.[10] We had a very excellent game supper, also some muscal bread as given to us by our packed mule friends. This is the kind of bread eaten by the mountain Indians and is the roots of the muscal cacti which they bake in the ground by digging a trench around the root of the plant at sertain seasons of the year and when sufficiently cooked they pull it out up by the tops, leaving the hard baked crust in the ground. It is very good eating when you are in such a condition as not to be able to obtain any other kind of bread. The evening was rather cool.

Monday, June 18, this memorable day (to me), "the 18th of June 1815 now thirty-four years ago, on which that celebrated battle [Waterloo] was fought and which decided the fate of the greatest general of modern armies. I was present at that battle altho but a boy not yet nine years old, still I recollect many incidence of the field of battle and the lines of march of the army up to Paris."[11]

Our line of march today was pretty much the same sort of travelling as yesterday, meeting with tremendous wide and large river beds intirely dryed up and wide enough to contain all the water in the

[10] David Jordan (June 17, 1849) commented that the red berry "tasted very much like what we used to call in Maryland the 'Sarois berry.' The guide eats them where ever he can find one." It was also this day, he noted, that they passed the place where Kearny abandoned his wagons in 1846.

[11] See "Introducing William Robinson Goulding," this volume.

Mississippi and presenting the appearance of the deserted beds of onced large and turbulent rivers. On the table lands, at times for two or three miles, a compleat level covered over with a burnt clinkered like stone, with now and then a small spot of grama grass and accasia with miriads of lizzards of all colors running in all directions.

The mirage presented its singular and deceptive water views. Its appearance is like a sheet of water disturbed by the winds. Some of the company riding ahead some distance would loom up and looked like the masts of ships and the mules legs as if someone was walking on stilts. Our animals evidently began to shew the effect of hard travelling, for many of them became tender footed, and about four o'clock we struck the river and camped for the last time beside this singular river of the Del Norte. Our party were now very busy in putting on shoes on the mules and such as did not have shoes enough took off the hind shoes to put on the fore feet of such as did not have any. Horse nails became in great demand. Our little camp ground did not cover over more than three or four acres where was grass, and our sleping places was close to a sandy, pebbled, high bank, and all around us for miles seemed to be compleatly barren. The evening was very fine and the most of the company enjoyed a bath in the river, which at this point appeared to be quite still and smooth water.

It was the turn of my mess to grub our worthy guide, so he supped with us this evening, and I found him a very intelligable sort of fellow. He pointed out to me from this camp the mountain where is the hiding places of the Navajoes, who, when few in number, descend upon the valleys in the night time and carry off the fruit, sheep, and cattle, and after, the women and children of the Mexicans. And when in large numbers, they used to come in the day time and levy their dues. Their retreats and caverns are at a distance to the west in high and inaccessible mountains where the troops of the United States will find great difficulty in subduing them and where the Mexicans have never had the courage of penetrating. The Navajoes may well be termed the Lords of New Mexico. Few in number, disdaining the cultivation of the soil and even the rearing of cattle, they draw all their supplies from the valley of the Del Norte [Emory extract omitted]. Our guide gave me his name this evening, which is "John Olearous."

12

Rio Grande to Rio Mimbres

During 1849, nearly five hundred emigrants of various companies climbed out of the Rio Grande Valley in the vicinity of Alamocitos to begin the next leg of the journey, which would take them along the Gila River to its junction with the Colorado River at the Yuma crossing. The rugged pack trail that would become known as the Gila Trail meandered through New Mexico's Gila National Forest, passing the Santa Rita copper mines and Arizona's Pima villages. Lieutenant William Hemsley Emory, traveling with General Stephen Watts Kearny and his Army of the West, took this route in 1846 with Kit Carson as guide. The area had not yet been mapped, and although the Native people, frontiersmen, and Mexicans knew it well, they used physical features as guideposts. As a result, Goulding and others frequently consulted Emory's book, Notes of a Military Reconnaissance *(1848), to find their way.*[1]

John Charles Frémont had terminated his disastrous fourth expedition in January 1849 at Kit Carson's house in Taos and was anxious to return to California. There is no doubt that Carson encouraged Frémont to take the Gila Trail and even provided a guide. Frémont did not travel the full length of the trail, however, but turned south at the Mimbres River. Thus, Goulding's party, led by one of Frémont's guides, appears to be the only group of forty-niners to follow the Frémont cutoff. In addition to recounting adventures along the trail, Goulding describes some interesting encounters with the Apaches.

---

[1] For further clarification, the reader is referred to George Ruhlen (1957), who made a detailed modern reconnaissance of the route and compared Emory's observations with the creeks and rivers in the area.

Tuesday, June 19, this morning just before day, my attention was atracted by a hissing kind of noise, when at daylight I got up and to my surprise found rather a cold comrade close to my head in the shape of a huge rattlesnake. I soon alarmed the whole camp by a "reveillee" in the discharge of a pistol at the unwelcome Mexicano. He had nine rattles on his posterior extremity, which I soon cut off and put in a small tin box containing several more of the same sort, already accumulated during our travels over the Great Desert, and this was the first rattlesnake I seen since my arrival in southern New Mexico. This one differed in color from any that I have seen on the plains, it being a light brown color. In fact it was just the same color of the soil of our present camp ground.

Our squadron being all formed, we again proceeded on our march by the river till just nine o'clock. Our guide now informed us we are to leave the "Rio del Nort" [Rio Grande] altogether as we must now take the trail leading towards the "Rio Membres" and which now runs into a deep and gloomy revein occasionaly meeting with dry streams of white sand in which our mules would sink up to the knees. Large clay buttes of all sorts of forms in our sight. Our trail some times so obstructed by bushes that we found it very difficult in getting our packed animals along, but by a little coaxing and any quantity of Spanish "refined literature" in the way of "Vamoise Mulee," Cha——ho &c., our guide at last led us out on the ridge land or plains, over which we travelled till the afternoon, when we came to a large river bed compleatly dried up, with some timber such as cottonwood and oak. On decending into this mighty ravine, we flushed several covies of quail and doves. Also a solitary black bear was sloly trotting along in the middle of this great sand bottom and would sit on his "behinds" and look at us as contemptable as if he despised our approach on his dominions. Sergt. Lovely [Rogers] and some others of our corps who were excellent shots started off to give chase to his Bruin Majesty, and the hunt was very exciting for a short time. In chaceing him up the bed of this ravine they flushed a flock of turkies, of which they shot two very large cocks, but their black Zarr was better acquainted with the grounds than his enemies, so they abandoned him. They, however, discovered a very fine little brook of spring water boiling up out of the sand as clear as cristal and makeing various turns in hundreds of serpentine forms through the bottoms, became into a small runing stream in which was numerous quantites of small pearch, numbers of which were caught.

During our camp this evening in this place were several large trees presenting in appearance as if some extencive raft had at one time been floating and had run aground just at this point. Some of our men built a fire against one of these trunks, which during the night took fire and made a general conflagration, which was grand in the extream and was the death of numerous night hawks and doves, who plunged into its blazing flames to be devoured by its mighty element.[2]

Next morning, Wednesday, June 20, after partaking an excellent breakfast of meat, fish, and fowl, we commenced to ascend up the steep bank to the west revein, all hands leading their animals and climbing up some two hundred feet above the valley. All the packs did not get up till nine o'clock, it being so steep and difficult, being obliged to make the assent in an obliqued manner in opposite directions to gain the top, where was apperantly a level plain covered with cactus and the mezquite bushes in endless varieties growing up amongst the bassalt and clinkered like surface. We now proceeded on our march. At 10 AM the mirage again made its appearance and looked in the distance exactly like a splendid lake. Two distant peaks loomed up before us and looked for all the world like a fore-and-aft schooner at anchor.[3] As we were observing this natural deception, our advance guard came to a halt at the very edge of a steep precipice.

[2] Ruhlen (1957) writes that Emory left the Rio Grande at Alamocitos (Truth or Consequences) and traveled south for four miles before turning west at Elephant Butte. Here he ascended a 200-foot tableland. Emory wrote about crossing arroyos and ravines, the first two of which Ruhlen identifies as Seco and Animas creeks. Emory made camp near a "fine leaping mountain stream" known as Percha Creek, five miles directly east of modern Hillsboro and twenty-four miles from where he started at Truth or Consequences (Ruhlen 1957, 221). Jordan called it a brook of "beautiful clear water" (June 19, 1849).

[3] Phineas Blunt (1849) saw the same mirage of a schooner when he passed by on June 26, as had Emory (1848, 57) in October 1846.

Below were green trees, two of which explained the misterious vessel. Here was a luxuriant foliage, the sure indication of water. Makeing a circuit, we decended into this valley and found a running stream of clear, limpid, and cool water fringed with a small growth of cottonwood and a new kind of evergreen oak with leaves like the holly, also a new kind of ash and walnut with the nuts about half the size of those of the States and endless quantities of wild grapes. Six miles further brought us to another valley or ravine in which was another creek of clear water running sluggishly and like the last about the size of a mans waist. In this valley were also many large trees uprooted, presenting the appearance of newly made ground.[4] [Emory extract omitted.]

Our guide informed us we shall not meet with water for nearly eighteen miles from this place, so we concluded to camp for the night in the most extensive looking buttes and high mountains I ever seen. I amused myself during the afternoon in drawing a sketch of the profile of the views about us.[5] Several quail were shot, of which we cooked for our supper.

Thursday, June 21, in consequence of one of the men being very ill, we did not proceed this morning until one PM. We packed up and marched over some fine rolling country, our guide telling us we are now approaching the mountain [in] which the waters of the Rio Membres first takes its rise. The soil in the valleys of which we now pass, and even to the hill tops, are covered with grama grass [Emory extract omitted]. We seen several of the black tailed deer quietly grazing on the sides of the hills, and rabbits were as plenty as the quail. Towards evening we traversed by some small streams of pure water fringed with cane breaks and stunted growth of walnut, live oak, and ash, and some new varieties of cactus, one a miniature tree with the stalk six inches thick. At one of these streams we camped for the night.

[4] Goulding has combined his own observations with Emory's (1848, 57) in the preceding paragraph. According to Ruhlen (1957, 223), this camp was near the present-day Nunn Ranch at Berenda Creek, three miles west of Lake Valley, with the Mimbres Range to the west.

[5] Sketch missing.

Friday, June 22, our invalid being much improved this morning, our squadron was all formed in column and commenced our line of march at seven o'clock, determined if possible today to strike the Rio Membres, which our guide says is about nine leagues from this camp (27 miles), when about nine o'clock a party of Mexicans came in sight, a trading party on an expedition to the Apaches and other mountain Indians. First we met a poor mule with two packs of maze on his back, which we drove along [Emory extract omitted]. We soon overtook the main party which consisted of ten men and one small boy whom our guide was acquainted with. They had some twenty packed animals, all loaded with maze & bread and articles suitable for Indian trading.

We were now fairly in the pass through the mountains, which shifted our front to all points of the compass; sometimes our trail became quite narrow and full of a shattered kind of stone and rocks as if they had just fell or rolled down from the tops of the huge mountains on our right and left. All at onced an oppening made its apperence of about half a mile wide with the mountains ranging all around us. Here we left the trading "laderons" to camp, here a "trail crossed our trail" at right angles just as we approached the defile to the opposite mountain, and by its apperance, as well as the trail we were on, and on which we have been ever since we left the Del Norte, had been there and [been] beaten by the feet of these natives for centuries.

Our guide informed this trail that crossed the trail to the copper mines at the head waters of the Gila River where he says he has been on three different times.[6] When I told him of the Americans in the United States giving the credit to Fremont for makeing this rout first, he laughed right out,[7] a regular jackass laugh, in which his donkey on which he was then a riding joined in a mighty corous, which

[6] The men had been trudging along Dry Gavilan Creek and Gavilan Creek and were indeed coming to a crossroads when they reached the Mimbres River. Goulding and friends turned south at this location (Ruhlen 1957, 226).

[7] The guide was well aware that Kit Carson and the Native people frequently used the trail, and of course, General Kearny had followed it in 1846. Frémont had trekked the route in 1849, four months before the Goulding party (Frémont 1849).

gave such an innumerable number of echos through these mountains that I thought the hills were full of bouricks [little donkeys]. Seems that several mountains here form canons just at this opening and is a wonderful curiousity to the passers by. A few stunted live oak trees is all that is growing just at this point. The narrow and rocky pass caused us to walk to spare our tender footed animals. At last we decended in an arroyo which led us towards the Rio Membres, very narrow and full of shattered stones, the sides covered with a thick growth of stunted live oak. In full view nearly the whole time of our decent was a mountain of a peculiar shape and symmetry resembling the segment of a spheroid or dome.[8]

Near the base of this mountain we struck on this beautifull valley of the Rio Membres. At this part it is about one mile wide, of rich fertile soil and densely covered with great varieties of timber of large size with beautiful young growth of trees and flowers of endless varieties. Just at this season almost everything you looked at was in bloom. About one hundred yards from the bank of the river, we found an old Indian camp with several of their lodges as made of bushes still remaining. This place being open and like a kind of field, free of underbrush, we formed into an oblong coral and camped. Indications of rain, and for the first time since we entered New Mexico their was thunder and lightning. So for the first time also since we left the prairies, we pitched our tent and which we found very comfortable during the night for it was quite cold.

This Rio Membres is an independent river rising in the mountains and emptying its waters in the sands some eighty miles south. The river is a rapid stream from fifteen to thirty feet wide, and in some places, opening out into large gullies or ponds, affording sufficient water to irrigate its beautiful valley. There is great quantities of fish in its waters, such as black trout, roach or sunfish, and gudgeon. Its banks are lined with large cottonwood trees as well as the ash and walnut. The blue quail, partrages, and turkies have great cover in this

[8] The dome was visible as they descended Gavilan Creek. It is Blue Mountain on modern maps and it is three miles northwest of modern Dwyer, Grant County (Ruhlen 1957, 226). Goulding paraphrased some of the foregoing material from Emory (1848, 57–58).

valley and our men had great sport both in their fishing as well as shooting till late in the evening. The dried branches of the deserted wigwams serving us for ready firewood to cook our plentiful supply of meat, fish, and fowl.

Saturday, June 23, this morning we proceeded towards the south, following the trail on the east of the river, flushing great quantity of all sorts of game as we moved on. At one time three black tail deer jumped right through our ranks, leeping instantly into the thick cover where it was not prudent for our men to follow. A fine, large grisley bear was seen by the advanced guard, who fired six rounds into his hide, but he succeeded in getting into the thick swamp, leaving his blood only for his disappointed hunters to look on. Sergt. Lovely, the two Baxters, and the others lost nearly two hours after him, but said it was not possible to get in where he was shot. During the delay searching after Bruin, the rest of the company were busy in eating red and white currants which were now ripe and in great abundance and of a delicious and sweet flavor, much larger and sweeter than the Dutch or English currant of the States. Grapes and gooseberrys were also growing in this valley, but not as yet ripe.

Eight miles below our last camp our trail led us directly on to the river, where we forded. At this place it was not more than two feet deep and about thirty feet wide and the bottom of sand and pebbles with some cottonwood trees on the west side and a cane swamp on the side we just left. Here we found an open kind of field or small plain, with some deserted lodges, same as those we had in our camp last night. The grass in this place was of a most excellent quality, resembling trefoil, a kind of clover. Here we stoped to noon and feed.

When scarsely were our animals staked, our party became alarmed at the apperance of a body of men on the opposite side of the river advancing rapidly towards us. We could only see their heads every now and then. Consequently we instantly saddled and formed our party into close column and six of the party went to reconnoiter and soon returned with ten new men, all mounted on good horses, with each of them with a packed mule. They were Missispians who have been travelling in our trail all the way from Socoro, forceing their marches to endeavour to overtake us.

They gave us a thrilling account of an engagement at the Placers in New Mexico between the Americans and the Camanches and that their was several killed on both sides but that the Camanches were defeated and several of them taken prisoners. They also informed us of a company consisting of sixty men, mostly Texans, now on the way, makeing forced marches to overtake us. They came into Socoro the same day that they left but they had lost several of their mules and ponies in crossing and would have to wait to purchase a new supply in the vicinity of Socoro, when they intended then to proceed at onced. We were quite refreshed with the exciting accounts recited by these men. Our party now numbered sixty eight men and one hundred and thirty four animals, sixty-six of which were packed mules, all in good trim and all securly packed. So we made quite a formadible apperance.

At two o'clock we again proceeded on our coarse. As we advanced, the valley became more open and clear of timber, with rolling green hills on both sides of the river. Leaving the valley or river bed, about half a mile wide, covered with cane break and swamp grass, with here and their an odd tree or bush and the huge towering looking mountains in the distance all around us, we saw some objects perched on the hills to the east of us which were at first mistaken for trees or cacti, but our guide exclaimed, "Indians, there are the Apaches."[9] His more practised eye detected human figures in our shrubbery. By the manner they were acting, it was very evident they had not a favourable opinion towards us. Soon we notised these Indians in all directions on the hills, intirely surrounding us both front and rear. A council being called of the whole company, it was deemed adviseable to form into a close and compact form of coral with all our packed animals in the center and await the result of an

[9] The emigrants were crossing the territory of the eastern band of the Chiricahua Apaches, which extended west from the Rio Grande to Quemado on the north, the Hatchet Mountains on the west, and the international boundary on the south.

attack or an interview with these Lords of the Mountains. The larger body of them being on the opposite side of the river, we concluded to send a party with our guide over to them and seek a talk with them, but our guide, who was more experienced in these matters than we were, vollenteared to go himself alone, telling us at the same time that he could manage them more successfully when aloan than when he had others with him.

Our position being now on a small rise or knoll in a level field of some twenty acres, we dispatched our guide to the Indians on the opposite bank of the river, awaiting the result of his interview with them with anxious eyes gazing in all directions. The Indians were also equally disturbed and wondering what formidable looking party we could have been that dared to travell on their dominions. The attitude just at this moment was indeed very interesting and warlike. Every man except the picket guard dismounted, standing to his horses head, bridle in hand, ready to mount at a moments warning and intensely gazing at the approach of our guide, who now had nearly arrived to the banks of the river, leading his donkey through the cane breaks. He now mounted and plunged into the river—he sinks, he swims, he's lost—no, he's all right. He assends the bank, waveing the small but glorious American flag of the Stars and Stripes. The Indians rather reluctantly walked a few steps towards him but hesitated a few minutes, talking apparently with each other, when one of them more bold step'd forward and talked with our guide, and being satisfied with his discours as to who we were, he raised up his hands and shouted, when the Indians all through the hills arround gave a yell and one of them instantly set fire to some grass, which was the "signal of peace." Such a gallopping of Indians as was then to be seen in all directions. Even for many miles from the base of the mountains was seen Indians mounted and on foot, running in all directions.

Seventeen of the Indians, all mounted, crossed over to us, all in Indian trail, following our guide in the swamp. They all dismounted and led their horses up the banks, approaching our level position.

Several parties were also approaching us in the same way. All dismounted from all sides of us. I went towards our guide to meet them with Capt. Carter, and our guide introducing the Capitano and the Seignior Doctoro, they manifested to me the greatest of respect and commenced hugging me at a great rate, in fact much more that what I had bargained for. Parties now came in from all sides and all hands got hugged to their fullest satisfaction. Their were several women with these Apaches, which we now learned was the name of the tribe to which they belonged and these woman were all mounted on horses of a small size "A la Duchess de Berry," (astride like men) and we could not distinguish them from the men untill they were within our lines for some time.

About forty of these fellows were of the warriors of the tribe and resembled the Camanches in some respects. Their hair, instead of being laced on long straps of buffalo hide as the Camanches were, was loose and cut off about six to eight inches long and left flying in the air and looked in the distance like a mopp. They were armed with bows and arrows in leather quivers. Spears, all with steel or iron blades, tied on poles by a firm twine made of rawhide cut while green. For the purpose they carried shields made also of green rawhide of animals, the hair still on the inside, with a strap on the top for the arm to pass through and a hand hold also of leather, apparently worked into the solid hide. Three of the party had English made fuzzies, had the tower mark (the broad A) on the lock.[10] Several of them was tattooed and painted on the body and stripes of blue, green & red on the face. Some were of a pale slate color and others striped and looked about as interesting and facinating as did our Grisley Lord in the morning scenes. Some had brass rings of a large size in their ears and two had them in the nose, and all the warriors had large no. 8 wire of brass on their arms.

[10] A fusee or fuzee is a fusil (a light flintlock musket commonly found in the North American Indian trade). "British-made ordnance and equipage are always marked with the broad arrow, which looks like an arrowhead. It is both proof mark and symbol of the British Ordnance Department" (Andrew Masich, personal communication, 2007).

To their women we gave some trinkets such as beads, rings, and pieces of blue and red cloth and flannel, figs, raisins, and biscuit, and to the men with the muskets we gave a few charges of powder and balls and large shot, also some plugs of tobacco and clay pipes, of which they thought much of. After fully satisfying ourselves with the apperence of these singular looking creatures, we mounted all at onced, which took these people all by surprise, and instantly forming into close ranks, took up our line of march, our guide taking the lead with some eighty of these Indians escorting us. When going a distance of a mile, they commenced to leave us in squads of three or four until we were again left to our own numbers.

We learned something by this visit from these people in their method of protecting their animal[s'] fore feet from the stones, rocks, and the enfermal prickley pear cacti. It was a very simple contrivance of a moccasin made of rawhide and formed when wet and green over an old hoof of the dead animal and this extending up the limb and simply tied around the fetlock. It is made sufficiently large to admit several thicknesses of the thick rawhide so as to make it easy to the foot or hoof of the beautiful mustang horses which all of them had, for they all had horses. I did not see a single mule with this party.

Our trail led us west and apparently leaving this beautiful valley. About five PM we approached a narrow pass through a mountain, some half mile through which we gradually decented into a small valley with a kind of knoll or mound. Nearby were some salt springs and excellent grama grass and bull rushes. Here we camped. Their was but one solitary tree near to the base of this mound, at the root of which my mess made our campfire. This knoll was at one time a crater, for all around its assent was covered with burnt lava in which was cradles or basins of fine, clear water, quite warm, and which was overflowing from the reservoir on the top, where was an cavity of some thirty feet in diameter with the water boiling up sufficiently hot to make tea or coffee. This mound was about two hundred feet in hight and covered some twenty acres of ground. The water at its base became cold and was excellent to drink. During the evening, our men, many of them enjoyed the luxuries of the bath in the natural lava tunnels formed on its walls.[11]

We were also visited by several Indians mounted on mules loaded with muscal dried and prepared in various ways, also dried meat and lumps of suet rolled in sand and leaves to keep it from melting by the heat of the climate. These Indians evidently had been used to trafic with the white man before, for they knew well the use of money. The Spanish quarter and pistareen [silver piece] they were quite familiar with, and when we offered them the United States half dollar and the quarters, they became quite enraptured at the brightness of its appearance, and the eagle took their fancy very much, and after biteing the pieces of coin with their beautiful white teeth, and gingling them on the rocks of lava laying at our feet, they then were convinced that they were pure placca. They were very anxious to dispose of anything they had, to get possession of the quarters. We had another slight rain with distant thunder and lightning just before night and which caused these Indian pests to vaumise the campo in a tremendous hurry. They are very superstitious and dread to be out during night and they fear thunder very much.

[11] Goulding is describing geothermal springs that poured from a tufa dome created over millennia by flowing mineral water. The springs have been tested at 130 degrees Fahrenheit and were well known by the prehistoric Mimbres people and later the Apaches and western explorers. Known since the late nineteenth century as Faywood Hot Springs, they are located near City of Rocks State Park, Grant County, New Mexico, and became a popular tourist resort (Bishoff 2001, 22–23).

13

New Mexico's Boot Heel

Reaching the Mimbres River, the gold rushers began to descend from the mountains and enter a vast, dry plain composed of volcanic and sedimentary rocks. Coming to Cow Springs, they were funneled into a road opened by Philip St. George Cooke and his Mormon Battalion in 1846. They passed future Separ, and moving south, drove along Brockman Hills and Coyote Hills, reaching Playas Lake. Once across the dry lake and Whitmire Pass, the men found themselves in verdant Animas Valley. Ahead was the greatest challenge of all: a rocky trail snaking over the Guadalupe Mountains and dropping into a splendid, tree-lined canyon watered by a free-flowing stream. They crossed into what is today Sonora, Mexico, and reached the deserted San Bernardino Rancho, where they had an opportunity to repeat the excitement of the buffalo hunt as they ran down wild bulls, a remnant of the ranch's cattle herd.

Sunday, June 24, this morning our men were all in very fine spirits as well as our animals, and I have no doubt but it proceeded from the beneficial effects from the drinking of this mineral water as runing from this hot spring. Yesterday and in fact for several days past, their was much ailing in the corps with a kind of dierea or griping pains, and this morning not a man complained. At some future day, no doubt, this same spring will rival anything of this kind in the United States and perhaps in the whole world. I have never in all my travels through Europe ever seen any thing to come up to it either in size or its pure water. Our guide pointed out to us a short cut across a dark looking sort of plain, "hornado" [jornada], he called it, about twelve miles in extent, which he said by crossing would save us some two days march than if we followed the usual trail as the one we are now on, and which led to a place or town in Sonora [Chihuahua] which he called Janos.

With much reluctance on the part of the men as well as was manafested by our mules at the leaving this camp, we at last commenced our line of march across this hornado. About 12 at noon we came up to some chalk hills at the base of a mountain, by which we travelled for some miles, when suddenly we turned towards the south, when opened to our view another barren plain of some twenty to thirty miles in width. Traversing directly across this black and dismal commons for about two miles, we came to a swampy hole or quagmire all surrounded with a coarse sort of grass and rushes and trampled all about its soft, muddy bottoms by the savage beasts from the adjoining mountains.

Here all at onced our guide, and who was now far ahead of us, dismounts and when we came up to him, he says, campo "De la Awa de Vacha" [Cow Springs].[1] It was now but 3 PM and we very reluctantly stoped to camp, as we had no other alternative, for our guide informed us that their was no other water for 15 leagues from here (45 miles). This is a singular camping place, but the grass and water is always the object for the traveller in these regeons. The name given to this place is well applied—"Cow Spring"—as the water obtained at this place, and which oozes up out of the earth in several places, has the taste as if it was impregnated with the manure of that animal. Some of the company dug fresh holes, thereby to get sweeter water,

[1] Cow Springs/Ojo de Vaca, is three miles east of the Luna county line, New Mexico, and has for centuries been a well-known watering hole midway along the trail between the Santa Rita copper mines at Silver City, and Janos, Chihuahua. The spring is currently surrounded by the buildings of a large working ranch and protected by a circle of rocks under a canopy of ancient cottonwood trees. There is no public access (Hackler 2005, 142–43). The Mormon Battalion under the leadership of Lt. Col. Philip St. George Cooke watered here in 1846, and by 1858, the springs had become a regular stop on the Butterfield Overland Stage.

and which we did, as regards its cleanliness, being pure from the mineral springs from which it sprung. But as for the taste, it was much improved in the flavour of the "Suty muty." It was so much so, that some of the stomachs were turned of the most delicate of our party. When the water was boiled, it was just as sweet as the best spring water, and this fact being discovered, all became satisfied.

Our guide, "Jeone Occuans," leaves us at this place, so the fifty dollars as promised him was now collected and given to him and we gave him some provisions.[2] So he left us, makeing tracks to the north. During the evening the same party of Mexican traders which we passed last, came up to this camp. Some ravens were shot and eaten by our men and this was the only hint of game we seen about this place. The night was a dreary one, much more so than any camp as yet we had met with. The savage and wild beasts came here to drink from the extensive ranges of mountains towering up all around us, some of them shooting their heads up into the clouds far above the blue sky. During the night, which was dark, the roar and yells of these beasts were continually echoing through the distant hills, some of these savage animals coming here to drink during the night, and one of them, more courageous than his companions, made bold to come between our guards, and he, not knowing the Yankee password, got shot, and his carcas laid there in the morning in the shape of a black wolf.

Monday, June 25, the early part of the morning was spent in boiling water and cooling it preparatory to our journey over this barren and dismal looking hornado. Our officers and those appointed for the purpose had much dificulty and perplexity with those traders, endeavouring to get one of them to guide us to the camena highway from Chawawa [Chihuahua] to the Gila, and finally made an arrangement with one of them to go with us for 30 dollars. He said he would put us on the "Passa Grande" [Guadalupe Pass] in six

[2] Unfamiliar with the Spanish language, Goulding wrote words as he heard them. In Chapter 11, he refers to the guide as "John Olearous." As previously noted, Frémont reportedly employed the same guide to lead the way to California. His name is not among the guides listed in Frémont publications.

days.[3] At two o'clock we commenced our march over this awful desert covered all over with basalt and burnt clinkerd looking stones and copper ore. As we advanced into it, their seemed to be no kind of vegatable growth and inhabited only by the lizzard and which were of all sizes from as big as your little finger to as large as your forearm and of all colors in the rainbow.

We travelled without stopping till midnight, when it was so dark and we were so fagged out that we formed as close as possibly to each other, dismounted, unsaddled, and everyman holding on to his rains, we camped on the spot, and well our poor beasts knew the state of our camp, for the moment the saddles were off, down they laid as quiet as lambs and they seemed to revel in the stop as well as ourselves. We now gave each of our animals a scanty drink of our prepared water and which we carried in gourds, canteens, and gum elastic tanks, which were of overhawls [overalls] with boots attached and when filled would hold about six gallons of water and were the best things I have seen during the rout. Except with a cold bite and a drink of farena and water, we went to bed supperless.

"Near the dawn of the day,
Our mules began for to bray."

Tuesday, June 26, the morning was fine and the air refreshing, and all hands were soon in the saddles giveing to our animals the last of our Cow Spring water. We again proceeded on our march amidst views of the most extensive & ragged mountains bounding the entire horizon that man's eye could look upon. About six o'clock the soil began to indicate a better aspect, for we began to see some small patches of ground grass, then the short acasia, and now the low mezquit, and by eight o'clock we came near the base of the mountains when very extensive fields of the prickley cactus, then the muscal in great abundance. The stalks of the latter, some of them as high

[3] Goulding and company crossed the continental divide before following a track between Ben Moore and Bessie Rhoads mountains, Grant County, as they headed southwest toward Separ on modern Interstate 10. Emory named Ben Moore Mountain after a member of the First Dragoons who was killed at the Battle of San Pasqual in California in 1846. In 1856 it was renamed Soldiers' Farewell Hill.

as fifteen to twenty feet and many of them in full blossom with their splendid white lilly heads. One of the party discovered a hole of water in a rock close by us. This too was impregnated with this delightful odor of the cow, but nevertheless it was now drunk by all with the keenest relish, our animals browsing a short half hour on the grama grass.[4]

We again continued our march through this pass, which is about two miles through, when again presented to our view another terrible looking barren desert like the last, but our guide proceeding on ahead of us on his mule, so as a matter of coarse proceeded on after him. Some eating a biscuit and chewing some dried meat, and some smoking and talking various stories of our very interesting travels. When about eleven o'clock the appearance of a lake came in light and our decent became quite gradual, and the soil changed from the black basalt and burnt lava and stones to that of a green sod with very good grass. All this was very cheering and we became quiet flattered, antisipating a fine camp by the lake, and to enjoy our good suppers again of meat, fish, and fowl.

The nearer we advanced towards this lake, the more thirsty we got and the further it appeared to be from us, and by one o'clock we finally came to its banks and found we had all been most cleverly deceived, for it was a compleat dry bed of what was onced a lake [Playas Lake].[5] That wonderfull and singular phenominon, the mirage, had again been displaying its beauties on the hard and sun cracked bed of this race coarse. Where we crossd it, it was about half

---

[4] The Knickerbockers went southwest across a dry plain to Brockman Hills before moving on to Coyote Hills, Grant County, where the old road, now used by local ranchers, follows the contours of the terrain. In 1849, travelers had no trouble negotiating the road, but when I made a reconnaissance in 1993, I found many locked gates and was unable to follow the trail in one continuous segment, despite obtaining permission to be on the land. The travelers found water in various pools along the way, one being Vista Tanks, which is marked on Emory's map as having water for fifty animals.

[5] A splendid view greets a modern traveler reaching the summit of the Coyote Hills. Looking to the east, one sees the Little Hatchett (6,639 feet) and Big Hatchett (8,441 feet) mountains, and to the south and west, Animas Mountain at 8,532 feet. On the flats of the Chihuahuan Desert is a silver streak, which, as one moves closer, becomes a shimmering lake, wet or dry depending on the rainfall. This is Playas Lake, an irregular and elongated lake bed. It is one of a number of bolsons, "large purses," or inland basins with no drainage to the sea (Jaeger 1967, 33).

a mile wide and upwards of ten miles in length. As we advanced, the deceptive water apperance would retreat and again advance in our rear, giveing the apperance of the water about the feet of our animals. Of those in the rear or in front at a distance of a hundred yards, also to our right and left, it so appeared, reminding us of the beautiful passages of Scripture where the Isrilates crossed the Red Sea, the waters of which rolled up before them as they advanced on its surface.

The mirage in this instance was intirely different from what we had seen before, being confined to the surface. I supposed was caused by the serene and condenced hot atmosphere, as not a breath of wind or air was their apparent, and the sky a perfect sheet of lovely blue without a solitary speck or cloud to mar its quilt of heaven. When we had seen this singular element before, the air was riffled by wind and clouds, hence the deception in looming up apperances of ships, sloops, and men rideing on horses as if walking on stilts. The bottom of this dryed lake was as hard as marble and not a particle of sand was on is surface. It was all full of fine sun cracks and as our animals walked on it, those which had on shoes made a noise as if walking on tiles or marble slabs.[6]

On arriving on the west side, their was numerous banks of white sands and small pebbles and varieties of small broken shells. These sand banks had the apperance of been at times drifted by the winds. Beyond them again was quagmires of bul-rushes and all varieties of such weeds as general grow about the banks of ponds and lakes. In these we found some water holes but mostly so salt that we could not drink of it. After some considerable searching we discovred a hole full of black beetles swimming in sweet water, which we streined through a silk handkerchief and by this means we all got a drink.

[6] Goulding's travel companion David Jordan had a similar experience that day: "as we entered the bed of the lake we could see, about 150 or 200 yds, on either hand what appeared to be a beautiful sheet of clear water, but it was like the ends of a rainbow, you could get no nearer to it. Several of the men thought it was water & started at full speed to water their animals—rode several miles & come back without having got any nearer than when they started" (June 26, 1849). John Russell Bartlett (1854, 1:218), while midway across the lake, noted the sudden appearance of a mirage that led him to believe he was actually rolling across a body of water. David Brainard rode over "a beautiful hard, polished surface, equal to the finest cement" on September 9. This editor has driven on the lake bed leaving nary a trace.

Our guide said about two miles up by this enchanted lake he had, on one occasion, found good water, so we continued on tramping through these sand hills, twisting and winding around them in all directions until we made our direction now compleatly south and the lake bed became several miles longer. In fact we never assertained its correct size or extent.

To the north of us on the hills we discovered wild cattle for the first time since we left New Mexico.[7] Our guide informed us we would soon come in regens where their were any quantity. At last we heard the crack of a rifle as a signal from the advance party, denoting the good news of our camp. We soon spurred up our nags to the place. Here was indeed any number of water holes apperently even with the surface with excellent grass on the hills all about.[8] One of my mules, more thirsty than the rest, plunged right into one of these wells of water, and unfortunately for my mess, was the very mule which had our panyards of biscuit and our blankets and bedding on the top. With a good deal of dificulty we succeeded in getting the develish thing out almost drownded. Instantly we spread all the buffaloes [robes] and clothes we had and on them placed our biscuit to dry, changing with several messes in the company for dry bread or flour so as to consume as much as possible of the wet bread during this camp.

During the evening, several Indians visited us from the adjoining hills, some on foot and some mounted, but they were far inferior looking than any that we had seen before.[9] Two of them spoke a little bad Spanish. One of them handed me a piece of paper on which was written: "These Indians are Carribelles and have treated us

[7] The "wild cattle" had wandered from San Bernardino Rancho, Sonora, on the other side of the Guadalupe Mountains, which the travelers were about to cross.

[8] The travelers found a number of water holes as they moved along the shore of the dry lake. William Hunter of the Callaway County (Missouri) Pioneers noticed a spring with an outlet raised above ground level. "The matter which it voided," he said, "was of the consistency of honey, a greyish blue color. . . . The earth around for a circumference of 35 or 40 feet rocked violently up and down, on jumping on it near the orifice" (1992, 129). Local residents in 1992 did not recall geothermals near Playas Lake but said that there were many in the area and that they come and go.

[9] These American Indians belonged to the southern band of the Chiricahua Apaches, whose territory is mainly in northern Mexico, and they may have come from the Sierra Caballero, a range northwest of Lago de Guzmán in Chihuahua (Opler 1983, 402–403).

friendly. (Signed.) Nolen and Brown, January 1849." They grinned like a badger in a trap when I handed them the "passa," as they called the paper, saying that it was "muncho a waino americano, caballero vaumis a la grande cameno." By signs and bad Spanish we made to understand from them that they had been watching our movements all the afternoon. They had been in ambush laying in the grass. Their lodges are in the hills to the southeast of this about three miles, and seeing us looking for water, they came down to assist us.

They told us that their fathers informed them that these numerous water holes which they say are now all along its south banks drank up all the waters of this lake on account of the wickedness of the Montezumens, but that in a few more years or moons, it would all go back again. These Indians had balls of fat rolled in sand and leaves and muscal bread, the same as the Apaches had a few camps back, and which we bought of them for shirts, pieces of cloth, and some quarters. Near dark these Indians all left us and after dark they set fire to the grass on several of the hills, which made a magnificent and grand sight.

During the night, this singular phenomina, the mirage, made its apperance as grand as in the day. I was on guard during midnight, and there was all the natural appearances of a real lake, even the rustling of the flags and bul-rushes, the ruffling of the waves, as if the water ebed and flowed. The noise of a wind blowing through the cane brake, and at the same time, their was not a breath of air or wind to be felt, but as still as death, except now and then the bellowing of a wild bull some distance off. There we stood, six of us on guard duty, to witness one of the most singular and grandest deceptions that man ever witnesed. It made me think more of the great works of our wonderful Creator than I ever did before and I have no doubt it had with the whole company.

Wednesday, June 27, this morning it was scarcely day light when our camp was all surrounded with the Indians of all ages and sizes from the old elephant-skinned looking woman with her teats like two old Dutch bolongne sausages, to the little cribbed up popoos, some on good horses; and on some horses you would see them four and even half a dozzen small boys and girls, all [illegible] like so many saddle trees hanging on a fence, all grinning like chimney sweeps eating ginger bread. The signs and gestures and the grunting—growling noises in discoursing with one—another was very amusing to all of us, several of their woman riding on poor old jaded horses a "La fashion de La Duches de Berri," with the body of the horse all covered with bunches of dried meat, muscal, and pieces of fat and lumps of suet enough to supply a brigaide of the regular army. They had some paste or thick molasses, the extract of the mezquit beans, and the acorn mixed up with it. These pot shaped looking creatures was the most odd looking sight of the Indian race we had met with since we came into the rocky mountains.

Several exchanges were made by our men for their fresh ones, giveing in boot as a numeration to induce them to swap, some half blankets, buffalo robes, pieces of cloth, and paint, of which they appeared to have a great desire for, particularly the red and green. They were very anxious to have us swap our pistols and rifles for their animals, but that was peremptorily refused. Our people did not purchase their vegetable sort of stuff with as much spirit as they had anticipated we should. Consequently, great murmering and grumbling was caused amongst them. And one of their old ruff looking fellows and who manafested all the time rather an unfriendly feeling towards us, and he got into the center of their crowd and went on jabbering at a great rate. Our guide told us that he understood from one of the chaps who had the passa, as they termed it, this was their old warrior chief advisor, and was telling them we were "Mexicanoes" and we were on our way to the Sonora ranchiaros to assist the people their in war against the "Montezumas," of which their ancestors these Indians boasts of decending from. He was explaining to them as the reason why we would not let them have any of our arms, of which we had so many of, and which was a fact, for every man of us was well armed. Seeing their women and children stealthily leaving our camp gave us warning that their intentions were not very flatering. One of their women laid down an infant about two months old by my saddle, and which was laced on a kind of wicker basket frame in the shape of [a] kite. Their features were flat and much more negro-like than those we had seen before.

They are a deceitful-looking set of Carobello Apachees and altho they smirkily will swear eternal friendship, when at the same moment they have a mental reservation to rob the first American or Mexican they would come across unprotected. The greater part of these fellows were armed with the lance and bow. They were small legged and short in stature, big bellied, and broad shouldered. At nine o'clock, all our packs and kits being ready and securly saddled, we instantly formed squadron into line. This had the desired effect. It made these cowardly, contemptable looking beings stare and tremble, and one of the men fired off his six shooter into the air close by one of these fellows, and he looked with perfect astonishment seeing the six blazing reports all coming out of one barrel at one time. They all gave a yell of amazement, and we quietly proceeded on our journey, not one of these fellows following us one single inch.

Our guide led us on down the south side of this dry lake with the mirage, as yesterday, displaying all her magic graces of deception before us to close our eyes, the rolling sand hill still by its banks in mighty heaps. After two miles in the sands, our guide leding us west over rolling hills and valleys for about ten miles, when we came to the base of the mountain, travelling through a pass some five miles long and three hundred yards wide with their tops upwards of four thousand feet high on each side. We opened on another extensive open plain some 20 miles in dimension with extensive range of mountains all around it.

To the far west of us we could see a green range of some bottoms which denoted to us of their being a river. Our travlling was over some good land with all varieties of cactus—century plants, some of them in blossom, and at times, the bayonet cactus, some so thick and close it was difficult to pass. We travelled for nearly twenty miles before reaching these green bottoms, when we were sadley disappointed, the river being entirely dried up. Parties were sent out to explore the diverse tributaries of this river bed for water. Our guide, also seeing signs of Indians on the mountains to the south of us, had gone over to them, our main body with the packed mules starting up the bed of the sand river, when we heard the crack of a rifle which was the signal that water was found, so that by 4 o'clock at the base of a large mountain we camped near some holes of water fast a drying up in the bed of this extensive flooded river at certain times. Our guide, with a few of the Apache Indians, came and as usual supplied us with fat, muzcal &c. Some gan[n]et was seen, and I shot a mess of quails & doves which were very plenty near our camp. I took a drawing of the camp with the valley of the river bed & mountain.[10]

Thursday, June 28, we were again surrounded with Indians this morning, endeavouring to trade, but we were near pretty well supplied with all we wanted of them. One of them wanted to sell us a boy, a Mexican captive, but was declined. They wanted 100 dollars for him, or 2 mules. At 7 o'clock, we took up our march over this level plain covered with the American aloe or century plant in all its variety and thousands of the different species of lizards running before us as we advanced. After passing some 1/2 mile from the river bed, this species of plant ceased, when that of the acasia & mezquit took its place and the ground became more barren. During the afternoon, we passed several extensive dog towns,[11] where we again struck a river bed, which we followed to the foot of the mountain, where we found water and camped at 4 o'clock. Seen a few black tailed deer & some hairs and antelopes.

Friday, June 29, our guide informed us he knew a shorter way through the mountains but the "camena" was rather ruff and rockey for our animals, but if we wished, he would put us on the great Chiwawa camena before 3 o'clock if we would follow him. But we could not reach it till next day by making the circuit of the mountain, so a

[10] (Sketch missing.) The gold rushers had reached the southern extremity of the Animas Mountains, which are connected to the Sierra Madre in Mexico. They were about to cross into the Animas Valley by way of Whitmire Pass, with the Peloncillo range in the distant west. Animas Creek indeed disappears into the sand at intervals. This area is one of the most ecologically diverse in the United States and is currently under the protection of the 500-square-mile Gray Ranch through the Animas Foundation. The foundation is dedicated to protecting the natural assets of the ranch while maintaining the cultural and economic heritage of the area (Sayre 2005, 8).

[11] Prairie dog towns were eliminated there many years ago.

voice of the company being taken on the subject, we concluded to follow our guide over the mountain, good or bad, for we were now pretty well tired out of these valleys, jornadas & mountain passes. At 8 o'clock we saddled, and takeing a good supply of water, we commenced the assent [which was] very rapid, the hills steep and the footing insecure, but the scenery grand and romantic.[12] We had to walk and lead our animals over 5 miles, the travelling being so steep & rockey and in some places nearly perpendicular. We would have to decend sometimes into deep dykes or reveins and then climb up these spires almost perpendicular, which gave us an opportunity of seeing what a mule could do and how well they are calculated for travelling through such a country.

A great variety of new plants were seen; at one view, also the cacti and the small leaf acacia and a species of sedge. In places we would meet with open spaces of bare gravel. Great varieties of beautiful insects & bugs runing over the rocks & ground, of the most brilliant colours. A huge black bear, looking down from a ragged looking clift far above us, yet was looked at with rather an unfavorable opinion of his good feeling to us. In one place I met with an extensive bed of the turks' head cactus with the fruit on them ripe. Sticking a fork in the berry, which is the size of a large straberry, and with a small knife cutting off the prickley outer rind, the inside is delicious and has the flavour of the garden straberry at the north.

We now began to descend gradually, through, as it appears like, one ancient orchard of the stunted live oak and some few ceders, when at 2 o'clock we met with the great valley of Chihuahua Pass. Here was wagon tracks, enough to satisfy us we were now on the regular rout for California. We discharged our guide and paid him 30 dollars and off he went in a trot in another direction from the way we came. When after resting a short time, we proceeded on west

---

[12] The men negotiated a pass in the Guadalupe Mountains (6,450 feet) in the Peloncillo Range four miles east of the Arizona border with New Mexico and just inside the international boundary. It was here that Lt. Col. Philip St. George Cooke and his Mormon Battalion pulled and pushed wagons over the hills in 1846 to become the first group to open a wagon road to the Pacific. Goulding has done a fine job of describing the difficulty. This editor had the pleasure of traveling there and photographing the terrain on horseback in 1983 and found it as the travelers described.

FIGURE 9. View of Animas Creek, Animas Valley, Hidalgo County, New Mexico, 1985. The San Luis Mountains appear far to the south at the international boundary. *Photo by Patricia A. Etter.*

FIGURE 10. Modern view of capped rock, Guadalupe Canyon, Hidalgo County, New Mexico, 1983. *Photo by Patricia A. Etter.*

through this extensive valley. Through it was a small river bed makeing its twistings or serpentine turns in all directions through a narrow forest of all kind of heavy grown timber such as oak, ash sycamore, hickory walnut, prickly ash, and the everlasting cottonwood and great varieties of creaping under brush and flowers. Some huge, gigantic rocks presented to our view as we passed on. Under one of them, right in the road, was a very large cave sufficiently large to hold 10 or 12 men directly in the solid rock. The trees were cut or marked with the names of several hundred who had passed this rout, several of which were Americans, and recently cut as well, a great many Masonic emblems & Odd Fellows, some of them very well executed on the huge cottonwood trunks. Many small birds and wood guests flushed up before us, and some few turkies were shot by the party.[13]

After travelling & crossing several times through the sands of this river bed for some 6 miles west, our road led us up on the plate land, where we met with the old fashioned, dreary plains again, and this looked more so than any that we had yet seen, for it had recently been burned, and the splendid bayonet cactis and century plant now looked awfull, being partly burnt. An extensive, green looking valley appearing to our view, which encouraged us, and at 5½ o'clock we came up to it and camped in grass up to our horses knees and some excellent spring water in a stream all around our camp.

Saturday, June 30, we saddled up at 7 o'clock and proceeded on our march. Not far from our last camp, on riseing a hill, a fine open plain came to our view with the apperance of a deserted rancheria all in ruins. About 3 miles of travel over some as fine arrable land as could be, we came up to this onced fine village. The valley by apperance was onced under cultivation. A small pond of good water and alive with small fish watered the whole place and got its supply from springs nearby the ranches. There must have been upwards of [illegible] acres of land about this place. From the remains of the quantity of ox hornes, head & bones scattered about the old camp fires, their must be cattle in great numbers in the vicinity of this place. I took a sketch of the ruins of this place which will better describe it than I can other wise.[14]

In my walk about the old center court, and which I supposed was

---

[13] The gold seekers funneled into Guadalupe Canyon and moved along a rocky stream bed. It is indeed a wonderland, as Goulding described it, but Benjamin Stevens, a Baptist minister from Hannibal, Missouri, became downright poetic: "The hand of Omnipotence has scattered here and there in wild profusion some of the most fantastic and sublime scenery ever beheld. Here are caverns, precipices, deep ravines, flowing fountains springing from the solid rock, two hundred feet high and gurgling streams with fragrant flowers and shrubbery all combined make it appear almost the enchantment ground" (September 14, 1849).

[14] (Sketch missing.) In 1822 the Mexican government granted 73,340 acres, known as the San Bernardino Rancho, Sonora, to Ignacio Pérez, who was forced to abandon the site fifteen years later because of continued Apache raids. The bulls, now wild, were descendants of his early herd. H. M. T. Powell (1931, 125–26) found the ruin of a large establishment, originally built in a quadrangle enclosing some three acres. Along the remains of adobe walls were the main building and offices, and on the north, houses or rooms extended the length of the walls. Long bastions occupied both the north and southeast corners.

their chappels, I seen several human skulls and bones. Therefore came to the conclusion that the inhabitants of the place must have been murdered and all communication cut off from them by the treacherous Indians. From the apperance it had not been inhabited in many years. An imense flock of black birds hovered about the place and by a remark made by one of our men, an Irish Catholic, that they were the souls of the ancient inhabitants of this place. If so, their must have been upwards of 5 or 6 thousand.

Our trail led directly through the place, when we struck into a plain of scrubby chaperal, and at 11 o'clock we made the range of mountains, grand & raggetty in apperance. Here we met a pass; about 2 or 3 miles winding thrugh it brought us out with an open prairie covered with the everlasting prickly chaperal with a kind of grama grass amongst it. Here our road was frequently crossed by the tracks of cattle, numerous herds now to be seen in all directions grazing on the Indian ruins. A party was now selected from the corps and sent in ahead to hunt, and provide some fresh meat for our next camps. Our march was hard with us today, as we must make the next range of mountains before we can camp. A heavy rain during the afternoon rather impeaded our progress. We made the mountain range about 6 o'clock, where we camped by pools of rain water and bad grass, our poor jaded animals pretty well tired out.

During the afternoon on our line of march one of the company, a Mr. Williams, found a mule, saddle with his bridle on, mouthed but the rains over his head, quietly grazing amongst the bushes, and in searching all about, could find no tracks whatever of the rider, neither dead or alive. Some pieces of fresh beef, apparently 3 or 4 days old, was hanging on the pommel of the saddle. Search was made in all directions and fires made conspicuously during the night, but found no owner, but drew the wild bulls bellowing around us all night. Our hunting party had a young bull, the steaks of which we enjoyed very much.[15]

[15] Almost every emigrant tried to shoot a wild bull for dinner. One had an ox for dinner instead, since he missed the bull and killed his own animal (Ricks, August 3, 1849). This could have been a good site to hide a murder in any year, as the ranch had been abandoned for so long. By the twenty-first century, the old hacienda had settled to a mound of adobe.

14

Sonoran Desert Adventures

The overlanders had been in the Mexican state of Sonora since leaving the San Bernardino Rancho. In 1849, Arizona's land south of the Gila River belonged to Sonora; it became part of the United States with the Gadsden Purchase in 1854. Goulding and his comrades crossed the path of Isaac Duval and his hotheaded crew, who stirred up trouble in the village of Santa Cruz. After leaving the village, the Goulding group traveled north along the Santa Cruz River through Tubac, the missions of Tumacacori and San Xavier del Bac, and the presidio of Tucson. They were now crossing the Arizona Sonoran Desert, where July temperatures can reach well over one hundred degrees, water is scarce, and the native cacti provide little shade. Moving toward the Pima villages across some ninety miles of scorching, rock-strewn terrain took its toll on both men and animals.

Sunday, July 1, the heavy rain during the night drenched several of our packs, but the sun soon dried up everything and about 7 o'clock we commenced our journey.[1] The road was very good all day, traversing through very high mountains on our right & left, some times varying from 2 to 10 miles from us. About 3 o'clock, a heavy rain came up again. Our gum elastic capes & caps came into use again. We seen a great many antelope during the day but no Indians. At 5 o'clock we met a fine camping place and stoped for the night in

[1] Leaving the rancho, the Knickerbockers headed west to Blackwater Creek (Agua Prieta), Sonora, opposite modern Douglas, Cochise County, Arizona.

excellent grass and water. Our animals began to show the effects of the journey. Most of the country which we passed today is as fine arable land as I have ever seen and capable of sustaining a large population, even to the tops of the hills and mountains, and covered with foliage and grass. The present camp is in a valley of fine meadowland with excellent salt grass, a fine pond of water alive with fish, and any quantity of black birds. During the night a heavy dew fell, which is the first time since [we] left Chotous [Chouteau's] plain [that] we experienced any dew during the night.

Monday, July 2, we saddled up and continued our march at 7 o'clock. At 12 o'clock we came to a narrow stream of running water in a bog of considerable extent. In crossing the marsh we discovered a deserted rancheria apparently in ruins, also to the right of our road, but we did not go to it, being too far out of our way. At 1 o'clock we came to the beutiful little stream called San Pedro, alive with trout. The water was so clear and pure, the fish looked like birds flying about in it. We crossed it and about 1-½ miles up the river by a rocky mountain we camped. All the lines & fish tackles in the company was now fetched into use and some fine mess of trout was now served up on our tin plates in preference of anything else. In some small gullies close by the river, several mud turtles were taken by the hook & line and made an excellent stew. The howling of the wolfs was very alarming during the night and denoted to us we had fairly got out of the great ranges of the rocky mountains, as the wolfs [were] seldom heard in the mountains.

Tuesday, July 3, the howling of the wolfs wakened us up bright and early this morning, and saddled up and proceeding on our journey, following the waggon road for some 4 miles, to our left, south of the road, we discovered an abandoned rancheria on a hill. I viewed it with my glass but it was all in ruins. I took a sketch of it from the saddle. Again we struck the river San Pedro and followed it south for about a mile. Close by the river at this place is an abandoned village or extensive rancheria, but all in ruins. See sketch.[2] We

[2] The deserted ranch was probably on the 1821 San Pedro, Sonora, grant belonging to Rafael Elías Gonzales (Officer 1987, 357n55). Like others in the area, the ranch was abandoned due to Apache attacks. (Sketch missing.)

met with several such places during the day all allong this valley and was [illegible] in a fine state of cultivation. At 11 o'clock we stoped to let our animals have a bite of the beutiful grass & clover [that] was in this valley. Several huge mountainous-looking rocks like plum pudding were met in our route during the forenoon, and the eco by these rocks was very amusing to us.

The mountains in the front of us were very high. In aproaching near to the port of them we discovered that the waggons had counter marched and we did not observe where they had turned off. So, on reconoitering a little we found they had turned off about a mile back of this mountain and made another rout to circle the mountain.[3] During the afternoon we seen several deer & antelope. Struck into another splendid valley with good grass. On rising over a hill we discovered a number of wild cattle grazing over the hills beyond the next valley. On making the latter valley & finding plenty of good water & grass, we camped, and a party was soon out after the wild cattle. Not long after, we heard several cracks of the rifle and soon a messenger [came] in for five mules to be sent out to fetch in 4 fine oxen, which the hunters were now dressing. Soon, the camp wood being plenty, all hands set to work making [illegible] and preparing the beef by cutting it up into strips and drying it in these [illegible] with a continual fire underneath. Although the turkies were so plenty running about our camp, we could not see anything but fresh beef.

The bellowing of the wild bulls and the howling of the wolf was the joy bells to this glorious Wednesday, July 4. All hands were up bright and early, and by a vote of the company, it was resolved to spend the Glorious 4th of July at this camp. The day was spent in the barbecuing of beef. One of the hunters fetched in a fine antelope which we enjoyed for dinner. Several wild horses were also seen during the day as well as cattle. During the evening we had a heavy thunder storm.

Thursday, July 5, we packed up and took up our march at 7 o'clock

[3] Back in 1846, Philip St. George Cooke, with the Army of the West and leading the Mormon Battalion, had turned north at the San Pedro River, then marched west to Tucson. Few forty-niners, if any, took that route in 1849. Instead, they all stayed on a sort of trail to the Sonoran village of Santa Cruz. Goulding and friends became lost as they tried to negotiate the rugged and circuitous mountain path but eventually reached Santa Cruz.

this morning. We followed through this beautiful valley for about 8 miles, flushing up before us any quantity of game of all sorts as well as horses, cattle, and antelope. Then we struck on table lands or [illegible] of a poor kind of redish colored soil, our road making a semi circle of about 4 miles, when we struck a dry river bed apparently springing from the high range of mountains to the north of us. This we followed some miles when we gradually assended the plate lands again, when about 3 or 4 miles off ahead of us we discovered several horses & mules.

In looking again with my glass, I discovered objects moving amongst them like men, and nearing them, discovered them to be a body in camp in the valley. On coming up with them, we found them to be a company of Texans commanded by Capt. Duval and were on their way to California. [They] had been here some two days recruiting their animals on this San Pedro River. About 3 miles south from this camp [is] the little village of Santa Cruz containing about 500 Mexicans from whom we got a supply of flour at $2 the allemo (about 2 quarts).[4] They informed us that the mountain Indians had robbed these people some few days since of their wheat and several mules & horses and some few head of cattle, which they drove off before their eyes in open day. They [Duval and company][5] made a great time with several of our party to go against the Indians

[4] The small village of Santa Cruz, Sonora, in a curve of the Santa Cruz River, was under constant threat of Apache attacks. Samuel P. Birt of the La Grange Company arrived on August 3 and reported that seventeen Apaches had dashed through town "killing three men and one woman & carried off 2 boys besides driving off nearly all their horses & gentle cattle" (1967, 197).

[5] Isaac H. Duval, a no-nonsense leader, had already done battle with a number of Apaches in both Chihuahua and Sonora. He again stirred up trouble in Santa Cruz, and on July 5, 1849, David Jordan recorded that the "Texians were real desperattoes. They steal and plunder whenever they get a chance." Duval himself admitted that he had battled with the "hostiles" (Apaches) near Santa Cruz and ordered his men to fight them. This resulted in three badly wounded forty-niners, four dead Apaches, and a number of severely wounded animals. "The men dragged the dead hostiles down the trail and left them there," Duval wrote (1987, 96–98). The Duval Company brought the cattle stolen by the Apaches back to Santa Cruz, where the alcalde wanted them driven into the public corral. "By war we won these cattle, by war we will keep them," Duval reportedly said. "Instead of driving them into the public corral we will drive them down our red throats!" The following day, they did slaughter some animals and distributed meat to the Santa Cruzians before tossing the entrails into the alcalde's yard (Harris 1960, 74–75). Fortunately, later travelers were better behaved and found the residents friendly and helpful.

and that they would give us 100 dollars for each Indian head or scalp we would bring them in, and 500 for each of their chiefs.[6]

Duval's company having assertained from the Mexicans that we could pass through the mountains near our camp and which would shorten our road some 20 miles as the regular road went round by Santa Cruz and then down the other side of the mountain now close to our present camp. All parties being ready at 3 o'clock, we again proceeded on our march, following the river for 3/4 of a mile, where our guide led us in a very narrow trail gradually assending into the mountains, when soon the banks in each side of us became gullied and almost impassable arroyos or holes. We travelled in this way for several hours, [in] some places having to take off the packs from the mules and lifting the plunder over, and such incessant toil to the men and misery to our best animals we never before experienced. Copper ore and lead seemed to be in great abundance, several pieces of which was picked up by the men.[7]

About eleven PM we gained the [Santa Cruz] valley on the other side of the mountain when we dry camped. Some did not reach camp at all but stoped in the mountain all night. The whole rout through was a succession of steep ascents and descents paved with sharp, angular fragments of rocks and metalic looking clinkerds [illegible] with copper ore oosing out of the fisures or cracks, and the rattling of the mules shoes against the rocks, the high black peaks, and the deep dark ravines, and the dreadful oaths and language of the Texas Rangers all favored the idea that we were now treading on the river of the infernal regions below. Several animals gave out. One of my mules, packs and all, fell headlong down a precipice, but to my surprise, got up and made a circuit rout, and headed us off on

[6] The Apaches had become such a threat that the Mexican governments in Chihuahua, Sonora, and Durango declared all-out war against the Indians and offered a bounty of $150 for the capture of each Apache woman and child, $250 for a warrior, and $200 for the scalp of a dead warrior (R. Smith 1964, 17). As a result, a number of emigrants took time out to go into the scalp-hunting business.

[7] One of the nicknames for Arizona is the Copper State. Nearly half the world's copper is produced within 175 miles of Tucson, in the area where Arizona, New Mexico, and Sonora meet (Walker and Bufkin 1979, 50).

the direct rout. Mr. Wm. Ford, one of my men, was thrown from his mule and had his carbine broke in two by the lock and was slightly injured himself. Our camp was very much scattered.

With a supper of some penola and water, I soon fell asleep and slept until three o'clock in the morning of Friday, July 6, when we quietly hitched up and proceeded for the river, which was only two miles from us. Now we all stoped to camp. The river was alive with a small black trout, which we soon had numbers of them in the pans frying for breakfast. All the rear of the company being up and all hands being refreshed, at 1 o'clock we again proceeded on our march through the valley, when about 5 miles on our rout we came to a deserted ranch or casa. It had the appearance of defence or barracks for soldiers, it having port holes flaring from the inside to point the mussels of their guns. It was two story high and built of adobes and sufficiently large to contain 200 men. A well of water full of bull frogs in the center of the inner court is all that remained of the former occupants. 3 miles further on we met with another casa of small dimentions but similarly constructed. This valley had the appearance of having been under cultivation at some time as their were small drains or ditches which led from the river apparently intended to irrigate the land.[8]

After traveling some 25 or 30 miles we came in view of a splendid looking hicienta [Tumacacori Mission], which took us all by surprise.[9] The remains of a portion of the fences were still standing amongst the wildflowers and grass. Some Indian lodges also were

[8] The Knickerbockers had entered the Santa Cruz Valley, where the river's course was revealed by the cottonwood trees lining its shores. The Santa Rita Mountains formed a backdrop to the east. The men noted deserted cattle ranches as they moved up the river: San Lazaro, Santa Barbara, San Luis, and Buenavista, the latter described by David Brainard on October 11, 1849. This site, he wrote, contained the remains of a mill for grinding corn or wheat, and many large vats and other machinery, suggesting that the proprietors were smelting precious metals. It appeared to have been heavily fortified.

[9] Jesuit friar Eusebio Francisco Kino celebrated mass for Tohono O'odham residents in Tumacacori in 1691 and built a church there in 1757. The Franciscan order took over in 1767 and with the help of the Tohono O'odham residents constructed the present Mission San José de Tumacacori. Except for the bell tower, the church was completed by 1822 and abandoned during the harsh winter of 1848, not long before Goulding and his companions arrived.

still in ruins. Here we camped in as fine grass as I ever seen. After partaking of some refreshment, I went down to this deserted hicienta. I took a drawing of it in pencil with the outlines of the raggetty looking mountains imediately on the back of it.[10] My position was in the bathing place in the outer court yard, and which was onced a garden. After taking the drawing, I walked all through it. The belfrey is built of brick. The top of it is much fallen off. It had 5 places for bells, 3 of which were now hung in it, which our boys amused our camp by ringing them for some time. Their [are] 2 other large bells below, not mounted, apparently to have fallen down. The interior of the chapels was onced splendidly painted and ornamented in stuco. Some remains of the furniture such as chairs, tables, forms, stools, images of saints, candle sticks & crosses are scattered all over the place. The onced beutiful white plastered walls are defaced wih the names & initials of the various passers by with charcoal or cut with a knife. The marble slabs of the altar are broken and fragments of them scattered about. The bones of the dead, a laying about in corners of the church so that we came to the conclusion that the inhabitants must have been murdered by the savage and left the place desolate. The swallow, batts, and the night hawks are the only inmates now.

In walking over this place, I found the principle entrance was to the chapel is from the south side, B, which is a large plaza surrounded with the ruins of many small adobe casas. Onced connected togther, in rear west, C, is also a plaza with a row of adobe casas apperently

[10] Sketch missing. Goulding's description is one of the best. The Indian "lodges" are to the south and west of the church, and have melted to a mound of adobe. The convento east of the church has seen a similar fate. At one time, these housed various activities that supported the mission, such as ironwork, carpentry, and weaving. The "river running through it" was the acequia, or irrigation ditch, that led from the Santa Cruz River a mile upstream. To the east of this was the garden and orchard where grew quince and other fruit trees. The "raggetty looking mountains" are the Santa Ritas, twenty miles distant. According to resources manager and archaeologist Jeremy M. Moss of the National Park Service, burials were found beneath the church floor, and the bones Goulding saw could have been human remains disturbed by treasure hunters or rodents (personal communication, 2008). By the time Charles Edward Pancoast arrived in October, the church had been tidied some and had caretakers he called "Indian Prophets." He also wrote about the "well-preserved Spanish Bible" left open on its pedestal, which they would not let him touch (1930, 235).

used as a fort. They having port holes in the rear of them on the right, D, is also a number of similar small casas. In the front, and by the arches, E, is a yard, 40 foot wide and 200 long. In through any of these arches leads you to the court yard of the chapel. There is a large plaza in the front, and was onced surround[ed] by a mud wall of some 6 [acres?] of ground in which one still [finds] the bathing places of the priests. In one portion of it are still a number of quintz trees and [they] will have a large quantity of fruit, and with a few plum trees [and] peach trees is all that remains of once a fine garden. The enclosure of this place is very extensive, upwards of 2,000 acres of land at least, and already of an excellent quality with a small Santa Croix River running through it. The doors no. 1, 2, 3 are white. No. 3 is much destroyed. At sunset, I returned to my camp and on my way shot 3 fine partrages & we had a slight sprinkling of rain during the night.

Saturday, July 7, at 7 o'clock we proceeded on our march, passing some deserted casas and numerous fenced in lands, with now and then the wild Indian lodge showing us plainly that the savage had left this place desolate. At 10 o'clock we came to a village all in ruins. In the chapel their was still a solitary bed remaining. A great number of fruit trees, particularly peaches, was in the different gardens about this place. About a mile from this place we raised again from this valley and our road led us on the dreary desert and mesquit. Again the pillow & beehive [barrel] cactus made its apperance. See drawing of the last one I seen, which will better describe them.[11] As we advanced in this desert, the cactus became very numerous, as also the Cereus giganteus, a huge vegetable tree from 20 to 40 feet height, of 2, 3 & 4 massive arms projecting from the main trunk and all in prickly rows from the bottom to the top.[12] The day was excessively warm, and the desert sandy, and the day's march very fatiguing, it being 9 o'clock at night before we reached water. After partaking of some supper I soon enjoyed a good night's rest.

---

[11] Sketch missing.

[12] *Carnegia gigantea* (formerly *Cereus giganteus*), or saguaro, is a major feature of the Arizona Sonoran Desert; virtually every emigrant described its grandeur. Its fruits provided food, and when fermented, they became a sweet liquor for the desert dwellers. The wooden stalks from a fallen giant were used for building houses and fences. The Gila woodpecker pecks out its own nest hole in the huge plant.

Sunday, July 8, several of the company not getting up to camp last night, it was concluded to remain here for the day, being in the neighbourhood of a pueblo of Indians, as well also of a small Mexican village, and several messes with waggons were here in camp on their way also to California. Some of them had come through Mexico and some by the way of Texas. During the day I visited the Mexican village and compared it to the drawing of the "onced Indian abbey" or chapel, but now going much to decay. Here we got abundance of poultry, tortillas & milk & eggs. Here I assertained the name of the place we left yesterday to be "Toboka" [Tubac].[13] The Apaches, they told us, destroyed the place and robbed the inhabitants of all their produce and cattle and killed any that molested them. The same river, Santa Croix, waters this place, and during the evening I caught a fine mess of trout and shot a hair which weighed 9-½ lbs. a few yards from camp. Several of the Pueblo Indians, which are a quite inoffencive kind of people, fetched abundance of flour, farina, and penola unto us so we laid up a good supply. For a shirt, they would give about 6 to 8 quarts of flour. We spent the evening very socially, visiting one another and talking of our different travels.

Monday, July 9, I visited the village again this morning, and taking my seat on the top of a small casa in front of the plaza, I finished my sketch of "Santabien" [San Xavier del Bac].[14] During the time I was making the sketch, several of the Pueblos made great time about

[13] The deserted village of Tubac was four miles down the road, where the Spanish established both a presidio and a mission called Saint Gertrude de Tubac in 1752, with 50 military men to protect 400 villagers. It was from this village in 1775–76 that Presidial Captain Juan Bautista de Anza and 240 immigrants covered 1,200 miles in about eighty days to settle the town of San Francisco, California. One can follow the emigrants on a 4½-mile segment of the Juan Bautista de Anza National Historic Trail between Tumacacori and Tubac. H. M. T. Powell (1931, 142) wrote that he saw holes that had been punched in the walls for "musketry" and found some old military papers in one of them, which he took as a souvenir. Many changes have occurred since 1849. The modern village of Tubac bustles with tourists, and artisans tend boutiques and shops. The presidio and church are well preserved and open to visitors, while French, Italian, and Mexican restaurants ensure that no one in this day will suffer either thirst or hunger.

[14] Sketch missing. Mission San Xavier del Bac, the "White Dove of the Desert," is considered by many to be the most beautiful mission in the Southwest and is an outstanding example of Spanish Baroque architecture. Construction was begun in 1776 by the resident Papago Indians (Tohono O'odham) under the supervision of Franciscan missionaries. A mission school run by the Sisters of Charity from Manitowoc, Wisconsin, continues to serve the Native children. The church holds regular services and is open to all.

FIGURE 11. San Xavier del Bac, Mission Road, Tucson vicinity, Pima County, Arizona, circa 1900. Papago (Tohono O'odham) dwellings encircle the church.
Courtesy of the Prints and Photographs Division, Library of Congress.

it and thought the drawing a great wonder to them, and indeed it is a very great wonder to me to see so much expence laid out as had been on these church's or "haciendas" when the inhabitance are such a poor, miserable set of ignoramouses. But it appears that they lavish all their wealth on their priests & churches and live in filth & ashes themselves. This appears to have been their religion.

I walked all over the Indian pueblo, which consisted of 63 small straw huts shaped something like a beehive from 8 to 12 feet diameter round and about 7 to 8 foot high. In the center, they creep into a small hole large enough for a mastiff dog to go in at. Some of them have a kind of temperary shed made in front of the beehive house of twigs or limbs of trees, under which they work at grinding wheat & corn into flour between 2 stones. These Indians are intirely naked except the breechcloth and the shirt which some of them had obtained from our company. These are a well featured looking tribe and are all copper colored. The women, as with all Indians, do all the work. They are called Pimos [Pimas]. At 3 o'clock we packed up and proceeded on our march to Teuson [Tucson], it being but 10 miles from this place. At 5 o'clock, within 1 mile of Teuson, by the same river of water which supplies it, we camped for the night.

Tuesday, July 10, I visited this Mexican town of Teuson early this morning.[15] It looks like all these Mexican towns which I have as yet seen, similarily, like an extensive brick yard. It contains about 500

---

[15] Emigrants' impressions of Tucson in 1849 were varied and colorful:

> *Fandangos* were going all the twenty-four hours of the day Harris 1960, 79);
>
> Here we got plenty of grapes, onion, eggs, and cheese, all in exchange for a little salt (Brownlee 1986, 65);
>
> Spanish and Indians of both sexes came to camp with pumpkins, muskmellons, peaches and quinces (Bouldin, October 2, 1849);
>
> Attended day-long funeral of a four-year-old child (Forsythe, October 6, 1849);
>
> No time to sketch the town, not worth the trouble (H. Powell 1931, 8–9);
>
> The soldiers make a contemptible appearance (Clarke 1988, 68);
>
> Poor looking place (Stevens, October 5, 1849);
>
> Tucson, with its delicious nights out of doors, under the refulgent moon (Nugent, March 23, 1878).

One of them, Asa Bement Clarke, visited a blacksmith and observed a piece of native iron being used for an anvil. The artifact is now known as the Tucson Meteorite and is housed in the Smithsonian Institution. Its story is told in Richard Willey, *Tucson Meteorites* (1987).

inhabitants. [There is] a barracks containing 2 troops of Mexican lancers of about 100 men, and if these are a sample of the Mexican dragoons which Gen. [Winfield] Scott & [Zachary] Taylor whipped, then I don't begrudge them the honour of such victories. Their was not a man in the whole of our party but what could throw down at least a squad of these fellows with a look. I rode up to the gate of the so called casa, where I seen a sentry standing with a carbine in his hand, when he instantly held my horse, having the appearance of a military man myself. The whole guard imediately turn[ed] out, as well as the officer of the day, who I soon found out to be very much the gentleman, and who soon introduced me to the major in command of the squadron and the doctor of the post. Four could speak very good French, and as being more fluent in the "Parly vous," I soon became quite a lion amongst them, and which had the desired effect of making the reseption of our whole party very well welcomed in the whole place. The guards, on their parts, were ordered to salute me with a present in my passing, and sentries which were before neglected, I notised were now posted.

I wanted to get a mule for my mess and which was soon obtained for me on very reasonable terms. The umbria that had the mule I wanted would not "vend" it less than 60 dollars, but when I told the officers respecting the mule & the price, in less than 10 minutes I had the mule with a soldier mounted on him standing before me. When the officer said, "I should have him for the price which was twenty pacis [pesos]." They were very kind to us all and sold us at very reasonable rates all the "polonced" (maple sugar) they had in the town.[16] The officers and soldiers would make the inhabitance sell us the same as they did to them. I also purchased an ass here and had my gum elastic bags filled with water so as to have this animal to carry our water across the desert which we have to cross between here and the Gila River. We employed a guide here, an Indian Pueblo who would guide us to the Rio "Hela" a much nearer way

[16] This was not maple sugar but a syrup, *sitol*, that the Native people boiled down from the pulp of the ripe saguaro fruit. Sitol was also made from the graythorn (*Ziziphus obtusifolia*) or from the juice of the baked heart of *Agave deserti*. The syrup was stored in clay ollas (Rea 1997, 252, 257).

than the waggon road. After getting all our supplys at this place, we returned to camp and packed and formed and marched into Teuson in regular military order. The guards turned out and showed us all the horses they now have; several of the squadron escorted us some ways out on the desert.

It was 6-1/2 PM when we left Teuson. The early part of the night was dark. About 11 o'clock, the moon rose and gave us light. Their being so many of us that a rush was kept up during the whole line of march till about 1 o'clock when we got pretty well tired out and dry camped by our animals, every man by his own saddle. I divided the water immediately amongst my mess. One of our pack mules was missing, but to look for it then was out of the question. It happened to be the pack mule that had our clothing and extra bedding, which we did not want very particularly. The sean now was rather singular to many of us. The moon was up in its glory and to see the men, horses & mules in all positions scattered in all directions as if in the "battlefield." After partaking of some water & penola, I laid my head in the saddle and slept till dawn of day, when the mules they commenced then until morning to bray.

Wednesday, July 11, 3-1/2 AM, all hands hitched up, every man his own beast, and "vaumised" after the guide for the "Rio Hela." We kept the regular waggon road till 9 o'clock, when our guide turned due north on a narrow trail with high mountains direct[ly] in front, some 30 or 40 miles from where we expected to find water, and many expected to find the Gila River running at its base but were sadly disapointed. When coming up to the mountain at 5 o'clock, we found nothing but a dry river bed with plenty of hot sands and well garnished all round with the Cereus giganteus, mesquit, and many other varieties of the cactus tribe. Several attempts were made by digging to get water in the bed holes of the sands, but no, not a drop. The train now became very much scattered. The guide, being disappointed himself in not finding water in the mountain, knew well the result, so he cut for the Gila River, which was some 30 miles from this place. Showing us now, it would have been nearer and much better for us to have kept the waggon road when we would have made the distance but 104 miles from Teuson to the Pimos village. But now, our distance will be upwards of 150 miles.

The rush now was tremendous. The best horses and mules kept the advance. I had plenty of water for my own mess till this morning, but now we were intirely out. Mr. [John A.] Hunter of my mess gave out, as well as his mule, and had to drag along at snails pace during the greater part of the day. About 6 o'clock a short thunder shower came up, when I spread my gum elastic cape and collected a few sups of water, thereby quenched the thirst for a short time. I also cut off with my sword (by standing in the saddle on my horse) several figs from the cactus giganteas and which was now nearly ripe. This, however, caused too much delay at such a time; therefore I proceeded sloly till dark, when from the fatigue my poor horse also gave out, as many others did. And therefore, I had to walk and lead him at a snails pace, passing many horses and mules on the way, abandoned by their owners, leaving even the packs on them and going on themselves with only their empty canteens, water being the only thing ever thought of. I entertained in this very way till 10 o'clock at night, when I heard the voices of one of my men, a Mr. Jones of Texas. The poor fellow was almost dying with the thirst. He could go no further and actualy was not able to unsaddle his horse. Their being mesquit [and] chaperal close by, I soon unsaddled and made our horses fast in these bushes, which gave the poor things some feed, their being a sort of bean of which the mules & horses will eat when they cannot get anything else.[17] I recommended Mr. Jones to strip off intirely naked and lay on his horse blanket, and which has the effect of keeping off the thirst so long as you keep laying down during the night. Mr. Hunter came up to us but had to leave his mule and kit behind. He was compleatly broken down. Have drunk nothing since morning. I gave him the [phrase illegible] and the last sip of brandy in my G.E. [gum elastic] canteen, when he soon fell a sleep.

---

[17] The screwbean mesquite (*Prosopis pubescens*) is primarily found near river bottomlands, while the honey mesquite (*P. glandulosa*) and velvet mesquite (*P. velutina*) spreads over all drainages in Arizona. Mesquite meal was a primary food aboriginally and (as Goulding discovered) provided feed for the animals.

At the dawn of day, 3-1/2 AM, Thursday, July 12, we saddled up, and cutting down some beehive cactus and eating the inside relieved us of some of the thirst.[18] The inside is very much like a turnip, the water juice being rather tastless. Some of them are better flavored and more juicy than others. We proceded on slowly, passing several who were compleatly broken down, giving them information of the benefit of the beehive cactus, and which they readily received and were much relieved. Between 5 & 6 o'clock we met with one of the company coming out to meet us with a supply of water, having all the canteens and water gourds he could get from all the companys now at the Gila River some 5 miles ahead of us. After taking a hearty drink, we proceded on with rather a more cheerful feeling. We soon met others coming out to feed their fellow comrades, when within a mile of the camp, I met Mr. Ford coming out loaded with water for us.[19] We soon reached the camp, when we had plenty of good coffee and stewed quail.

Here we stoped all day. The River Gila is about 1/3 mile from us, there being a flat bottom with cane brake, cottonwood, willow & mezquite and alive with quail, rabbits & other small game, numbers of which were shot. I gave a Chilian Indian that belonged to Dr. Jordan's mess $5 to go back after Hunter's mule & kit, giving him another mule loaded with water in the G.E. bags and provisions for himself, enough for 3 days. So off he started at 10 o'clock. The grass is rather poor & scarce on this place but our animals eat hearty of the young willow tops and the mezquit screw bean, another species of that shrub we met with here. During the day, several of the company came up very much broken down. Several had gone back with water to regain their animals, some of which were altogether lost with their packs on. We had a slight shower of rain during the night.

Friday, July 13, this morning the foraging party reported good grass some two miles further down the valley, so all hands saddled

[18] A thirsty traveler is not likely to squeeze enough bitter liquid to quench his or her thirst from this now protected species of barrel cactus, *Ferocactus acanthodes*.

[19] "Such suffering I never saw," wrote David Jordan, "one man jumped right into the river & laid down & opened his mouth & let the water run in he laid there about an hour—others were unable to get to camp but laid down in the road" (July 11–12, 1849).

up and we proceeded on our march. The blue quail was in great quantities.[20] Every few paces we flushed up covies of them. I shot 26. On coming to the grass, which was indeed excellent, and near the river, we camped. I cooked my partridges and had an excellent dinner. In the afternoon I went to the Gila River where I took a comfortable bath. Several of the company caught some fine black trout of which this river abounds. During the afternoon, the Chilian returned to us with Hunter's mule and saddle, informing us as soon as he gave the beast the water, he followed him in trust all the way. He travelled all the night and did not rest except about 1/2 an hour since he left us, being anxious to be with us to the Pimos village. We had some heavy rain during the evening. That, and the terrible howling of the wolf, was the drama of the night.

Saturday, July 14, about 8 o'clock we saddled up and proceeded on our march. We passed two old Indian encampments and met with broken pieces of pottery and appearances of the places being deserted at some remote time. The river valley varieing much, some times not over 1/2 mile wide and at times from 3 to 4 miles wide in the extreme. Land on both sides of the river is of a barren appearance, the Cereus giganteus growing in its grandeure. We traveled till 8-1/2 PM, when we camped in good long grass not far from the river. Capt. Carter and all the men of his mess took sick from eating the remains of the cold dried meal they had for breakfast, and which was caused by it remaining in the sun camp kettle all day. Haveing medicine by me, I soon relieved them. A heavy rain fell during the evening and made our camp rather uncomfortable during the night.

---

[20] Gambel's quail, *Callipepla gambelii.*

15

The Gila Trail

After recovering from their brush with death from thirst, the gold rushers enjoyed their stay with the friendly Pima and Maricopa Indians who lived in scattered villages along the Gila River. But more hard times were ahead as they short-cut a deep bend in the Gila River and trudged across forty-five miles of waterless desert. Their only relief was an occasional burst of rain from the summer monsoons. They also traveled at nighttime to avoid the unrelenting heat. At least one of the Knickerbockers, Reverend Ira Allen, succumbed to the rigors of the journey and was buried somewhere on the banks of the Gila. The group passed the names of previous travelers scratched into Independence Rock dating back to 1845 and were fascinated by hundreds of ancient petroglyphs (now preserved in Painted Rock Petroglyph Site). They struggled through miles of sand, the trail marked out by the discarded belongings of those in advance.

Sunday, July 15, the morning was fine and the sun soon dried up all our traps, and Capt. Carter and his mess being well, we saddled up and proceeded on our march. The valley continues wide and shows continuously the mounds of former cultivation.[1] We were met by several of the Pimos Indians during the morning, coming out to meet us with maze flour & mellons. We travelled some 15 miles and crossed to the north side of the river and camped. The grass was poor, but the Indians fetched us plenty of corn fodder for our ani-

[1] The mounds were ancient Hohokam.

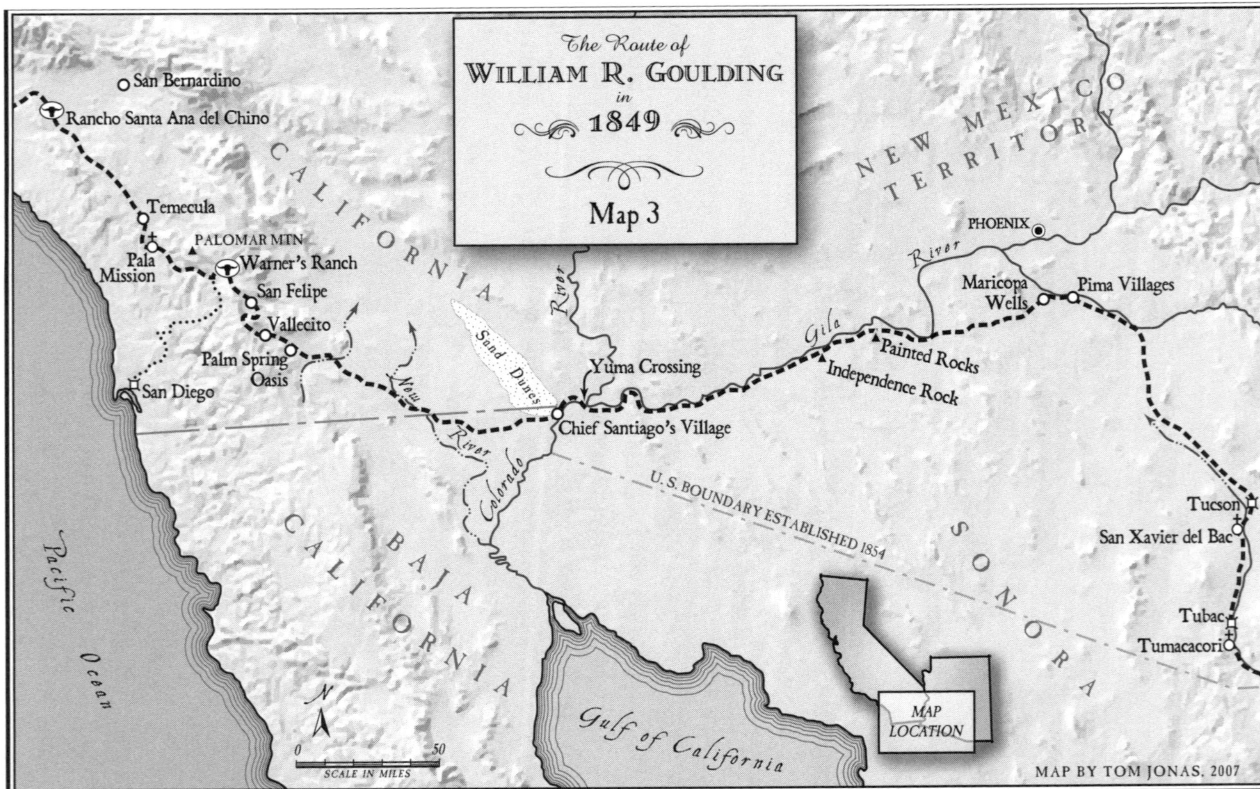

MAP 3. Tucson to Rancho Santa Ana del Chino

mals. We were but 2 miles from the Pimos village. The company became very much scattered about in small parties, some going on to the village and some stopping near the river to rest and recruit the broken down animals, others waiting for some one of their messes behind in search of their animals on the desert. Our camp was filled with men, women, and children during the day with baskets of corn, frijoles or meal, mellons &c. [to] traffic. Beads, red & blue cloth, blankets & shirts were the articles demanded in exchange. They did not seem to care for money. The conclusion of each bargain was manifested by a grunt from the Indians, so the trading went merrily on. We had plenty of hot corn and rested well during the night.

Monday, July 16, we saddled up early this morning and recrossed the river and arrived at the Pimos village by 6 o'clock, and we were all very agreably surprised to see such an extensive settlement of what is called the wild Indians, surpassing many of the Christian nations in agriculture and little behind them in many useful arts, and far before them in honesty and virtue.[2] We were soon surrounded by their women and children—all desirous to camp by them, so we found a suitable place and camped for the day, one of my company, a Mr. Pucket, being taken very sick. These people fetched us abundance of corn, both for ourselves and our animals. I took a strole through the thatched huts of these people. [Emory extract omitted.]

Corn, wheat, and straw are in these beehive like houses [and] were stowed in large earthenware jars & baskets filled with mezquit beans, corn, wheat, and some few mellons. A few chickens and dogs were seen but no other domestic animals except horses, mules & oxen. Their implements of husbandry are the axe of iron and small hoes (shaped thus) ——, shovels and hammers, and a long hooked shaped stick used as a plough, thus ——. This is the end of which they hitch on an ox.[3] The soil is very easily pulverised.

---

[2] Goulding is paraphrasing Emory (1848, 54).

[3] He sketched three items from the Pima farmer's tool kit. The "hoe" or digging stick, *eskud,* was flattened and sharpened at one end and was about as high as the farmer's elbow. A primitive wooden plow, *uus giiki,* pulled by oxen, prepared the ground for planting. Both the hoe and plow were fashioned from desert ironwood, *Olneya tesota,* with cutting faces of iron or steel (Rea 1997, 43–45; Russell 1908, 98).

Goulding's sketch of a Pima axe, small hoe, and plow

Penola and the mesquit bean seamed to be their chief article of food at this time of the year, as well as roasted Indian corn. Penola is the heart of the Indian corn, baked dry and ground up and mixed with molasses dissolved in water and is a delicious beverage and is very nutritious. They have molasses put up in large jars hermeticaly sealed and which they express from the figs of the Cereus giganteus [saguaro].[4]

The crop of wheat was all in and each family had their share of the grain laid up in large crocks of burned earthenware, some of which I notised was as large nearly as a flour barrell. They grind the flour between 2 stones by rubbing them in the ground by women on their bended knees. In one of the arches I notised the kind of loom consisting of 4 stakes drove in the ground, and the stalks of corn fastened by the cotton twine were attached to them and the ball of cotton is passed by hand from one side to the other. The drawing taken on the spot will better explain the contrivance.[5] The 2 beams are about 2-½ inches in diameter and 6 feet long each and are tied fast with mescal thread to the 4 stakes in the ground about 18 inches up this frame. 2 women or girls pass and repass the shuttle from one side to the other. The shuttle is about 2 feet long and contains the ball of cotton thread, which is spun by another rude and singular process. The material is imbedded in sand and the spinner twisting it with and between the fingers as she draws it out from the top of her toe from the ground, the foot pressing gradually on the mass of material.

[4] Goulding has borrowed many phrases from Emory (1848, 85) to describe the preparation of "molasses" and other particulars of the Pima villages.

[5] Sketch missing.

I did not notise any method amongst them of smith work, therefore came to the conclusion that they must have obtained the iron axes & hoes of some Mexican traders who perhaps at intervals comes amongst them. There proces of useing the hoe is they sit down on there knees or legs and poke the knife shaped hoe in the loamy kind of soil and by that means only soften the soil and which is all thats nesesary. A storm came up so I returned to my camp, and we had a very disagreeable night of it, as it rained all night.

Tuesday, July 17, the sun came out bright and pleasant and all our trappings were soon dried up, and [we] again sadled up our animals and proceeded on our march. [After] travelling for about 4 miles through these people where we found some 10 more of our company encamped in a stubble corn field, and their being a good grazing lot, we also unpacked and camped at 9 o'clock AM. After partaking of a good breakfast, I took my gun and strolled off through these settlements. I found in one of these arbors a man in a kneeling position, sitting as it were on the calves of his legs, in the act of weaving a cotton belt of many colours. To a stick drove in the ground was attached a round stick about 10 inches long to which was fastened the different collored thread, red, blue, and green, and he passed a white thread through them to fasten each time he moved the cross piece near his body. A girl also was busily imployed in makeing a small basket of willow and which was so closely fabricated that it would hold water and was beutifuly made by her fingers and by the assistance of only of a small piece of willow chip to prop the folds together.

I discovered some onions growing in one of their gardens, of which I purchased some as well as 3 fine water melons. I also got some molasses which is very thin and is obtained from the mesquit beans and cactus figs. I was very much amused seeing an old granny intirely naked sitting down on her legs and rolling with a small smooth stone, on a another larger one of the same kind, wheat boiled in water in an earthen pot shaped vessel. Dipping her hand occasionally in a vessel of the thin watery kind of molasses and by this mode, rolled it into small rolls like stick candy or smaller. 5 little copper coloured and naked urchins all a lying around her, watching her hands, as fast as she made the rolls and putting in their mouths. This way she continued until they had a sufficiency to satisfy their meal.

During my walk I struck upon a very extra cabin amongst these people. They had a fine lot of chickens of which I purchased 3 for one dollar and then returned to camp and assisted in cooking and enjoying a first rate dinner with my fellow messmates. During the afternoon were visited by numbers of their women with abundance of flour and of which we laid in a good supply. We had a big thunder storm during the night but slept very well nevertheless.

Wednesday, July 18, our company was very much scatered overall about this Pemos Indian settlement and all endeavoring to recruit their animals as well as themselves with the abundant supplies of corn, fodder, vegetable, meat & flour as obtained from these industrious tribes of Indians. This morning quite a scene of confusion came off at my quarters in consequence of a misunderstanding between a party of "Duvals" company, some of my company, and one or two of the Coco Maracopa [Maricopa] Indians in regard to the whereabouts of some certain gold mountain, which was said to be in existence some where to the north of this place, and of which this Maracopa Indian guide said he would take the parties for some given amount. A Mr. Tyler and one Shaw, not being very well versed in Spanish, as well as the Indians also, were led into a wrong understanding. So, the old governor of the tribe having called on me that morning, to whom these gold hunters aplyed, about 30 in number, all mounted, armed to the teeth, supplied with 10 days rations, canteens & calibashes of water &c., Indians along with them, and when the parties were prepared for the start, the Indians, "mule like," didn't know how to lead the way but brayed Americano vaumis the camenia and the Indians would show them muncho awa a la notchia.

The difficulties were all explained and settled by the aid of Judge McLellen, who could speak very excellent Spanish, and having also with him a Mexican servant, on a parley with the old governor, chief "Juan Antonio" [Lunas], and his interpreter, who was a Maricopas by birth.[6] This fellow looked very much like a woman in the countenance, had a splendid head of hair as thick as your arm behind and tied up like a horses tail, his fore locks were also long and as low as his waist, a very neat gold ring with pearl drops in his nose, with a blue blanket about his body. This comprised his whole costume.

The governor had on a white shirt, a blue U.S. Infantry jacket with only one button behind & 2 shoulder nots of white worsted, the elbows out through the coat and shirt as if fashioned in that state. This, with a cotton handkerchief to tie up his hair, and a pair of blue cloth pants and sandals, composed his Excellency's morning dress. On this very interesting occasion, the gold hunters being all fully satisfied as to the mistake in regard to [illegible] not being nearer than the Sacramento River, made their minds up together and dispersed to their various camps.

The old governor staid with me the whole forenoon and was quite amused when I showed him his likeness from Emory's work. This tickled him very much and is a very good likeness of him and so he was dressed just at the time. His colour is like all his tribe, a "copper colour." He sold our company 3 young steers for $20 ea., which we slaughtered and barbecued, by being dried on stakes with a little fire under. They have a large number of cattle and use the oxen in the plough, some of which were now to work at this time, as they were planting their second corn crop. I had made a chicken pot pie for dinner of which the old governor partook and parted us very friendly.

At 2 o'clock my party hitched up and we proceeded on our march over these peoples lands—all under cultivation. We travelled about 10 miles, about 1/8 of which is under cultivation with corn, wheat, cotton, and gardens of mellons, fenced in mostly. Passing their huts

---

[6] According to David Jordan's journal entry on the same day, the men wisely gave up the gold-hunting idea when they determined that they had misunderstood the proposed guide.

The Pima chief, Juan Antonio Lunas, befriended and welcomed the many travelers who trod through his village, including both Philip St. George Cooke and Emory in 1846. The Quaker forty-niner Charles Edward Pancoast offered the best description of Lunas: "a noble specimen of Manhood, six feet four inches in height and built in proportion, with large, bright expressive eyes, and an intelligent, benevolent countenance" (1930, 243).

in small groups all the way, I notised 2 mounds or high hills in the middle of their settlement, on which they have guards to watch the aproach of any other of their Indian enemys. Most every family have dogs and a kind of pet eagle or hawk, which is used in the place of a cat, the latter I seen now. Our road led us to the base of a large mountain where this peoples village terminates and which near it is the most thrifty part of them. After turning the left of this mountain, we again came out on the everlasting chaparel, through which we travelled for some 5 or 6 miles, when we made our salt grass encampment. During our march the last few miles we flushed several bevey of quail of which this country abounds, and getting a good supply, we enjoyed an excellent supper and retired for the night. Our camp was visited by gr[eat] numbers of the Maracopas with abundance of corn, penola & flour and mellons, some of which were very large and good.

Thursday, July 19, we had a heavy rain during the night which wet our packs and trappings very much. We were much angerd by several hundreds of these Maracopa Indians and who required much watching. These tribes are not as honest as the Pima. One of them stole a silk handkerchief belonging to me, and several of the messes complained of having things stolen. I noticed also some of their women were not so virtuous as they have the name of being.

This camping ground is somewhat noted here for its excellent salt springs and grass which is very excellent, but the land about abounds with deep rivers or dykes of clay & mud in which many of our animals got pretty well painted and gave some of our boys some work to do. This is the last grass or water for 45 miles of a hornada or desert [on] which we intend to take up our march this afternoon.[7] So having

[7] The gold seekers were at the site of Maricopa Wells on the Gila River Reservation, Pinal County, about twenty-four miles west of the Pima villages. Maricopa Wells was the last place to obtain water before negotiating a route through the "forty-mile desert," which cut off a bend in the Gila River, thus saving many miles. The Butterfield Stage built a station here in the mid-1850s. Waterman Ormsby (1988, 98–99), a rider on the company's first overland stage to San Francisco, wrote that six or eight wells were contained on a large plain of alkali soil and coarse grass. This is the traditional area of the Yuman-speaking Maricopa tribe. Tribal permission is required to enter the area.

FIGURE 12. Old emigrant trail (Butterfield Pass), Maricopa County, Arizona, 1994. *Photo by Patricia A. Etter.*

boiled 2 fine large fowls and ½ dozen quail and with a good supply of tortillas or flap jacks and 2 fine large water melons which I had lashed across one of my mule's packs, my party took up our march towards the mountain rampart at 4 PM, which lay west of us. We soon made the foot of these mountains, and the travelling now became very hard and rocky, with extensive forrests on all sides of us of the great Cereus giganteus in all its various shapes from the pillar shape to the 3 & 4 great armed ones, some of them upwards of 40 feet high.[8]

[8] Butterfield Pass (known as Maricopa Pass before the stage went through) contains a glorious cactus forest. Because the gold seekers restricted travel here to nighttime, lengthy descriptions of the area are rare.

At 8 o'clock we came to a halt and prepared our animals for the night travel. That is, lashing our packed mules and each man leading one or more as he could or most conveniently, the night being dark, and we must make at least half of this desert before midnight. No accident disturbed our travel till midnight, [when] we met the chaperal so very dencely thick it was impossible to get along, our leading packs so frequently would get entangled, so we camped about 1 o'clock, all as close as possible, making fast our animals to the chaperal, and unsaddled and lay down till the dawn of day. The boiled chickens & mellons became now a delicious morsel and which we all very much enjoyed at 3 [AM].

The day dawned Friday, July 20, [and] we imediatly saddled up. One of my pack mules, Allice, sprung her lariet during the latter part of the night and made tracks on the back trail and rather put me to some trouble to rescue her, which I did about 8 miles in the rear, where I once took her, going back to the Maracopa salt springs. As the approaching daylight appeared, this forrest of chaperal and the scattering Cereus gigantea look most grand and beutifull to the eye. The great plain behind us and to the left of us extending as far as the sight could reach, with the great mountains to our right and in front of us, through which we have to pass a gap now making its grand apperance in front of us. During the night, we frequently heard the roar of the wild bear of the forrest and which made the [scene] most grand and awfull.

At 11 AM we made the mountain pass, which is about 2 miles through the pass, when we opened on to a large plain, gradually descending for some 6 miles, when we again arrived at the Gila River. After making some 40 miles travel, here the Gila or the Hela, as the Mexicans call it, is much wider than when I saw it before, and very heavy mesquit & cottonwood bottoms alive with abundance of game. I seen some signs of beaver in this part of the river. We kept down the river for some 5 miles, when we found some excellent high grass, where we camped by the river bed. We were all very much fatigued from our last march of the 2 days and 1 night, but our animals had now abundance of both grass and mesquit beans and without even going out of our camp fire smoke for it. After making dinner and supper of barbecued beef &c., I soon had a good sleep.

Saturday, July 21, at 8 o'clock this morning, finding ourselves all very well refreshed, we again saddled up and marched, keeping by the river for some 5 miles, when the river gradually here makes a bend north by some miles and our road leaves it and goes west, which we kept for 8 miles, when we were soon assending a small but very steep mountain of the blackest kind of stone or rock you could look on. Here we all dismounted and lead up. After this we descended into a deep revein or river bed. Here one of my packed mules, "Little Taddy," showed "simptons of giving out." My old and faithful companion, Mr. W. F. Ford, had to coax and lead her along by putting her pack on his mule, Bentley. This mountainous pass is about 4 miles in extent. When we again decended towards the river, it is on this decent that the large heaps of rocks which lay in your road are discovered, and which are traced with hieroglyphics or unknown characters, the mark of human hands. Several of them I copied. These were [of] undoubted antiquity and the signs and symbols intended doubly to commemorate some great event. One stone bore on it a figure of a mastodon, a horse, a dog, a man &c., their heads all facing to the east and some of them were well excecuted.[9] No doubt but this region of country was onced settled by some inteligent race of people, and if we had time to explore about, many more remains of this kind could be discovered.

We soon came up to the Gila River again, which now opens out

[9] Goulding has cribbed from Emory (1848) to describe what is now Painted Rock Petroglyph Site in the Sears Point Archaeological District east of Gila Bend, Maricopa County. Hundreds of petroglyphs dating to 900 A.D. have been scratched into the desert varnish on the rocks (Boma Johnson, personal communication, 1994).

much wider than we have heretofore seen it, with very extensive marshs or flats covered with many new growths of willow, cottonwood, and masquet grass, coarse and [illegible], a great many islands which are made by the many turns or branches of the river. About 4 o'clock we crossed the river and camped very comfortably on one of these islands with plenty of good feed for the animals and lots of quail for ourselves. A party of 3 of our company came up late but were not able to find Smith's horse, which was no doubt stolen by some prowling Maracopas Indians which had been doging us for some several days. We were much annoyed during the night by moschetoes.

Sunday, July 22, at 7-½ this morning we again proceeded on our march, all in good order. Crossed and recrossed several branches of the Gila, all of which are very shallow and sandy. About 10 o'clock we again struck up on the plate land, leaving the river to our right. The appearance of the surface over which we are on now was indeed dredfull, black burned basalt and clinkard stone, and such going we never before experienced. For 8 miles we continued over this sort of travel, when we again decended to the river. After travelling thirty miles till 3-½ PM, we camped in a fine grove of young willows. Close by this camp a large, black, rocky bank or hill was there [and] was also marked in some places by the names of many that had passed by here before.[10] Being camped close to the river, we all of us enjoying a comfortable bath in this great Gila River.

We were visited by a party of Indians who appeared to be friendly. Supposed them to be Coco Maracopas by there heads and face. They were all well armed with bows & arrows, shields, and spears—but no guns—we treated them kindly and separate them amongst our different messes and they staid all night with us. The howling of wolf was the principle music of the night, softened a little by the piano notes of the delicate moscheto.

[10] Independence Rock is about twenty-five miles west of Painted Rock Petroglyph Site, close to the Gila River, also in the Sears Point Archaeological District (Boma Johnson, personal communication, 1994). A number of overlanders stopped long enough to carve their names on the rocks for posterity. Joseph R. Simmons (November 9, 1949) copied three into his diary: Benoit, Maxwell, and Hatcher. As it turns out, L. Benoit was there with Frémont in 1842 and Lucien Maxwell was there with Kit Carson, date unknown (Wells 1982). Simmons met J. L. Hatcher, the mountaineer, in person at New River, California, on Hatcher's trip back to New Mexico.

Monday, July 23, at 7 o'clock we were all again on our march, all in good spirits. About 10 o'clock we assended to the table lands on which we travelled over a barren, stoney or gravel kind of earth till 1 o'clock when we again struck down on the river (on this last table land we met with the remains of 2 deserted waggons, all scattered about, and broken to pieces as well as the harness belonging thereto. No doubt the parties got sick of the waggon business and packed what they could and continued on their journey). Here we discovered many old encampments and trails in all directions through the bottoms. After watering our animals we again proceeded on our journey making our march on the table lands. Although being harder, we still preferred it to being continually bogging with our packed mules as is the case if you keep [to] the river beds. About 3 o'clock we met a small patch of grama grass, and our poor animals went at it like so many hungry wolves at a dead mule. So we camped, although we were 2 miles from water. But better to carry our water so far than deprive our animals of this great luxury of a bite of grama grass. The animals of all the company soon began to give out and showed the fatigues of the journey very much. My horse, "Camanche Bob," gave out during the day and did not get up till late. Although camped on the open plate lands, we camped very comfortable.

Tuesday, July 24, their was considerable distruction of property this morning in consequence of the giving out of many of our animals. Clothes and ammunition, medicine, it had to be left, no "jacks" being here to purchase. All had to be left to lighten the packs. At 7 o'clock we proceeded on our march. We struck the river at 9 o'clock and at 10 o'clock we met with some grass and camped by the river to breakfast, where we staid till noon. Being well revived by the grass, we again proceeded till 5 o'clock, passing 4 waggons which had been abandoned last fall by [Lawrence P.] "Graham" on his way to Monterey.[11] My poor horse, Bob, had to be left today, all we could do could not build him up, so we left him in the last grass

[11] Maj. Lawrence Pike Graham of Virginia was breveted for gallantry at Palo Alto and was returning to California from duty in 1848 following his participation in the Mexican War (Couts 1961, 48n4).

to recruit to the benefit of those who might come up that way, or to the wolves.

We passed a party commanded by a Mr. Lane from Mexico during the day, consisting of 13 waggons and about 40 men, mostly Mexican peons, all well armed and under good discipline of this Lane.[12] They were a comical looking set of fellows to us. This evening we had a dry camp in the plate lands, which we preferred to the bottoms in consequence of the annoynce of moschetoes. During the night I was suddenly surprised in my sleep by the wolves. I grasped my rifle and was just on the moment of leveling my piece when the muzzel struck the leathern pulles of my long boots, and which I took in my sleep to be wolves ears. When I woke again it was day light.

Wednesday, July 25, proceeded on our march at 7 o'clock. At 7-½ we again struck the river, when the base of the great range of the southern mountains begins leaving just room enough for a horse to pass by it and the river. The great range of mountains, we have had in our front for several days passed. One of my mules got bogged here in the Gila and gave us much trouble to save her, with the loss of wetting the packs considerably and the injuring of my sword scabbard against the rocks. The rocks projecting on the end of this mountain range had various heirogliphics similar to those already discribed. We traveled till 3 o'clock by the river pretty much, when we got into the most dence forrest of cane brake, brush, chaperal I ever seen, which continued for some 5 miles, when we came out again by the banks of the river, when we camped for the night. Several of the company did not make camp till late, dragging or leading their poor jaded animals along at a snail's pace.

Thursday, July 26, we left camp this morning at 6-½ AM. The travel today was very oppressive. Our trail led us through immense

---

[12] Lane is mentioned numerous times by gold seekers, and all efforts to find his first name have failed. William Chamberlin (1945, 255) noted that Lane started from Peres, Mexico, with nine wagons and fifty mules. Lilbourne Winchell (1933, 19) writes that a Mr. Lane was among the first miners to reach the San Joaquin River in Mariposa County, formed a partnership with J. M. Cassaday, and mined eight miles upstream at Cassaday's Bar. It was not long before Cassaday was killed by Indians, at which time Lane disappeared from the record.

forrest of some large mesquit trees loaded with beans, which we allowed our animals to indulge in, but the poor jaded things—these beans are not the kind of nourishment that they want. At 3 o'clock, as we came up, we discovered a sign up turning by a trail to the right towards the river, and seeing it fresh made, took it to be from the head of our own company. So we soon discovered we were right and found the camp formed by the River Gila. We were now but 2 miles from the Colorado River at the junction of the Gila. Several small companys of Americans were encampd all along between here and the Colorado, recruiting their animals in the good grass which is along this bottom. Here we formed our camp and right glad were most of us, for the days journey was a hard one.

16

Oh! Praise the Lord All Ye Pack Mule Men

There was much excitement as the emigrants crossed the Colorado River into California and strong Yuma Indian swimmers pulled them to the opposite side, sometimes successfully, sometimes not. Their course now took them across a barren wasteland and into Baja California in order to avoid the shifting Algodones Sand Dunes. A surprise was in store when they reached a point near modern Seeley, Imperial County, California—pools of water not present during Emory's visit in 1846. The group named it New River. When Goulding saw the running water, he fired off his double-barrel shotgun and cried out, "Oh! Praise the Lord all ye pack mule men for having brought you safe through the desert!" It was time again to fill up canteens before marching onto the Colorado Desert, where they trudged over a parched plain toward Carrizo Creek and, they hoped, fresh water.

Friday, July 27, we did not move camp today in order to make a refit and give our poor mules and horses an opportunity to pick what little grass they could before taking the desert of 90 miles which lies on the other side of the Colorado River between us and good water. Captain Carter and myself saddled up about 9 o'clock to visit the junction of the Gila and Colorado, which we found north of our camp about a mile and a half distant. On our way, we passed several encampments of Americans waiting to rest their animals, and some were busily engaged constructing rafts from the floating drift logs and small trees obtained on the banks of the Gila River. The day was windy, blowing from the north [Emory extract omitted].

On the bank of the Colorado their were upwards of fifty naked Indians employed in carrying across the kits and effects of some company on the way to California, and the sight was a novel affair. On a raft of about twelve feet square were piled on saddles and packs, valises, and bundles covered with blankets and buffalo robes and sitting on the top, some half dozzen Mexicans stripped to the flannel, and some others holding on to the lariets or ropes attached. Some twenty naked savages [were] pulling it along with the current, and such a shoutings as they made is only to be compared to that of whipping in to the death of a stagg or a fox hunt. The sight was so interesting I sketched it from my saddle in my note book.[1]

We came down to the point of crossing, where were another party just in rediness for crossing. They informed us that these Indians had a canoe made of raw hide, but yesterday one of their company on crossing over got upset and both him & canoe have not been found. These Indians are of the tribes of the "Garroteros" (or Club Indians), and Cochinears (or Dirty Fellows), Tontears (or Fools), Coyataros (or Wolf Eaters).[2] I should think the latter name was applicable to any of them, for on our return trip by the Colorado, we came on some dozzen of them in the act of roasting the limbs of a drownded mule and some of them devouring the meat off the bones with as much relish as our eppicurean would do from the leg of a chicken at the [illegible].

[1] Sketch missing.

[2] Emory (1848, 96) used these terms. He was unaware that "Garroteros" was the Spanish term for the River Yumans, who called themselves Quechan, practiced floodwater agriculture, and lived in low, rectangular, earth-covered houses. Many emigrants counted on Yuman swimmers to carry their goods across the Colorado. They had to be watchful, however, for the Indians, in need of protein, had cultivated a taste for horse meat.

George Churchill (August 7, 1849) said the men swam like ducks and that he had seen both men and women dive into the water and catch fish with their hands. The "Cochinears" were likely the nearby Cocopah, whose name had numerous variations over the years. "Coyoteros" was a term often applied to the Western Apaches (Stewart 1983, 1–2).

We found Captain Lane & party all comfortably encamped about half a mile from the junction. He informed us he had sent two men to reconnoitre and examine the lower crossing, as he had been informed that a fording place was their whereby he could ford his wagons, of which he had thirteen. I got a small supply of sugar from him (4 lbs.) and much information respecting Mexico, where he came from in the state of Chihuahua. His party consisted of a Capt. Gunn, an American, his brother-in-law, a Spanish gentleman, and a young Mexican gentleman (don), with their attendance consisting of forty men, mostly peons & hired Mexicans Pueblos, all of which were well armed with carbines, knives, pistols, and revolvers &c., and plenty of flour and provisions. After partaking of refreshment with these hospitable fellow travellers, we retired to our camp, where we found our whole company cooking supper of fried quail and fish, which they had caught in great abundance. With the exception of the annoyance from the moschetoes, we slept well during the night.

Saturday, July 28, our company were all busily engaged constructing a suitable raft on the banks of the Gila River about half a mile below our camp on a small island where was a good supply of drift timber. The raft being made and ready for launching, in the evening all the corps returned to camp. I called on Capt. Lane on my return and he informed me his party had not been able to find the reported fording place and had sent 4 of his waggons with 25 men for suitable timber to construct some rafts. He was going to move his camp in the next morning on the edge of the Colorado for the purpose of building and landing them their in preference of the manner others were doing in the Gila River and working them down through the thick brush and cane brakes.

Next morning, Sunday, July 29, all hands bright and early were packing and some moveing towards the great crossing place while others were gone to launch and work the raft around to the bank of the Colorado. By nine o'clock all our company were on the ground awaiting the party who had the management of the raft. There was a scene which beggared anything we had ever seen before, as a large number of emigrants had arrived and were makeing arrangements all along the bank of the river with the savages to either take their baggage or themselves over and drive their mules across. Here was a perfect menagerie into which was crowded French, Dutch, English, Irish, Scotch, Americans & Mexicans of all kinds and sorts, both of colour and complexion. Here was a scene of naked arms, bodys, and legs as was never seen before in a bathing scene. Here was the Indian savage from the Wolf & Mule Eater, the Dirty Club Indian, to the neat, blue-painted cheek Maracopa Indian, all mixed in together in a glance, and the language of the Spaniard, the mongrel Mexican, and the Yankee trading with the Indians & to take him over for his blanket (indeed the scene can be much better imagined than discribed). So the trade went merrily on and each bargain was announced by a grunt.

After some time, we discovered our raft coming sloly up by the bank, and when we came to get all our baggage on, we found it was not sufficiently large enough. So I engaged a small raft from some savages for 3 blankets to take over the ballance and drive over all our animals. So all our kits, panyards and sacks, saddles, and in fact everything we had in the world, except just the clothes on us, were properly secured on this raft and Messrs. [Gerard] Banker, [Andrew] Smith, [and] Hunter placed on the top. The savages, like water dogs, all ready panting to move off, when Ford and myself were just in the act of going on, we discovered, or rather were informed, that two of our mules had come back on this side. Consequently we pushed off the raft and removed to get our mules, which proved to be Banker's mule and our water donkey. After giving the shirts and coats off our backs to those savages and wanting to see them safe across, we then found a chance for Ford to go over with Mr. Carson and Sprages' raft and I went up to Mr. Lane's party to cross over with them. On going, I observed a raft upset in the middle of the river and all its contents, raft and all, went to the bottom. Fortunately there was no Americans on it, being altogether the stores of some of the parties carryed over by Indians. On arriving at Capt. Lane's camp, we found them busily engaged making large rafts. Mr. Carson being also left, as well as myself, we were cordially treated and welcomed with Capt. Lane's party during the night.

Next day, Monday, July 30, Capt. Lane's company had constructed three very large rafts. The largest was 30 feet square and I named it the (Big Gun) in compliment of Capt. Gunn, and the other two, the Gila and Colorado. After breakfast we commenced loading the Big Gun, and after piling on the wheels and then the bodys of four waggons, and in them placing the provisions &c., Capt. Gunn, Dr. Craig, the Mexican gentlemen, Carson, myself, and five Mexicans—all of us with paddles constructed by Mr. Carson, and all of us strip[p]ed to the buff, we were launched off on the yawning gulf with three hearty cheers from those on shore. [We were] followed by some thirty savages who either swam after us for sport or for a chance to plunder in the event of some accident which might happen to us. But our raft made good her way and when in the middle of the gulf, these Indians left us and swam for the shore, leaving us to our fate. Our craft was too large and unyielding for us to manage, and owing to the drift, we were carried down the stream for four miles, makeing over fifty compleat turnarounds as we sailed along. All of us [were] working with our paddles to endeavour to get her out of the center of the river, but proved utterly impossible to do so at the point of the opposite bank which we intended to disembark.

After we all came nearly exhausted and worried out, our bark took a sudden turn by stricking one of these movable sand bars, and at the same instant, Capt. Gunn plunged into the deep with a rope around his body, aided also by our Mexican don. They lost the rope and by the jerk, our bark took an [illegible], rapid course towards the opposite bank, leaving our corageous comrades to extricate themselves the best they could. They did make out to swim for the shore, and after much difficulty, succeeded in landing amongst the thick chaperal, of which the whole steep bank was covered.

Our bark continued her course for upwards of a mile below where they landed, and by herculean efforts we were able to drift her against the steep bank, by which the water was shallow, but we were intirely out of sight of every living one of our party. By fireing a few shots from revolvers and holloring, we were found by our worthy companions, who were all torn and scratched by the prickley chaperal. After a few jovial remarks at our fortunate and miraculous escape from death, we partook of some refreshment, and then by the aid of spades and a pick axe, we made a landing place. And by chopping with axes and our Bowie knives, we made a passage through the thick brush for over two hundred yards. Here, Carson and myself left our Spanish friends and went in search of our company, whom we found encamped in a grove of mesquit beans some three miles further on. Hunter had been waiting all day for me at the landing but did not know till now of my whereabouts, supposing I had been lost, as he seen one of Capt. Lane's rafts go down with all its contents. It was now six o'clock, and as I found all our animals were safe and all our baggage, with the exception of getting wet, I soon went to rest and reflected on this most terrible day of my life.

Tuesday, July 31, the morning being fine, I opened my pack to see how far my baggage was damaged and found all my instruments and books wet. Some of my lancets and small instruments were compleatly rusted with this brackish water from the Colorado. I dried up as much as I could and threw away such as I thought worthless. Our whole company being now in good order, it was thought adviseable to commence at onced to arrange for leaving this bean camp and proceed over the desert. So each animal, being supplyed with as much coarse grass and beans as could be well stowed in our equipments, at 3-½ PM we commenced the march through this thickly overgrown mesquite with willow and cottonwood for some four miles, when we descended into the wide bed of the Colorado. Here we came abreast of the old (as reported) fording place.[3]

We then travelled over a sandy plain with rolling sand hills, which

[3] Emigrants had three Colorado River crossings to choose from. The upper crossing was where the river channel was compressed by cliffs. A modern bridge on Interstate 8 located there currently eases the crossing to California. Seven miles to the west is a middle crossing at a geological formation known as Pilot Knob (de Anza called it Cerro San Pablo). At this point, the river turns south, and at four miles is a third crossing known as the lower crossing. It appears that Goulding landed in the vicinity of Pilot Knob on the west bank of the Colorado and camped. The next day, he traveled some four miles south to "the old fording place," or lower crossing, which had been used by Kearny in 1846. Pilot Knob, Mohave County, is so named because steamboat captains later navigating the river used it as a guide (W. Barnes 1988, 331). For in-depth information and stories by emigrants at the Colorado crossings, see G. Ellis (1995).

keep continuously moveing so as to make it difficult to keep the track. At seven o'clock, we noticed a number of savages playing and rolling in the white sand hills to the south of us, and being atracted by our formidable appearance, they gave a tremendous yell and disappeared for a few moments, but again were in much more numerous bodys. On our near approaching them, we found them to be of the Umas [Yuma, or Quechan] tribe and live here in a community cultivating the land and grow maize, corn, wheat, mellons &c. We desended into the wide bed of the Colorado again, immediately by the village of these Indians, and which appeared to be large and had a population of upwards of a thousand persons.[4] The Colorado is near to this village and seems much wider than at the crossing, and the banks much lower, not more than four feet high, when at the crossing they were upwards of 16 to 20 feet high. Judging from indications, sometimes this part of the Colorado overflows. Its general appearance at this point is much like that of the Arkansas with its turbid waters and many shifting sand islands. We obtained a few mellons from these Indians and proceeded on our journey by the edge of these immence sand hills until about 10 o'clock, when we halted at a dry arroyo in which we found a hole some six feet deep.[5] So we soon furnished all our animals with a hearty drink of water. By appearances (about this place, as well as over some we travelled since leaving the village) of the acequias for watering the land of the farm settlements of Indians, which settlements it is probable have been cut off by the continual drift of these immense sand hills incroaching on the wide bottoms of the Colorado.

The night was extremely beautiful and clear as day, almost. So every man on horseback with his bunch of grass and bag of beans tied behind him on the cantle of his saddle, we traveled some five or six miles along these sand buttes about south. We then mounted the

---

[4] The village is shown as "the Village of Santiago Chief of the Yumas" on a November 1849 Whipple map, "Mouth of the Rio Gila," reproduced in G. Ellis (1995, 22).

[5] The well was Cooke's Well, or First Well, Baja California, some thirteen miles west of the Colorado, and was located in a deep cleft at the base of a thirty-foot cliff on the dry bed of the Rio Alamo, an ephemeral overflow channel of the Colorado River (Jonas 2008).

buttes and found, after a short distance, a firmer footing covered with agates stones, and we were now fairly on the desert. At one and a half o'clock we camped, every man keeping his own animals in his own hands till the morning, Wednesday, August 1, when the braying of our mules woke all hands up at 4-1/4 AM.[6]

Partaking of a cold breakfast of penola and water and some cheese and a dram of Mexican brandy which we had obtained of Capt. Lane, we proceeded over this dreadful desert, passing the remains of dead mules and skeletons of many horses with portions of harnis, saddles & packs, old hats, and clothes of all discription as having been left by those who had preceded us on this to be dreaded road. At 10-1/2 AM we came to what is termed the Alamo [Mocho] or cottonwood [Emory extract omitted] we found two deep holes. In descending into them, we were inabled to dip up with a tin cup, by pressing it into the sand, a sufficiency of water to make coffee and give our animals a drink.[7] So by the aid of some boards taken from the remains of four waggons left here, we made fires and had fried bacon and flap jacks for our dinner. Our whole company coming up, we remained here till 4 PM, when we found our animals had eaten up the remains of our supply of beans. Again we left this dismal and gloomy sepulcher of death and travelled north till 6 o'clock, when we met with a sort of revein or dyke in which we found a number of the mesquite trees, loaded with beans. Here we stoped till 8 o'clock, loading our animals with beans, when we again proceeded. Our course was a very winding one to avoid the sand drifts which were again nearing us on our right. We disengaged ourselves intirely from

[6] Goulding's fellow traveler David Jordan said he tied his animals to bunches of juniper bushes, adding that it was a beautiful night to travel, "Clear, & moon within 3 days of full" (August 1, 1849).

[7] The gold rushers had covered nearly twenty-two miles before arriving at Alamo Mocho. It had been a tough go. On August 9, Churchill wrote of passing dead animals, discarded wagons, and even the arm of a man. George W. B. Evans (1945, 163), arriving at Alamo Mocho in September 1849, wrote that recovering water from the well was a slow process as it was twenty-eight feet below the surface of the desert and the sand at its sides kept falling back into the well. Based on several exploratory trips to Baja California, Tom Jonas (2008) was able to map Alamo Mocho's exact location near the Mexicali airport, using topographic maps and the technique of retro-photography.

their view by our trail turning due west over an immense level of clay, hard and as smooth as a bowling green.

The desert was now almost destitute of vegetation. Now and then, [there was] a low bush with small, oval, plaited leaves and a few bunches of coarse, prickly sort of grass. The heavy travelling through the sands had proved too much for our poor animals and now the hard marble like surface. With all the efforts of their drivers, we could bring them no farther than the middle of this dreary desert. Now 12 o'clock, we concluded to stop and dry camp as we did last night, giving each of our animals his share of the beans and a scanty sup of water. We slept on our kits till the daylight did appear. Our company had now become much scattered. Some had made better progress ahead and many were in the rear.

Thursday, August 2, we had not proceeded but two miles from our last camp when we met Dr. Baxter looking for his seven mules, which stampeded during the night from a lake of water by which they had camped some half a mile farther on. This was indeed a singular news to us, for the meeting of a lake of good water on this desert was something we had never heard of. We soon were up by the edge of this fairy representation of a lake, which indeed it was, for as far as the eyes could see was covered with good clear water, apperently as if it had been an overflow from some great river.[8] It certainly could not be from the Colorado, as its waters are of a redish hue, and we therefore concluded it must be from the mountains of the north. The head of our party being here, we camped all day, part of the time picking beans from the scattering trees about our camp, and sleeping under our moscheto nets to keep off numerous swarms of a large species of house fly which was a very great anoyance to us.

---

[8] Coming on New River was indeed a surprise; the area was dry when Emory passed four years earlier. It was an intermittent stream, running only when the Colorado was in flood, that no doubt saved the lives of the Knickerbockers and oncoming emigrants. David Jordan watched as Goulding came along the road and "as soon as he seen the runing water he fired off his double-barrel gun & then cried out at the top of his voice '*Oh! Praise the Lord all ye pack mule men for having brought you safe through the desert.*' Then took off his hat & gave 3 cheers, created quite a shout in camp" (August 3, 1849).

During the afternoon, Dr. Baxter found his mules, and at 6 o'clock we prepared for the march again and travelled very well till about 10 o'clock, when we were overtaken by the Mississipian Company, and they being anxious to get ahead, led us off the regular track, and at last we found ourselves wandering about. At midnight the moon had gone down and here we were up to our [illegible] in a soapy quagmire as it was, and our animals much tired out. We stoped, and finding the first spot, each mess dismounted and camped till daylight, when our stoutest animals now showed signs of ailing, and scarcely a man was seen mounted.

On the morning of Friday, August 3, it was now discovered the cause of losing the trail. The advance were intercepted by a river apperantly crossing them at right angles, and which were by all appearances been in existence at some very remote period before, as the rounded banks would indicate, but had now only been recently occupied by this new freshet or supply of water from the northern mountains. By 6 o'clock the trail was again discovered and which led to the very edge of this New River, which was soon forded by the tallest men wading in and carrying over all our effects to the opposite bank, then driving our animals over, all of which was done by 8 o'clock, when on the opposite side we made fires and had a tollerable good breakfast of fried bacon & coffee.

The sun was very oppressive and made our progress very slow. With the imense mountains in our front, nothing could be more desolate in appearance, but the gap through which we had to pass became nearer to our view, and that gave us encouragement to progress. Our passing views were indeed more terrible even than yesterday, our path strewed along with dead and dieing animals and every discription of articles thrown away; even guns and rifles and ammunition now became compleatly werthless to the owners. About 12 o'clock we found ourselves entering the gap in the mountain which had been before us the last three days. The plain was now crossed, but we had not as yet found any comfortable looking place whereby to recruit our animals. [Emory extract omitted.] The first valley we reached was dry. We seen some holes in which water had been onced obtained, but several skeletons of animals being near prevented us exploring any further searches. [Illegible] proceeded on at a snail's pace, all leading our worn down animals. At 5 o'clock we reached the long expected "Cariso Creek."[9] Here we halted and camped in little squads all about this little cane creek, a narrow but pure spring water. All our company came in by dark and once more we were all together after crossing the dreadful desert of 90 miles. The growth about our camp was cane rushes and coarse grass such as you will find on the sea. There are some few mesquite bushes; such was the state of our present camp. [Emory extract omitted.]

---

[9] The travelers had negotiated a desolate twenty-eight-mile stretch of of alkali desert to Carrizo Creek, located in the Vallecito Mountains in Anza-Borrego Desert State Park, San Diego County. Jordan (August 4, 1849) wrote on the same day that he had been living on bread made of flour, water, and salt; "coffee" was a concoction from dried peas. But arriving at the creek with Goulding, he found a freshwater spring with good grass. J. R. Forsythe [1849] wrote of the area when he arrived on November 22: "It is impossible to imagine the complete waste & sterile appearance of those peaked, Jagged, Pointed, and Hillocky mountains. The Genius of Solitude, Desolation & Death rains over all . . . at no time are you ever out of sight of Dead Mules, Horses, or Oxen."

FIGURE 13. Paul Etter on the old emigrant trail near Carrizo Badlands, Anza-Borrego Desert State Park, California, 1980. This was an historic route of Indians, trappers, forty-niners, and the Army of the West. *Photo by Patricia A. Etter.*

17

California! At Last!

The remnants of the Knickerbockers now arrived at what is today known as the Anza-Borrego Desert State Park in Southern California. Few named sites existed there at the time—the only one Emory referred to was Palm Spring Oasis, which he described as a spring with "cabbage trees" (1848, 104). Nevertheless, Goulding and friends probably found and followed tracks left by both General Stephen Watts Kearny in 1846 and Major Lawrence P. Graham in 1848, as the latter marched his troops to the Pacific Coast following occupation duty in Mexico. Vestiges of the old emigrant trail are preserved in the park, and the modern visitor can view them from the road or hike along segments of the trail.

The environment began to change at the Indian village of San Felipe at the north end of the park. Our argonauts began to feel blessed as they followed a path over rolling, grassy hills dotted with trees and streams and inhabited by friendly rancheros. The adventurers headed for Warner's Ranch, but instead of stopping there, headed north on a trail along the San Luis Rey River west of Palomar Mountain. It was not long before they reached the ruins of the Asistencia de San Antonio de Pala Mission, the Indian villages in Pechanga Canyon, and the Temecula land grant.

Saturday, August 4, the howling of the wolf woke us up early this morning to enjoy this refreshing sulpher spring water. About 9 AM, our company were all in good trim, considering our late fatiguing journey over the desert, and sloly proceeding on our march. As the coarse cane & grass at the spring and about our last camp was anything but desirable for our horses, and what their was left was very scant oweing to the great number of companies which had previously passed this rout, this last consideration would not prevent our giving our animals a day's rest wherever grass could be found.

We followed the dry, sandy bed of the Cariso nearly all day at a snail's pace. The valley all along our march was about half a mile wide, and on each side are mountains of grey granite and quartz, sand, and clay rising from 1,000 to 3,000 feet above it. At about noon our attention was attracted by several scattered objects seen projected against the cliffs. They were the cabbage or palm trees, and by them we found a hole of bad tasting water and a small patch of grass, which was soon devoured by the few animals that went over to see these trees.[1]

We rode for several miles through thickets of the cacti and centennial plant, tho sharp thorns terminating every leaf of this plant were a great annoyance to our dismounted and wearied men as well as the feet of the jaded animals they were coaxing and leading along. [Emory extract omitted.] My companion Mr. Wm. Ford was far in the rear endeavering to get his poor mules along. I waited until Ford came up, tugging the halter of his animal along. After refreshing ourselves, we again proceded, when about 5 PM the soil and the appearance became suddenly changed. The valley becomes smaller and the sight of green on the mountains as well as on the ground now gives us, as well as our poor jaded brutes, new vigor and energy. And at six o'clock we arrived at a number of water holes with plenty of excellent grass, which now was a "feast night" for our animals as well as a "feast day" for the packs of wolves which kept close on our track all day, seizing our deserted brutes and making the air resound with their howls as they battled for the carcasses. The water comes to the surface in pools at this place. It is a valley surrounded by high,

[1] Goulding has paraphrased this portion from Emory (1848, 103–104) along with his own observations on Palm Spring Oasis, Anza-Borrego Desert State Park.

bleak mountains, destitute of vegetation and seamed in many places with volcanic matter. The grass, which is coarse, extends for nearly two miles along the valley, and some few Indians reside in small huts and cultivate the land in small patches.[2]

The next morning being Sunday, August 5, and notwithstanding the water was saltish and in pools with plenty of small snakes swimming therein, yet we were compelled to avail ourselves of it for a day to recruit our animals. The day being extremely hot and our camp being exposed to the raise of the sun, we made our Indian lodge of small willows, and covering it over with our blankets, this made us comfortable quarters during our encampment. At this place I visited the Indian's lodges and was much amused at their manner of making cord out of the fibers obtained from the muscal plant. [To] one of them, an old man, I gave a plug of tobacco, and he made me a piece of cord. First he took a roll of the flax like fibers of the plant, and wetting them, put them in a hole in the sand, and placing his foot on the top of the hole, which being covered with sand, stamped down, he then hooked up a small portion of the flax through his toes and so on to his thigh; then he would roll it with his hand in a quick manner, and drawing it occasionally through the hand using suet and wax as an assistant in the formation of the cord, and it was realy astonishing how fast he would spin it out on his naked thigh. I notised a skull cap also made in the same way and worn by one of their woman. They had mellons, pumpkins, and plenty of corn. (I notised several old adobe houses in ruins, indicating that at some remote time, this place was inhabited by Mexicans.)[3] By signs and grunts I made out considerable information.

---

[2] Though it was only about six miles to the next site at Vallecito, travel was torturous, as August air temperatures were in the low hundreds and ground temperatures even higher. At this point, they had no name for Vallecito, which William Hunter (1992, 194) called "Los Bayocitos" and George W. B. Evans (1945, 166) termed "El Yseta." A Butterfield Stage stop would be built there about ten years later.

[3] A group of desert-dwelling Ipai, whose language was classified as Diegueño, lived here in small bands in dome-shaped, thatched huts (Luomala 1978, 592–99). David Jordan also noticed the "mud houses or parts of them" on the same date (August 5, 1849). These had been thrown up by Maj. Lawrence P. Graham during his winter camp in the area in 1848, according to William Chamberlin (1945, 249), who passed through on August 16.

After shooting a few brace of quail, I returned to our camp and indulged in a comfortable dinner of fried quail and pork. A company of Mexicans consisting of some ten men passed us on their way to the state of Sonero [Sonora]. They had been at the mines, but Mexican-like, we could get but little information from them. The most was "muncha ora" and "muncha Los Yankee laderona"—I wrote a note and gave [it] to one, informing Capt. Lane of our adventure over the desert.

The next morning, Monday, August 6, all our troop were in the saddles this morning, which told us fairly the advantage of our Sunday's rest. Here also was a few of the same apparent tribe of Indians consisting of some 5 or 6 lodges. This valley was apperantly alive with quail and hares. Several of them we shot. Our trail ascended again through a narrow pass or defile, very rocky and romantic in the extreme.[4] In some places their was not room for two packed mules to pass each other, and all the points of the compass was made several times before we got through this narrow defile of the "Mount Saint Bernard" of California. For to such it strongly resembles according to the discription of that wonderful mountains of Switzerland over which the Great Napoleon passed.[5] Through this pass we also met a small party of Mexicans on their return from the mines. Some of the more unthoughtful and bad thinking minds of our party made some remarks as to the practicality of stoping them, and which could be very easily done and would no doubt be carried into effect had it not been that the majority of our corps were of men

[4] Emory (1948) did not mention the next long climb over Campbell Grade, where vestiges of the trail can be seen from the modern road that traverses the park. This editor has walked the steep, rock-studded trail and was amazed at what these gold rushers were able to accomplish. The road descends into Mason Valley.

[5] Jordan wondered if they were even on Kearny's road, and wrote that they passed sites that had not been mentioned in Emory's report. For example, he recalled a "narrow pass," as did Goulding, "which was several miles in length and in some places so narrow that a single wagon could not more than pass" (August 5, 1849). The pass was Box Canyon, where Philip St. George Cooke, following in the wake of Kearny and Emory in January 1847, trudged through a circuitous, sandy, and narrow wash where his men had to chisel the rock walls to widen the trail to the width of one wagon. I am not sure how Goulding could compare this to Napoleon's trek over the Alps, having easily trudged through Cooke's narrow canyon myself.

composed of much more concientious feelings than robbing these poor, worn out looking Mexicans. Altho we afterwards heard every one of them were robbed and killed by the Umas at the crossing of the Colorado.

Trees of various kinds began to present to us that we were fast approaching that long wished for [California; Emory extract omitted] for we had got heartily tired of quail stewed with rusty pork [illegible] and flap jacks and it is hard to satisfy the cravings of hunger with such indifferent food. Quail is excellent with toast and butter, but of these latter we only had to think of. We gradually decended into the valley of the deserted village of San Fellippe,[6] and our eyes were gladdened with the evergreen oak and ceder with the willow bean tree, and now the beautiful velvet leaf shrub sage impregnating the air with its fragrant smell as we rode along. Occasionally, the beehive and bayonet cactus presented itself to our view and some of the "Agave americana" or centennial plant, some of which were in full bloom.

About 4 PM we came up to this ruins of San Fellippe. Here was some 30 small, rude constructed huts occupied by Pueblo Indians and Mexicans. Several enclosed gardens with mellons, beans, onions &c. These people seemed much better informed than any that we had heretofore seen since entering the south mountains of California. Their were many women amongst them and all were busily employed in drying and cleaning their maise and acorns, and grind nuts and berries of various sorts, particularly a species of the elder, both red and white, which they had spread on sheets of muslin in the sun. Also some had large vessels full of the figs from the cactus, of which they make a sort of sugar. All these woman wore frocks or peddicoats and caps as before discribed as made from the fibers of the mescal plant.

---

[6] The company made one more challenging climb between Blair and Earthquake Valley before descending to San Felipe Indian village. Goulding copied the term "deserted" from Emory (1848, 104), but as Goulding and others witnessed, the village was far from empty. The inhabitants belonged to another band of Ipai people. San Felipe later became a stop on the Butterfield Stage.

Our camp was pitched in a long field like of grass, three or four miles in extent, through which flowed a small stream towards the north, abreast of the village, which at this time was all in ruins, on the base of the high mountains which still range on all sides of us from 3 to 5,000 feet high and to the north was close to our camp. We collected sufficient dry sage and scrub mezquite roots and bushes with which we made fires to cook our supper. The same here as all over the Indian or Mexican settlements, the woman is the worker and slave to the men. Two of these woman passed my mess fire with large, hamper-like baskets on their backs loaded like a mule with acorns and berrys which they had been collecting in the hills during the day and now returning to their wigwams as happy and as jovial as any young maiden and felt proud in telling us they were "now Americans" and "no more Mexicans." Numbers of their women and children fetched us "latha" (milk) and tortillas, a sort of griddle cake mixed with flour and fat and molasses. The latter I only seen used at this place. I shot some black-birds and one meadow lark (the first I have seen since leaving Arkansas) and with abundance of cactus figs, we had a very fine supper.

We were joined at this camp by several of our former associates who had been detained on and over that dreadful desert. They informed us of the melloncholly news of the death of a Mr. Ells of New York, who died on the desert at the Allimo and was their buried by the Massachusetts waggon company, who had fetched him so far, sick, on one of their waggons.[7] Our night was comfortable passed with exception of one of the nightly serenades. A wolf made free with our frying pan about ten feet from my head. The ringing sound of his licking the pan woke some of the boys up and [illegible] him to some other quarters.

On the morning of Tuesday, August 7, early, our troop was on the march [Emory extract omitted] and for the first time since leaving

[7] Goulding wrote about Ell's death in the Rancho del Chino Register Book (Bynum 1934, 5). The trip from New River to San Felipe, nearly eighty miles of almost waterless, boulder-studded, sandy trails with steep grades and switchbacks, took its toll on both the emigrants and their stock.

the Arkansas, we saw what would even their be called large trees. We passed some few more Indian lodges, and by one of them we seen some peach trees and grape vines under cultivation. Emerging from these we saw in the distance a beautiful valley called the Agua Caliente (Hot Water Valley), where we expected to find some American settlers.[8] Leaving this small valley, we ascended the hills to the north covered with mezquite & shrub sage [Emory extract omitted].

There was some twenty thatched huts near to and about the farm yard, in which lived a lot of half naked Indians who were held in a sort of serf-dom by their former masters but now were even worse off than they were before they became Americans, as they themselves would imply. Some of their women were painted or tattooed on the face, breast, and arms. We could not get any satisfactory information from the French or Dutch man who was here of the whereabouts of the proprietor and therefore concluded that they pretended ignorance on account of so many passing just at this time by whom they had been much annoyed. We however obtained some suet and beef, flour and [Emory extract omitted].

To the south and down the valley of the Agua Caliente is the road to San Diego, to which some of our party now left us and went there, being tired out of the pack mule travel which has still some 700 miles to go. Having seen enough of this place, we travelled on some few miles further, passing by several springs and a beautiful rolling country, at times passing some fine large oaks. About six o'clock, we came to an Indian village of several hundred souls, but having a plenty of provisions, we did not visit them but camped near an extensive grove of trees in which was a number of rocks. Feeling a desire for a change of diet, I strolled amongst them and shot sufficient to make a "corbo fricko a la Francais"—a large crow pot pie.

---

[8] Jonathan Trumbull Warner's ranch house was near the junction of San Felipe Road (County Highway S22) and State Highway 79, San Diego County. Warner was not in residence at the time, so the emigrants could not replenish supplies. Some four miles from the ranch were the Cupeño village of Kupa and a number of hot springs, also called Warner's Springs. Many an overlander welcomed a soak in these waters, but Goulding passed them by and followed the trail on the west side of Palomar Mountain (State Highway 76). He passed modern Rincon Springs and Pauma Valley before arriving at the ruins of Pala Mission.

I also shot a large rattle snake with nine rattles, which I cut off and carried home with many others of the same sort. A Mr. Wood joined us here, having lost his mule at the last camp, and not being able to find it, abandoned his search and concluded to foot soldier it the rest of the rout.

On the morning of Wednesday, August 8, we proceeded on our march bright and early, over hill and valley and the mountains, until nearing us at eleven o'clock we came up to a camp of some of Capt. Duval's company busily employed in dressing a young steer which they had just killed and from which we got a few lb. of steaks.[9] We passed by several small villages of the native Pueblo Indians intermixed with Mexicans during our march,[10] and several heards of cattle ranging in the sides of the base of the mountains in all directions, denoting to us now fairly that we were getting into the heart of California.

Our travel was very romantic, and some passes through which our trail led us was very difficult, and our troop became very much scattered. The feeling now was to hurry on to the mines, many of our boys having got sight of some "rocks of the gold" in the hands of those Mexicans which we were continually now meeting on their return from the mines, and as we were now out of danger from the uncultivated and wild Savage, no further attention was paid to guard duty, and each and every mess became its own independent company. Some had six or eight men, but the majority were of even smaller parties and which kept passing and repassing each other several times during our march. Those who now had the best horses or mules fared the best, at least they imagined so. But I found that at most of the Indian settlements and small rancherias we could always get a sufficient supply of what they had by being civil to the inhabitants. Some few were rather cold and unfavourably disposed to Americans, as might be naturaly expected under the present excite-

[9] Isaac Duval's (1987, 116) diary does not define his route or give a date of travel between Warner's ranch and Los Angeles. This new information could be helpful to those researching this segment of trail, since most emigrants used a trail on the east side of Palomar Mountain that went directly to Temecula.

[10] The villages were of the Luiseño people, whose territory extended from the Pacific Ocean to Palomar Mountain (Bean and Shipek 1978, 551).

ment of travelling going on in their country and which many of them thought was over.[11]

After travelling through a narrow pass for upwards of an hour up to our horses knees in water part of the time, with mountains towering high above us on both sides, we came out into a very extensive plain with large heards of cattle and a large flock of sheep. Nevertheless, with all the immence heards of cattle, there is still the appearance of a sort of desolation, and which so far all the rancherias present, and is little calculated to impress us with favorable notions of the agricultural resources of this part of California. The land in the narrow valleys is good but surrounded everywhere by high, barren, and rocky looking mountains. And where the land is good, the seasons are too dry for men to attempt cultivation without facilities for irrigation.

We met a Mexican umbra who informed us that this place in our view looking like some ancient castle was the Mission of San Luis.[12] We arrived at the base of the hill of the rancheria about 6 o'clock, and not finding any grass about the place, we pushed on and encamped a mile below or by a small pond where was onced a fine orchard and garden, by the appearances of the ruins all about, and close by were some fifty Indian huts, all apperantly peacibly disposed and happy.

One of them, a fine, athletic looking fellow and the most polite and best informed one we as yet have met with, came and shewed us the best spot to pitch our camp,, both for ourselves as well as animals and on the morning of Thursday, August 9, our Indian friend fetched us a pail full of new milk. And now, as we were thined out to our own mess, and not caring to hurry on our animals, we concluded to stop here a day and rest. So we requested our Indian friend to bring us a fat sheep. During the morning I strolled over to the ancient looking castle which first attracted our attention in this valley, but after a very

---

[11] Goulding is referring to the fact that California had recently come under American control; some residents were still suspicious of the newcomers, while others welcomed them.

[12] The Asistencia de San Antonio de Pala Mission (established 1815) was a branch of San Luis Rey Mission twenty miles to the west, and had served a thousand Luiseños until secularization in 1833. The campanile, which was intact during Goulding's visit, still stands apart from the modern chapel (Crump 1985, 56). The Cupeño people at Warner's Springs moved to this site in 1903 (Hoover, Rensch, and Rensch 2000, 342–43).

fatigueing walk of nearly two miles, on arriving thereto, I found a place of desolation. The outer adobe walls which gave the place some appearance from the distance, were in a tolerable state of preservation oweing to their immence thickness, being about two feet thick. But all the inside partitions and court yards were in ruins and was now used at times as a coral to protect the sheep in from the storms. A solitary cat was the only occupant at the present time and was the first of that tribe that I have seen in many months. All I could do could not induce the poor puss to become friendly with me, so I returned on my way to camp.[13] I shot several black birds from an immence flock of them. Passing several old vineyards and gardens all neglected and in ruins, I arrived in camp, where Mr. Ford & Hunter were busily imployed cooking mutton chops.

During the afternoon, the Indians in our immediate neighbourhood were out in their best, and evident signs of some jovial time or entertainment was about to be cellebrated, and about three o'clock a party came along escorted by a fiddle and tambereen and the parties a dancing and singing at a great rate. We were informed that a wedding of one of the young senoretas of this village was about to be cellebrated with one of the young dons of Tomascall [Temescal], another village some few miles from this place.[14] These people seams more enlightened and much better informed than any that I have before seen. The Roman Catholic creed seems to be their religion in a part. They dress better and are more secluded in their manners, particularly the female part of this community. Their politeness is not surpased by the most refined and educated Mexicans I had seen in New Mexico or Sonero. When night closed in, we had no other accompaniment than the howling of myriads of wolves, attracted by the smell of the entrails of our fat sheep which had been thrown in the edge of the pond not far from our camp.

Friday, August 10, the morning was cold and raining, with a heavy

[13] Travelers and miners, who had been away from wives, children, and animals for so long, often looked for the comfort of a pet. Robert Brownlee (1986, 129) wrote from Agua Fria mines that he was selling kittens to the miners for sixteen dollars or an ounce of gold.

[14] This was the Luiseño Indian village in Pechanga Canyon on the Temecula Land Grant, which was patented to Félix Valdez in 1844 (Cowan 1956, 101; Bean 1978, 551).

FIGURE 14. Asistencia of San Antonio de Pala, Mission Road, Pala, San Diego County, California, 1936. Campanario and cemetery gate are shown. Photo by Henry F. Whithey. *Courtesy of the Prints and Photographs Division, Library of Congress.*

fog, a new feature to us, and indication that we were not many leagues from the ocean. A party of very respectable looking Spaniards on their way to Mexico visited us, of whom I purchased a fine white horse in exchange for my cloak and sword, now two articles of no further use to me, and a good riding horse being just the thing I now wanted. These men had a large number of horses and mules and were anxious to sell more of them to us. I endevored to dispose of some few instruments but did not succeed. Having rested ourselves pretty well at this place and the weather clearing off fine, at 3 PM we commenced our march, travelling over a variety of country till 7 o'clock when we camped in a sand bed near some good grass and was well pleased with my new horse, who gave evident demonstration of his superior qualities. To our right and north of us we noticed a volcanic mountain with large volumes of smoke issuing from the side of it.[15] We met with no

[15] The smoke was from a brush fire, not a volcano.

FIGURE 15. Palomar Mountain from Pachango (Pechanga) Canyon, circa 1895.
A Temecula (Luiseño) Indian village is in the foreground. Photo by C. C. Pierce.
Courtesy of the University of Southern California, on behalf of the USC Special Collections.

Indian lodges or travellers during our afternoon ride, and our camp was a dreary one, which we enlivened by a pan full of fat chops with the duplicate next morning, Saturday, August 11, at 8 o'clock.

We proceeded at 11 o'clock. We came to a lake [Elsinore] about 12 miles in circumference with large heards of cattle in all directions.[16] Several trails passed our trail. At noon we stoped at a small casa where was some umbras dressing beef from whom we got a supply of beef and salt and suet. Travelling over many hills and valleys with several volcanic mountains continually in view, amusing our eyes with the volumes of smoke now and then bursting therefrom, at 6 o'clock we arrived at Tomascoulla [Temescal] Rancheria, near to which we camped by some Indian lodges or huts.

At this ranch the proprietors were very polite and were well informed Mexican descendants having plenty of everything we wanted. We laid in a good supply and the lady sent us a large dish full of hot cakes and a bottle of vinagar with a pot full of stewed beans. This was the first house we have met with since leaving New Mexico where the people have the Delph ware. The plates and bowls and the glass tumbler became a luxury to drink a draught of sulphur water out of, being used only to the tin cup for months back. We visited these hospitable people during the evening and was much amused with their conversation respecting the late war and the exploits of the American cavelries in getting the Mexican rulers out of the country. The rancherier of this place was one of the first, with [Jonathan Trumbull] Warner, [Joseph] Snooks, [James] Stokes, and [Isaac] Williams, who lent their aid to Gen. Carney [Kearny] and his associates, in gaining the South of California out of their possession.[17] I was much amused by the singular method of

[16] The emigrants were moving north along Old Temescal Road, which parallels the Corona Freeway, Interstate 15 (Gudde 2004, 389), and had arrived at Lake Elsinore.

[17] Goulding and friends had reached Bernardo Yorba's Rancho La Sierra, now the town of Corona, Riverside County. This ranchero apparently told Goulding about the various individuals who had lent aid to General Kearny's Army of the West before it arrived at San Pasqual, where the army battled the Californios under Andrés Pico in 1846 (Hoover, Rensch, and Rensch 2000, 294, 346; Cowan 1956, 98). Both Jonathan Trumbull Warner and Isaac Williams had been residents of California since the 1830s; Dr. James Stokes was a prominent English merchant in Monterey; and Capt. Joseph Snook, an Englishman, had been in California since 1834, becoming a naturalized Mexican citizen in 1833 (Davis 1967, 13, 322).

light given to us during our visit. An Indian Pueblo boy was kept holding a shock of some sort of dried cactus and occasionally rubbing it with a piece of suet or tallow and which burned equal to any gas or torch you could produce, and by the aid of one such, the night being very dark, we were lighted to our camp.

Sunday, August 12, 1849, early this morning these hospitable people sent one of their sons to our camp, desiring us to come and breakfast with them. Accordingly, we packed up our kits, and leaving our animals to feed on a plentiful supply of corn fodder thrown them by the Pueblos attached to the ranch, we went up to the house, where for the first time since leaving New Mexico, we sat down to a table set out with knives and forks and white plates, with a large bowl of good strong coffee which the Spanish senoras are famous for makeing. The middle of the table was strewed with fine white bread cut in pieces, two glass decanters filed with wine, and our dishes were served separately with chilé stewed with chicken and small pieces of mutton, but the first mouthful brought the tears trickling down our cheeks, very much to the amusement of the family, with their leathern lined throats, who, like the Mexicans, are well accustomed to this sort of stew, the chilés, red peppers, stuffed with small minced up garlic and mutton dried in pepper.

The senora, whose name was Margareta, was very talkative and discribing to us the rancheria of Col. [Isaac] Williams and of his goodness to them and to all the people in the country, and his ranch being the next stopping place, the senoras put us on our direct rout and we parted and proceeded.[18]

[18] About this time, Benjamin Butler Harris (1960, 97) of the Duval Company mentioned "nooning" at the Yorbas' on his way to Williams's rancho. Señora Yorba dispensed the same hospitality to Goulding and company. At one time, the Yorba ranch covered close to eighteen thousand acres. Its history is recalled on California State Landmark 738, erected in Corona City Park at Sixth Street (Hoover, Rensch, and Rensch 2000, 294).

18

Rancho Santa Ana del Chino

On leaving the Yorba ranch, following the Santa Ana River, Goulding and his friends arrived at the much-anticipated Rancho Santa Ana del Chino. Isaac Williams's rancho spread over 35,600 acres between the San Gabriel Mountains and the Santa Ana River in San Bernardino County, California. The modern cities of Chino and Chino Hills lie within the boundaries of the former rancho. In 1830, Williams had joined the Bean-Sinclair fur trading company, along with Ewing Young and Jonathan Trumbull Warner, and had trapped in the Gila River and the lower Colorado before arriving in Los Angeles in April 1832. Williams earned a living by hunting sea otters before managing a mercantile business in Los Angeles. He liked California, and despite being a foreigner in Mexican territory, he was active in local affairs and was warmly received by his neighbors. Former Texas Ranger Horace Bell thought Williams a perfect specimen of the frontier gentleman: tall, handsome, elegant, and courtly in his manners. Williams took the oath of allegiance in 1839 to become a citizen of Mexico and was re-baptized as Julian. Soon after, don Julian took as his bride Señorita María Lugo, daughter of Antonio María Lugo, a prominent Southern California landowner. In December 1841, Lugo deeded Rancho Santa Ana del Chino to his son-in-law. Williams later added another 13,366 acres to his holdings.

Now, in 1849 and 1850, thousands of fatigued and impoverished gold rushers arrived on his doorstep and had reason to be grateful to don Julian for his generosity, hospitality, and assistance. Fortunately, Williams liked to have people around, and, as we learn from William Goulding, he was a gracious host to all who stopped at the ranch.

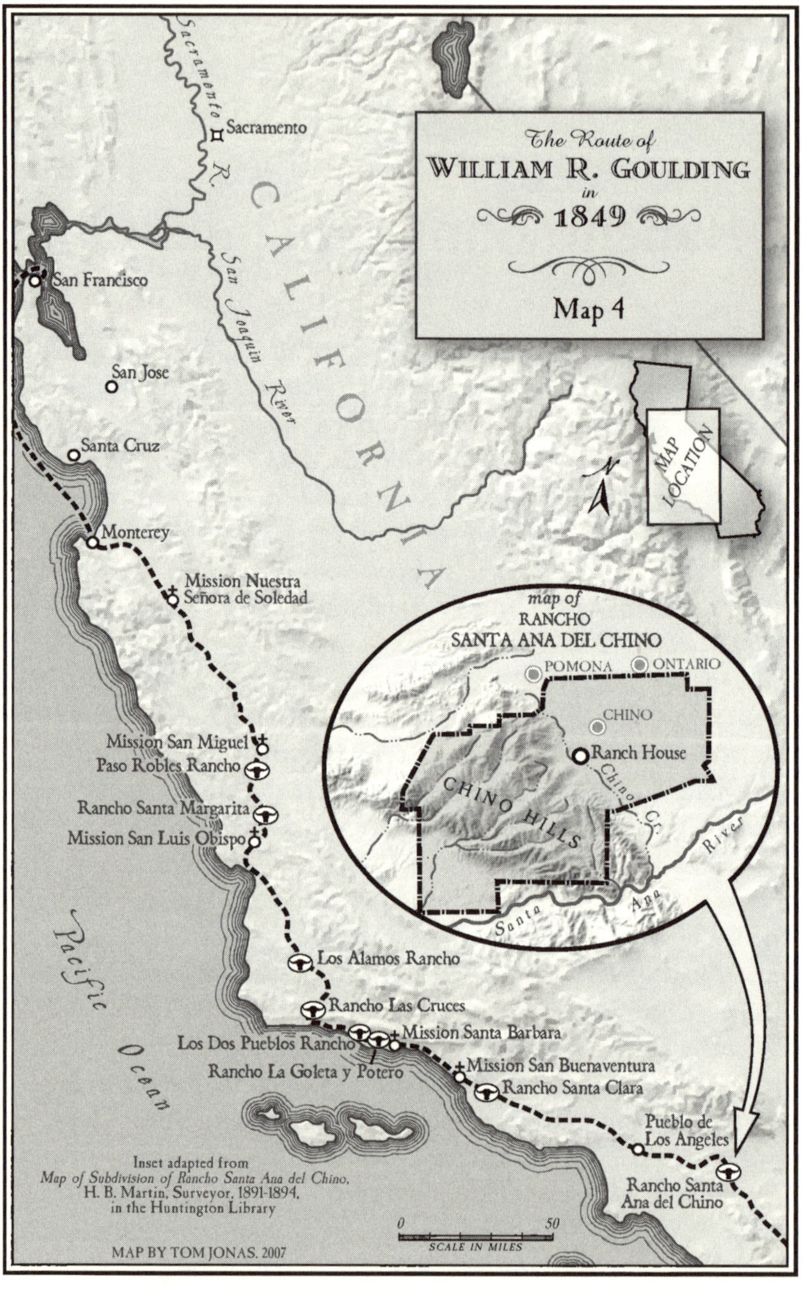

MAP 4. Rancho Santa Ana del Chino to San Francisco

Many have given brief descriptions of the ranch, but Goulding records economic activities there that have never before appeared in print.

Sunday, August 12, continued travelling over very fine arable land, the hills covered with cattle luxuriously feeding upon wild oats and mustard, which this part of the country is covered with, on the rolling hills. Twelve miles from our last camp we met with a small casa or rancho occupied by only seven or eight persons. Here we stoped to noon. The river Santa Anna, a small, rapid but shallow stream, is close to this house and is the boundery line on the south to Williams land. We forded this stream, which is some twenty yards wide and at this time not more than 8 or 10 inches deep and flowing full of gold colored mica and black sand. Imediately after fording this river, to the right of the road is a large casa or ranch which belongs to Col. Williams and is used for a coral for his immense herds of cattle, now grazing over his lands in all directions as far as your eyes can see.[1]

Two leagues from this river brought us in sight of this celebrated "Rancho del Chino," owned by the famous Col. Isaac Williams, and a splendid appearance it makes to the view when within a mile of the mill, which is the first point we came to. This mill is built of timber and sunburnt bricks (adobes) and being painted white, looked as if it was a stone fort erected to protect his house, which from this point looked like some ancient castle without turrets. In front of this mill and imediately on the road is a large pond of water which is supplied from the river Santa Anna and which is used as a reserve basin to irrigate the land and gardens in and about the premises. The valley is extensively cultivated by irrigation and is now covered with corn

[1] The exact location of Williams's ranch house has caused controversy over the years, which is surprising, as it became a stop for the Butterfield Stage in 1858. The house stood until 1865, when Williams's daughter María Merced Rains tore it down to build a new house on the site. A granddaughter believed the house site to be on the stage road that ran from Rincon to Pomona, about three miles south of modern Chino and close to the dairy house of the California Junior Republic (Beattie 1940, 62–69). A map by surveyor H. B. Martin (1891–92) appears to uphold this theory.

and wheat, and in the rear of the mill, a very extensive vine-yard and peach and plum orchard and a few apple trees.[2]

As we advanced to the left of the mill pond, we came abreast of a large brickyard looking ranch, which we were informed was Williams extensive soap and candle works by a Mr. [Theodore] Foster, an American who approached us and who was like ourselves a recent mountain voyager and who had a few days since arrived at this place and was now participating the hospitality of the famous "Rancho del Chino."[3] A few hundred yards brought us immediately in front of this spacious one story edifice some hundred feet square built of mud bricks and white-washed, the roof flat and covered with asphaltum cement, built in the Spanish style on a square. The interior of the square is an open court and the principal rooms open into it, and nothing can exceed the comfort and convenience of the interior, the thick walls making it cool in summer as well as warm in the winter.

Our worthy host now approached us, and being introduced by our fellow traveller Mr. Foster, Mr. Isaac Williams kindly invited us to his hospitality as long as we wished to stop. We found Mr. Williams to be an open-hearted and frank American and expressed all he said with his mouth, with his eye, and with his hands too, for he instantly assisted us in unsaddling our packed mules as well as our riding [gear?] and led our horses into the wheat field immediately by the house, which was fenced in for his own riding horses, and treated us in every manner as if we had been his own relations. During the evening we amused the worthy family with a brief account of our journey over the deserts and rocky mountains, in which our worthy hosts two daughters were much interested. Mr. Williams

[2] On April 22, 1847, Philip St. George Cooke ordered a noncommissioned officer and six men of the Mormon Battalion to Williams's to protect the ranch and "operate under his guidance," which included cutting grain and building a race for his mill (Tyler 1969, 278). James Bouldin observed that Williams had "a good mill . . . formed by a dam like basin by daming a cannion then a race from the basin some 200 yards to the mill" (November 28, 1849).

[3] Theodore Foster had been staying at Isaac Williams's "hospitable residence" for several days and was there to welcome Goulding when he arrived on August 12. According to a Foster letter (1849) published in the *Missouri Republican*, he had arrived in Los Angeles by way of Mazatlan and may have been working for Williams. We have scattered information on Foster. William Rice (1947, 4–5) wrote that by 1850, Foster had become a laborer on John Rowland's ranch near the Chino ranch. That same year, Foster tried but failed to establish a newspaper for Los Angeles.

was a widower, having lost his senora some two years since, and he had but these two girls, Francisca and Margareta [María Merced].[4]

Their was but two Americans with him, but he had some two hundred Indian Pueblos in the gardens and fields about the rancho in small huts and some few in the ranch who acted as servants in cooking. Also a black smith and a shoe maker, also Indians who were there to work and were learned these trades by him. He informed me he had at one time all the different trades he desired for his own use, even tanners. And all these Indians he instructed through the means of books which he had imported from the States. He kept one principal major domo who was also an Indian who governed and attended to the direction of all his out-door affairs.[5] And during the time of the revolution in this country he had over five hundred of these Indians under his control and acted as serfs to his will in any matter he might order or direct.

At one time he done a large business in hides, having a very extensive range of land upwards of twenty leagues long and nearly as many in weight and every day used to kill from twenty to thirty head of cattle expressly for the tallow and hides. The tallow, he used in making mould candles, and the residue was converted into soap of a superior sort and for which he used to receive a ready market for at San Diego and San Pedro, to which places he kept continually teams going to and from, loaded with hides and soap and candles too, and in coming home used to stop at his coal hills and load up a cargo, which he used in his melting furnace large quantities both of coal and asphaltum. I stoped at Williams twelve days and during my leasure their I drew him two views of his place and which pleased him very much.[6] During my visit their on one night there was some rain, the first they had seen for the last eight months. Mr. Williams informed me that during two years he at one time had not seen a drop of rain.

On the morning of Tuesday, August 14, Mr. Williams and myself took a ride over his lands. After riding through immence fields of

[4] Williams and María Lugo's two daughters, Francisca and María Merced, both later married Americans, and their future lives could easily be the subject of a book of its own.

[5] The mayordomo was José Popé, a Gabrieleño (Hoover, Rensch, and Rensch 2002, 299).

[6] Sketch missing.

wild mustard and oats, when about nine miles from his house, we came to the summitt of a hill on which an immence field of coal crops out the surface of the soil, the seam being at the place where he opened was twenty feet deep.[7] We rode for two miles along the top of this coal hill, from which we had a distant view of the Pacific Ocean, but owing to a dence fog there I was not able to distinguish any objects with my glass.

In the chain of mountains running south were several large white masses, and on looking at them with the telescope were concluded to be white limestone or granular quartz. The view all around was very oposing and grand, the geological formation of the extensive range of mountains in all directions looking like a succession of castles or pirimids piled up on top of each other. These mountains are formed principly of sandstone and lava.

Mr. Williams informed me he had visited them with a party of his Indians some years ago and his account was very interesting. The range to which he was with his party were almost bare of verdure, mere brown piles of barrenness sprinkled here and there with a cluster of briers, small shrubs, or dwarf trees, and a few ravines having an odd large tree therein. Among the ridges are a few spots to which the sweeping rains have spared a little soil. There are also some places near the bases of these mountains which are well adapted to tillage and pasturage.[8] But the principal difficulty with that region is the same common to all countries of volcanic origin, a scarcity of water; the porousness of the rocks allows it to pass underground. His lands extends over to the base of the mountains to the east, and his object of exploring in these mountains was for timber and coal, as at the time, he did not know of coal being to the west of his house, but 8 or 9 mile distant he says the general aspect is far from pleasing. There was such a vastness of monotonous desolation as he travelled up the

[7] Seams of coal were readily available from Coal Canyon in nearby Chino Hills (Stephen Williams, personal communication, 2006).

[8] Goulding could look in almost any direction for a magnificent view. To the north were the San Gabriel Mountains; to the east, the San Bernardino Mountains; and to the south, the Santa Ana Mountains.

range towards the north, the surface became dry and so blistered with volcanic fires, and at last, after four days wandering through them, it became so forbidding to the wants of his thirsting and hungering men and mules, he gladly turned his eyes towards his home. While he was in some of the ravines, they fell[ed] several large pines and trimming the tops from them, and on different occasions after, he sent with teams and oxen to haul them to his place and were used in constructing his numerous buildings about the premises.

In the neighborhood of his coal hill there is a small lake or pond and on the surface of which is covered with asphaltum or resin gum with which he has all his buildings semented on the roofs and which answers a very good purpose so far as warmth and keeping off the rain when there is rain. But I pity the feet of those who may venture to walk on the top of one of the roofs in the heat of the day, as the suns rays melts it into a sticky sort of tar which nothing but spirits will eradicate.[9]

On our ride home Col. Williams gave me a very interesting account of his troubles in this country and the jealousy of the old Spaniards had against him as well as all the Americans and Britons in the country and of the revolution in '36 and '40 and of the villany of Jose Castro and Alvarado, in a conspiration or junta, concocted at Monterey, by which they had imprisoned a great number of the foreigners in the country. Altho it was these same Americans and Britons who had but a short time before placed them by their courage at the head of California, independent of the old Spanish yoke. Even his wifes brothers and kindred, after his father in law died, became jealous of his enterprise and prosperity and even went so far as to attack his rancho with an armed force and was besieged for nearly a week within the mud walls of his house, and in several places to this day is the remains of bullets fired into the window frames and gate posts of his rancheria. And all this hostile feeling was worked up throughout the country by the personal enmities and jealousie of half a dozen scoundrels, who, disregarding the most

---

[9] Natural asphalt and tar seeps dotted wide areas of Southern California, the most famous being La Brea Tar Pits in Los Angeles.

sacred pledges to their friends, would rob them of their property and sacrifice their lives.[10]

Since the revolution of '36, the Californians and Spaniards had been convinced that the Americans and Britons were vastly their superiors in skill and courage, and now they became the galants of the land, for it was and is a fact now that the senoritas, the dear ladies, in the plenitude of their taste and sympathy for foreigners, preferring them as husbands. Hence the jealousies of these dons of the country. "Jose Castro," one of the kindred of his wife, was heard to say before the Junta of Monterey that such indignities could not be borne by Castilian blood, for a Californian cavalier cannot woo now a senorita if opposed in his suit by an American sailor, and that these heretics must be cleared from the land.

On arriving near the house, Francisca, the youngest daughter of my worthy host, came running to meet us, holding in her hand a huge bat, which she had caught in one of the out houses, and had it stretched out like a skin of a rabbit on two pieces of wood with a segareta in its mouth, puffing away the fumes as if it realy enjoyed the smoke of tobaco, when at the same time the poor animal was breathing its terable fears and sufferings of its stretched out body to the excited enjoyment of its little executioner. Bats of a very large size are seen in California measuring nearly two feet across the wings.[11]

Messrs. Ford, Dorsy, and Foster volunteered to go to the Pueblo of des los Angeles for Mr. Williams to purchase some provisions &c., and returned on Saturday bringing us some New York papers, the first we had seen now in the last six months, also some segars and lots

[10] Goulding is referring to the "Battle of Chino" in 1846, when a group of Californios who were Mexican sympathizers attacked the Williams house, believing that Williams and his neighbors supported the American takeover in California. When they set his roof on fire, Williams surrendered along with his two daughters; his neighbors Benjamin Wilson, John Rowland, and Louis Robideaux; and others who had taken refuge in the house. The men were arrested and jailed in Los Angeles until things settled down between the Americans and the Californios (Beattie 1940, 62–69; Ingersoll 1904, 15–108). Williams eventually asked for and received military protection, which came in the form of the Mormon Battalion. Daniel Tyler was one of those who drew duty at the rancho and worked with his colleagues to dig a race to set a small mill going, the one Goulding noticed when he first arrived (Tyler 1969, 278, 291–92).

[11] Francisca may have captured an exemplar of the largest bat species in the United States, the western mastiff bat (*Eumops perotis*), whose wingspan is about two feet.

of other luxuries. Des los Angeles is but thirty miles from the "Rancho del Chino." They also brought with them a Mr. Weber, one of Williams old fellow companions and neighbors in this country for many years past and who had gone off with the excitement created in the country by this gold fever, and now after being their nine months returned here with his health and constitution compleatly broke down with a fever of a more terrible nature than gold even, that fever of death. For I understood he only lived to get home to his family, and after reciting to us of his adventures in the gold mines, some of us began to think we wished we never left home.

Gen. [Bennett C.] Riley, the then governor of California, had issued a proclimation that all foreigners excepting those who came from the United States should quit the mining district, and this created considerable trouble in the mines, and hence the reason why so many of these Mexicans were daily passing us on their return to Senora and Durango in Mexico. The prices of all provisions at the mines were very high and alarming and many things could not be had for any money. Flour and pork was selling at from six to twelve shillings a lb. and other things in the same proportion, and his general views and accounts of the mines were rather dubious.

Several parties of Americans arrived and passed on by Williams during the week and all of which were abundantly supplied with fresh beef and vegatables gratuously by this worthy man, and in many instances where their mules and horses were broken and jaded out, gave them fresh ones instead, without any remuneration whatever. Such was and has been the general character of this Isaac Williams. And the same philantrophic hospitality he gave to Col. Fremont and the army attached to Gen. Kearny, the "Army of the West." Altho he was promised to be paid by those great "Warriors of the West" for his mules and horses and cattle, he should be paid, but up to the present time he has never heard any responce from those brave men. Nevertheless, the celebrated Col. Fremont had been writen to on several occasions, to make right the pecuniary obligations he was under to Col. Williams, if nothing else. At the time Fremont was at this place, he made overtures to Williams to purchase his Rancho, and thereby gained his confidence and has now forfeited by his neglect and ingratitude.[12]

The major domo every morning used to kill one or two small cattle, and the scene was rather amusing. Two of the Indians, mounted on spirited horses, would single out such a steer as was desired from the heard in the coral near to the house and chase him up near to the spot where they kill in front of the house, and in an instant one would through the laso over the head and fore feet while the other threw in like manner, making fast the hind feet, then galloping there horses in contrary directions, by which means the beast became hooked by the sudden jerks, and would instantly fall in the side, with the head & fore legs fast in the stretched out laso, and at the same time the laso of the other rider drew up the two hind legs also on the stretch, when the major domo quietly walked up to the fritened animal and cuts his throat with a large knife. In a few moments the riders slacks their lasos, and rolling them up, throws them on the [illegible] of the saddles, and in less than two minutes the animal is skinned, cut in quarters, and hanging up in the shambles of the court yard, and in less than an hour after, not a drop of blood, intestines, or remains of the creature is left except the bones of the head, but what is devoured by a flock of hungry "turkey bussards," and the bones left are better picked before the next morning by the hungry wolfs.[13]

One morning I was much amused at their rude method of thrashing. A large coral occupying nearly an acre of ground was appropriated to this rude thrashing machines. The grain being placed in the center of the ground of clay previously swept clean, their major domo turned in some twenty more horses, and two of the Indians mounted bare backed on two of the most spirited of them and set them gallop-

[12] At this point, John Charles Frémont probably could not afford the ranch. Many biographies about him describe the complex of issues he faced.

[13] Both Bayard Taylor and Edwin Bryant were impressed with the strength and agility of the Mexican vaquero as he selected a beef from the herd, caught it with his lasso, threw it to the ground, bled, flayed, and quartered the meat and tossed it on hot coals in an incredibly short time. Taylor commented that the meat, "dripping with rich juices . . . was remarkably sweet and delicious" (1988, 94), while Bryant noticed the piles of cattle bones strewn about, showing "terrible slaughter . . . and a prodigious consumption of flesh" ([1849], 17). Beef was the staple diet of the Californios, in addition to providing the major source of income through the sale of hides—known as the "California banknote."

ing, and with whoops, yells, and blows from the laso, used as a whip, they keep the affrighted brutes constantly in motion. To seperate the wheat from the chaff, they used a winnow machine imported from the United States, but the Indians and Mexicans, who have never seen such, use [a] simple hand-barrow with a bottom of raw beefs hide perforated with holes, and against this they shovel the grain, and being fixed in a proper position, the wind carrys off the chaff. Mr. Wiliams had over sixty acres of wheat now ripe and could not get hands for any money to reap it and was obliged to leave the greater part to shed its grain on the soil. The gold excitement was so high that most of his people had gone to the mines.

On the afternoon of Thursday, August 16, when quietly sitting drawing Col. Williams Rancho,[14] my attention was attracted by a cloud of dust over the vast fields of wild mustard to the south of the mill, and on coming over that way to see the cause, I was agreeably surprised at meeting a number of our old company, "the New York Knickerbockers," who had attached themselves to some packed mule companies and had left San Tafee June 1st over the northern mountains by what was called the Spanish Trail. A Mr. Shaw and Captain Day were the so styled comadantas of these go-a-head companies. The accounts I received from Mr. John Hoyt, who was one of my own mess in the corps of Knickerbockers, was very thrilling and filed up with many difficulties, trials, losses, and disappointments. He told me he kept a journal of most of his route in pencil.[15] Some of them were defaced from wet and exposure. The party encamped by the coral near the house and both them and their animals were plentifully supplied with all they wanted by our worthy host. Mr. Hoyt was again received into my little company and he expressed his regret ever leaving us as he did at Santa Fe and making such a wild goose chase as they did over the Spanish Trail.

---

[14] Sketch missing.

[15] When John P. Hoyt split off from the Knickerbocker Company, his new group was headed by a Captain Day. Hoyt signed the Register Book of the Rancho Santa Ana del Chino on August 21, 1849, and other members of Day's group signed in on August 28, 1849 (Bynum 1934, 9–10). Goulding copied the contents of Hoyt's journal into his own (see in appendix C). There is no record that Hoyt's original journal has survived.

19

California's Mission Trail

BEFORE QUITTING THE RANCH, Goulding agreed to deliver a letter from Isaac Williams to Governor Bennett C. Riley in Monterey, asking for protection against Mexicans and others, returning from the gold fields, who were helping themselves to his livestock. Following a brief sojourn in Los Angeles, Goulding, Hoyt, Ford, and a Mr. Gunn started out on the long-established Mission Trail to Monterey, each mission a day's travel or about thirty miles apart. The men observed the missions in decline. Without knowing it, Goulding was witnessing the final days of California's pastoral period, during which prominent Spanish and Mexican families controlled thousands of acres of land along the coast and exploited Indian labor to supply the needs of their families. It would not be long before squatters and immigrants hungry for land changed all that. In the meantime, the Californios offered their fabled hospitality to both friends and strangers, and Goulding was one recipient of their largesse.

On Sunday, August 19, we were very much amused at Col. Williams amusing method of spending the Sabath. All the females portion of his Indians came to his rancho, and all cleanly dressed (this is the first place I met where respect was shown to the Sabath) with skirts and spencers, but all sported that everlasting Mexican piece of furniture, the "reboso." After reading a chapter in the Bible and reciting a prayer, Mr. Williams discoursed a few words in Pueblo to the people,[1] and then he called one of the old ladies, and blind-folding her with a handkerchief, he commenced by taking up a patern of fancy calico sufficient to make a skirt and would ask her, who shall have this, and the blind-folded lady would call out the name of one of the assembly. Thus the scene went on for an hour, until all present had some gift from their werthy and benevolent master. At some periods of the decisions, considerable jealousy was manifested, as some homely looking serf would happen by chance to get some flashy red & blue stripe or figured piece of muslin, or a flaming red cotton "reboso" with a six inch long blue fringe tipped with yellow, then their black eyes would flash fire and the teeth would grit sometimes so as you could here them across the plaza. However, Williams had a way of so reconsiling them to their wished for choises, as he always had duplicates and used to so maneuver as to exchange with them who manifested any extravagant jealousy in the decision.

Numerous companies of Mexicans kept passing Williams from the mines on their way to Mexico, and they were in many instances robbing him of his heards of horses and mules. Some companies of Americans on coming up to Williams rancho had his branded mules and horses with them, which Mexican parties had sold them in exchange for their worn out and jaded animals, and giving them thirty and even fifty dollars to boot at times. This was indeed very gratifying to him. Williams had no redress as to the scoundrels who was guilty, but he sent his major domo and a party of Indians and drove off his heards and caviats to the mountains for the north east, out of the way of the present excitement.

On Thursday, August 23, Capt. Lane and his party came up to Col. Williams place, but his party was considerably broken down from the effects of the crossing of the Colorado and the route over the desert. He lost seven of his waggons and sixteen of his mules and twenty three hundred silver dollars, which went to the bottom of the

[1] Goulding's words suggest that Williams was either speaking the language of his Native workers or Spanish, which many understood.

Colorado in a small trunk with the whole contents of the raft, two waggons with all the stores and provisions therein.[2] But his brother in law, Seignor Duc——, and the eight peons on the raft made out to swim to the west side with only their carbines and revolvers. His account of the crossing was a terrible afair and serious loss to him. With his party their were some more Americans, the Boston Company, and a small party, men of the Knickerbockers, consisting of Messrs. Shuyler Hoes, [J. Alfred] Kanouse, [Hiram] Green, [John M.] Hendricks, [John] Jackson, Hamilton, Anderson, and the two brothers Metcalfs, and Messrs. Orlando Dunham of Boston, Norwood of Portland, and eight others of their party.[3] The two men as supposed to be murdered by the Humas at the Colorada belonged to this company; their names were [Samuel B.] Kingsley and [S.] Spaulding.[4] Mr. Lane sold his small riding waggon to Col. Williams and took to the saddle the remainder of the journey. My little squad being now in good health and well rested at this place during the last twelve days and our animals now in good trim, we decided on taking up our march with Capt. Lane tomorrow morning.

Friday, August 24, this morning my party and that of Capt. Lanes hitched up all in the most excellent and best of spirit, for Col. Williams exchanged all their broken down and jaded animals and gave them fresh ones, and with a bountiful supply of fresh beef and flour & the squadrone (for their was upwards of seventy all mounted) gave our hospitable and worthy host nine hearty cheers and the cavalcade proceeded. Col. Isaac Williams then wrote a letter to the Governor, Gen. [Bennett C.] Riley, stating to him the unprotected state of this section of the country and the nessescity of imediate force sent in a military strength to protect the American settlers in this part of the country. At eleven o'clock he gave me the letter to

[2] Lane's loss is recorded in the Rancho del Chino Register Book (Bynum 1934, 8).

[3] See appendix A for a partial list of Knickerbocker Company members.

[4] Jack W. Smith wrote in the del Chino Register Book that the two Bostonians were captured by the Yuma Indians at the Colorado River crossing and were thought to have been killed (Bynum 1934, 6). It turns out, however, that they escaped after being stripped of all their clothing, and they began trekking naked toward Los Angeles, when a party of emigrants found them suffering from sun and thirst, revived them, and brought them to the mines (Harris 1960, 91).

deliver as soon as possible. Parting with his family rather reluctantly, I proceeded in company with John P. Hoyt and Capt. Gunn.[5]

After travelling some twelve miles over a most beautiful section of rolling hills covered with wild oats and mustard and extensive valleys with immence heards of cattle, we overtook our party at a place called the Mills. This place, with the country through which we have travelled some twelve miles at the south side of Col. Williams, is what might [be] better named the Garden of the South of California, as irrigation appears all along every mile you come to. At this place their was some eight or ten splendid rancherias, all nearly as magnificent as Williams, and roads crossing in all directions as if this part of the country was thickly settled.[6] Over two hundred Mexican miners passed us during our days march. We passed two small rivers, and at 6 o'clock we camped by a branch of one of them in a small copse of wood and got at our old amusement again in frying flap jacks and beef steaks.

Saturday, August 25, at eight o'clock we proceeded on, crossed the

[5] Williams's letter, which Theodore Foster forwarded to the *Missouri Republican*, dealt mainly with two items: the relief he had provided to hundreds of emigrants who had been deprived of goods and animals by Yuma Indians at the Colorado crossing, and the problem of having livestock stolen by returning Mexicans, which they in turn sold to incoming emigrants. He noted that some twenty thousand people had passed his home in the past twelve months and he fully expected to see five to ten thousand more. "How far and to what extent this state of things is to continue it is not for me to say," Williams wrote, "but I see no reason to doubt but that it may go on and increase in intensity, until the people of this section are robbed of their entire stock." When forwarding the letter, Foster wrote that "Colonel Golding, so well known in New York as a surgical instrument maker," would deliver the letter to General Riley (T. Foster 1849). I postulate that both Foster and Goulding helped Williams compose and make several copies of the well-written letter, which contains fourteen paragraphs and 1,137 words. It was dated August 24, 1849, the same day Goulding departed from the ranch.

[6] Goulding and friends were crossing Rancho La Puente, some eighteen miles east of Los Angeles, a Mexican grant of forty-nine thousand acres that had been deeded to William Workman and John Rowland in 1842 (Beck and Haase 1980, 37). In twenty-first century terms, the land grant includes the cities of La Puente, Industry, Hacienda Heights, Covina, West Covina, Baldwin Park, Whittier, Diamond Bar, and Rowland Heights. Both men were easterners who settled in New Mexico, becoming good friends and Mexican citizens. Both had been involved in the Taos trade and trapping but moved to Los Angeles in 1841 when life became dangerous for naturalized foreigners in New Mexico. As Mexican citizens, they were eligible to apply for land grants in California and shared the Puente rancho, which once had been part of San Gabriel Mission lands (Rowland 1999, 61–87, map 161).

Fernando River [Los Angeles River] and the battle ground of the "Army of West,"[7] and by ten o'clock the beautiful "City of the Angels" came in full sight. Here on the top of the ravine (which seams to be in front of the town) we waited till our whole party came up so as to make as respectable a looking appearance as possible. Passing several respectable looking casas (houses) and gardens, we formed our camp on a green field by the side of the running stream of water in the ravine.

The population of "des los Angeles" [El Pueblo de Nuestra Señora de los Angeles] is about two thousand souls. It is the centre of wealth of the California people and was heretofore the seat of government and was the center of military power of California, it being near the base of the mountain and commanding the passes to Sonora, cut off from the north by the pass of Santa Barbara, where all the revolutions have had their origin, and it may be said is the point where the last battle was fought in which decided the achievement of the country to the United States. Some twenty American fashioned houses were in the town and nearly as many more partly built, but oweing to the thirst for seeing the mines, all the mechanics had banished the place. The foundations of some fine stores were on the centre square or plasa and a few Americans were here doing some business. A small fort is on the side hill west and commands the town. It was erected by the United States troops during the late war with Mexico.[8]

---

[7] The Battle of La Mesa (also known as the Battle of Los Angeles) was the last skirmish of the Army of the West with the Californios. The battle, led by generals Stephen Watts Kearny and Robert F. Stockton, took place on January 9, 1847, in Cañada de los Alisos at the confluence of the Los Angeles and San Gabriel rivers. This followed the defeat of Kearny's army by the Californios at the Battle of San Pasqual near present-day Escondido in December 1846. The Battle of La Mesa ended resistance to American occupation with the signing of the Treaty of Cahuenga on January 13, 1847 (Gutiérrez and Orsi 1997, 344; Rolle 1978, 187; Hayes 2007, 83).

[8] The fort that Goulding noted as a result of consulting Emory was designed by Emory in 1846 and constructed by members of the Mormon Battalion. It was dedicated as Fort Hill on July 4, 1847, and was renamed Fort Moore Hill for Capt. B. D. Moore, killed in the Battle of San Pasqual (Hoover, Rensch, and Rensch 2002, 170). The fort and hill were later leveled to build the Hollywood Freeway. The fort's site was northeast of the junction of Temple and Spring streets, close to historic Olvera Street (Ord 1849; Prudnan 1862, map).

Figure 16. William R. Hutton, *Fort Moore: American Fort at Pueblo de los Angeles from Mr. Pryor's house, July 10, 1847.* Also known as Fort Moore Hill. *Courtesy of the Huntington Library.*

Mr. Ford, Capt. Lane, Gunn, and myself rambled all over the town, and it seamed like a holiday amongst the natives. Drinking, gambling, and dancing appeared to be going on like as if it was their regular business.[9] In one of these adobe built houses was assembled a large party of Pueblo Indians, women old and young, the old ones squatted down on the floor and the young senoretas dancing the everlasting Spanish waltz with Mexican umbras of all shades and size and with all sorts of Spanish fantastical dresses, from the silk red sash to the red flannel shirt, and boots with huge spurs, with rowels four inches in diameter or the size of [a] wind wheel from an old English wind mill, and every variety of figure was here introduced that could be imagined.[10]

In one place just on the outskirts of the town, we was attracted by a large party about a number of fires. Here they were roasting beef by throwing a large chunk into the burning cinders, and cutting or tearing off a portion, would throw it in again for the next friend. In fact, as a general thing throughout the whole country, the natives prefer nothing more than the fresh meat of a bullock cooked in this rude way; sitting down to a meal of bread, tea, and coffee is scarsely ever done by this class of Californians, and the white teeth of the Californians and the blood tinging in their cheeks of their olive coloured faces would seem to prove this beef, in the manner they eat it, to be [a] very healthy diet. We returned to our camp about 11 o'clock, considerably tired out from our perambulations.

Next morning, Sunday, August 26, saddled up and left camp by 9 AM. I sold a few surgical instruments in amt $20 to one Dr. [Alex W.] Hope,[11] a resident of this place, and made some few purchases

---

[9] Most emigrants agreed about the fandangoes, gambling, and drinking taking place. However, James Bouldin reported that the "introduction of the Yankee whiskey is creating some fears with the growers of their vines and think the whiskey ought not to be brought in" (September 12, 1849). The padres had been growing wine at the missions since the 1770s, and many ranchos had extensive vineyards by 1849.

[10] Rowels are the round, rotating wheels attached to the back of spurs. Goulding is referring to the "star rowel" that contains four or five spikes, each over an inch long, sometimes called "can openers." They could cut a horse badly but were often worn for style (Slatta 1994, 94, 358, 362).

[11] Dr. Alex W. Hope, U.S. Army surgeon (1826–56) and native Virginian, had been a Los Angeles resident since 1848 (Bancroft 1964, 787). Goulding also met William Rich Hutton, assistant to Lt. Edward O. C. Ord, surveyor of public lands. Hutton (1942, 33) mentions the "arrival of Dr. Golden, a celebrated surgical instrument maker from New York," in one of his letters. From these, we learn that Goulding met and conversed with Hutton about the military men he had seen in both Santa Fe and Albuquerque, including Lieutenant Pleasonton and Dr. Lewis Edwards.

of provisions, when the main body proceeded on their march from the City of Angels—more properly should be called a City of the Devils and Male Imps—meeting many Americans here, and so many questions to answer that some few of our party were detained until the noon time, when we parted with these new settlers, and about 3 PM we overtook our main party. We passed some few ranches and some fine cultivated country and camped under some cotton or willow trees, our camp much divided.

Next morning, Monday, August 27, left camp at 7 AM all in good order. Traveled in consort with Capt. Lane's company. We were passed by a great many returning Mexicans from the gold mines, stating to us that the American miners had turned them, all the Mexicans, out of the mines. We traveled through a long range of mountains during the day and camped at 3 PM in a fine valley with a small rancho where Mr. Lane purchased a young beef and we had it slaughtered for the general benefit of the party. Cost $5.00. We were much amused during the evening by the stories of Mr. Lane and his men, particularly Capt. Gunn.

The next morning, Tuesday, August 28, our march during the day was very fatiguing. The pass through the Coast Range of mountains were very difficult and much the steepest we have met in some time.[12] During the day, my party, being comprised intirely of packed animals and well mounted men, we parted with Mr. Lane with his wagons as they had to make circular roads which we could much better avoid, so we camped in good grass after making 25 miles.

Next morning, Wednesday, August 29, we were passed in camp by Capt. Lane's party, they making an unusually late start. We travelled

[12] Leaving Los Angeles, Goulding and friends negotiated Cahuenga Pass and turned west near present-day Studio City, essentially following present-day Highway 101 toward San Buenaventura Mission. At Newbury Park, they descended Conejo grade, leading to the Santa Clara Valley. George W. B. Evans agreed with Goulding's description of Cahuenga Pass, writing that he climbed the "highest and steepest mountain met with in California" (1945, 191). Both Goulding and Evans mentioned meeting Mexicans returning from the mines—with their gold hidden in goose quills, according to Robert Brownlee (1986, 105). It would not be long before California passed a foreign miners' license tax aimed at driving noncitizens from the mines. In the meantime, David Jordan made out nicely, selling his gun, powder flask, and shot pouch to a returning Mexican miner for thirty-two dollars on August 14, 1849.

in company 12 miles, when we came to Santa Clara Mission,[13] where we nooned until 3 PM, when my party proceeded till 5-½ PM, when we came up full breast to the long desired Pacific Ocean. And when I beheld the large and rolling green waves, I praised God for his safe diliverance to me [illegible] country I have just passed. At 6 PM we came up to the ruins of a town called "Bueno Vantura" [San Buenaventura], formerly a Mexican [mission] on the Pacific Coast.[14] We camped close by the adobe walls of the onced fine chapel with the noise of the noise of the ocean to lull us to sleep. We found good and hospitable cheer at a coastlines house where we got plenty of cigars and liquers and much information.

Next morning, Thursday, August 30, during our march today, we were for 20 miles constantly on the beach, sometimes the surf flowe-ing over our feet. At 4 PM we came to a ranch near the beach, where we camped and enjoyed a good supper of crabs and mussels and some mellons bought of the ranch people.

Next morning, Friday, August 31, at 10 AM we arrived at Santa Barbara, a very fine little town 12 miles from our coast camp. There is no hotel here, but a Mr. Wood had a kind of restaurant and furnished us with the first baked pies we had since we left the States. That, with some other refreshments, we passed our noon camp very well, when we again left the place, passing by in our view the grand double spired chapel or Mission of Santa Barbara, onced a very fine and extensive cathedral.[15] At 5 o'clock, we arrived at Mr. [Daniel Antonio] Hill's ranch, which a Mr. [Isaac J.] Sparks, a storekeeper

[13] Rancho Santa Clara del Norte is on the Santa Clara River and is south of Saticoy in Ventura County. The 1837 grant belonged to Juan Sánchez (Beck and Haase 1980, 36; Cowan 1956, 91).

[14] San Buenaventura was the ninth mission founded by Franciscan friar Junipero Serra in 1782. According to Spencer Crump (1985, 64), in the early days worshipers were called to services by its wooden bells. Overlanders camped on the nearby beach and fished or ate fruit picked from the still-producing mission gardens. Following along in March 1850, H. M. T. Powell (1931, 211) set up on the sand with Santa Cruz Island in view while he sketched the mission buildings, while others walked along the water's edge, marveling at the huge vertebrae of whales that had washed ashore.

[15] Mission Santa Barbara, the "Queen of the Missions," was dedicated in 1820 after an earlier structure was damaged by the 1812 earthquake. This is the only mission where the Franciscan order has served continuously over the years (Crump 1985, 66).

of the town we nooned at, told us it was but 9 miles from here, but we made over 15 miles, often in our track passing some very extensive heards of horses and cattle. After pitching our camp for the night, I went up to the casa of Mr. Hill and found him, a clever sort of man, was a native of Lowell, Mass., had been in this country some 30 years, married a lady of Spanish origin (Castillian), had 13 children, 7 boys and 6 girls; not one of the family spoke English. He was now erecting an additional building to his ranch and was the owner of a 20 league grant with extensive ranges of cattle.[16] After much pleasing information from him of our continued rout, we retired to our camp fire under the broad canopy of heaven with our saddle for a pillow and our durable gun and revolver for bed fellows.

Saturday, September 1, we were detained this day until noon in consequence of some of our animals straying off with the caviats of horses and mules in the vicinity of Hill's domain. With the assistance of two of Mr. Hill's men and their fleet horses, we got our animals back after many miles galloping. Dr. Dean [Nicholas Den] of the latter tour came here today and we were highly pleased with [t]his gentleman['s] information, which is not unusual by the nature of his country, the land of [illegible].[17] From the information received and it being received Saturday, and desirous to get at our next camp, the mission

[16] Daniel Antonio Hill (1787–1865) arrived in California from Massachusetts on the American ship *Rover* in 1826. His Rancho La Goleta y Patera totaled 4,426 acres. Hill was a farmer, carpenter, and mason and constructed his adobe at 35 La Patera Lane, Goleta, presumably his house on the rancho, in the 1840s. He married Rafaela Ortega, cousin of doña María Conception Ortega de la Guerra, whom Goulding would soon meet (Rolle 1978, 125; Hoover, Rensch, and Rensch 2002, 414–16; Bancroft 1964, 785).

Isaac J. Sparks (1804–67) arrived with Ewing Young's party of trappers in 1832. Though he kept the only store in Santa Barbara, he mainly engaged in hunting otter along the Santa Barbara Channel. Sparks was the grantee of the 22,153-acre Huasna Rancho and the 8,839-acre Pismo Ranch, both in San Luis Obispo County (Bancroft 1964, 729; Storke 1891, 392–93; Beck and Haase 1980, 35).

[17] Dr. Nicholas Augustus Den (1812–62), an Irishman, arrived in Santa Barbara on the *Kent* in 1836. His Rancho Los Dos Pueblos was on the Santa Barbara plains near Naples Beach and contiguous with Daniel Hill's La Goleta. Den had married one of Hill's daughters. He had served as alcalde of Santa Barbara and was known as a stockraiser of considerable wealth and reputation (Bancroft 1964, 785; Bryant [1849], 82, 107; Beck and Haase 1980, 36). William Heath Davis thought Den "as homely a man" as he ever saw, but he had a lovely wife with "luxuriant hair falling to her feet" (1967, 93).

of Sta. Margaretta [Santa Margarita Asistencia], to rest and keep the Sunday, I went on ahead of my company. And following the trail as directed along by the coast at times, the way strewed with flowers and the green foliage of the trees, and now and then descenting into a small valley and through a small, cristal, running stream emptying its contents into the calm and splendid ocean of the Pacific, again raises in a hill covered with wild mustard and oats, where to my surprise, I was met by two black wolves, the first I have seen in this country. Instead of attacking me as I expected they would, one of them sat on his haunches like a dog and look [illegible] at my passing as unconcerning as if he were blind. The other trotted off when I fired my revolver at the setting wolf, when he too trotted off, yelling and pawing his head as he went up the hill into some brush wood. Pursuing my course, thinking I was on my right road, till I came to a camino pass which led directly through the mountain, the span of which seemed to come on directly. At that point the apperance of a deserted casa or ranch near to this place with some few apple trees, but it being now nearly dark night and thinking that my expected mission of Santa Margaretta would be come to view, I continued through the pass, being now fairly in the narrow defile, mounted on my spirited California horse, with the noises of the water gushing through the rocks and the screach owls and the emence numbers of bats. This, with the darkness and lonesome position I was now, it made me think, indeed, that I was really out of quarters, and came to the conclusion that I certainly mised the trail in the mustard fields. At last I came to a river which was evidently for me to ford, where I met a trail leading up a hill, when I dismounted, and finding the time to be there 9-½ o'clock, I kept on for nearly a mile, but not the least sign of a house or even bark of a dog or anything to indicate civilization. I staked out my horse, and placing my saddle and camp blanket as usual, after taking some refreshment which I had in my holsters, I slept till day light.[18]

[18] Goulding was still in Santa Barbara County, near Gaviota, some thirty-three miles west of the city of Santa Barbara. He was wandering along the Las Cruces Trail, an old ranch road that crosses coastal grasslands to Hollister Ridge and overlooks the rolling hills and canyons near Refugio State Beach.

Sunday, September 2, seeing now my true position on the top of a mountain, the continuation of the same spur noted last night by the Pacific Ocean, the portal through which I passed was formed of immense buttes of clay and rock and sand, with large flakes of mica and seams of gypsum. Nothing could be more forlorn and desolate in appearance, now to me all in full sight at the bottom of this high observatory which I was led to by the well-beaten trail made by the immence herds of cattle to be seen to the far west and quietly grazing in the valley and side hills now in my view. My horse now showed signs of his [illegible]. I saddled up and followed the cow trail back the way I came. The grass at the river I found much better than I had seen, so I let my horse browse and I heard a distant noise of the tramp of horses and then the voice of a native singing as the Californians do when galloping on a cattle drive. Soon, the major domo, a Mexican, was up with me and who informed me of my wrong road, being now some 10 miles from Sta. Margaretta Mission and on the direct road to De Los Cruces (Lost Cross), the very place we were particularly directed by Mr. Hill and others to avoid going. It being 3 miles to this latter place from my present position and but 2 miles back to the coast, I concluded to return through the same lovely defile which I traveled last evening. I was much amused with the grand and romantic appearance of the pass, but it still was fully wide enough for a waggon to go through, and in some places the river widened and branched off in all directions through the mountain range. In one place, a ridge formed apparently a complete circle with a water basin in the center. Adjacent to it was a heap of stones with a wooden cross, no doubt put there by some of the natives, who are still some of them very superstitious in their Roman Catholic errors. Some portion of this range of mountains (and of which this forms the spur ending on the Pacific) is lofty, the base in most places is covered more or less with pine, ceder, and scrub oak [illegible] mixed with many varieties of cactus and acacias. Approaching the ocean again and near to the old casa and orchard as discovered last night, I observed my companions in camp in the hill of wild oats, quietly awaiting my resital of the adventures of the night. There being abundance of blue quail in the brush all about us, we soon had a pan full frying for our Sunday morning breakfast.

Mr. Lane and his party now again came up, so we all proceeded to this defile on our way to de las Cruces, where we arrived by 11 o'clock AM and quartered for the day. We found the seignor rather inclined to be more obliging than we were informed about him, but he seen our party were rather formidable, and as we had the dollars to pay him, no doubt he thought it the wisest for him to be civil, and through the influence of "Don Lorenzi," one of Mr. Lanes gentleman companions, we all got provided with plenty of the good things of his ranch—our animals too, instead of roaming about the fields, were put into the coral and abundantly supplied with corn stalks and trefoil clover, all done by the Seignor Aseintus de la Geurios [Guerra] (De la Rancho del los Cruses).[19] When we first came to his place, however, some grumbling was manifested to some of the (one) party by his sons in law and the word Vaumis Las Americanos used, but on approaching the old man and becoming acquainted with him, matters became general[ly] civil and hospitable. The son in law showed some of my companions where the ripe mellons was and where the good fruit could be got and the senoria found white sugar for my coffee and a room was provided for the mucha weyno Senior Doctoro Americana.

In fact, nothing was too good for us, and on the morning of Monday, September 3, we found our company escorted by their sons of our werthy host [to] a newer rout over his land and through his extensive fields of wheat and oats to the main road to Santa Rosa Mission, giving us much information of the various people we should meet with, those who we would find civil and those who were unfriendly toward the Americans. I was presented with a new hair lariet for my horse. At 1 o'clock we stoped at Santa Rosa at a Mexican ranch 12 miles from our last place on the top of a knoll or

---

[19] Rancho Las Cruces, granted in 1836 to Miguel Cordero, was near Santa Ynez Mission and occupied some 8,888 acres (Beck and Haase 1980, 36; Cowan 1956, 31).

hill, with a tiled roof.[20] There was some few Americans recruiting here after recently coming over, as we have done. Near to this place we were joined by a Capt. [Thomas E.] Ridley and 8 men, part of a camp on the way to the mines.[21] Passed some very fine cottonwoods country abounding with cattle and horses with some few ranchos in view to our right and left. We ascended a very steep mountain, having all to dismount and lead our animals up and down on the other side into another splendid valley of plains covered with horses and cattle. Here we struck a wide waggon road.

Travelling on for two miles, we came to the splendid Hicienda of de Alamal [Los Alamos], owned by the Lady Senora Conception Ortega and her three amiable daughters, Catherena, Deloras, and Weynus.[22] Being in advance of my troop, I was cordially received by these ladies, who instantly had my horse unsaddled and put up in the adjoining coral by their major domo, a very polite and well dressed young Castillan. When I gave the senora my introductory letter from Seignor Hill and his lady, who are cousins, they were exhilarated to the highest degree and all but "Catherena," the eldest, lent a hand to my reception, but she was the first one to present me with 'una' segareta "a ma fabrica" [illegible]. I was highly favoured by these people during my stop with them. My companions in camp close by

[20] Goulding had arrived at Francisco Anastasio Cota's Rancho Santa Rosa, of some 15,526 acres granted to him in 1839. Cota (1781–1851) had been a soldier at Santa Barbara presidio. His old adobe has been renovated and stands near Mail and Santos roads six miles west of Buellton (Beck and Haase 1980, 36; Gudde 2004, 348; Hoover, Rensch, and Rensch 2002, 419).

[21] Thomas E. Ridley and John Hoyt signed the Rancho del Chino Register Book on August 21, 1849, after their trip along the Gila Trail. Ridley wrote that the men lost "19 mules and at least $1500 worth of money & baggage taken from us by the Indians" (Bynum 1934, 8). Ridley later obtained a license from Mariposa County to operate Ridley's Ferry at Benton Hills (Mariposa County Court Records, 1852).

[22] Goulding and company had arrived at the 49,000-acre Los Alamos Rancho, Santa Barbara County, granted to José Antonio de La Guerra y Carrillo in 1839 by then governor Alvarado. Born in 1805, Guerra was the son of José Antonio de la Guerra y Noriega (1779–1858), native of Spain and family patriarch, then living in Santa Barbara. The Los Alamos ranch house is a National Historic Landmark 3½ miles west of the town of Los Alamos on California 135 (Beck and Haase 1980, 36; Hoover, Rensch, and Rensch 2002, 420). María Conception Ortega and José Antonio de la Guerra had six children; Bancroft (1964, 768–69) lists the girls as Catarina, Dolores, and Juana (probably Goulding's "Weynus").

were supplyed with abundance of tortillas and carney by this ladie's directions to her paeons, of which she had a great many in small casas close by. But I was their imediate guest and was not allowed to go in camp during the night. The family appeared to be religious in the Roman faith and said prayers during the evening, and in the sal[a] was spread out for me a fine cott with the richest sort of blanket for me to sleep in. I was much amused with the ladies during the evening till a late hour, they learning Spanish to me and me English to them.

Tuesday, September 4, up early this morning and galanting Deloras and Weynus about this beautiful hicienda until breakfast time, when the whole family were about at the table, with their paeons in the rear of the sal on their knees till a prayer was given by the senora herself, when a fine, hot breakfast of stewed meat with chile colorado and frijoles and chocolate and coffee and several sorts of bread and fruit and cheese &c. About noon, with great reluctance, I left these good and hospital people on our march.

We passed various changes of country, some small, sandy desert and some prairie dog towns and ground squirls, also some sand hills, and again approached in sight of the Pacific Ocean, traveled over a long and dreary, white, sandy beach with green, extensive prairies to the right covered with extensive herds of cattle belonging to Capt. Denny, whose ranch we arrived at about 5 o'clock.[23] Here we found encamped a waggon and a party consisting of 3 men, apparently sailors. With 3 women and some clothing they had come all the way by land from Wisconsin. The head of this family was a Mormon on his way to Salt Lake to join his people. The proprietor of this rancho, Capt. Denny, was absent down to the coast, where it was reported a wrecked ship was laying. We got a good supply of meat and camped in good grass for the night.

---

[23] Captain Denny was probably a neighbor of the de la Guerras. He had returned to his ranch by September 21 when David Jordan arrived. Jordan wrote that Denny had been living there for some twenty-six years, adding that his wife was thirty-six and the mother of eighteen children, "and looked like she could have 10 or 12 more." In spite of having such a large family, she managed to serve him a good dinner for fifty cents. Jordan also noted that he counted 132 Mexicans passing on their way back to Mexico.

20

Sojourn in Monterey

Predictably, the first thing Goulding did on arrival in Monterey was to find his way to the U.S. Army post. He delivered his letters of introduction and had a long-awaited interview with the military governor of California, General Bennett C. Riley. The general had been responsible for promoting a constitutional convention for California, and members were gathering in town for meetings in the brand new California capitol at Colton Hall, which had been constructed in 1847 by then alcalde Walter Colton. The United States had not provided for the establishment of a territorial government in California; thus, the citizens decided to write a constitution and create an instantly functioning government. Delegates began meeting on September 3, 1849, and at the end of six weeks had a constitution to hand to the voters. Goulding had a rare opportunity to meet some of the delegates, including John Augustus Sutter, on whose land gold was first discovered; Stephen C. Foster, alcalde of Los Angeles; Edward Gilbert, editor of the Alta California; and Caleb Lyons, secretary of the convention. Goulding also attended a high-society dinner and grand ball and has provided us with an inside look at the people of Monterey and events surrounding the constitutional convention.

Wednesday, September 5, during our march this day we travelled by a very level and well watered country, several small ponds, and flushed up several flocks of wild ducks and other kinds of water fowl. Flushed a drove of wild pigs—belonging to, no doubt, some distant ranchero. One of them was shot, but the meat was very rank and impalatable. Arrived at Santa Louis Mission [San Luis Obispo] at 4 PM; against thereto we camped.[1] This was indeed a beautiful place, but like to the rest of these missions in this country, was now all in ruins—and only inhabeted by a few ignorant Pueblos and two or three Mexicans.

Next morning, Thursday, September 6, we had some hills to go over today which made up for yesterdays deficiency. About noon we arrived at the Mission of Santa Margaretta [Santa Margarita Asistencia], built of stone but out of order, with 2 or 3 deserted casas built of adobes and white washed, and the inside of them were very tastefully painted.[2] We past several uninhabited casas during the day and at 5 PM camped in the garden of one, apparently but just deserted. The garden had much fruit of which we indulged in. A runing stream or brook of water run directly through this place. Several casas. Wolves came around our camp tonight.

Early this morning, Friday, September 7, we proceeded and at 9 AM we arrived at Santa Robes [Paso Robles].[3] Here we found one Mexican family and several serfs or Indians. At noon we came in sight of the Mission of Saint Migule [San Miguel Arcangel], and for nearly 2 hours march it made a grand appearance to our view, but at 2 PM, on coming up to its walls, we found not a soul to give us any information.[4] Even the ground squirls, which heretofore we had seen in great numbers abut these deserted missions, at this one they

---

[1] San Luis Obispo de Tolosa, founded in 1772 by Father Junipero Serra, is restored and currently serves as the parish church in the town of San Luis Obispo (Crump 1985, 72).

[2] Santa Margarita, San Luis Obispo County, extended along the bottomlands of the Salinas River valley and was granted to Joaquín Estrada (Hoover, Rensch, and Rensch 2002, 387–88; Beck and Haase 1980, 35; Cowan 1956, 93).

[3] Pedro Narvaez's Rancho Paso de Robles was southwest of the modern town (Beck and Haase 1980, 35; Cowan 1956, 68).

[4] Word had not yet trickled down to Goulding and friends, but John Ross Browne (1950, 59–68) had recently witnessed the murder of four members of the Reed family in an adobe structure near San Miguel Mission. That did not deter Phineas Blunt (October 9, 1849) from making a tour of the establishment. Under the porch he found church bells bearing a casting date of 1822 and examined the room where the murder was committed, noting bloodstains on the wall and door. James Bouldin (January 6, 1850) was also fascinated by the large, deserted structure and described it minutely.

all seemed to have disappeared. We found the remains of a dry well, so we continued our march over a barren and sandy ground. About 5 PM we came to a better looking soil, when we shot some quail and camped.

Next morning, Saturday, September 8, we had a very tedious and unpleasant day's march through a very barren and sandy, dreary country till toward night, where we came into some old river beds with some trees and grass. Flushed a few hairs and shot one and camped to feast on his meat.

Next morning, Sunday, September 9, after a good breakfast of hair stew and coffee, we took up our march until 11 o'clock, when by a small stream we found a casa where we got a supply of flour and meat, and meeting with an American who had the mails from San Francisco, who told us that for the next 20 miles there was no water, so we camped at this place for the day. This man knew Isaac Williams very well and gave us a true account of the Rancho del Chino. He had resided 9 years at the Pueblo des los Angeles. His name was Eliga Nolton, a native of Canada, feeling anxious to gossip. On going, we hitched up again and travelled some twenty miles, meeting another American mounted on his way back to des los Angeles—also we were passed by 20 Mexican miners returning to the state of Senora, heartily sick of the mines. About 8 o'clock we camped in a mountain pass amongst some few trees with plenty of bears tracks in the land all around. The country through which we have passed for the last three days is as desolate almost as that through which we passed on the Gila River.

Next morning, Monday, September 10, this morning our road fetched us parallel to the Salinas River, the banks of it covered with some very fine timber and aparently a river that will at some future time give life and power to the northern sawyers of timber. In some places the road is 4 to 5 miles wide. On coming to an old casa, deserted, with a large wooden cross nearby, we left the bed of the river and crossed an extensive plain or small desert, passed by 200 Mexican miners on their way home from the "muncha mala oros!" At 4 o'clock we arrived at the Mission of Soledad. We camped on the banks of the Salinas River about a hundred rods from the casa of Seignor Felisiano Soberanes.[5]

At this place we met with one of Capt. Duval's company, Joseph Bittick, who was thrown from his horse a few days back and was left to have his arm set or rather his shoulder.[6] On examining the man, I found a dislocation of the os humeris. The shoulder had become quite flat and much swollen, with violent and severe pain. I instantly placed the patient in a low chair and put my foot on the chair and my knee in the axilla to act as a fulcrum and depressed the arm, and pressing upon the acromonius process, in consequence of the enflaimed state of the arm, I was unable to reduce it, so I relaxed the muscles by bleeding &c., and thus made an extension and a counter extension of the arm at right angles to the body by means of a sheet folded diagonally, passed under the axilla. I then fastened it to the door post with another sheet made fast to the fore arm and wrist, then with "traction" made gradually, & in a few minutes reduced the difficulty and then placed a roll of cotton cloth and bandage and slung his arm up—in a short time after, my patient moved his fingers and wrist and kept on improving, and next morning, Tuesday, September 11, I was satisfied the man was out of danger.

The Senora Mariana Tomer Roderegus [Rodríguez] was of French decent and manifested a very great attention to us—particularly to myself, in consequence of my successful operation of the young Texan. The evening before, she insisted upon my whole party partaking of our breakfast at her casa, had sent her son (named) Jose Loberias [Soberanes] early to our camp with the invitation. A better breakfast we did not have during our whole march. I made out to understand that their family was not all at home, that two of her daughters were in Monterey at their residence, as some time they all

[5] Feliciano Soberanes purchased the mission property, Nuestra Señora Dolorísima de la Soledad, on the Salinas River, Monterey County, in 1846 for eight hundred dollars (Cowan 1956, 99).

[6] Joseph Bitticks had been a lively member of the Duval Company and B. B. Harris kept track of his shenanigans as they moved westward. He once put up an irreverent prayer for rain and within an hour was inundated with a cloudburst. Following that, whenever thirst threatened, he refused to pray for water (Harris 1960, 62).

FIGURE 17. Soberanes Adobe, 336 Pacific Street, Monterey, California, 1960. Photo by Jack E. Boucher. *Courtesy of the Prints and Photographs Division, Library of Congress.*

resided in town.[7] Even our mules were fed at her door with sweet lattes. After taking down the particular address of the casa at Monterey of Seignora de la Soberanes, we took upon our march from off the grand camino to the gold mines, leaving all our old comrades, Capt. Ridley and party, and with Mr. Ford, Hoyt & Hunter, I proceeded towards the coast again through the valley of the Salinas. We spent all day flushing all kinds of small game, and at a willow which we were passing through, three beautiful antelope flushed up right under our very feet and were instantly lost in the endless underbrush of this extensive valley, the river and its various little tributaries run-

[7] The Soberanes adobe "house with the blue gate," built in 1830, State Historical Landmark 712, where Goulding later visited the daughters, is preserved at 336 Pacific Avenue, Monterey (Hoover, Rensch, and Rensch 2002, 232, 235).

ning in all directions, crossing and recrossing every half hour. When coming to a large orchard-looking plain in which were two ranchos, we camped for the night under a large oak tree with mirieds of ground squirels all over us.

Wednesday, September 12, 1849, for the first time during my whole rout across this country, I now had an attack of dierhea and therefore was to travel very slow. At 1 o'clock we came to a casa where we met an Englishman, a carpenter, to work putting on a new addition to this Spaniard house. He gave us much information about this country. We also were met by the mail carrier going to San Francisco. We were now but 6 miles from Monterey. We passed several small farms and haciendas, and at 6 PM we camped in a small orchard ½ miles from the town.

Being very unwell myself, I remained in camp until the morning of Thursday, September 13, when we road into the town of Monterey, which made a very imposing and grand apperance as we approached it. The first person I met to speak to happened to be the French Consul, a very gentlemanly man who directed me to the quarters of Doctor [William Shakespeare] King of the U.S. Army Med. Post at this place. The Dr. received me courteously and introduced me to the quartermaster, Capt. [Franklin] Howe,[8] who received my letters, commission, and dispatches from Col. [John M.] Washington, Capt. R[obert C.] Brent, Lieut. [F. D.] Thomas, and Dr. Picily and Dr. [Joseph Howard] Bailey, and Dr. [Lewis A.] Edwards, also a letter to Gen. [Bennett C.] Riley from Isaac Williams, all of which being placed on the quartermasters table, he then ordered all our animals to be placed in the government coral and unpacked, and our party were all quartered in the soldiers casas. A room was given to myself in the hospital and my name placed on the mess rolls.

At 10 o'clock General Riley and staff came to the Adjutant Generals Office, where I was introduced to the old and ruff old warrior. After taking about a dozzen pinches of snuff, he said,

[8] George Churchill said he met "Dr. Golden and John F. Hoyt" as they rode into Monterey that day. First, Goulding met William Shakespeare King, who was assistant surgeon until 1852 and served in numerous posts all over the United States (W. Powell 1890, 332). Quartermaster H. Franklin Howe had been in California since 1846 with Company C of the First Dragoons (Bancroft 1964, 788).

> So you have just arrived over the plains, pretty ruff march, I suppose—got no soldiers here to spare. Williams must arm his serfs and civil Indians and take satisfaction out of the Mexicans himself, he knows how to do it. He done it before, by the Eternal G——, he must not expect any help from us. We could not help ourselves just now, so many deserters gone to the mines, no stoping the traitors, all for gold—cannot get help enough to saddle a horse or mount a guard at the magazine. Isaac Williams must trash the Senorians himself. If they take his horses, he must go and take them back again, that's all. Be G—— I can do [nothing] for him.[9]

So, taking a few more pinches of snuff and cursing some terrible oathes, all apparently to be a mere habbit of his, he commenced laughing and flung the (Williams) letter on the clerks desk, and looking at the other letters, he handed them to his clerk—and commenced his various questions of my journey, but politely handed me some cigars and desired Capt. [George Clinton] Westcott to consider me one of the mess.

During our conversations the general was several times interupted by persons calling for various privileges such as permission to pitch a tent on such and such places and build cabins and boarded booths and also some complaints by the inhabitants agst Captain of vessels arrived in port and some of the trivial natures, when the old fellow would blow out with a blood and [illegible] and a G—— D—— their eyes, at the same time taking a tremendous pinch of snuff.—"Go and flog them D—— and take satisfaction out of these same hides yourself. What do you come here a boddering me for." It was at times really laughable to see the gestures of these Mexicans and Pueblos & Californians natives with their humble and bowing demenior attitudes, beging off for redress or satisfaction for injuries done to them.

During the day, I sold the Commissariat Capt. [Elias Kent] Kane my horses and mules—in all with pack saddles, panyards (some of

---

[9] Brig. Gen. Bennett C. Riley (1787–1853) was the last military governor of California, appointed on April 12, 1849, and serving until November 13, 1849. He joined the military in 1812 and enjoyed a long and distinguished career. During his tenure in California, he promoted the formation of a state convention to prepare a constitution for governing the state. Riley has been described as "bluff, hardy, and plainspoken," a fact with which Goulding would most heartily agree (Starr 2005, 91).

these very fine, covered with bears [illegible]), and riding saddles—all for $500, which he paid me for all in silver and gold. After I had sold my stock, I took one look at my poor old mules, who so well fetched me through my journey, and my better or weaker feeling came over me, and thinking of my family of whose names I had given to all of those animals, I left the scene with regret. Talking with Capt. Westcott, he said "Doctor, you feel just as I did when I first crossed the plains, but you shall not long have them here to look at for long. I shall send them off this very night packed with provisions in the mines of Tulley [Tulare] Valley and all I am waiting for is a suitable mule team to go with them." I at onced proposed Mr. John Hunter to him, one of my men, who I had fetched with me at my own expense, and who proved an ungrateful scamp, and with difficulty I got him along so far—I proposed the chance to him and he acepted and was engaged at near $150 a month and left this same night.[10]

At 3 o'clock we dined at the mess—Capt. Westcott, whose wife and her sister and two little girls had come to the country the year before across the plains. The Chaplain of the department also boarded here as well. Also as the Hon. Caleb Lyons (of Lyons Dale, State of New York), recently from China as pleniopotentiary extraordinary, a very gentleman and poetical scholar. Had a very agreable siesta and walked around the suburbs of this beautiful harbor in company with Lieut. [Matthew Rider] Stevenson of the 6th Infantry and the Hon. C. Lyons until 9 PM, when I retired to my quarters as prepared by Dr. King [illegible] in the hospital [illegible].[11]

Friday, September 14, early this morning I was [illegible] from the balcony of the hospital looking at this fine and beautiful harbor of

[10] Churchill sold the commissary sergeant four mules and a horse for $430 and was also offered $100 a month to drive one of the teams when he arrived in Monterey on September 11. The military was transporting vegetables to soldiers and emigrants in the mines who were suffering from scurvy.

[11] Capt. George Clinton Westcott was regimental quartermaster on General Riley's staff (Heitman 1903, 1:1020). Caleb Lyons (1822–75) of Lyonsdale, Lewis County, New York, was a delegate to the California state convention in 1849 and its assistant secretary (*Appleton's Cyclopedia* 1887–89, 4:66). Matthew Rider Stevenson was the son of Col. Jonathan D. Stevenson, whose regiment of New York volunteers reached California by sea, too late to be of service in the war with Mexico (Davis 1967, 322).

Monterey, having the appearance of a basin or small lake. Some eight or ten vessels were laying at anchor and the attraction caused by the gold mines had too thined their crews as well as the numerous deserted casas of which we had recently traveled by. This harbor, no doubt in some day not too distant future, will become the sight of a great commercial town. At present it has but one warfe with a number of boats passing to and from the vessels with a signal flag port on the end. In the distance was seen the white cliff at the entrance to the harbor and the numerous herds of cattle grazing on the adjoining hills belonging to the Mission of Santa Cruz, which you can just see a little of its onced extensive spires. Also in view to the east is the Castle of Monterey where the custom house barges are in readiness to board all vessels entering the port. And here, too, are the dungeons wherein many an innocent and brave tar, both Americans and Britain, were placed in confinement by the treachery of the meniels of "Alvarado and Castro" during the days of the "Junta" and its fiendish designs at the time of the revolution.[12]

After partaking of a comfortable breakfast, for the first time I had a regular American table to set down to since I left the mess room of the Santa Fe Percussion Mess. I gave Mr. Ford, my comrade, $50 as his share in our mule trading. I went to visit my friends of the Soberanes family, escorted by Lieut. Stevenson, who was well acquainted with the young ladies, and we were much amused with their obliging Espanola, and a great time we were in anticipation, as the Grand Convention Ball was to come off this evening, and they were making preparations in their silk and satin velvet dresses for to be their. Their was considerable excitement manifested now all through Monterey as the members from all parts of the country were arriving in town for the purpose of the Convention, which was to be opened with a splendid ball given to the inhabitants of the place.

[12] In 1849, Santa Cruz Mission could easily be seen across Monterey Bay. The 1794 structure was destroyed in the 1857 earthquake. The Monterey Custom House had been the most important building in Alta California since 1814, and all trading vessels were required to sign in and pay duties. It is California Registered Historical Landmark no. 1. The California criminal justice system at the time required that Monterey prisoners be sent to San Diego or Mexico, and those from the south to Monterey (Hague and Langum 1990, 91).

During the day, I had a long walk with Hon. Lyons along to observe the castle and by the rocks along the entrance to the harbor, and was much amused in the conversation of this gentleman. We returned and dined at 3 PM and made preparations for our evening's entertainment, when at 9 o'clock, in company of Capt. Westcott and his ladies, Dr. King and his senora, Lieut. Stevenson and the Miss Senoretas Sobranes and their brother, and a numerous host of officers of the Post. And at 10 o'clock their was an assembly congregated in the Convention Hall as respectable and as extravagently dressed as I had ever seen in the halls of New York. In fact, the ladies vied with each other in their costly robes—with excellent musik—the ball was open and everyone appeared to be happy and pleased.

Their were some twenty Americans and English ladies and about 100 Native ladies or Spanish senoretas and senoras—some of them had come over a hundred miles for the occation. Dancing was kept up till 1 o'clock, when all the ladies were escorted to the supper table, and all being seated, the gentlemen standing behind them helped them plentifully with the immence good things set their. The table was heaped up with abundance of all kinds of meat, fish, and fowl. And in all sorts of cookeries the skill of the caterer to be in no way a novise of the art. When all the ladies were satisfied, they were escorted to the ballroom and left to their recreation in smoking segaretas and cracking amonds. And the gentlemen then returned and sat down and done justice to the good things provided without end. Such a "dejuner de porchet" I never before sat down to. Their was all the rancheros and Lords from all the haciendias from all parts of the new state. The veretable and celebrated Captain [John Augustus] Sutter sat next to me and whom I got to be quite sociable with.[13] Several speeches were delivered and toast and sentiments drank until a late hour or rather an early hour.

---

[13] Thousands of travelers exiting the northern trails would find themselves at John Augustus Sutter's fort in Sacramento. Like Isaac Williams in the south, Sutter provided sustenance to exhausted, hungry travelers. In January 1850, the California legislature passed a resolution honoring the two men for their contributions. However, political enemies forced Williams's name to be stricken from the record. Some ninety-two years later, Senator Ralph E. Swing offered Senate Resolution no. 24, January 12, 1942, to reverse the decision. William's letter was entered into the *Senate Journal* and the resolution was adopted unanimously (California Legislature 1942).

FIGURE 18. Colton Hall, Monterey, California, 1887. Old State House, where the first California constitutional convention was held in 1849. Photo by C. C. Pierce. *Courtesy of the Huntington Library.*

In the morning of Saturday, September 15, at 10 AM, Mr. [Stephen C.] Foster of des los Angeles, one of the delegates to the convention, and the Hon. Caleb Lyons called and waked me up, so we waited on Mr. [David Estevan] Spence, one of the principle and oldest residents of this place. We were cordially received and welcomed by this old Scotch gentleman and his very polite senora. We were much amused with his account of the revolution in this country, through which ordeal he passed and witnessed the many changes that took place. We were joined here by the young cavalero Soberanes and Lieut. Stevenson, Capt. Sutter, an editor of the Alta California from San Francisco named [Edward] Gilbert, and several other guests.[14] This old citizens garden seems to [be] the general loafing or retreating rendevous for all the bloods of this garrison, and being a jolly good and clever fellow who can tell and hear a joke and drink a bottle of wine as well as anyone, and of such he, too, has a goodly stock, as well as some of the best brandy and Holland I have ever drank—so we spent the day in a siesta until the bugle sounded the mess call.

During our siesta I gathered much information from their guest. Capt. Sutter says that the Valley of Sacramento and that of San Joaquin are the most fruitful part of California, which is capable of producing all the fruits of the temperate as well as the tropical climate and likewise offers extensive pasture grounds for cattle—this region comprises a level plain from 15 to 20 miles in width extending from the Bay of San Francisco beyond the mission of that name, north and south, and may be termed the Garden of California. The two principle rivers in Upper California are the Sacramento and the San Joaquin. The only navigable stream is the Sacramento. The harbor of San Francisco is one of the largest and most magnificent harbors in the world. The yield of wheat, small grain, and vegetables is said to be great, but as agriculture can not succeed in Upper California but by irrigation, it has hitherto happened that it has been principally occupied as a pastoral country. The numerous animals which are slaughtered for little more than their hides and tallow do not putrify or become offensive as they would in other climates, and the hooves are generally used instead of wood for garden fences, sometimes interwoven with the prickly pear cactus, and makes a very durable fence.

Mr. Spence's account of the revolution by Alvarado, aided by [Isaac] 'Graham' and other Americans and English new settlers in the country was very interesting [. . .].[15]

---

[14] Stephen C. Foster (1819–98) was the alcalde of Los Angeles and a state senator (S. Foster 1949, 318–21); Scotsman David Estevan Spence (1798–1875), conservative, energetic, and widely respected, was claimant to Rancho Encinal y Buena Esperanza in Monterey County (Hoover, Rensch, and Rensch 2002; Crump 1956, 33); and newspaper editor Edward Gilbert (1819–52) was elected as the first congressman from California in 1849 and died as the result of a duel three years later (Bancroft 1964, 756).

[15] I have omitted Goulding's attempt to repeat David Spence's story of the Graham affair, as he tried to put it in context, but did not get it quite right. See Ramón Gutiérrez and Richard J. Orsi, *Contested Eden* (1997), for a history of California before the gold rush.

On arriving at Capt. Westcotts, we were introduced to the celebrated Colonel John C. Fremont, who had just arrived from San Francisco via San Jose, and his dear lady, Jessey, who through her sickness on rout had caused his delay. During the evening I was much amused in the company of Fremont, as he too had to take his quarters up with myself in my room in consequence of the great number of people now arrived in town from all parts of the states to participate in the events of this state convention.

Sunday, September 16, I wrote a letter to Isaac Williams stating to him of my interview with Fremont and his answer in declining to purchase any portion of the Rancho del Chino as he had agreed to do when at the place,[16] and rather insinuated a disregard or respect to Mr. Williams claims on him altogether, and to which I was much surprised, for Mr. Williams had stated to me all the affairs relating to his assistance to the army and particularly to Col. Fremont and his party, who had been fed and feasted at the Rancho del Chino in a most hospitable manner for several weeks—and no compensation had ever been given to Mr. Williams by any of the Army of the West, and all of which had been treated kindly by him and his people during the campaign in the South of California. With a discourse by the Reverent Chaplain of the post and a walk during the afternoon, the Sunday was closed and retired to.

Monday, September 17, visited a family resident about ½ mile from the town this morning with Doctor King and constructed a trip to a child having a congenital hernia—the first case of the kind I have met with amongst the Spanish race. During the afternoon, I was ingaged assorting my kit and preparing for to leave, for we expected every moment, the arival of the steamer from Panama, and at 8-½ PM, when quietly smoking a segareta in company with Senoreta Soberanes, we were greatly alarmed by the report of the gun fired off at the castello, a signal that the steamer hove in sight. Parting with all our friends, myself and Mr. Ford and Hoyt got our baggage reversed to the dock and at 10 o'clock we were safely on

[16] The Frémont saga is a story in itself, and there are hundreds of books and articles about him. Frémont's offer to purchase the Williams ranch never materialized. Instead, he became involved with his northern properties and other matters.

board the steamer Oregon from Panama, loaded with passengers. Our fare was $20 each to San Francisco. I was very fortunate to get a state room and Berth E, the only one vacant on board, as just vacated by a passenger who left at Monterey. Had a pleasant nights rest and at 7 o'clock next morning found our craft safely anchored.

Tuesday, September 18, in the Bay of San Francisco, I was much amused to see the activity and hurry, endevors of the great number of passengers—450 from the States [Kip extract omitted].[17]

At 9 AM we were climbing up the unfinished new warfe & after some herculean efforts we got all our baggage on that part of the dock that had just been floored and planked over. [Kip extract omitted.] One of my party after some time got a cart owned by some of our old comrades of the Knickerbockers, and who for two dollars carted all our luggage up to the American Hotel, where we engaged board at twenty one dollars per week. [Kip extract omitted.] I opened several letters I had rescued from the Post Office, having been there since several days before my arrival.

Goulding's journal ends here, leaving us in the dark about his return home from San Francisco. It was not unusual for overlanders to end their diaries abruptly; many stop writing at the Colorado crossing at Yuma. Goulding seems to have felt it necessary to create a satisfactory conclusion to his trip by adding a few descriptive paragraphs about San Francisco from an 1850 pamphlet by Leonard Kip. As mentioned, many hopeful scribes of the day "borrowed" from others.

I suspect that Goulding re-boarded the steamer Oregon in San Francisco and returned home by way of Nicaragua or Panama, as most did (records of passengers on return trips were not kept until later). At this point, plenty of miners and adventurers had grown tired of the whole adventure and were happy to get out of California with nothing but the clothes on their backs.

---

[17] Passages from Leonard Kip, *California Sketches, with Recollections of the Gold Mines* (1850), have been omitted.

We may never know if Goulding went to California expecting to make his "pile" in the mines. Starting at Fort Smith, he had met other professionals who probably boosted his initial confidence about the trip and provided him with letters of introduction to officers at United States forts along the way. He also made good use of his background as a surgical instrument maker and doctor to meet others.

A number of unexpected events perhaps altered his plans, starting with Goulding's sojourn at Isaac Williams's ranch. He may originally have intended to go to the southern mines (centered around Stockton) by another route. Instead, he went to Monterey to deliver Williams's letter to California's military governor, where he met a number of California's present and future leaders. He no doubt learned from them that life in the northern mines, especially during the winter, was no picnic. Because of rains and high water, mining would have ended for the season. Miners spent the winter crowded in tents or makeshift cabins. Expenses were high. As we have followed Goulding on his journey, it has been obvious that he enjoyed his comforts and privacy.

Goulding had become sick for the first time and felt sentimental about selling his animals, each named after a member of his family. To be sure, the money he received from the sale of his animals was more than he would have made as a miner during the coming winter. Perhaps a letter from home and a sense of responsibility to his family helped him make the final decision to leave California. If Goulding started out with the goal of making it rich in the mines, his experiences on the trail, the individuals he met, and knowledge he gained no doubt changed his view. By the time he reached Monterey, he probably felt he had had enough adventure and was quite simply ready to go home.

Appendix A

Constitution
Of the Knickerbocker Exploring Company,
of the City of New York

Fort Smith (Arkansas) Herald, March 21, 1849

We, Gentlemen of the City of New York and its vicinity, in order to form a company for the purpose of migrating to California in quest of business to better our condition, and secure for ourselves, for our families, and our friends, the blessings of an enterprise in which so many of our countrymen have so successfully engaged in, influences us in common, with others, to feel a high degree of interest, as we claim it our right and privilege to enjoy, and reap the advantages which the history of the times, and the daily events present to our knowledge, and to promote our general welfare, and secure to us an economical and safe journey to our place of destination, by augmentation, do ordain and establish this Constitution; and for the protection of each and every person enrolling as members of this Company, we do solemnly and mutually pledge to each other, our lives, our fortunes, and our sacred honors, looking with a firm reliance on Divine Providence for protection.

	Name		Age	Residence	Occupation
Captain,	John A. N. Ebbetts,	M	33	New York	Merchant
1st Lieut.,	George H. Blake,	M	24	Troy, New York	Jeweller
2nd Lieut.,	Abram A. Van Gelder,	M	26	New York City	Music Dealer
Treasurer,	Peter Lodewick,	S	28	151 Prince St.	Artist
Secretary,	James P. Burr,	M	41	108 Grand St.	Book Keeper
	Gerard Bancker,	M	33	181 Wooster St.	Coal Dealer
	Phineas U. Blunt,	M	39	New York	Soapstone worker
	B. C. Wilson,	M	30	361 Brown St.	Wood Turner
	Wm. F. Ford,	M	29	New York	Surg. Instr. Maker
	Stephen Hyde,	M	53	163 Prince St.	Boot & Shoe Maker
	Alx. H. Reed,	M	35	30 Barkley St.	Merchant
	John Flynn,	M	38	158 Lawrence	Cartman
	George Derrick,	W	48	404 Broadway	Harness Maker
	James Spencer,	M	45	123 Walker St.	Artist
	Andrew Smith,	S	29	Norwalk Is., Con.	Printer
	Jessee Brush,	M	40	31 Charlton St.	Artist
	Wm. S. Ross,	S	30	225 Thompson St.	Pharmacopolist
	Wm. Canfeld,	M	33	119 Spring St.	Jeweller
	Wm. W. Wyckoff,	S	26	133 Thompson St.	Prac. Engineer
	Hiram Green,	S	26	New York City	Clerk
	Barnabas Pike,	M	44	New York City	Dry Goods' Man
	Cornelius Cornwell,	S	28	New York City	Grocer
	John M. Hendricks,	S	23	New York City	House Smith
	James E. Baker,	S	23	67 Norfolk St.	Mahog. Door Maker
	George Churchill,	S	21	Troy, N.Y.	Grocer

Name		Age	Residence	Occupation
Wiliam Moore,	S	32	New York City	———
James Helms,	S	29	New York City	Brass worker
Charles Churchill,	S	25	Troy, N.Y.	Miller
Edgar Seabury,	M	28	Troy, N.Y.	Tailor
James H. Cooley,	M	25	117 McDougal St.	Painter
Joseph Van Doren,	M	28	286 Spring St.	Oil Merchant
James Brown,	M	24	50 King St.	Hatter
Patrick Garvey,	M	33	38 Haumersly St.	Tailor
Oliver B. Oakley,	M	33	Cor. Carm. & Bedf'd	Silver Plater
James Lockhaert,	S	28	172 6th Avenue	Cartman
Jas. Broadmeadow,	M	29	226 Greenwich St.	Steel Manufact'r
John Murphy,	M	29	Harlem, N.Y.	Stage Proprietor
John Jones, Jr.	S	28	94 White St.	Grocer
Sam'l Griffiths,	M	26	9th Ave & 35th St.	Dock Builder
John H. Bogert,	M	26	62 Gansvort St.	Comb Maker
H. M. Sturges,	S	24	Western Conn.	Clerk
Ira M. Allen,	W	53	New York	Clergy & Geol't.
Rob't. W. Nevins,	S	41	51 W. Wash. Place	Merchant
Samuel Kelly,	M	47	165 Canal St.	Exchange Brok'r.
John P. Hoyt,	M	32	165 Canal St.	Merchant Tailor
James L. Byers,	S	20	272 Bleecker St.	Dry Goods Clerk
Joel G. Candee,	W	45	20 Park Place	M.D.
Schuyler Hoes,	M	43	Newark, N.J.	Clergyman
J. Alfred Kanouse,	M	34	Newark, N.J.	Lawyer
Josiah H. Bruen,	M	36	Newark, N.J.	Farmer

Name		Age	Residence	Occupation
John Price,	M	29	Newark, N.J.	Spec. Manufact'r.
John Jackson,	S	17	New York City	—
Wm. McClelland,	S	19	New York City	Clerk
T. L. Sturges,	S	25	Wilton, Conn.	Farmer
James Mac Nally,	S	28	New York City	Iron Founder
John Hempseed,	S	24	333 Hudson St.	Sad. & Har. Mak.
John A. Hunter,	S	29	New York	Surg. Inst. Maker
Wm. R. Goulding,	M	42	New York	Surg. Inst. Maker
Samuel Y. Lum,	S	27	Newark, N.J.	Student
Melvin S. Gardner,	S	25	Bowdoinham, Me.	Ship Master
E. L. Hughson,	M	[30?]	Newark, N.J.	Baker
E. O. Crane,	M	27	Newark, N.J.	Tailor
Wm. Larison,	M	24	Newark, N.J.	Journalist
J. F. Hough,	S	20	New York City	Clerk

Appendix B
Rancho Santa Ana del Chino Register Book

WILLIAM R. GOULDING wrote the very first entry in what became known as the Rancho Santa Ana del Chino Register Book, a rare manuscript now housed in the Huntington Library (figure 19). With the support of Isaac Williams, Goulding undoubtedly promoted the idea of the register. Hundreds of gold seekers were arriving daily at the ranch and were probably encouraged to sign in on arrival. This offered a way to reconnect with colleagues who had gone on ahead or were yet to arrive. Some, like Goulding, briefly described their trip, while others simply noted their name, home state, company, and date of arrival.

Most of the travelers, arriving fatigued and impoverished, had good reason to be grateful to Williams for his generosity, hospitality, and assistance. In a way, he did not have much choice, for the migrants were exiting major trails that intersected the ranch. Some accused Williams of an ulterior motive—asking people to sign their names in order to obtain reimbursement later from the California government. Robert Brownlee thought he had "a very dishonest heart" (1986, 93), while L. N. Weed, arriving on September 14, accused him of being a "Yankee of the most grabbing kind" (1857). After 1850, entries by gold seekers declined, but the register contained sporadic additions up to about 1895, long after Williams's death in 1856. The later entries were mainly by locals who noted lost and found animals.

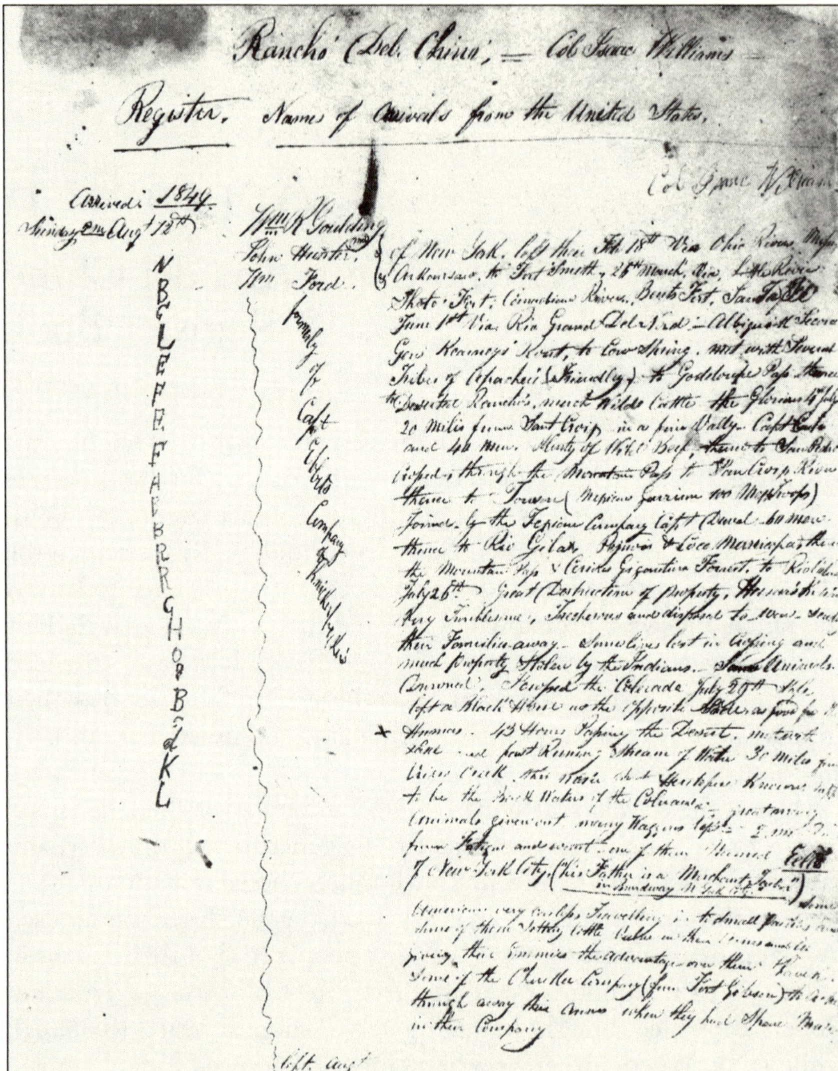

Rancho Del Chino, — Col Isaac Williams —

Register. Names of Arrivals from the United States.

FIGURE 19. Rancho Santa Ana del Chino Register Book, showing 1849 William Goulding entry. *Courtesy of the Huntington Library.*

We find some interesting statistics between August 1849 and September 1850. Close to 586 travelers representing fifty-six companies of prospective gold miners left a record: tragic stories of accidents and death, stories full of hope, memories of encounters with Indians, and a few amusing tales. The emigrants came mainly from the southern states and New York. They had followed the Fort Smith–Santa Fe Trail; the Cherokee Trail; various trails out of Texas; the Santa Fe Trail out of Independence, Missouri; the Gila Trail; the Old Spanish Trail out of Salt Lake City; and trails through Mexico.

In addition to some murderers and scamps, an interesting array of characters is represented, all of whom took part in building California. Here was a future sheriff and mayor of Sacramento; the discoverer of Yosemite; a justice of the California Supreme Court; some who were murdered and others who were murderers; the founder of the Los Angeles Star; prominent mountain men, ranchers, and ferrymen; Texas Rangers; elected officials; nine future members of the Mariposa Battalion; the father of author Edna Bryan Buckbee; the deputy county clerk of Sacramento; the first county recorder of Tulare County; and finally, one who inherited a large estate in England and left as quickly as he came. Therefore, Isaac Williams's register is more than a list of names. It gives us a composite picture of the character of men who came to California and found gold in other ways. It helps us learn how these people traveled, the companies they traveled with, and the routes they followed. These migrants were mainly male, although some families were included in the register. A published version by Lindley Bynum is available as "The Record Book of the Rancho Santa Ana del Chino" (1934).

William Goulding's Entry in the Register Book
Rancho del Chino—Col. Isaac Williams
Register. Names of Arrivals from the United States

Arrived 1849 Sunday PM Augt 12th	Wm. R. Goulding John Hunter Wm. Ford Formerly of Capt Ebbits Company of Knickerbockers	of New York. Left their Feb 18th via Ohio Rivers Missis & Arkansas, to Fort Smith, 26th March. Via Little River Shoto [Choteau] Fort, Canadian River . . . Bents Fort [Texas] Santa Fe June 1st via Rio Grande del Nord—Albiquick Secora Gen Kearney's Rout, to Cow Spring. Met with several Tribes of Apacheis (Friendly) to Godiloupe [Guadalupe] Pass thence to Deserted Ranchos much Wild Cattle the Glorious 4th July 20 miles from Sant Croix [Santa Cruz, Sonora, Mexico] in a fine vally—Capt Carter and 40 Men. Plenty of Wild Beef, thence to San Pedro Crossed, through the Mountain Pass to San Croix River thence to Touson (Mexican Garrison 100 Mex Troops) Joind by the Texian Company Capt Duval, 60 men thence to Rio Gila, Pemos [Pimas] & Coco Maricopa, thence the Mountain Pass & Cerious Gigantica [Saguaro] Forrest. to Rio Calerado July 26th—Great Destruction of property, Humas [Yuma] Indian Very Troublesome, Trecherous and disposed to war—sending their Families away—some lives lost in crossing and much property Stolen by the Indians—Some animals Drowned. I crossed the Colerada July 29th Safe left a Black Horse on the opposite Side, as food for the Humas—43 Hours passing the Desert. Met with a Lake and fast Runing Stream of Water 30 miles from Crisso Creek [New River]. This water not heretofore known.

Left Augt.	Supposed to be the backwaters of the Colerada—great many Animals given out—many Waggons left—2 men died from Fatigue and want—one of them named Ells of New York City. ("his Father is a Merchant Tailor in Broadway N York City") Americans very careless, Travelling in Small Parties Some of them Setting little value in their Arms and Amunition Giving their Enemies the advantage over them. I have known some of the Cherokee Company (from Fort Gibson) to actualy through away their Arms when they had Spare Mules in their Company.

Appendix C

Reminiscences of John Hoyt, Member of the Knickerbocker Company of New York, and His Travels on the Gila Trail

John P. Hoyt's reminiscences, reprinted here without annotation, originally formed chapter 19 of William Goulding's journal. Hoyt was a member of Goulding's mess when the Knickerbocker Exploring Company first set out from Fort Smith, when he was listed as a thirty-two-year-old merchant tailor in New York. After reaching Santa Fe, he was among those Knickerbockers who opted to switch to pack animals and follow the Old Spanish Trail. Turned back by flooding and bad weather, his group continued south along the Rio Grande and left the river near Truth or Consequences, New Mexico. His group followed the full length of the Gila Trail west, passing the Santa Rita copper mines near Silver City and Mangas Springs, New Mexico, where they reached the Gila River. They followed the river's twists and turns through mountainous terrain all the way to the Pima villages in Arizona before continuing along the river to the Colorado crossing at Yuma. Hoyt reunited with Goulding at Isaac Williams's Rancho Santa Ana del Chino in California. His trip can be followed in detail in "The 1849 Diary of Stanislaus Lasselle" (1991).

Goulding copied Hoyt's reminiscences into his own diary and wrote:

[Santa Fe, May 31, 1849] Their was twenty eight of them all well mounted and armed, and every man had a packed mule with from two to two hundred and fifty pounds of provisions. They several times met with Indians but none of them would approach their body altho at several times they endeavored to speak with them for as they had not guide they had lost their way and were wandering about for a week and had at one time came up to their own camp which they had left three days before.

This fetched them to council amongst themselves of what was best to be done. Here the true Yankee spirit of partyism presented itself. One was for going on the same route they had previously gone over, while the rest were for returning back to the Rio Grand. When they were in the height of their argument they were surprised by a party of Indians who were returning from a fray for they all appeared to be mounted on fresh mules and horses. Several of them having the well known Mexican brand in their shoulders and thighs and they were dressed in all sorts of a fantastical style. The Mexican dress and saddles predominated, showing where they had chiefly made up their wardrobe. Several of them wore beautiful helmets, decked with black and white feathers, and they looked like a band of antique Grecian warriors returning from the wars, but with the short shirt, waist belt, bare legs, and buckskins, and Mexican Toggery showed the Indian mountain Apache in his true costume.

These Indians have no fixed homes, their houses are of twigs and deserted with indifference. They hover around the beautiful hills that overhang the del North [Rio Grande River] and along its banks to the states of Chihuahua and Sonora, and woe to the luckless company that ventures out unguarded by a strong force, the light and graceful manner in which they mounted and dismounted always upon the right side, was the admiration of all present. Seeing we were well armed and more than a match for them in a bunch, they were very polite and by signs they informed us a way out of this trap or den of the Apaches. After two days we met with a river or stream running at the rate of six miles an hour so we erected a raft, and in the first attempt in crossing, the raft upset and everything was lost but the four men narrowly escaped being drowned. A second attempt was made and the like result, and the third attempt was made and by lashing six of their mules to the raft when all were carried down the flood and but one of the mules succeeded with the five men in getting back again to the bank some half a mile below where they started from.

Now with the los of most of their provisions and all their extra clothing, they were obliged to retrace their steps to the Rio Del Norte, cursing "Kit Carson," "Coons" [Benjamin Franklin Coons of El Paso], and all the quarter-master sergents that Uncle Sam ever had who advised them to go to California by these infernal high roads. Barefoot and bare breeched, many of them was, when they came out on the Rio Grand at Albequek [Albuquerque].

There they recruited and got fresh supplies and after a rest of three days proceeded down the East side of the river till they came to Limitar where they again crossed the Rio Grand aided by the Pueblo Indians which turned out in great numbers along its banks. Here we were met by a French man, the alcalda, who gave us information of our former associates in the Knickerbockers. The Indians had a number of small canoes and rafts by which we soon got over all our provisions and kits. We then proceeded to cross our cavalcade, some of the horses were first driven in the swift current and went bravely over. Others were very troublesome and we were obliged to imploy Indians to swim them over. After a short time the remainder of our animals seeing their companions enjoying the luxuriant grass, they were all hunted with a terrible yell into the river where they arrived safe on the opposite side. Some had to struggle hard to get up on the banks in addition to the steepness were covered with a coating of mud. It was a beautiful sight to see all on arrival plunging and springing through the swift stream to see the splash of spray as it showered around when the horse would disappear and again to see the noble animals rise above the wave. Snorting and dashing the waters from his mane as he swam for the opposite bank. The Indians seemed to enter into the spirit of the scene. One of them seized the lariet of one of our most spirited horses and dragged him down into the water. He stood for a moment, and then plunged into the stream throughing his arms alternately as he dashed across.

It is in such scenes as this, the Indian exels their fine limbs, dark hair, and flashing eye and wild grace of motion. The picturesque of attitude that such occasions develop. We stopped at the town of Secoro for two days and were handsomely treated by the troop of dragoons stationed at that place. We travelled then over the same trail passed by our former companions to the Rio Membres.

Here we camped for nearly two days amidst an old Indian encampment. We were joined at this place by eight Texians who with us proceeded toward the Rio Gila travelling over a succession of hills and valleys, ravines and trap dykes with huge mountains of reddish [illegible] and brown sandstone dispersing in regular strata. Noticed a large pile of volcanic glass brittle in strata about a half inch thick, the character of the country different from any we had seen before. Several new plants and shrub with some new kinds of cedars and pines and live-oaks in the small valleys. In many places the path was strewed with huge fragments of hard rock, making it difficult for our animals to get along.

We turned by the north of a round looking mountain and struck into a fine extensive valley which we supposed to be an arm of the Mimbres. Here we camped by some deserted and ruined adobe houses some twenty or thirty of them. Evidently the remains of large copper mines for we noticed all over, specimens of the copper ore and in several places, large holes and dykes apparently where the former occupants had worked. The entire surface of the hills all around is covered with iron pyrites and the red oxide of copper. Some of our party made attempts to find gold but did not succeed. Two Apaches Indians came to our camp from whom we got some Mescal roots and molasses mixed with suet rolled up in the leaves of some sort of cactus. We continued down the valley and came to an extensive spring of sulphur water. Here the valley opens out large with the mountains ringing all around. At the distance of ten to fifteen miles here was several Indian lodges, evidently their place for large meetings. Proceeding we soon came into a most terrible creek or river bed, which we thought we never would get out of, but go ahead was the password and we travelled all night at a snales pace stoping to rest at midnight a few hours. Our curiosity was excited to see at daylight to see what sort of place we were in. The valley we had been travelling all night, was narrowing by the intrusion of high precipices and the proximity of great mountains in confused masses, indicating some remarkable change in the face of the country. We were in truth but a few miles from the Gila, which by ascending in the ridge of the ravine we soon arrived at and camped.

Several Indians visited us and soon the whole camp was busily engaged in trading. These Indians had mules, lariets, ropes, and dried beaf, fat and mescal and one of them had a bag ful of hard biscuit which was soon purchased for the best striped shirt I had in my kit. Blankets, red shirts, pieces of red & blue cloth, knives, needles, thread of any colour, handkerchiefs, large bone beads and brass rings of large size is the only articles they seemed most to desire in exchange for their articles. They had extravagant notions of our wealth. They were very eager for traffic, and we had some difficulty in getting our line of march formed. Finding we were indifferent in continuing for trading, they began to scamper off in various directions.

We followed the course of the Gila for many miles and saw great numbers of the blue quail. The bottom of the river is narrow, covered with large round pebbles. The growth of trees and weeds very luxuriant, the trees chiefly cottonwood, sycamore, mesquite, cedarwood, birch, pines, with the wild hop and grapevines creeping through them.

It was the custom of our men, in riding along, to carry their rifles laying horizontally across the pommel of the saddles, and to be ready for a shot at a bear or anything else. [They] used to have their pieces always capped and the underbrush now became so thick and the trail narrow, one of the packed mules in its haste in passing one of the men, so jarred his rifle that it snapped and discharged the ball into the thigh of one of the party a Mr. David Buchaning [Buchanan], a werthy and good man who was some ten feet from the rifle sitting a "la Madame" easily jogging along. His brother a young doctor one of the party made an attempt to extract the ball but it was well lodged in the posterior part of the pelvis (on the coctis) and did not succeed.

Some of the ingeneous of the party constructed a frame litter of willow poles whereby the unfortunate man could lay in the mules back as it was not possible for him to sit up in the saddle. In this way, our worthy companion was carried for several weeks.

We crossed and recrossed this Gila river some dozzens of times, some days, for hours, pursuing its river bottom to evade the deep loose volcanic dust and fragments of rocks which occupied the banks of the river and the steep ascents and descents occasionally met with shifting the packs and cutting our mules back dreadfully at times made us prefer the river where it was practicable to go ahead. In some places it would wind and twist around that we were obliged to take the table lands.

We camped in the ruins of some very extensive town according to the appearances of the earth. For upwards of two miles the earth was strewed over with broken pottery and the clay buttes in the distance looked like ancient castles making all kinds of shapes as washed away by the rains. Nothing but the most fantastic looking mountains that could be imagined. On one side [of] our camp the bold outline of a castle presented itself with the tops of the walls horizontal. The corners vertical and apparently bastioned in the front but in examining with the spy-glass the whole construction was nothing more than clay buttes and the naked eye, the delusion was compleat.

During our march we passed two more extensive masses or broken pottery and visible signs of irrigating ditches in all directions for miles and the foundations of some very large houses. The stories forming the supposed foundation was round and unhewn, and the cactus of all varieties growing in all directions.

A party of Indians were in camp and were much surprised at our sudden visit. They were the most miserable looking objects we ever beheld. Their legs were large and muscular but their faces and bodies were one mass of wrinkles almost like scale. The men were armed with spears and bows and arrows, none of these spoke Spanish and our communication was by sign. Their chief talked in a tongue resembling the bark of a dog more than the voice of a human person. They seemed indifferent to our company so we passed on and left them. We supposed them to be the "trembles" or "Cayotes" tribe. We passed by some of the cereus giganteus cacti upwards of fifty feet high during this day and camped in an extensive grove of the same during the night. At last we arrived at the Pimos village where we stoped almost a week to recruit our animals as well as ourselves.

These are the most enlightened Indians we have met with during our travels over the mountains. We visited the Coco Maricopa Indians which also cultivate the soil and weave blankets and cotton cloth caps and live in a state of hospitable and friendly community having laws and order and governed by one head chief.

We left these people and travelled by night over the desert of fifty five miles covered with an immense forest of cactus in all its varieties, and the howl of the panther a Mexican lion with that of the wolf and the screaming of the screech owl was our music during the [illegible] of the night. During the following day, we camped by the two extensive piles of rocks which were covered with hieroglyphic simbols of unknown characters. We then continued buy the Gila for several days and at last arrived at the junction of the Gila and Colorado rivers, where we found several companies encamped, waiting to recruit their animals before undertaking the crossing of the Colerado and immediately in the other side have to encounter the great 90 mile desert. Supposed to be without wood or water.

At this camp we were joined by Capt. John Ebbets and a party of the old company of the New York Knickerbockers and learned the mellancholy news of the death of the Rev. Hiram L. Allen who died in July on the Gila River. Also of the death of John Flynn who died from fatigue and want on the desert near Touscn. The suffering of these men was dredful and painful but now the worst feat of crossing of the mighty element the Colorada. After resting at this camp our party continually on the watch with a continued state of fearful anxiety from the continual reports of the depredations committed by the Umas [Yumas] Indians. Now at the crossing in great numbers and who had taken possession of all the former rafts constructed by the different preceeding companies and now were extravagant in their demands from the emigrants crossing and so much so that some companies had to resort to taking the rafts from [them] by force as they had it in their power to give them blankets and shirts enough to satisfy their reckless and unreasonable demands.

In one of these rows two of the Americans got murdered and twenty six of their animals were stampeded and driven off by these reckless vagabonds. Our camp was nearly two miles from the place of crossing and it became necessary for the parties now to be numerous when their, as they would rob and plunder every small party. On the day our party arrived at the banks of this stream or gulf of death, there was upwards of two hundred Americans. That is all parties from the United States. ("As in this country or any place amongst Mexicans they call everyone from the United States Americans") and such a motely and fantastic looking assembly never was together before. There was all nations all tongues and all sorts of dispositions, the gentleman and the beggar, the soldier and the plebian, the General and the Corporal, the lawyer and the Judge, the master and the slave, the Mexican Don and the Pueblo Serfe, the parson and the vestry with all its different ways of thinking of this method of Baptism but the day and the time was come and into the deep we all went as fast as we could pile our plunder in the hundred and fifty rafts, for at this time their was any quantity of them and we gave the Indians liberally of blankets, shirts, cloth, tobacco, and trinkets to satisfy them to swim over and pull us to the other side.

We were very particular in having our lariats and ropes attached to each others raft, and the sight was grand and thrilling in seeing us all go over in a huge body with the glorious American flag, the stars and stripes flutering in the breese as we floated down and over this mighty Gulf of the Colerada. The day was one of the finest that could be. Not a breath of air except a little in the stream caused by the movement of the water. No accident occurred to us in crossing except the loss of some flour and the wetting of our plunder but seven of our mules were drowned in the rush of the whole parties cavalcade, which we drove in and over in front of us and which was discovered on our arival.

The Indians on the opposite side were even to be more feared that those we left and it was dangerous for less than six or eight of us to be together but we kept a strict watch till our whole party was over.

When at four o'clock in the afternoon we commenced our march over the dessert and all our suffering before were no comparison to the jaded mules and horses now could go no further and the pass word now was "Legs do your duty" Some made out to lead their poor brutes into the mountains or California but I made out to lead myself for I left my poor Nell puss at the clay [illegible] river of mud in the dessert. She could go no further so here am bare breeched and barefooted.

"Thus was the notes and statement of my old fellow messmate, John Hoyt, Esq."

Bibliography

Abert, James W. 1970. *Through the Country of the Comanche Indians in the Fall of the Year 1845*. Edited by John Galvin. San Francisco: John Howell Books.

———. 1966. *Western America in 18461847: The Original Travel Diary of Lieutenant J. W. Abert.* San Francisco: John Howell Books.

Aldrich, Lorenzo. 1851. *A Journal of the Overland Route to California*. Lansingburgh, N.Y.: Alexr. Kirkpatrick, Printer.

Anderson, H. Allen. 2008. "Adobe Walls, Texas." *Handbook of Texas Online.* www.tshaonline.org/handbook/online.

Appleton's Cyclopedia of American Biography. 1887–89. New York: D. Appleton.

Archambeau, Ernest R. 1954. "The Fort-Smith-Santa Fe Trail Along the Canadian River." *Panhandle Plains Historical Review* 27:1–26.

Arizona Atlas and Gazetteer. 1993. Freeport, Maine: DeLorme.

Audubon, John James. 1940. *Audubon's America: The Narratives and Experiences of John James Audubon.* Edited by Donald Culross Peattie. Boston: Houghton Mifflin.

Bailey, Joseph Howard. 1849. "Letter." *Fort Smith (Arkansas) Herald,* February 14.

———. Small manuscript subject file, Arkansas History Commission, Little Rock, Ark.

Bain, Alexander. 1890. *English Composition and Rhetoric.* New York: D. Appleton.

Baker, T. Lindsay, and Betty R. Harrison. 1986. *Adobe Walls: The History and Archaeology of the 1874 Trading Post.* College Station: Texas A&M University Press.

Bancroft, Hubert Howe. 1964. *Register of Pioneer Inhabitants of California 1542–1848.* Los Angeles: Dawson's Book Shop.

Barnes, Joseph K. 1864. Letter to William R. Goulding, September 28, 1864. Enlistment Papers. United States Army. National Archives Microfilm Publication, RG 94 M1064, Roll 92 G-542. National Archives Building, Washington, D.C.

Barnes, Will C. 1988. *Arizona Place Names.* Tucson: University of Arizona Press.

Bartlett, John Russell. 1854. *Personal Narrative of Explorations . . . During the Years 1850, 1851, 1852 and 1853.* 2 vols. New York: D. Appleton.

Baur, George. N.d. "Journey of William Robinson Goulding, Jr." Unpublished manuscript in the editor's files. 17 pp.

———. N.d. "Journey of William Robinson Goulding, Sr., across North America." Unpublished manuscript in the editor's files. 25 pp.

Beale, Edward F. 1934. "Survey of a Wagon Road from Fort Smith to the Colorado River." Edited by Grant Foreman. *Chronicles of Oklahoma* 12 (March): 74–96.

Bean, Lowell John, and Florence C. Shipek. 1978. "Luiseño." In *California.* Vol. 8 of *Handbook of North American Indians.* Washington, D.C.: Smithsonian Institution.

Bearss, Ed, and Arrell M. Gibson. 1969. *Fort Smith: Little Gibraltar on the Arkansas.* Norman: University of Oklahoma Press.

Beattie, George William. 1940. "Where Was the Battle of Chino Fought?" *Historical Society of Southern California Quarterly* 22 (March): 62–69.

Beck, Warren A. 1982. *New Mexico: A History of Four Centuries.* Norman: University of Oklahoma Press.

Beck, Warren A., and Inez D. Haase. 1980. *Historical Atlas of California.* Norman: University of Oklahoma Press.

———. 1979. *Historical Atlas of New Mexico.* Norman: University of Oklahoma Press.

Benson, Henry C. 1860. *Life Among the Choctaw Indians and Sketches of the Southwest.* Cincinnati: Pub. by L. Swormstedt and A. Poe, for the Methodist Episcopal Church.

Berlandier, John Louis. 1969. *The Indians of Texas in 1830.* Washington, D.C.: Smithsonian Institution Press.

Biographical Dictionary of Indians of the Americas. 1991. "Black Beaver." Vol. 1. Newport Beach, Calif.: American Indian Publishers.

Birt, Samuel Pearce. 1967. "The Journal of the La Grange Company: Being the Record of a Journey from Texas to California in 1849." Edited by Carlo D. Ferrari. *Quarterly of the Tuolumne County Historical Society* 6 (January–March): 193–98.

Bishoff, Matt. 2001. *Touring New Mexico Hot Springs.* Guilford, Conn.: Globe Pequot Press.

Blunt, Phineas. 1849–52. Notes of Travel from New York to the Gold Region of California in the Year Eighteen Hundred and Forty Nine, February 5, 1849–January 14, 1852. Manuscript. Bancroft Library.

Bouldin, James E. 1849–50. Diary of Captain James E. Bouldin, 1849–1850. Typescript. Department of Special Collections, Stanford University Libraries.

Boyd, William T. 1855. "Mortgage Sale of Surgical Instruments." *New York Times*. May 12.

Boyer, John. 1849. *Arkansas State Democrat* (*Little Rock*), September 7.

Brainard, David. 1849. David Brainard's Journal, Delaware, March 20, 1849–November 29, 1849. Manuscript. Bancroft Library.

Browne, John Ross. 1950. *A Dangerous Journey: California 1849*. Palo Alto, Calif.: Arthur Lites Press.

Brownlee, Robert. 1986. *An American Odyssey, The Autobiography of a 19th Century Scotsman*. Edited by Patricia A. Etter. Fayetteville: University of Arkansas Press.

Bryant, Edwin. [1849]. *What I Saw in California*. [New York: D. Appleton.] Reprinted by Indy Publishing.

Bynum, Lindley. 1934. "The Record Book of the Rancho Santa Ana del Chino." *Historical Society of Southern California* 16:1–55.

California Legislature. Senate Resolution no. 24. Relative to Colonel Isaac Williams, perpetuating his communication to the Senate dated February 15, 1850, and commending him for his benevolence and humanity toward early pioneers. *Senate Journal* (January 12, 1942): 117–20.

Candee, Joel G. 1850. "From an Overland California Emigrant." *Hartford* (*Connecticut*) *Courant*, September 14.

Chamberlin, William. 1945. "From Lewisburg, Pa., to California in 1849." Edited by Lansing B. Bloom. *New Mexico Historical Review* 20:24–57; 144–80; 337–44.

Chatham (*New York*) *Courier*. 1970. "The Little Brown Church Keeps Tradition Dating Back to 1847." December 17.

Churchill, George. 1849. Journal of an Overland Trip to California. Manuscript. ARC 561 Churchill. California History Room and Archives, Monterey Public Library, Monterey, Calif.

Clarke, Asa Bement. 1988. *Travels in Mexico and California*. Edited by Anne M. Perry. College Station: Texas A&M University Press.

Columbia County, New York, Historical Society. Research notes in editor's files. Various dates.

Constitution of the Knickerbocker Exploring Company, of the City of New York. 1849. *Fort Smith* (*Arkansas*) *Herald*, March 21.

Cooke, Philip St. George. 1937. *Exploring Southwestern Trails, 1846–1854*. Vol. 7 of *Southwest Historical Series*. Edited by Ralph P. Bieber. Glendale, Calif.: Arthur H. Clark.

Couts, Cave Johnson. 1961. *Hepah! California! The Journal of Cave Johnson Couts . . . During the Years 1848–1849*. Edited by Henry F. Dobyns. Tucson: Arizona Pioneers' Historical Society.

Cowan, Robert G. 1956. *Ranchos of California: A List of Spanish Concessions 1775–1822 and Mexican Grants 1822–1846*. Fresno, Calif.: Academy Library Guild.

Cowper, William. 1889. *The Poetical Works of William Cowper*. Edited by William Benham. London: Macmillan and Co.

Crump, Spencer. 1985. *California's Spanish Missions: Their Yesterdays and Todays*. Corona del Mar, Calif.: Trans-Anglo Books.

Daily Alta California. 1864. "Explosion of the Steamer Secretary: Thirty Lives Lost, Many Persons Wounded." April 16, p2, c2.

Davis, William Heath. 1967. *Seventy-five Years in California*. Edited by Harold A. Small. San Francisco: John Howell Books.

Dockstader, Frederick J. 1977. *Great North American Indians: Profiles in Life and Leadership*. Van Nostrand Reinhold.

Domenech, Emmanuel. 1860. *Seven Years' Residence in the Great Deserts of North America*. 2 vols. London: Longman, Green, Longman, and Roberts.

Dott, Robert H. 1960. "Oklahoma's California Road, 1849." *Chronicles of Oklahoma* 38:154–79.

"Douglas Hospital." Finding guide, Old Military and Civil Records Division, National Archives and Records Administration, Washington, D.C.

Dun, R. G. & Co. New York City. Vols. 374, 377, various dates.

Dunbar, Seymour. *History of Travel in America*. 4 vols. New York: Tudor, 1937.

Duval, Isaac H. 1987. *Texas Argonauts: Isaac H. Duval and the California Gold Rush*. Edited by Richard H. Dillon. San Francisco: Book Club of California.

Ebbetts, John A. N. 1853. "Pacific Railroad Survey: Report of the Exploring Party, the Country in the Neighborhood of Walker's Lake . . . Major Ebbetts Report." *San Francisco Daily Herald*, December 19–20.

Edmonson, James M. 1997. *American Surgical Instruments: An Illustrated History of Their Manufacture and a Directory of Their Makers to 1900*. Novato, Calif.: Norman Publishing.

Ellis, Franklin. 1878. *History of Columbia County, New York*. Philadelphia: Everts and Ensign.

Ellis, George M. 1995. *Gold Rush Desert Trails to San Diego and Los Angeles in 1849*. San Diego, Calif.: San Diego Corral of the Westerners.

Emory, William Hemsley. 1848. *Notes of a Military Reconnoissance from Fort Leavenworth, in Missouri, to San Diego, in California, Including part of the*

Arkansas, Del Norte, and Gila Rivers. Ex. Doc. no. 41, 30th Congress, 1st Sess. United States Army Corps of Topographical Engineers. Washington, D.C.: Wendell and Van Benthuysen.

Etter, Patricia A. 2000. "On the Southern Route, San Miguel del Vado." *Overland Journal* 18 (Spring): 18–19.

———. 1998. *To California on the Southern Route, 1849: A History and Annotated Bibliography.* Spokane, Wash.: Arthur H. Clark.

———. N.d. Rancho Santa Ana del Chino. Unpublished manuscript.

Evans, George W. B. 1945. *Mexican Gold Trail: The Journey of a Forty-Niner.* Edited by Glenn S. Dumke. San Marino, Calif.: Huntington Library.

Faulk, Odie B., and Billy Mac Jones. 1983. *Fort Smith: An Illustrated History.* Fort Smith, Ark.: Old Fort Museum.

Fletcher, Patricia K., Jack Earl Fletcher, and Lee Whiteley. 1999. *Cherokee Trail Diaries.* Sequim, Wash.: Fletcher Family Trust.

Foreman, Carolyn Thomas. 1946. "Black Beaver." *Chronicles of Oklahoma* 24 (Fall): 269–92.

———. 1932. "The Choctaw Academy." *Chronicles of Oklahoma* 10 (March): 77–114.

Foreman, Grant. 1968. *Advancing the Frontier 1830–1860.* Norman: University of Oklahoma Press.

———. 1939. *Marcy and the Gold Seekers.* Norman: University of Oklahoma Press.

———. 1934. *Five Civilized Tribes: Cherokee, Chickasaw, Choctaw, Creek, Seminole.* Norman: University of Oklahoma Press.

———. 1925. "Early Trails Through Oklahoma." *Chronicles of Oklahoma* 3 (June): 99–119.

Forsythe, John Robert. [1849]. Diary. Peoria, Illinois, Public Library.

Fort Adobe. N.d. Pamphlet. Canyon, Tex.: Panhandle Plains Museum.

Fort Smith (Arkansas) Herald. 1849. "Knickerbocker Association." March 14.

———. March 15, June 28, 1848; February 14, March 21, 1849.

Foster, Stephen C. 1949. "I Was Los Angeles' First American Alcalde," *Historical Society of Southern California* 31 (December): 318–21.

Foster, Theodore. 1849. "Rancho del Chino, August 24, 1849." *Missouri Republican*, November 21.

Frémont, John Charles. 1970. *The Expeditions of John Charles Frémont.* Edited by Donald Jackson and Mary Lee Spence. Urbana: University of Illinois Press.

———. 1849. "Letter from Taos, New Mexico, January 27, 1849." *New York Tribune*, March 20.

Fugate, Francis L., and Roberta B. Fugate. 1989. *Roadside History of New Mexico*. Missoula, Mont.: Mountain Press.

Giese, Dale F. 1995. *Forts of New Mexico*. Silver City, N.Mex.: Dale F. Giese.

Gilmer, Jeremy Francis. Papers. No. 276. University of North Carolina, Chapel Hill.

Goodyear, Charles. 1853. *Gum Elastic and Its Varieties . . . and of the Discovery of Vulcanization*. Vol. 1. New Haven, Conn.: Goodyear.

Gottschalk, M. C. 1999. *Miguel Romero y Baca and the Early Settlement of Las Vegas, New Mexico*. Las Vegas, N.Mex.: M. C. Gottschalk.

Goulding, Warwick. N.d. Family tree. Unpublished manuscript in the editor's files.

Goulding, William R. Addenda to journal, July 1864–April 29, 1865. 61 pp. Yale Collection of Western Americana, Beinecke Rare Book and Manuscript Library.

———. Journal. February 18–September 18, 1849. 325 pp. Yale Collection of Western Americana, Beinecke Rare Book and Manuscript Library.

———. Certificate of Membership in the Independence Guard, 264th Regiment, New York State Infantry, 1844. Copy in the editor's files.

———. Enlistment papers. United States Army, 1798–July 14, 1894. Records of the Adjutant General's Office, Record Group 94, Box 297. National Archives Building, Washington, D.C.

———. Letter to Brig. General J. K. Barnes, Surgeon General of the United States, September 28, 1864. Enlistment papers, United States Army. National Archives Microfilm Publication M1064, Roll 92 G542. National Archives Building, Washington, D.C.

———. Letter to William R. Goulding, Jr., October 10, 1864. Manuscript in the editor's files.

———. Letter to Henry S. Van de Carr, January 31, 1865. Addenda to journal.

———. Letter to John Wolfel, December 20, 1864. Addenda to journal.

"Grand Old Belle Point." 2006. Printout in the editor's files. http://members.aol.com/BP20FAM/page8.html.

Greene, Peter. 2006. *Mike Butterfield's Guide to the Mountains of New Mexico*. Albuquerque: New Mexico Magazine.

Gregg, Josiah. 1990. *Commerce of the Prairies*. Edited by Max L. Moorehead. Norman: University of Oklahoma Press.

———. 1941–44. *Diary and Letters of Josiah Gregg*. Edited by Maurice Garland Fulton. 2 vols. Norman: University of Oklahoma Press.

———. 1926. *Commerce of the Prairies*. Edited by Milton Quaife. Chicago: Lakeside Press.

Gudde, Erwin G. 2004. *California Place Names.* Revised by William Bright. Berkeley: University of California Press.

Gutiérrez, Ramón, and Richard J. Orsi. 1997. *Contested Eden: California Before the Gold Rush.* Berkeley: University of California Press, for the California Historical Society.

Hackenberger, Mary A. 1942. Records of the Families of California Pioneers. Vol. 11. Manuscript. California State Library, Sacramento.

Hackler, George. 2005. *The Butterfield Trail in New Mexico.* Las Cruces, N.Mex.: Yucca Enterprises.

Hague, Harlan, and David J. Langum. 1990. *Thomas O. Larkin: A Life of Patriotism and Profit in Old California.* Norman: University of Oklahoma Press.

Handbook of Texas Online. www.tshaonline.org/handbook/online/.

Harris, Benjamin Butler. 1960. *The Gila Trail.* Edited by Richard Dillon. Norman: University of Oklahoma Press.

Hayes, Derek. 2007. *Historical Atlas of California with Original Maps.* Berkeley: University of California Press.

Heitman, Francis B. 1903. *Historical Register and Dictionary of the United States Army from Its Organization, September 29, 1789 to March 2, 1903.* 2 vols. Washington, D.C.: Government Printing Office.

Helm, Thomas B. 1886. History of Cass County, Indiana. Vol. 1. Chicago: Brant and Fuller.

Henry, Robert S. 1964. *The Armed Forces Institute of Pathology: Its First Century, 1862–1962.* Washington, D.C.: Office of the Surgeon General, Department of the Army.

Herndon, Dallas. 1922. *Centennial History of Arkansas.* Vol 1. Little Rock: S. J. Clarke.

History of Columbia County, New York. 1878. Philadelphia: Everts and Ensign.

Hollon, W. Eugene. 1955. *Beyond the Cross Timbers: The Travels of Randolph B. Marcy, 1812–1887.* Norman: University of Oklahoma Press.

Hoover, Mildred Brooke, Hero Eugene Rensch, and Ethel Grace Rensch. 2002. *Historic Spots in California.* 5th ed. Revised by Douglas E. Kyle. Stanford, Calif.: Stanford University Press.

Hunter, William. 1992. *Missouri Forty-Niner: The Journal of William Hunter on the Southern Gold Trail.* Edited by David Robrock. Albuquerque: University of New Mexico Press.

Hutton, William R. 1942. *Glances at California, 1847–1853: Diaries and Letters of William Rich Hutton.* San Marino, Calif.: Huntington Library.

Ingersoll, Luther A. 1904. *Ingersoll's Century Annals of San Bernardino County, 1769–1904.* Los Angeles, Calif.: L. A. Ingersoll.

Jaeger, Edmund Carroll. 1967. *The North American Deserts*. Stanford, Calif.: Stanford University Press.

Jonas, Tom. 2008. "Alamo Mocho: The Mexican War Trails of Kearny and Cooke through Baja California." Unpublished manuscript in the editor's files.

Jordan, David. 1849. "Dr. David Jordan Diary, 1849." Photocopy of manuscript. California State Library, Sacramento.

Julyan, Robert. 1996. *The Place Names of New Mexico*. Albuquerque: University of New Mexico Press.

Kanouse, Jacob A. 1849. "Incidents of a California Journey." *New York Daily Tribune*, July 20.

Keoke, Emory Dean, and Kay Marie Porterfield. 2002. "American Indians and Lacrosse." In *Encyclopedia of American Indian Contributions to the World*. New York: Facts on File.

Kendall, George Wilkins. 1935. *Narrative of the Texan Santa Fe Expedition*. Vol. 1. Austin, Tex.: Steck.

Kidder, Alfred Vincent. 1968. *An Introduction to the Study of Southwestern Archaeology with a Preliminary Account of the Excavations at Pecos*. New Haven: Yale University Press.

Kimball, Yeffe, and Jean Anderson. 1968. *The Art of American Indian Cooking*. New York: Lyons and Buford.

Kip, Leonard. 1850. *California Sketches, with Recollections of the Gold Mines*. Albany, N.Y.: Erastus H. Pease.

Lamb, Daniel Smith. N.d. "A History of the United States Army Medical Museum 1862–1917: Compiled from the Official Records." Unpublished manuscript. Otis Historical Archives, National Museum of Health and Medicine, Washington, D.C.

Lasselle, Stanislaus. 1991. "The 1849 Diary of Stanislaus Lasselle." Edited by Patricia A. Etter. *Overland Journal* 9:2–33.

Little, Elbert, Jr. 1939. "The Vegetation of the Caddo County Canyons, Oklahoma." *Ecology* 20 (January): 1–10.

Luomala, Katharine. 1978. "Tipai and Ipai." In *California*. Vol. 8 of *Handbook of North American Indians*. Washington, D.C.: Smithsonian Institution.

Malinowski, Sharon, et al., eds. 1998. "Creek." In *The Gale Encyclopedia of Native American Tribes*. Detroit, Mich.: Gale Research.

Mapes, Ruth B. 1965. *Old Fort Smith: Cultural Center on the Southwestern Frontier*. Little Rock, Ark.: Pioneer.

Marcy, Randolph P. 1859. *Prairie Traveler*. New York: Harper and Brothers.

Mariposa County Court Records, Agua Fria, California, August 12, 1852.

Martin, H. B. 1891–94. *Map of Subdivision of Part of Rancho Santa Ana del Chino*. San Francisco: Lith. Britton and Rey. Huntington Library, San Marino, Calif.

McArthur, Priscilla. 1986. "The Women Who Stayed at Home." In *Arkansas in the Gold Rush*. Little Rock, Ark.: August House.

"Military Hospitals." Finding guide, Old Military and Civil War Records Division, National Archives and Records Administration, Washington, D.C.

"Military Surgeons." Finding guide, Old Military and Civil War Records Division, National Archives and Records Administration, Washington, D.C.

Möllhausen, Balduin [Heinrich Baldwin]. 1858. *Diary of a Journey from the Mississippi to the Coasts of the Pacific*. 2 vols. London: Longman, Brown, Green, Longmans, and Roberts.

Moorehead, Max. N.d. Moorehead Collection. Western History Collections, Oklahoma History Center, Oklahoma City.

Morris, F. C. 1941. "The Country Explored by Lieutenant A. W. Whipple." In *Pathfinders of the Southwest*. Edited by Grant Foreman. Norman: University of Oklahoma Press.

Morris, John Miller. 1997. *El Llano Estacado: Exploration and Imagination on the High Plains of Texas and New Mexico, 1536–1860*. Austin: Texas State Historical Association.

Morrison, W. B. 1938. "The Saga of Skullyville." *Chronicles of Oklahoma* 16 (June): 234–40.

Mott, Valentine. Biographical Note. Valentine Mott correspondence. MS C 281. Archives and Modern Manuscripts Program, History of Medicine Division, National Library of Medicine, Bethesda, Md.

———. 1846. "Mr. Goulding's New Truss." *New York Journal of Medicine and the Collateral Sciences* 6 (May): 135–37.

New York Times. 1855. "Court of General Sessions . . . Jan. 17. Before His Honor Recorder Smith: An Important Case of Forgery," January 18.

———. 1854. "Forgers Upon a Bank," August 15.

Niles' National Register. 1844. Vol. 66 (June 11): 224.

Nugent, John. 1878. "Scraps of Early History, 4." *Argonaut* (San Francisco, Calif.) 2, no. 11 (March 23).

Officer, James E. 1987. *Hispanic Arizona, 1536–1856*. Tucson: University of Arizona Press.

Oklahoma Atlas and Gazetteer. 2003. 2nd ed. Yarmouth, Maine: DeLorme.

Opler, Morris E. 1983. "Chiricahua Apache." In *Southwest*. Vol. 10 of *Handbook of North American Indians*. Washington, D.C.: Smithsonian Institution.

Ord, Lt. L. E. 1849. Map of Ciudad de Los Angeles. Manuscript. Huntington Library, San Marino, Calif.

Ormsby, Waterman L. 1998. *The Butterfield Overland Mail*. Edited by Lyle H. Wright and Josephine M. Bynum. San Marino, Calif.: Huntington Library.

[Otis, George Alexander]. 1865. *Reports on the Extent and Nature of the Materials Available for the Preparation of a Medical and Surgical History of The Rebellion*. Surgeon General's Office, Washington, November 1, 1865, Circular no. 6. Philadelphia: J. B. Lippincott.

Pancoast, Charles Edward. 1930. *A Quaker Forty-Niner*. Edited by Anna Paschall Hannum. Philadelphia: University of Pennsylvania Press.

Pattison, George K. 1849. Letters. *Newark (New Jersey) Morning Eagle*, April 3, 11, 23; May 15, 17, 23; June 2, 27, 28; November 20, 21.

Payne, John Howard. 1932. "The Green Corn Dance." Introduced by John R. Swanton. *Chronicles of Oklahoma* 10 (June): 170–95.

Pearce, T. M. 1965. *New Mexico Place Names: A Geographical Dictionary*. Albuquerque: University of New Mexico Press.

Plan of Lincoln U.S. General Hospital. N.d. Printed diagram included with the William R. Goulding journal. Yale Collection of Western Americana, Beinecke Rare Book and Manuscript Library.

Post Returns from U.S. Military Posts, 1800–1916. Records of the Adjutant General's Office. National Archives Microfilm Publication RG 94 M617; Albuquerque Post, Reel 13; Socorro Post, Reel 13; Fort Marcy, Reel 745; Las Vegas, Reel 602. National Archives Building, Washington, D.C.

Powell, H. M. T. 1931. *The Santa Fe Trail to California, 1849–1852: The Journal and Drawings of H. M. T. Powell*. Edited by Douglas Watson. San Francisco: Book Club of California.

Powell, William H. 1890. *Records of Living Officers of the U.S. Army*. Philadelphia: L. R. Hammersly.

Powers, Stephen. 1849. "Sketch of John A. Fairchild." Manuscript C-E, 65:42. Bancroft Library.

Prince, Bradford. 1912. *The History of Fort Marcy, New Mexico*. Santa Fe, N.Mex.: New Mexican Printing Company.

Prudnan, Charles. J. 1862. First American Protestant Cemetery and Fort Moore, Los Angeles, California. Map. Huntington Library, San Marino, Calif.

Rancho del Chino Register Book. 1849. Manuscript. Huntington Library, San Marino, Calif.

Rea, Amadeo M. 1997. *At the Desert's Green Edge: An Ethnobotany of the Gila River Pima*. Tucson: University of Arizona Press.

Register of Enlistments in the United States Army, 1798–1914. National Archives Microfilm Publication RG94 M233, Reel 29, 1864–1865, A-K. National Archives Building, Washington, D.C.

Rice, William Broadhead. 1947. *The Los Angeles Star 1851–1864.* Berkeley: University of California Press.

Ricks, Caspar Stinemets. 1849. Caspar Stinemets Diary [June 26–August 10, 1849]. Typed transcript. Bancroft Library.

Roads of New Mexico. 1990. Fredericksburg, Tex.: Shearer.

Rolle, Andrew F. 1978. *California: A History.* 3rd ed. Arlington Heights, Ill.: AHM Publishing.

Romero, Miguel Sena y. May 12, 1849, letter from San Miguel del Bado regarding his position as Alcalde. Donaciano Vigil Collection, 1727–1877. New Mexico State Records Center and Archives, Albuquerque.

Rowland, Donald F. 1999. *John Rowland and William Workman: Southern California Pioneers of 1841.* Spokane, Wash.: Arthur H. Clark.

Ruhlen, George. 1957. "Kearny's Route from the Rio Grande to the Gila River," *New Mexico Historical Review* 32 (July): 213–30.

Russell, Frank. 1908. "The Pima Indians." *Twenty-sixth Annual Report of the Bureau of American Ethnology* (Washington, D.C.): 3–389.

Sacramento Union. 1942. "State Senate Acts to Rectify Mistake—92 Years Late!" January 13.

Sayre, Nathan F. 2005. *Working Wilderness: The Malpai Borderlands Group and the Future of the Western Range.* Tucson, Ariz.: Rio Nuevo.

Scarborough, Asa. 1969. "Diary of a Member of the First Mule Pack Train to Leave Fort Smith for California in 1849." Edited by Bessie L. Wright. *Panhandle Plains Historical Review* 152:1–59.

Sherburne, John P. 1988. *Through Indian Country to California: John P. Sherburne's Diary of the Whipple Expedition, 1853–1854.* Edited by Mary McDougall Gordon. Stanford, Calif.: Stanford University Press.

Simmons, Joseph R. 1849–50. Diary, 1849–1850. Joint Collection, University of Missouri Western Historical Manuscript Collection, Columbia, and State Historical Society of Missouri Manuscripts.

Simmons, Marc. 1982. *Albuquerque: A Narrative History.* Albuquerque: University of New Mexico Press.

Simpson, J. H. 1850. *Fort Smith to Santa Fe Route, 1849.* Maps 1–4. United States Senate. Ex. Doc. no. 12, 31st Cong., 1st Sess., being the report of the Secretary of War, of January 14, 1850, transmitting the report and maps of the route from Fort Smith to Santa Fe, made by Lieut. J. H. Simpson of the Corps of Topographical Engineers. Washington, D.C.

Slatta, Richard W. 1994. *The Cowboy Encyclopedia.* New York: W. W. Norton.

Smith, Andrew. 1849. "Letter from Woods Creek." *New York Daily Tribune*, November 13.

Smith, Margaret Ross. N.d. "The Old Anthony House." Small manuscript subject file, Arkansas History Commission, Little Rock, Ark.

Smith, Ralph A. 1964. "The Scalp Hunter in the Borderlands, 1835–1850." *Arizona and the West* 6:5–22.

Sniffen, George F. 1849. Notes by the Campfire: Being a Narrative of an Overland Journey from the United States to California in the Year 1849. Digitized. John B. Goodman Collection, MSS 26. Mandeville Special Collections Library, University of California, San Diego.

Snively, Daniel, and Louanna Furbee. 1968. *Satan's Ferryman: A True Tale of the Old Frontier*. New York: F. Unger.

St. John's Evangelical Episcopal Church Cemetery records, Old Section. Stockport, Columbia County, New York. Copy in the editor's files.

Stanley, Francis. 1964. *The San Miguel del Bado New Mexico Story*. Pep, Tex.: N.p.

Starr, Kevin. 2005. *California: A History*. New York: Modern Library.

Stevens, Benjamin. 1849. Untitled manuscript. John Lewis RoBards Papers. Joint Collection, University of Missouri Western Historical Manuscript Collection, Columbia, and State Historical Society of Missouri Manuscripts.

Stewart, Kenneth. 1983. "Yumans: Introduction." *The Southwest*. Vol. 10 of *Handbook of North American Indians*. Washington, D.C.: Smithsonian Institution.

Storke, Yda Addis. 1891. *A Memorial and Biographical History of the Counties of Santa Barbara, San Luis Obispo, and Ventura, California*. Chicago: Lewis Publishing Company.

Suneson, Neil H. 1996. "Geology of Red Rock Canyon State Park." Reprinted from *Oklahoma Geology Notes* 56 (1996): 88–105.

Taylor, Bayard. 1988. *Eldorado, or Adventures in the Path of Empire*. Lincoln: University of Nebraska Press.

Taylor, Frank H. 1913. *Philadelphia in the Civil War, 1861–1865*. [Philadelphia]: The City.

Texas Atlas and Gazetteer. 2005. Yarmouth, Maine: DeLorme.

Thrapp, Dan L. 1995. *Encyclopedia of Frontier Biography*. CD-ROM. Lincoln: University of Nebraska Press.

Tiller, Veronica E., ed. 2005. *Tiller's Guide to Indian Country: Economic Profiles of American Indian Reservations*. Albuquerque: Bowarrow Publishing.

Tomer, John S., and Michael Broadhead, eds. 1992. *A Naturalist in Indian Territory: The Journals of S. W. Woodhouse 1849–50*. Norman: University of Oklahoma Press.

Tyler, Daniel. 1969. *A Concise History of the Mormon Battalion in the Mexican War, 1846–1847*. Glorieta, N.Mex.: Rio Grande Press.

Unruh, John B., Jr. 1993. The Plains Across: The Overland Emigrants and the Trans-Mississippi West, 1840–60. Urbana: University of Illinois Press.

U.S. Census Bureau. 7th Census of the United States, New York, 1850. National Archives Microfilm Publication, 4th Ward, M593, Reel 536, p. 79. National Archives Building, Washington, D.C.

———. 8th Census of the United States, Stockport, Columbia County, New York, 1860. National Archives Microfilm Publication, M593, Reel 738, p. 22. National Archives Building, Washington, D.C.

———. 9th Census of the United States, Stockport, Columbia County, New York, 1870. National Archives Microfilm Publication, M593, Reel 921, p. 8. National Archives Building, Washington, D.C.

U.S. Surgeon-General's Office. 1870–88. *The Medical and Surgical History of the War of the Rebellion, 1861–1865*. Washington: Government Printing Office.

Van Buren Arkansas Intelligencer. 1845. May 3.

Van Zandt, Howard. 1935. "The History of Camp Holmes and Choteau's Trading Post." *Chronicles of Oklahoma* 13 (September): 316–37.

Van Zandt, Roland. 1966. *The Catskill Mountain House*. New Brunswick, N.J.: Rutgers University Press.

Virtual American Biographies. Museum of History. Book. 1. Continental Discovery to 1899. http://famousamericans.net.

Walker, Henry P., and Don Bufkin. 1979. *Historical Atlas of Arizona*. Norman: University of Oklahoma Press.

The Waterloo Medal Roll: Compiled from the Master Rolls. 1992. Darlington, England: Naval and Military Press.

Way, Frederick. 1994. *Way's Packet Directory, 1848–1994: Passenger Steamboats on the Mississippi River System Since the Advent of Photography in Mid-continent America*. Athens: Ohio University.

Webb, James Josiah. 1931. *Adventures in the Santa Fé Trade, 1844–1847*. Edited by Ralph P. Bieber. Glendale, Calif.: Arthur H. Clark.

Weed, L. N. 1857. "Narrative of a Journey to California in 1849." Manuscript. Yale Collection of Western Americana, Beinecke Rare Book and Manuscript Library.

Wells, Dennis. 1982. "Arizona's Independence Rock." Unpublished manuscript in the editor's files.

Whipple, Amiel Weeks. 1941. *A Pathfinder in the Southwest: The Itinerary of Lieutenant A. W. Whipple During His Explorations for a Railway Route from Fort Smith to Los Angeles in the Years 1853 and 1854*. Edited by Grant Foreman. Norman: University of Oklahoma Press.

Whipple, Amiel Weeks, and Lieutenant J. C. Ives. 1856. *Reports of Explorations and Surveys to Ascertain the Most Practicable and Economical Route for a Railroad from the Mississippi River to the Pacific Ocean, 1853–54*. Vol. 3. U.S. Senate, 33rd Cong., 2nd Sess., Ex. Doc. no. 78. Washington, D.C.

Will de Chaparro, Martina. 2007. *Death and Dying in New Mexico*. Albuquerque: University of New Mexico Press.

Willey, Richard. 1987. *Tucson Meteorites*. Washington, D.C.: Smithsonian Institution Press.

Williams, Isaac. 1849. "The Overland Emigration, Rancho del Chino, August 24, 1849. Letter to his Excellency, Brigadier Gen. B. Riley." *St. Louis Missouri Republican*, November 21.

Winchell, Lilbourne Alsip. 1933. *History of Fresno County and the San Joaquin Valley*. Fresno, Calif.: A. H. Cawston.

Wislizenus, Frederick A. 1848. *Memoir of a Tour to Northern Mexico, Connected with Col. Doniphan's Expedition in 1846 and 1847*. Washington, D.C.: Tippin and Streeper, printers.

Woodward, Joseph Janvier. 1862. *The Hospital Steward's Manual: For the Instruction of Hospital Stewards, Ward-Masters, and Attendants, in Their Several Duties*. Philadelphia: J. B. Lippincott.

Writers' Program of the Work Projects Administration in the Commonwealth of Pennsylvania. 1940. *Pennsylvania: A Guide to the Keystone State*. New York: Oxford University Press.

Writers' Program of the Work Projects Administration in the State of Arkansas. 1941. *Arkansas: A Guide to the State*. New York: Hastings House.

Index